No Off Switch

'Andy Kershaw, without you we wouldn't
know nothin'! Rock on'

Joe Strummer (2001)

'Andy Kershaw has led an extraordinary life. His unrivalled role in bringing World Music to the ears of the west is just part of the story of this man whose zest for life, music, people, experience and travel made him the finest British broadcaster bar none. That his life has had its ups and downs is to say that the Alps have snowy peaks, but throughout this dizzyingly paced and often wildly hilarious book he brings alive his matchless career, and the cultural life of a Britain that seems to be vanishing. Forget Media Studies and a life of student debt: read *No Off Switch* and learn what it is to be a real broadcast journalist, a real achiever. A real someone ... I make it a rule not to puff books but Andy Kershaw's *No Off Switch* is sensational'

Stephen Fry

'Andy Kershaw is such an enthusiast. He made me travel a little further than I normally do. He has an ability to do things first and ask questions afterwards. Not a recipe for a safe, secure life, maybe, but it makes things a lot more interesting for the rest of us!'

Michael Palin

'Passionate and furiously funny – Andy Kershaw is unfailingly fearless'

Dame Ann Leslie

'A staggeringly good read. It takes a lot for me to laugh heartily. I'll be stealing openly from it. This book is magnificent'

Nigel Blackwell, Half Man Half Biscuit

'I cannot recommend Andy's book *No Off Switch* highly enough – a terrific read from a real rock-and-roll war correspondent. This is one of those rare things – a beautifully crafted and genuinely well-written book from a music-business veteran who has looked at both sides now. As rare as a penguin in the Gobi desert, as I know from my own fifty-year experience dog paddling in the industry of human happiness'

Keith Altham

'Andy Kershaw's memoir zooms along with the high-velocity recklessness of a TT racer. It's impossible not to cheer him on as he accelerates round the hairpin bends of his life, yelling hilarious defiance at anyone who tries to stop him'

Francis Wheen

ANDY
KERSHAW
No Off Switch

Virgin BOOKS

2 4 6 8 10 9 7 5 3 1

First published in the United Kingdom in 2011 by Serpent's Tail

This edition published in 2012 by Virgin Books, an imprint of Ebury Publishing

A Random House Group Company

www.randomhouse.co.uk

Addresses for companies within The Random House Group Limited can be found at
www.randomhouse.co.uk/offices.htm

The Random House Group Limited Reg. No. 954009

A CIP catalogue record for this book is available from the British Library

The Random House Group Limited supports The Forest Stewardship Council (FSC®), the leading
international forest certification organisation. Our books carrying the FSC label are printed on
FSC® certified paper. FSC is the only forest certification scheme endorsed by the leading
environmental organisations, including Greenpeace. Our paper procurement policy can be found
at www.randomhouse.co.uk/environment

Typeset by Palimpsest Book Production Limited, Falkirk, Stirlingshire

Printed and bound in Great Britain by CPI Group (UK) Ltd, Croydon, CR0 4YY

ISBN: 9780753541074

To buy books by your favourite authors and register for offers, visit
www.randomhouse.co.uk

For Sonny and Dolly

THANKS

THANKS TO Geoff Adams-Spink, Phil Almond, Geoff Alun-Jones, Marta Anicic, Florence Arpin, Lucy Ash, Jonny Barnes, Vic & Pam Bates, Glen Baxter, George Beale, Mark Begovich, Sarah Bennie, Ian Birrell, John Bisbrowne, Nigel Blackwell, Nick Bonner, John Bowes, Vanessa Bridge, Simon & Kate Broughton, Jane Buchanan, Sheena Bullen, Cyril Burgess, Matthew Burton, Anglin & Jen Buttimore, Rachel Calder, Martin Carthy, Greg Chamberlain, Iain Chambers, Mick Chatterton, John Cooper, Jo Crocker, Paul Crockford, Trevor Dann, Robin Denselow, Cathy Drysdale, Mark & Clare Ellen, Mark Ellingham, Issy Emeney, Colin Fenton, Andy Fingret, Stephen Fry, Luce Garland, Jonathan Garratt, Peter Greste, Sid Griffin, Steve Henderson, Chris Holmes, Simon Howard, Jonathan Irving, Susan Jeffries, Anna Jenkins, Peter Jenner, Fergal Keane, Stephen Kearney, Alan & Mike Kelly, Martin Kelner, Nigel & Nicky Kermode, Eileen Kershaw, Elizabeth Kershaw, Kathleen & Mick Kirkbright, Ann Leslie, Jenni Lewis, Togga Lord, Chris Lycett, Mark Makin, Dave & Lizzie McLean, Natalie Merchant, Carl & Alison Moody, Richard Morse, Beth Morton,Tessa, Harry & Emma Munt, Neil O'Brien, Lembit Opik, Michael Palin, James Parkin, Jim Redman, Gillian Reynolds, Paul Rider, Lorna Russell, Roger Short, Ralph Steadman, Sheila & Rodney Taylor, Al & Josie Thompson, Steve Tilston, Judy Totton, Pete Townshend, Catherine Turner, Terry Waite, Helen Walters, Marvin Ware, Malcolm Wheeler, Francis Wheen, Peter Wood, Dave Woodhead, Roger Wright, Andrew Zweck.

VERY SPECIAL THANKS to Joanna Coop, Noel & Pam Clegg, Shaz Nicol, Bill & Sheila Saner.

AND WITHOUT WHOM… Rachael Clegg, Debbie, Colin & Alice Law, Audrey & Tony Mansell, Barbara Shimmin, Chris Simpson, Bob & Jane Taylor.

CONTENTS

FLOATING IN A MOST
PECULIAR WAY

FAR BELOW ME was a bubbling multi-coloured broth of humanity – all toothpaste smiles, sunglasses, bare arms and bouncing bosoms. The crackle and murmur of anticipation was borne upwards on the warm morning air to my perch, high above the stadium. Tucked under the roof, I was leaning over a steel gantry, gawping at the immensity of the occasion but oddly divorced from the happiness, companionship and excitement of those down on the Wembley pitch.

Just seconds from presenting the biggest television event since man first landed on the moon, I felt, in the company of thousands in the stadium and millions who'd be watching around the world, quite alone.

I wished I could be down there, among friends for a carefree day as a participant in history. But it was too late to back out now. A BBC production assistant, with clip-board and stopwatch, was calling me from the football commentary box, our studio, along the walkway. There was nothing I could do but go for it.

It was 13 July 1985. This was *Live Aid*. I was 25 years old. Eighteen months earlier, I had been unemployed, in Leeds, without any real prospects or ideas of what I would do in life. Certainly, I'd never had any plans or ambitions to work in television. It was less than a year since my first television broadcast, less than two years since Billy Bragg and I had hit the road as rock & roll guerrillas. And just one week before this day of *Live Aid,* I'd presented for the first time my own programme on BBC Radio 1.

The technicians wired me for sound. I picked my way over the cables, between the cameras, settled on the presenters' sofa and looked into the black mirror of the camera lens. 'How many people are supposed to be watching this?' I asked one of the producers.

'Some say four or five hundred million. Others reckon it could be more than a billion,' he replied.

Not for the first or the last time in my life did a familiar question flash through my mind: 'What the fuck is *this*?'

IGNITION SEQUENCE STARTS

THE CAR HAD GONE through a low garden wall. It was a huge, voluptuous black saloon, its paintwork gleaming in the sunshine and its bumpers generous and glamorous even in their state of contortion. Masonry and windscreen glass had been flung across a precious lawn and the flowerbeds were ploughed and violated by deep wheel gouges. The car's unfortunate occupants had already been taken away.

It was, apart from birdsong, completely silent. Other bystanders just stared.

The house was Miss Whiteley's. I was on my way home from another happy day at Howard Street Nursery where the lovely Miss Whiteley was our headmistress.

Whoever was taking me home urged me to hurry along. But I didn't want to leave until I'd absorbed every shocking, incongruous detail.

Though the words were not then developed in my infant vocabulary, the sensation was one with which I would become more than familiar and actively seek, not just as an accidental television presenter at *Live Aid* but in all areas of human experience. A car through a wall on a lawn? What the fuck was *this*?

FROM ROCHDALE
TO THE MOON

IT WILL SURPRISE some historians to learn – as I arrived in the world on 9 November 1959 in Rochdale, Lancashire – that I was born towards the end of the Second World War. That hostilities had ended officially fourteen years earlier did not, however, diminish powerful legacies of the conflict which shaped my early years. Our town remained pretty much untroubled by dizzying post-war social dynamics: the class-barrier ram-raids; sexual revolution; youth culture upheavals; antiauthoritarianism; psychedelia and ill-advised trousers with which the Swinging Sixties liberated other territories. In fact, I would say Rochdale finally emerged from the Second World War some time around 1972.

Rochdale had been a major industrial centre, a cotton mill town, to which – unbeknown to me at the time, of course – a feckless teenager, John Ravenscroft, who would become John Peel, had been sent by his exasperated Liverpool cotton merchant father to work in a mill in the early 1960s. Spookily, the mill in which young John had his youthful brush with manual labour was not a hundred yards from the nursery school I was attending at the time. For all I know, I might have once watched him, through the playground railings, winching bales of cotton into the mill. Or avoiding winching bales of cotton into the mill.

If the Lancashire cotton industry wasn't exactly a magnet for the pubescent John Ravenscroft, it had been occasionally for the Luftwaffe. In the grounds of the nursery were old red brick air-raid shelters, dank, mysterious and inviting – inhabited, naturally, by ghosts, monsters and baddies. The Rochdale of my childhood was seemingly crowded by men with one leg, the other being somewhere on the Somme or at Ypres. The town centre never had a shortage of eager, self-appointed, shouting, freelance traffic controllers of a certain age. And there was a man who, on his frequent walks along our street, would claim to have designed and built, single-handedly, most of Rochdale's great municipal buildings. I would look forward to his appearances and to the scope and ambition of his latest achievement.

Both world wars were still very much living events. My paternal grandfather, Nat, had lied about his age to enlist in the navy at the outbreak of World War I and found himself, at the age of fifteen, on the battleship King George V at the Battle of Jutland. On his death in 1986, my dad gave to me Granddad Nat's service medals. The authorities, at the end of the war, had been compelled to acknowledge the gallant contribution of child combatants: his medals were inscribed 'Boy Kershaw'.

Granddad Wallace – my mum's dad – was a survivor, just about, of the second war. He'd served as a military policeman in North Africa and Cyprus. He didn't talk much about it, not even among his pals and fellow veterans propping up the bars of his various pubs around post-war Rochdale. We all just understood he'd had a bad one. In one incident, he'd ridden his motorcycle over a landmine in Egypt. Only after he died, did I learn he'd been ordered to take part in a firing squad to execute a fellow soldier. He had never once revealed this to anyone but my grandma.

For the rest of his life, Granddad Wallace was a tormented man, alcohol-dependent and clinically depressed. His marriage to my grandma was wretched. He once confided that he had come home from the war, to his marriage, his child and what turned out to be fifty years of misery, only for my mum. There

Granddad Nat (left), the original Boy Kershaw, soon after the Battle of Jutland, 1916; and Granddad Wallace, on active service in North Africa during WW2. *Unknown*

wasn't available then, to Granddad Wallace and his friends, after the war, the luxury of the recognised medical syndrome of Post Traumatic Stress Disorder to explain and accommodate their agony. Quiet, dignified suffering – and oblivion through alcohol – was their only way to cope.

For the working people of Rochdale, the wars had been their only opportunity to travel. Joining the Forces gave those men some perspective, albeit limited, of a wider world out there. For most of them it was, it seemed, a wider world from which they wished to beetle back to Rochdale as rapidly as possible.

Aside from travel in uniform, horizons were very limited. And wilfully so. People of that generation were satisfied simply to grow up, work, get married, have children and die without ever leaving their neighbourhood. Until the 1960s, very few young people struck out from the town, even to go to college. (An irritation with this lack of curiosity and ambition would, eventually, have a major impact on my outlook.) There was, unarguably, a benefit to this deprivation: the Rochdale of my childhood had a sense of community and neighbourliness which has now all but vanished. The disadvantage, meanwhile, was that for a curious child with a sense of adventure and a grasp of the possible, shown glimpses of a bigger world in the flourishing television age, Rochdale would become suffocatingly parochial.

HOWARD STREET NURSERY was – until the arrival of the saintly Miss Whiteley – a daily misery, alleviated only by the protection of my big sister, Our Elizabeth (fifteen months older than me), and the hot dinners. The permanent aroma of meat and potato pie sweetened an atmosphere otherwise of unwashed, post-war, bathed-once-a-week infants. But it was the regime of my first headmistress that had most impact – and helped to shape my anti-authoritarian inclinations, sense of justice and injustice and reflex tendency towards rebellion.

I can't recall the old dragon's name – which is probably just as well – though one of our confrontations is to this day a favourite in family folklore. For some perceived misdemeanour she had locked me up, alone in her office. I would have been no more than three at the time. After I stopped crying, I marshalled my thoughts and my anger. My mum and dad would have been at work but my grandma Norah was at her pub, less than a mile away. Remembering her number, I picked up the phone, called her and reported the news of my scandalous incarceration. Grandma Norah was a formidable woman of Irish Catholic stock. Within minutes she was on the premises and I was able to enjoy, through a window of the office overlooking the main room of the nursery, the spectacle of my grandma remonstrating with the headmistress. In a trice, I was sprung and carted home to be indulged with pop and crisps at my grandparents' pub.

Almost certainly the two events were not connected but, soon after, my old adversary retired and the seemingly dazzling, youthful and delightful Miss Whiteley took the helm.

That same office then became the centre for very different but equally formative experiences. Miss Whiteley, for some reason, favoured me and gave me periods of what amounted to private tuition. We'd look at books together and, to better examine insects and spiders I'd gathered in the playground, she let me use her magnifying glass while she explained the creatures to me. She was building all the time on a curiosity which my dad was cultivating in me at home.

I was also to learn, at Miss Whiteley's knee, that I am innately non-musical. I may love the stuff but it was apparent from very early on that I would never have the talent to play it. At nursery and beyond I was to be forever the kid who was assigned nothing more damaging nor discordant than the tambourine. (Years later I was to wish that many of those who considered themselves musicians and singers had also been troubled by this reality. And recognised it with similar humility.) My musical disability may, perhaps, explain my enthusiasm for music: if I were able to play the piano, say, I would not be satisfied unless I could play it as well as Albert Ammons or Jerry Lee Lewis. And if I could play as well as that, what fascination would their genius, and their music, hold for me?

MY DAD, JACK, was by 1965 the young headmaster of a Rochdale comprehensive school. My mum, Eileen, soon after was appointed head of a nursery school in nearby Oldham. Education was paramount at 28 Greenhill Avenue, an end-of-terrace house in which we lived until I was ten, and at our subsequent family home in Whitworth, on Rochdale's Pennine edge.

Both my parents were of that first generation in their families to go to college. (All my grandparents had begun their working lives in the mills, at the age of twelve.) The ethics of education and self-improvement were concepts Elizabeth and I just understood from birth. That meant not only drawing to the maximum on the formal education we received in school but gulping down at the same time the informal education we got at home, chiefly from my dad.

I was able to talk before I could walk and when I was no more than two, my dad would bring down off the bookshelves a weighty history of the Great War. To impress visitors to our home, he would show me in the book a photo of all the allied generals, lined up at some chateau or other, no doubt heroically

Uncommon AK camera shyness in Filey, 1962, with my mum (stripey jumper) and Grandma Norah to her right. Our Elizabeth is next to me, Cousin Linda is alongside her. *Unknown*

located many miles behind the front lines and battle-equipped with a most satisfactory wine-cellar. And I would name every single whiskered military man. (Today, I would be diagnosed with Asperger's Syndrome. Back then it was called – variously – learning, knowledge and curiosity.)

My mother's attachment to superstition and mumbo jumbo – in her case Roman Catholicism – sealed for me and Elizabeth a convent education. My dad, an instinctive atheist but an occasional tactical agnostic, went along with this as Rochdale Convent was known to be an outstanding school with wonderful teachers – staffed by German nuns who had fled Nazi Germany before the outbreak of war. It was located in the grand former home and extensive gardens of some wealthy Victorian mill-owner and philanthropist. So our playground was a whole private park.

Sister Illuminata, gentle and inspiring, was my first teacher and from September 1964 she took over where Miss Whiteley had left off. I was eager to learn, and before I'd left the infant classes other children had nicknamed me the Professor.

The curriculum wasn't dominated by religion but what there was I treated with a silent ridicule which I'd picked up from my dad. It was clear to me, even back then, that religion was a retreat from the rational. And when Catholic values did occasionally intrude they had ludicrous consequences. As on the occasion when an elderly nun found me reading the Ladybird book of *Your Body*.

On the inside back cover was a line drawing of the nuclear family: mum, dad, boy, girl, all naked. The ancient nun yelped in outrage, handed me a packet of coloured wax crayons and ordered me to draw clothes onto the figures. I thought that this was plain mad. I must have been eight years old.

WHILE NOT ENLIGHTENED in matters of the sub-navel region the nuns were, like just about everyone else on earth at the time, absolutely captivated and inspired by manned space flight. I was lucky enough to have, as the main backdrop to my childhood, the unfolding drama of man's greatest adventure since Columbus disappeared over the horizon.

My earliest memories were of the Gemini programme of the mid-1960s. Particularly vivid still is the awe with which I watched Ed White become the first American to walk in space in June 1965. If the images on the television resembled grainy, black-and-white animations, these were more than corrected by the rich colour photographs in a copy of *National Geographic* I fell upon some time soon after at school. The pictures of White, in his dazzling spacesuit, floating above a vivid blue planet made me giddy with excitement, a sense of the astronauts' achievement and a recognition of unfettered possibility. And, yes, he was *floating*. The concept of weightlessness was something beyond the experience of ordinary mortals. I wanted to be Ed White. I had to become an astronaut.

Manned space flight, and the fulfilment of President Kennedy's seemingly impossible 1961 ambition to put a man on the moon before the end of the decade and return him safely to earth was, irrespective of its Cold War imperatives, a stunning achievement. It was without precedent. There was nothing against which to measure it. The NASA scientists and astronauts were themselves, necessarily, making it up as they went along. To a small boy in Rochdale, Lancashire, watching all this through the fast developing medium of television, it was genuinely mind-blowing. And, for me now, in middle age, it still is. I am no less astonished today by archive film of a Saturn V launch than I was by that lift-off as a child. Yep, they sat on the top of that 364-foot rocket, a skyscraper-bomb of kerosene and liquid oxygen, lit the bugger up and, with six million pounds of thrust, rode it at *25,000 mph* to break free from their planet and into immortality.

Meanwhile, in the hallway at Greenhill Avenue was an oak bedding box which doubled up as a bench. And my space capsule. It had a hinged lid. I spent many a solitary but happy afternoon, during the Gemini years and into the Apollo programme, with the sun streaming down the hallway, emptying

I feel I've gone through much of life as the bloke with the pole in front of his face. At Butlin's, Ayr, 1962, with Grandma Norah, Our Elizabeth and Cousin Linda (now Mrs Weekes-Holt, a Cheshire Conservative councillor). *Unknown*

the blankets from that box and climbing inside to pretend I was Ed White or Virgil Grissom. Then I'd clamber out, very slowly, and make a space walk along to the kitchen or up the stairs. If Elizabeth came by as I was tucked inside my capsule, knees under my chin (it had about as much room as the Mercury astronauts had in their spacecraft), she would drop her weight down on the lid and not let me out until the brave little astronaut had banged and screamed to the point of near suffocation.

At the convent, when a space flight was in progress, the nuns seemed to recognise that this was history in the making. Any adherence to a timetable was abandoned. A television was wheeled into the classroom and for the rest of the day we would, as a class, watch the inspirational events brought to us by the hugely entertaining and educational partnership – certainly for the Apollo flights – of Patrick Moore and James Burke. For me and my pals, it was our football. I devoured, saved and stuck into scrapbooks everything on which I could lay my hands about space flight. I made myself a real expert.

Existential aspects of space flight and astronomy much occupied my childish mind. One or two of them still do. The most absorbing riddle of all was the concept of infinity. I would lie in bed and grapple with this one long into the night. If, I would reason, the universe ended at a brick wall, billions of miles out into space, then there must be something beyond that wall. And something then beyond that. And if space is indeed infinite (and already my previous reasoning had established that it is) then, mathematically, that meant there were an infinite number of possibilities, certainties in fact, out there. If there are infinite possibilities to infinity, that meant there had to be, unarguably, at that same moment, somewhere else in the universe, another little boy called Andrew Kershaw, who looked identical to me, lying in an identical bed in an identical room in a town also called Rochdale, having these same troubling thoughts. I never did get aroused by football.

On the night of 20 July 1969, pretty much as one, the world stood still. Except for my mum and dad. They went to bed. I was even told by my mum that I could not stay up to watch man's first moon landing as it was due to happen well past my bedtime. I had my own priorities. As soon as I was able to establish my parents were asleep, I took a blanket downstairs, lay on the sofa and watched Neil Armstrong, Buzz Aldrin and Michael Collins change the history of the human race.

2

OPENING TIME

UNTIL THE INTRODUCTION of the bossyboots smoking ban – no business of government – I had been going to the pub since the day I was born. Grandma Norah and Granddad Wallace ran them, in and around Rochdale, from the end of the war.

Their pub of my childhood years, the Green Gardens on the edge of Syke common in Rochdale, was notable for not having a garden. Of any colour. It did have a number of cosy little rooms until some brewery spiv breezed along one day in 1967 and announced it, like so many fine old idiosyncratic pubs in Britain at the time, was to be 'modernised' and made open-plan. Before and after these alleged improvements, I was happy there. Which was just as well. Busy parents, and my mother's professional preoccupations, compounded from 1964 by her election as a local Labour councillor, meant that Elizabeth and I were unloaded for much of our childhoods on to my grandparents.

This seemed to suit all of us. Our granddad loved to take care of us, picking us up from school in his little blue Ford Anglia and driving us straight to a sweet shop or a local cafe where he would spoil us rotten. Another huge treat was Granddad Wallace rushing round to collect me and Elizabeth whenever one of the local cotton mills had caught fire, as they often did. Half the town, it seemed, would turn out to watch the blaze and the efforts of the firemen to put it out. My grandma would also indulge us. At the pub, she'd always bring upstairs to where we were watching *Lucille Ball* or *Take Your Pick* together, bottles of pop and bags of crisps. She also loved to trail us around Rochdale Market, where she would treat us to childish luxuries or, for a true adventure, take us on the train for the overwhelming experience of shopping in Manchester and tea in its impressive department stores.

In many ways, I was happier at the pub than at home. Aside from the treats, our grandparents were simply more demonstrative in their love and pride for me and my big sister than our parents. Not for a moment am I saying we were deprived or unloved at home. Jack and Eileen just had a funny way of showing it. And not very often.

One regular indication of affection from my dad, in my early years, does stick, though, and it gives me one of those must-have-got-something-in-my-eye moments to this day. He was fond of sitting me, as an infant, on his knee, while singing the Al Jolson song *Sonny Boy*. ('Climb upon my knee, Sonny Boy...') It was chiefly for this reason that I named my own boy, born in August 1997, Sonny.

But that is about it. My mum was always 'too busy' or 'too tired' to give us much attention. And from my earliest stage of self-awareness, she led me to understand that I was naughty. Now, I struggle to think why. I can't actually recall any pattern of disobedience or bad behaviour. I was just brought up to believe I was bad. The terrors of original sin, which my mother was always eager to deploy as a control mechanism, made the possibilities of redemption seem hopeless. I couldn't understand why I was regarded like this. Usually, it seemed to me, as I slumped in the hallway or hid in my bedroom, weeping, that I hadn't done anything to deserve the latest scolding. She used to tell me that every time I was naughty I lost a jewel from my crown in heaven. I was distraught to learn this, picturing, with every chastisement, an increasingly drab celestial crown with big holes where the confiscated gems had once been. The other angels, I was certain, would mock me for this. It wasn't long before I had to conclude there must be no more precious stones left to lose.

At the pub, on the other hand, there was infinite care and affection and boundless possibilities for stimulation and entertainment. Elizabeth and I were my grandma and granddad's pride and joy. We adored them, too.

Two of my greatest friends in childhood were my grandma's dogs, Dandy and Kimmy. Dandy was crazy, a mongrel ball of fluff on long wiry legs who loved to marinade himself in cow shit on a nearby farm, then roll in grass clippings on the common before trotting back into the pub to the delight of the regulars. Kimmy was a big soft cross between a labrador and an alsatian. He was, when I was very small, gentle and patient enough to tolerate my riding on his back. Neither dog had a trace of malice or aggression. In his old age, and when I was old enough to ride motorcycles on the road, Kimmy could detect the tone of my bike's engine from all others and, as I approached the pub, would leave his habitual perch by the pub's front porch and trot four hundred yards across the common to greet me.

In the tap room, particularly, the old men would gather with

Grandma Norah and Granddad Wallace at the Green Gardens, Rochdale, in the late 1960s. Milk never really caught on. *Unknown*

pints of mild and let me sit among them. They filled my head with their experiences of the Western Front or D-day. With my granddad, we'd watch the black-and-white television above the bar. Those evenings and afternoons have left me not only with an encyclopaedic knowledge of 1960s television quiz shows, westerns and imported comedies, such as *Mr Ed* and *The Addams Family,* but suspicion and an anger about the capacity for what those in positions of power and authority – especially those who consider themselves to be superior – can put others through.

The television at the pub also left with me vivid memories of the assassinations of Bobby Kennedy and Martin Luther King, both in 1968. I must have been off school, either ill or on half-term for Bobby Kennedy's killing. There was no such thing in those days, of course, as a rolling news channel. We had, instead, the drama of, and morbid fascination with, a newsflash. (How, as a news junkie, I miss the newsflash...) The report that Bobby Kennedy had been shot came through, as I recall, around mid-morning, UK time. I was watching some schools programme or other which was interrupted. The same report and newsreel footage was then shown all day. What stuck with me was Kennedy's motionless body, oddly dignified in the chaos around him, as he lay on the floor of the kitchen of the Ambassador Hotel in Los Angeles. It was the first time I was aware of a breaking news story and I can feel the excitement still of knowing, aged eight, that I was – albeit via a pub television six thousand miles away – a witness to history.

In the afternoons, when the pub was shut between 2pm and 5pm, my granddad would take a nap in an armchair in their flat upstairs. With nothing better to do on one of these afternoons, Elizabeth and I – probably aged about five or six – rolled his hair into my grandma's curlers as he snored. When the first of his customers knocked on the pub door at 5pm, Granddad Wallace went to answer it, oblivious to the lurid pink rollers still adorning his head.

The days and nights at the pub were rich in every sense. Customers of the tap room became my friends and storytellers. I'd lend a hand (a very small one) in the dank, cool beer cellar. A large family of frogs seemed to thrive there, encouraged by my granddad who valued their tenancy as he said they ate slugs. Our grandma was always cooking. Her specialities were soups and pies.

On hot summer days, always fragrant with raspberryade and dandelion and burdock, Granddad Wallace would escort us to Syke Ponds on the common. We'd catch sticklebacks in a net, keep them and study them in a jam-jar until we returned them to the pond, before ambling back to the pub, via another sweet shop. My fascination with fish and fishing, and waters of all kinds, was probably born on these little adventures.

I also profited hugely, for a small boy, by offering to help my grandma by cleaning under the fixed seating along the walls of the tap room. A hand-brush swept through the darkness at the back, where the seat and a water pipe met the wall, could frequently yield a fat, friendly threepenny bit, a pretty sixpence or, sometimes even, a majestic half-crown. This, to a four year old, was wealth beyond dreams. And at night, Elizabeth and I would fall asleep in our beds above the pub, soothed by the babble from below of conversation and the cheery clatter of glasses.

3

FISH AND TWISTGRIPS

FOR SOMEONE WHO BECAME Mr Global Adventure – and at the last count I had visited 97 of the world's 193 countries – it is remarkable that I scarcely crossed the Channel until I was twenty-four. I did, however, as a child, see more than enough of Scotland.

With both parents teachers, Elizabeth and I were taken on long motoring holidays around Britain – particularly during the summer break – in our reliable Morris Oxford. These, invariably, would concentrate disproportionately on the country to which Radio 1 DJs would feel obliged to call 'north of the border'.

For the earliest of these trips we carried with us a family-size tent. This was later upgraded to a Sprite touring caravan. Both fulfilled my main requirements: to stay out of the endless Scottish rain; to give me somewhere to read; and to provide a bedtime sense of comfort and security as I lay there, soothed by the drumming of another downpour on the roof, against which there always seemed to be a soprano on the Home Service, battling to project her aria through the static. (Why don't those *Visit Scotland* television adverts ever feature these irresistible attractions?)

On these holidays I came to adore, and still do, the fragrance of wet vegetation after heavy rain. But not the music of those evenings. In my forties, before surgery to repair a burst eardrum, I was asked by the anaesthetist, a rather supercilious man, 'Are we allergic to anything?' as I stood on the weighing scales. 'Yes,' I replied. 'Opera.'

Our family holidays had, of course, an educational priority. And I'm glad they did. As children, we were soon familiar with most of Britain, particularly Scotland, and the bulk of its museums. We learned quickly and eagerly about our own country, its history (for that was my dad's enthusiasm), its geography and its wildlife. Kids who I possibly considered luckier at the time, because they were whisked off on exotic holidays to Mallorca (with sun), never knew their own homeland as I did. Among my primary school classmates, there were few other leading authorities on the battle of Culloden.

Before the decade was out, that fascination with history and a determination to know everything about a subject had turned me towards the debate over the assassination of President Kennedy. At the age of nine I read William Manchester's *Death of a President* and Mark Lane's *Rush To Judgement*. The JFK assassination became an obsession which has proved to be life-long and undimmed. (And since you ask – no, I am not a lone gunman adherent. Nor do my suspicions spread just to the Grassy Knoll. They extend to a third sniper who probably fired the fatal shot from the railway bridge over the Elm Street underpass.)

To keep us quiet in the car, and to prevent territorial disputes between me and Elizabeth over space on the back seat, we were pelted with books. I loved to escape into the world of the Famous Five, in which children, bound together by strong friendship and ties of close family, were largely independent of grown-ups. (Even as a child, I found Enid Blyton's attitude to working people outrageous but, unlike more tight-arsed critics, simultaneously hugely amusing. My favourite Famous Five assumption was that the juvenile adventurers were, by their breeding, quite within their rights to turn up unannounced at some remote farmhouse and expect to be fed. Equally, the hard-working farmer's wife was expected to drop everything, accommodate immediately the wishes of these ghastly public-schoolchildren and lay on a lavish spread. Without reward. And

On the beach, Fleetwood, 1963. *Dermot O'Leary*

working people, by definition those of the lower orders, always smelled unwashed.)

Paddington Bear appealed to me as the vulnerable outsider overcoming adversity. The anti-heroes of Richmal Crompton's *Just William* and Ronald Searle's *Molesworth* fed my germinating sense of subversion and rebellion. *Wind in the Willows* and the criminally-overlooked classic by BB (Denys Watkins-Pitchford), *The Little Grey Men,* picked up my love of aquatic life where television's *Tales of the Riverbank* left off.

THE RIVERS AROUND ROCHDALE were all heavily polluted by local industry. It is astonishing that this arrogance and selfishness was allowed to continue as long as it did. Even as I left home for Leeds University in 1978, our nearest river, rushing through a gorge of outstanding natural beauty, Healey Dell, ran navy blue – and dead – with effluent from a dye works up the valley. It gave off fumes which made one's eyeballs prickle.

The pocket-sized Observer's books formed the core of my childhood library. (Why have they been allowed to go out of print?) This began when my dad gave me the *Observer's Book of Birds*. Soon sated by sightings of the humble Chaffinch or House Martin, I began to spot the more exotic species around industrial Rochdale. I was forever catching a glimpse of the Montagu's Harrier – 'an uncommon summer visitor' – at all times of the year.

The addition of the *Observer's Book of Freshwater Fish* solidified my growing curiosity with what ought to be living in our rivers. Happily, as a cotton town, Rochdale had mill lodges and canals. Deep, dark and mysterious, these mesmerised me. I wanted to know which living secrets they concealed. Did they contain the fish in my book? But these were not enquiries of any interest to my dad. His own enthusiasm was for Rugby League – unsurprisingly, perhaps, as Granddad Nat, his dad, the teenage veteran of Jutland, had played for Rochdale Hornets in the 1920s.

I liked going to Hornets matches with my dad and we were as close then as we ever were. I felt his protection in those big crowds of tall grown-ups. But apart from watching Laurel and Hardy films together on the television, my dad seemed to have a problem with showing interest in my own growing passions. For my sixth or seventh birthday, my mum and dad gave me a child's fishing rod and reel. But that was it. Their contribution to my hobby ended there. Not once did my dad ever take me fishing. So desperate was I to go that, given parental indifference, the best I could manage, for years, was in my grandparents' pub, during its afternoon closure, when I would *play* at fishing in the long lounge bar.

This was odd because my dad was not without generosity or the capacity for self-sacrifice. When I was about five, I remember him – still a struggling teacher, before his promotion to Deputy Head and then Headteacher – selling his beloved golf clubs to pay for toy cupboards for me and Elizabeth. I cried for him when a man came to collect his golfing bag. On another occasion, a tramp appeared at our front door and asked my dad if he had a spare pair of trousers. I was terrified of this wild, shabby stranger but I also felt for him instinctive sympathy. I was appalled, outraged, that someone could be put through such indignity and humiliation. My dad went and found him a pair immediately. I was deeply moved by this and felt proud of my dad. Just as I did one morning when I was about five and getting ready to go to school. My mum was in hospital for some reason. My dad was struggling to look after me and Elizabeth alone. I found him in the dining room, trying to sew a button back on to my white school shirt. He was doing it with green cotton and he was sobbing. It was the only cotton he could find, he said. I recognised he was doing his best and I went to school quietly proud of his striking handiwork.

If my dad knew nothing about fishing and wasn't prepared to learn (perhaps his reluctance arose from ignorance of a subject in front of his son), then I was. I read everything in Rochdale Library's angling section, many times over. By the age of eight, I was an authority on angling theory, if not practice.

It is absolutely unthinkable now, in our age of Health & Safety zealotry and statistically unjustifiable paedophile paranoia, but by the time I was ten or eleven, I was, with my parents' consent or indifference, going fishing by myself on Rochdale's reservoirs, canals and mill lodges. These were – especially the mill lodges – alarmingly deep, with steep sides. And I couldn't swim. Although nervous, and frightened of the water and anyone who approached me (this was, after all, only six years and ten miles from where the Moors Murders took place), I had a glorious time. It was the beginning of my realisation that I was happy in my own company.

IN 1967, MY MUM AND DAD bought a static caravan on a site at Ulrome, south of Bridlington, on the east coast of Yorkshire. This represented an end to our tours of the UK. All subsequent holidays and many weekends were spent there. In the fullness of time, I found places nearby in which to fish. I learned to ride a bicycle at the caravan but the most revelatory two-wheeled experience took place there in, I think, the summer of 1971.

Two friends had a wealthy dad who bought for them anything that took their fancy. One day, they turned up with a brand-new child's off-road motorcycle, a 50cc Italian-made Italjet. We gathered in a field to admire it: grey and silver paintwork, knobbly tyres, real telescopic forks and a matt black two-stroke engine which gave off hot and heady fumes, sweet and pleasing. Then there was that twistgrip. That made it a real, living motorcycle.

I watched my pals take turns on their bike. It was something I knew I could never own. Even if my mum and dad could afford one, they would not fritter their money on such extravagances. And anyway, my parents frowned on motorcycles. They were still regarded, thanks to mid-1960s rockers and post-war ton-up boys before them, as dangerous instruments of anti-social behaviour. For that, of course, they fascinated me all the more. To the instinctive outsider, motorcycles were the *only* mode of transport.

Eventually, one of the boys offered me a ride – I had been too shy and too proud to ask. I couldn't believe this chance. In fact, I was at first terrified by the offer and alarmed by my breathless inability to resist. (What would my mum and dad say, if they found out?) I jumped on and stalled it straight away. Engine running again (what a *thrill* to swing that kickstart and feel the engine zip into life), one of the boys pushed me beyond the point where the clutch could again catch me out. I was off, at first wobbling slowly, certain it would not go where I pointed it and sure it would race out of control. But it didn't. After one lap of the field, without serious loss of life, my confidence soared. It was doing as I wanted. The feel of that twistgrip, spongy in the fist, and springy in its response, the obedience to it of the bright little motor, is still with me. Turning that throttle unleashed power, real propulsion. With a zing. It was *alive*. I was alive. And, instantly, I was hooked. What the fuck was *this*? On a motorcycle was, from that moment, where I wanted to be, where I felt comfortable and good.

My granddad, for his tap-room customers, ran an annual coach trip to the Isle of Man TT Races every June. This was less to do with an enthusiasm for motorcycle road-racing than an enthusiasm to get away from my grandma for a week. Already, as a small boy, Granddad Wallace held me spellbound with accounts of seeing the great Geoff Duke, in the 1950s, cock his head nonchalantly just an inch to one side, to avoid having it removed by a telegraph post when taking the Ginger Hall left-hander at the TT. In his store room, among the bottles of spirits and cartons of cigarettes, Granddad kept two scale models of racing bikes: a bright green Moto Guzzi and a glamorous, fire-engine red MV Agusta. I marvelled at their battle-readiness, their purposeful lines and deep, vivid livery. So, racing motorcycles were not as they were always pictured in the newspapers, all just black and white.

I wanted so badly, by the time I was twelve, to go to watch a bike race. And not necessarily all the way to the Isle of Man. I'd have been happy with Oulton Park, in Cheshire, our nearest circuit. But, no. My dad refused to take me. As before, with fishing, I had to settle, for the time being, with the ruddy books and magazines.

4

AUNTY BRENDA – WAS SHE
THE FIFTH BEATLE?

MY AUNTY BRENDA was a bit younger and much groovier than my dad. By the standards of Rochdale in the early 1960s she was startlingly sophisticated and cosmopolitan. Aunty Brenda had been to France. And liked it. She'd even lived there for a while.

This recklessness was regarded with a certain amount of circumspection by her father, Granddad Nat, the Great War veteran, and by my dad, who had been lucky enough, by the timing of his birth in 1928, to escape service in the Second World War. That good fortune did not prevent him from rushing to reinforce his father's view that the French were an unreliable lot, useless at fighting, and forever in need of the British coming to their salvation – for which they were always resentful and ungrateful. That was the French for you. It was imprudent to encourage my dad or granddad then to move on to the Italians.

My dad was also dismissive and contemptuous of youth culture. This was understandable. There had, it shouldn't be overlooked, been no such thing when he was growing up. The species later identified as the teenager did not exist in the UK until about 1956 or 1957. There was no youth culture until then because, pre-rock & roll, young people did not have music or any other cultural reference points of their own by which to distinguish their tastes from those of their parents. Jazz, trad and modern, made some advances in this generational delineation but achieved nothing like the social and cultural revolution brought on by rock & roll.

In fact, before the mid-1950s, young people did not exist at all. The bulk of those of my dad's generation and before, left school at fifteen or earlier, and the brighter, more aspirational among them got a steady, respectable job at the local bank, or similar. Few went away to college or university. Even if they did, there was still no concept there of youth culture. Young people, until liberated and electrified by Little Richard and his contemporaries, were simply a smaller, more junior version of their parents. They even wore similar clothes. This was my dad in the early 1960s – a young man bewildered by The Beatles.

Aunty Brenda was not. She loved them. And, inevitably, my first pop music memory (there was no rock until the Velvet Underground and Dylan's conversion to electricity in 1965) is of The Beatles.

At her bungalow in Rochdale, which she shared with Grand-dad Nat, Aunty Brenda presented me one afternoon with a child's red and cream plastic Beatles guitar, bearing, on its soundboard, the faces of the Fab Four. This was complemented by a Beatles wig – a moulded plastic, replica mop-top. (I wish I had them now. If I were to sell them on eBay, I could put the children through a good school...) It would have been 1963 because my chosen song for that afternoon's performance, which I must have learned from Aunty Brenda's record player, was *She Loves You*. This I belted out, standing on her kitchen table, as she squealed with delight.

THERE WAS, for better or worse, no Radio 1 until 1967. Even if there had been, Elizabeth and I would not have been allowed to listen to it; an official paternal ban on the station was still in place when I left home for university, although it was routinely flouted.

Music in the home, such as it was, was minimal in quantity and limited in scope. My dad had a fondness for Gracie Fields. Like most Rochdalians, he was proud of Our Gracie as the local mill-girl who became a huge international star of stage and screen. (One of my first freelance photographic successes was to sell to *Lancashire Life* some photos I took of Gracie on her last visit to Rochdale in 1978. She died soon after.)

My mum's Irish Catholic ancestry had handed down to her a romantic attachment to blarney in all its varieties. Musically, this took the form of a small collection of records by Irish light tenors, unloading of themselves sentimental yearnings for the old country, written in the main by Tin Pan Alley hacks in the United States who'd never set foot in Ireland.

She also had a couple of LPs of republican ballads. One of them had on its cover a man in a flat cap, scarf and scruffy tweed jacket. His head thrown back, mouth wide open and his eyes shut tight, he was pictured stretching an Irish tricolour over his head and appeared to be the worse for drink. It was called *Songs Of The Irish Rebellion*. ('And we're all off to Dublin in the green, in the green/Where the helmets glisten in the sun/ Where the bayonets flash and the rifles crash/To the rattle of the Thompson gun...') There was a period, during the regime of Mrs Thatcher, when my mother could have been shot dead by the SAS for owning this and similar albums.

For years, and until I was steered eventually to the real stuff, my mother's idea of country music and British folk music led me to believe, tragically, that both genres were irredeemably corny and not worthy of further investigation. The supreme achievement of Slim Whitman, Don Williams and the Spinners was to make very successful careers from stripping out the soul and raw emotion integral to the authentic variants of these styles. The Spinners, comfortable folk musicians for those who wore comfortable cardigans, had their own television show which ran for years. When they sang *The Day We Went To Rothesay-O*, as they always did, I could not imagine a group of blokes more unlikely to go on the rampage in Scot-

Aunty Brenda in her French film noir period – worryingly cosmopolitan for early 1960s Rochdale. And "The Professor", aged six, at Rochdale Convent, 1966.
Unknown

land on strong drink. The Spinners were to folk what the Bachelors were to pop.

Unavoidably, Beatlemania touched everyone's lives, except my dad's, in the early 1960s. But I was never moved by The Beatles. As I grew older, I came to respect them as trailblazers and outstanding composers of songs which were to become, very quickly, standards. Yet they didn't *excite* me. Just as I was never able to understand why anyone was convinced by Elvis Presley – manifestly plastic, second-rate and middle of the road alongside his genuinely dangerous contemporaries, Jerry Lee Lewis and Little Richard – I could not subscribe to the almost religious devotion to The Beatles. And once I became aware of the Rolling Stones, I recognised the true keepers of the rock & roll flame. Later, I would also hold The Beatles responsible for the creation of Rock as Art, and all the horrors which that pseudo-intellectual concept then visited upon us.

IN ABOUT 1968, I found in the back of a cupboard at home a forgotten and broken transistor radio. It was a dumpy, battery-powered Perdio model, with a chummy red leather covering and a gold-coloured sound grille. I can't recall why it didn't work or how I fixed it but I did. It was, most likely, the first thing I ever mended. My dad was pleased with my efforts and told me I could have it. I loved that little red box and was so proud to have it as my own personal grown-up appliance and as my connection to a strange, exotic wider world.

At night, especially, I would twist the dial across a clamour of competing foreign stations, bounced down to me on a shifting ionosphere. Sometimes I heard English and always I heard pop music, drifting in and out of my reception. Before too long, I'd found Radio Luxembourg and the American Forces Network Europe.

1968 and 1969 were years of upheaval, both musically and in terms of world events. I was becoming aware, largely through that little radio, of both. I have strong memories of being excited by that soundtrack as it was happening. And the record which moved me most in that period was one which, better than any other, caught the mood of the moment, the spirit of the age and most accurately mirrored turbulent global events: Thunderclap Newman's *Something In The Air.*

Let's just take stock of what happened in the space of those twenty-four months: Paris, May '68; the Prague Spring and the arrival of Soviet tanks to crush it; the first moon landing; the Woodstock Festival; the Battle of Grosvenor Square; the Vietnam war and opposition to it at its most intense; the assassinations of Martin Luther King and Bobby Kennedy; civil rights demonstrations in Derry, Northern Ireland attacked by the police and escalating into the Troubles; the British army sent into Northern Ireland (to protect Catholics); Enoch Powell's Rivers of Blood speech; the Biafran war and famine in Nigeria; Black Power salutes at the Mexico Olympics; Richard Nixon becoming US president; the start of colour television transmissions in the UK; the Rolling Stones free concert in Hyde Park (just a few days after the death of Brian Jones); the Charles Manson murders; the debut of *Monty Python's Flying Circus*; the My Lai massacre; Altamont.

Looking back, of all the records I should not have left out when I appeared on *Desert Island Discs* in March 2007, *Something In The Air* was the greatest omission from my selection of eight songs. It represents my awakening both musically and politically and, on a purely emotional level, evoking as it does popular solidarity and possibility – from fifteen-year-old Jimmy McCulloch's shimmering guitar opening through to the thrilling declaration of 'Hand out the arms and ammo, We're gonna blast our way through here…' – it still gets me *right there*. That Thunderclap Newman were one hit wonders renders drummer and singer Speedy Keen's song-writing achievement with *Something In The Air* all the more extraordinary.

The remarkable scale and speed of events of 1968 and 1969, and their reflection in an equally dizzying cultural revolution, made me yearn back then to be old enough to participate. In that summer of '69, my dad sat at the breakfast table and, tut-tutting, passed to my mum his newspaper on the front of which there was a photo of a lithe young couple dancing in foam, but otherwise naked, at a pop festival. It would have been either the Isle of Wight or Woodstock. Bubbles and suds obscured, tantalisingly, their most fascinating bits. 'Just look at that,' my dad sighed. 'What are things coming to?' I craned over the breakfast things but didn't dare voice my admiration.

Few people of middle age wish to be older but the little lad at the breakfast table still regrets, forty years on, not to have been born ten years earlier. Had I been nineteen in 1969, and not nine, I'm sure I would have been some central and, with hindsight, hugely embarrassing figure in British counter-culture, seeking out the likes of Joe Boyd at the UFO club or helping a hippy idealist music business maverick like Peter Jenner (with whom I would later work) to stage the free concerts in Hyde Park.

Cultural developments happened much faster in those days. Dramatic events seemed to be compressed into much shorter sequences. At the end of the 1960s, and in the space of just a decade, British music had moved on from Tommy Steele to Pink Floyd. Yet time, if not events, lapses slowly when one is young. That is because, at that age, any given period of time – a year or a decade – represents a much greater proportion of one's overall existence than it does later. My own involvement with concert promotion would begin to happen within ten years of the Stones in the Park but, in 1969, that was the equivalent of a century away and as yet unforeseen. Another cultural upheaval or two still lay ahead before I would slip into the music business.

I DON'T THINK there was a formal ruling at home that we were not allowed to watch *Top Of The Pops* but, certainly, we were scorned and ridiculed if we tried to do so. So, on those evenings of its transmission, if my mum and dad were out, Elizabeth and I would delight in what had to be a private passion. Or we watched with our cousin, Linda, at her house. Linda was a bit older than us, more worldly, went to discos and such, and was not subject to similar parental restraints. Alas, our occasional peeks at *TOTP* coincided with the early-70s explosion of Glam Rock. But beggars couldn't be choosers.

Of the silver-trousered, platform-perched Thursday evening performers, I was not convinced by the melodrama of The Sweet. Marc Bolan and T Rex were a little too fey and girlie. David Bowie could have his moments, although he had a tendency to self-importance. Spiritually, I was more aligned with Gary Glitter, the simplicity of his heavy-riffing, call and response, back-to-basics rock & roll, and with the loutishness of The Faces and Slade.

Totally unpretentious, Slade were one of few bands of the period who needn't have felt ashamed or threatened by punk. Indeed, Slade were proto punks and, I daresay, Johnny Rotten and his contemporaries learned much more from Slade than they cared to admit.

One afternoon in September 1972, I crossed a threshold. From a stall on Oldham market, which sold ex-jukebox singles for 30p, I bought a copy of Slade's 45, *Mama Weer All Crazee Now*. It was my first record. And, all the way home on the bus, I studied it, fondled it and fretted about how to get it undetected into the house. At the front door, I stuffed it under my duffle coat and hid it in my bedroom until my dad went out. Then I revealed it to Our Elizabeth. She was impressed. Before long she had slipped me 30p and an order for David Bowie's *Starman*.

It was only a matter of time before my record collection of one item was discovered by my dad. He seemed to feel genuinely betrayed and his response, which he would later regret and retract, was to hint strongly to me that this purchase, this fondness for pop music, was an indication of homosexuality. (Without, of course, his recognition or articulation of the existence of the preference.) This hurt and, for it, I resented him for a long time. But there was one positive, even life-changing, conclusion to this incident: my popular music proclivities had been outed. There was no going back.

5

PLAYING THE GAME
(AND PLAYING UP)

FOR SOME OF US at the Hulme Grammar School for Boys, Old-ham, the BBC television transmission of Michael Palin's *Ripping Yarns* pilot, *Tomkinson's Schooldays*, in 1976, did not represent the comedy landmark that it undoubtedly was but a milestone of serious investigative journalism. That none of us, during our seven years at Hulme, was caught and mauled by the school leopard, as Tomkinson had been at Graybridge, can be explained only by the school having been too stingy to employ, for security purposes, a similar big cat.

In all other respects, Hulme shared with Tomkinson's school so many similar ludicrous values and absurd tradi-tions, the justification for which even the most ancient members of staff could not remember. Just why, for example, was our playing field called 'Big Side' and not, well... the play-ing field? Did anyone really remember or care about the former pupils whose double-barrelled names were immortal-ised in gold leaf on huge oak boards in the school hall, of those old boys who had perished, in alarming numbers, apparently in defence of the colonies? Who on earth was the multi-initialled character who, according to his own personal and very generous memorial plaque in the hall, 'always played the game'. Which game? And why did his playing of it deserve a plaque?

By all the measures of educational achievement, Hulme was an excellent school. It was also one of those grammar schools that sheer tenacity, defiance and durability (founded in 1611) had conferred upon it – so the school imagined – the status of a public school, with all the pointless traditions and petty snobberies that went with that. And the full complement of nutcases in the staff-room that these institutions seem to attract.

I had left the cosiness and genuinely tender care of Rochdale Convent in the summer of 1970. Naturally, I was heading for my dad's secondary school in Rochdale. In fact, I went there for just one term. Then the local authority decreed all children had to attend their nearest comprehensive. There was to be no choice. Our nearest, alas, was a sink school, a hooligan academy. Even my mum and dad, who worked within, and were great supporters of, the state school system, realised that with a child's education there is just one chance. They decided to jettison principle and push me towards prestigious private schools. I passed the exams for both Oldham Hulme and Bury Grammar. In December 1970, parentally bribed into that exam success with the promise of a model Spitfire, I was packed off to the prep school of Hulme, fully nine miles away from home. I hated every single rotten minute of the spiteful, small-minded, dehumanising little torture centre.

As the new kid who'd arrived half way through the year, I was isolated by the other boys – when I wasn't being bullied by them. Most of the teachers (all male) were just as horrid, not even welcoming or sympathetic.

For seven months I sat alone in a shed in the playground during every break period and lunchtime. No one would play with me. No one asked me to join in. They were cruel – and smug with it. I loathed every single one of them with ferocity. In the shed, often bitterly cold through that winter, I read or just sat and thought. Sometimes I wept for the loss of my friends at the convent, who I missed terribly, as I did the happy industry of the place and the warmth of the nuns. Now, I was desperately lonely and miserable. No one, I vowed to myself, would ever humiliate me or push me around again.

This was not a resolution helped by my size. I was tiny for my age, but clever. Both of these characteristics are, to the cowardice and inadequacy of the bully, as irresistible as minnows to perch. (It was not until I was well into my second year at Leeds University that I started to grow.)

Those seven months were among the longest in my life. It even seemed to take for ever to get home to the far side of a distant town. And it was always dark, always raining, always cold. Back home there was time only for tea, homework and bed, in order to be up again at some ungodly hour to go through the hell of it all over again.

IN SEPTEMBER 1971, I was set free into Hulme Grammar's secondary school. Now, for my juvenile tormentors in the prep, the boot was on the other foot. The majority of the intake into the first year there were newcomers and outsiders like me. The bullies of the prep were no longer so smug.

Soon I had found a few kindred spirits. There was Mark Judkowski, with whom, for the duration of our school life, I would be a friend and respectful rival in excellence in most subjects. There were those who – like Jonny Barnes, Paul Taylor, Jeff Wharfe, Howard Johnson, Dave Brown (who decided he would change his very ordinary name to the very ordinary Derek Brown) and Simon Flynn – also had a sense of the absurd. Thank God, I thought to myself at some point during the first year, there are others here who understand, who also recognise just how ridiculous this place is.

I had a number of circles at school: those pals who also liked motorcycles, music, fishing and photography. Jonny, Flynny, Paul and Jeff weren't found together in all of these but we were otherwise bound firmly, and for ever it seemed, by our sense of humour, our instinctive anti-authoritarianism, a loathing of pettiness and injustice, and a delight in rebellion and subversion. We were also drawn together by our total lack of interest in football. Though there was not the tyranny of football that there is now, we resented even then the assumption that we should be obsessed by it. A liking for football, and – worse – admiring football culture, became very reliable indicators of the wanker.

Paul Taylor and I were more than friends. We were soul brothers and an inspiration to each other. Paul was genuinely wild, not in any violent or aggressive sense – he would never harm anyone – but he was without any apparent constraints on his thoughts and imagination. He terrified me, as I could never be sure what he would do next, and I adored him.

Much of our energy at school was expended on ridiculing the authority and the pomposity of certain members of staff, the prefects (we, in our group, were the only sixth-formers *not* to be made prefects), and particularly the Headmaster, Sid Johnson, a most unpleasant fellow with absolutely no sense of humour, who seemed not only to resent young people, and therefore his job, but actively to hate them. It always baffled me as to why he'd gone into teaching.

Soul brother. Paul Taylor growling out of the Geography classroom window. Hulme Grammar School, Oldham, 1976. He once managed to work the line, "I'm fucking boiling, me" into a public performance of *Hamlet*. AK

Paul and I were not, in the conventional sense, bad lads. Our subversion specialised in the kind of behaviour that Sid Johnson and his staff had trouble defining as an offence. There was, for example, nothing specific in the school rules to prohibit me and Paul spotting, one lunchtime on a tip near school, a wet, rotting sofa, from which much of the stuffing was hanging out. There was nothing either in the rules which proscribed us from sneaking that sofa into the school during a free period later that day, and slipping it on to the stage in the main hall, from which Sid Johnson would hold school assembly the following morning. By then, the mystery sofa was interposed – and giving off an offensive smell – between Sid and his staff. Cue Sid's spluttering indignation in front of the whole school, much mirth along our row, compounded by Sid's order to a couple of boys from the front to manhandle the foul furnishings away, with immense difficulty. This, of course, only prolonged the farce, Sid's visible exasperation, and our delight.

He stood there on another morning, his face empurpled, booming and yelling, his eyeballs about to burst. Some poor lad, you see, had been spotted that morning, ambling along to school, correctly dressed in uniform, in all respects, except for the unofficial adornment of a bush hat. To Sid, this was final proof that society was in meltdown and that the values for which he and the school were a bulwark against barbarianism (represented, on this occasion, by a popular item of fisherman's headgear) were facing massive onslaught.

I can't recall if the lad with the bush hat was flayed alive in front of the school there and then or hung, drawn and quartered during morning break, but Paul and I, on the victim's behalf, had hatched our revenge by lunchtime. In the school rules, I remembered, it stipulated that 'the only approved headgear is the school cap'. No one over the age of about nine had worn the school cap since before the war. But the school's own rules were about to become the instrument for their ridicule.

The next morning, after rummaging at the back of wardrobes the night before, Paul and I, aged eighteen and on the point of going to university, turned up wearing our school caps. Mine, which I'd not worn since the ghastly prep, resembled a pea on a drum. Paul, who was a chubby, bear-like fellow, looked even more ridiculous. Along the corridors that morning, there was much glowering and brow furrowing from the more establishment members of staff. I could see they were bursting to remonstrate with me yet they were unable to define and articulate what was wrong. For there was nothing wrong. I was, after all, only wearing the officially approved school headgear. And by doing so I was observing to the letter the school rules.

6

SURFIN' SAFARI
(THE BRIDLINGTON OPTION)

ALL SMALL BOYS aspire to, and affect, the tastes and behavioural patterns of older lads. This was true of a tendency towards cultural one-upmanship at our school.

More senior pupils sneered at my babyish Slade enthusiasms. Thirteen-year-old lads in my class, almost as self-defence, carried around progressive rock albums – not because they actually liked them or even listened to them, but because they thought they should do. So they tucked them under their arms just to be seen with them.

These LPs, examples of a style we doctors have come to identify as Big Lads' Music, were flaunted in the corridors or on the bus as badges of spurious maturity and sophistication. That they were absolutely unlistenable was neither here nor there. I've since been quite candid about this with Robert Plant and Rick Wakeman. I just didn't get it with Led Zeppelin or Yes, to name but two, and wasn't going to expend what little cash I had as a schoolboy on albums I didn't like. (I later came to appreciate bits of Led Zeppelin. But only bits.) By contrast, *Mama Weer All Crazee Now* spoke to me in 1972 and still speaks to me in 2011. It is a rousing, insolent record. And, by god, we need some musical insolence again now. I still own that original copy.

Slade were just the job, on one level, but my tastes were soon to be expanded. The milieu of the Beach Boys could not have been a more alien environment to a pre-pubescent in land-locked, industrial Rochdale – upon which the sun, when it shone, appeared to do so through Tupperware. I think it was my school pal – and still my pal – Jonny Barnes, who introduced me to the Beach Boys' carefree world of surfing, honey-coloured girls, gleaming teeth, infinite leisure time, blond crew-cuts, parental wealth, hot-rod cars and recreational road traffic accidents. Jonny probably picked up on the Beach Boys from his mum who, bewilderingly, when we were teenagers, appeared to be about twenty-five.

I adored the Beach Boys, for all those sun-kissed temptations and their glorious songs and exquisite harmonies. They seemed to promise gratification on an epic scale, just waiting around the corner in late adolescence which, for a while, persuaded me – a physically under-developed specimen, always overlooked or even ridiculed by girls – that to adapt a Beach Boys attitude to a life in Lancashire was my best hope of getting shagged.

To this end, when I was fifteen, I made an attempt at surfing. I embarked on this foolishness in the freezing grey breakers of Bridlington, with absolutely no knowledge of what I was doing, and barely able to swim. I nearly drowned and haven't tried to surf since. However, despite being the cause of my near death, I still love my Beach Boys records.

IF MY FLOURISHING PASSION for music suggests I was buying up vast quantities of vinyl every week, I wasn't. Pocket money, when I got it, had to be eked out across fishing tackle, maggots and, pretty soon, photographic materials, petrol and motor-cycle spares. As well as records.

One afternoon, in our kitchen, when I'd asked for a small sub to buy some photographic developer, my mum snapped at me, 'You know your trouble, don't you? You've too many bloody interests, that's what!'

I am so thankful I was never seduced, expensively, by clothes and fashion. When I was about twelve, I evolved a wardrobe – Levi jeans, T-shirts, sneakers (or rugged leather boots, never shoes), check cotton work shirts, and denim or ex-military shirts – which was unimaginative but hard-wearing, practical, time saving and never needed ironing. It was also time*less* in that, as it was never in fashion, it never went out of fashion. I've stuck with it ever since. It's versatile, too: simply by switching from a check shirt, with my 501s and sneakers, to a plain white T-shirt, I can advertise my rock & roll loyalties (black leather motorcycle jacket optional) instead of my acoustic Neil Young sensitivities.

One of my dad's maxims was, 'To be well dressed is to be suitably dressed.' I reminded him of that on the day we were burying my Granddad Nat. Within minutes of spluttering his complaint that I'd turned up at the chapel of rest in my customary blue-collar attire, the hearse broke down on the way to Rochdale Cemetery. It wasn't any of the mourners dressed 'properly' in sombre, dark suits who cheerily got down on the road surface and squirmed around under the car, grappling with the fan belt, until my granddad's coffin was again under propulsion. No, it was muggins, here – in his *Grapes of Wrath* costume.

Where were we? Oh, yes – disposable income. Or the lack of it.

Records were acquired piecemeal, purchases planned and agonised over weeks in advance of striding, with mock confidence and affected nonchalance, into Bradley's Records in Rochdale, to dump clattering piles of accumulated loose change onto the counter for the scrutiny of an implausibly sexy but indifferent, gum-chewing girl. This was a process made all the more humiliating if carried out, straight off the bus, in school uniform. Very often, I had to ease my way to the girl's attention by squeezing through a line of very tall, identical, willowy young men, in Afghan coats, constantly pushing back their lank hair from their faces, as they nodded and concentrated, on headphones, to the latest from Barclay James Harvest or similar, and pretended to like it.

On my infrequent shopping trips on the train to Manchester, there were record shops there – *record department stores* –

whose stock could bring me to a state of almost pre-sexual arousal. Rarely could I afford to buy a thing, but I'd go in there anyway, just to admire the sleeves, absorb the liner notes and fantasise about owning many of them.

I did, memorably, once splash out on one of these imported rarities. It was – and I had never anticipated this kind of thing was available on LP – an album of the March on Washington, of August 1963, when a quarter of a million civil rights demonstrators, black and white together, gathered before the Lincoln Memorial, to hear Martin Luther King deliver his *I Have A Dream* speech.

The speech, in its entirety, was on this LP, as was a song performed there that day, and badly recorded on location, by a young Bob Dylan. *Only A Pawn In Their Game* caught Bob in a moment of fleeting attachment to the civil rights movement and in his brief period of protest and righteous indignation. Soon after, chemicals – which informed Bob's greatest music – rather than causes became more important to him.

That LP embodied everything I yearned to be a part of. In trying to recapture the Sixties – of which I'd been an observer but in which I'd been too young to participate – I wanted to find myself now a place equivalent to one in that huge crowd, beside those ponds along that mall, terrifying the greedy, the powerful, and the corrupt, disarming them of their weapons of injustice and cruelty, with we-the-people solidarity and moral certainty.

This was, for the moment, and with a return ticket to Rochdale in my pocket, most improbable. But coming home with me that day, on that LP, was another scrawny, idealistic, misfit kid, with an appetite, a need and a flair for self-reinvention and, like me a hick from the sticks, who was to have – although I couldn't have predicted it at the time – a major impact on my outlook, my tastes and my life. Hello, Bob.

7

CHIMES OF FREEDOM

WE'VE BEEN THROUGH thick and thin, Dylan and I. Quite a lot of thin, actually.

I suppose I must have been aware of Bob since those early radio days with the little Perdio transistor and, around that time, no doubt, the detestable *Lay Lady Lay*. Small wonder I didn't latch onto him straight away. Pop music radio did not, as a rule, play *Stuck Inside Of Mobile With The Memphis Blues Again*.

The moment of revelation, and the instant, lustful consummation of our stormy and endless love affair, came with a second-hand copy of *Highway 61 Revisited* when I was about fourteen. I'd like to pretend, for purposes of posterity and historical accuracy, where it was, or from whom, I obtained this life-altering LP. But I simply can't remember.

I do remember playing it for the first time, bending over the record player and jolting back, as if I'd put my finger into the mains, when *Like A Rolling Stone* jumped out of the speaker. It was one of those moments – and I've been lucky enough to have experienced probably half a dozen of them in nearly forty years of meddling with music – in which, from the first few seconds of that torrential opening track, I knew that things would never be the same again. What the fuck was *this*?

Nine years earlier, at the time of the record's release in July

1965, fifteen-year-old Bruce Springsteen was being driven around New Jersey in his mother's car and listening to AM radio, when he heard *Like A Rolling Stone* for the first time. From Bobby Gregg's opening snare drum shot, which announces the song, Bruce later recalled that the experience was, for him, 'like somebody had kicked open the door to your mind'. I know exactly the blunt-force trauma that Bruce felt. Phil Ochs, a sharper protest songwriter than Dylan but who failed in his attempt to transfer to rock & roll and ended up hanging himself, said *Highway 61* was 'impossibly good' and wondered, 'How can a human mind do this?' The answer, Phil, was drugs. But that needn't detain us here.

Never mind in 1965, or 1974, *Like A Rolling Stone* and *Highway 61* retain still, for me, their capacity to shock and impress, to sound fresh, innovative and invigorating, dangerous and hip, forty-five years after they were recorded in the space of just six days in New York City that spring. (Dylan and his session musicians actually made up the arrangement of *Like A Rolling Stone* in the studio, over several takes.) Still I marvel at young Mike Bloomfield's lead guitar, elegantly winding up the tension over a pleasing and ascending C, F, G chord progression before releasing it, across Bob's invective, with the attack of a spitting cobra. I could put on *Like A Rolling Stone* now and still hear in it something new, a detail I hadn't spotted before. It is so *dense*. And, simultaneously, beautifully simple.

For the next two years, I didn't listen to another artist apart from Bob and those who Dylan cited – in all the books about him which I was collecting – as his inspiration. There didn't seem any need to do otherwise. The numerous incarnations of Bob Dylan, from Woody Guthrie protégé to acoustic love-song balladeer to psychedelic rock & roller, satisfied all my requirements. Aside from all his legitimate releases, I amassed an impressive collection of Dylan bootlegs, notably, and most influentially, his May 1966 concert with the Hawks at Manchester's Free Trade Hall (about which I would eventually make a radio documentary and track down, in 1998, the man who had, notoriously, heckled the newly-electrified Bob that night with a cry of 'Judas!').

This dramatic shift in tastes certainly kept them on their toes at Bradley's Records, Rochdale. If Dylan had kicked open the door to young Springsteen's mind he had shown young Kershaw the full sweep of a new musical horizon. Or perhaps a more accurate analogy might be that Dylan caused me to swerve from the middle of the road and into the rich and more interesting margins from which I would never again fully re-emerge. I had the staff in Bradley's ordering up albums by Big Bill Broonzy, Hank Williams, T Bone Walker, Johnny Cash, Woody Guthrie, The Carter Family and Muddy Waters.

If Dylan wasn't solely responsible for my awareness of the varieties of American music which shaped him, he certainly encouraged me to listen to folk, blues, country and gospel. He opened the door for me to Americana, thirty years before it was identified as a genre. Overnight, I lost interest in what was in the British charts. And, in time, an obsession with Bob pointed me, inevitably, towards his troubadour contemporaries, notably Neil Young, Joni Mitchell and Van Morrison.

Bob's protest period, and reading a great deal about its historical context, reinforced my instinct for the underdog, the oppressed, the outsider, and sharpened my sense of justice and injustice. Few songs have the power to reduce me to tears (The Oldham Tinkers' *Come Whoam To Thi Childer An' Me* springs to mind) but *Chimes Of Freedom*, Dylan's clarion for justice and human rights, can still make me fill up. Twerp that I am, I also left *Chimes of Freedom* out of my Desert Island Discs.

Later, with my glands by now in overdrive, I would listen endlessly to *Blood On The Tracks* – Bob's most romantic and last truly great album – as I drove home from another school friend's party, alone in my mother's car, across the darkened moorland above Rochdale, wondering why the latest girl, upon whom I had an unpromising crush, wouldn't even look at me. If those girls could have only glanced up for a moment from the broad shoulder of some barbarian knob-head who happened to play for the school football team, they might have noticed that the kid called Kershaw, the one who looked about eleven, bore striking similarities to the Rimbaud-ish bloke in *Shelter From The Storm,* did he not?

Hey, Mr Andy Kershaw, play a song for me. At Radio Aire, Leeds, 1982. *David Muscroft*

But then the record collections of all those Nicolas and Vanessas usually extended from The Electric Light Orchestra (how I loathed their bleatings) to *Saturday Night Fever*.

CHARISMATIC, ENIGMATIC, TANTALISINGLY PRIVATE, supremely hip, visionary, elusive, unpredictable, indefinable and mercurial, Dylan was a reservoir of mystery as well as magnificent music – and my secret soul mate.

But, most importantly and alluringly, he was never here. Since that 1966 tour, which had provoked almost civil unrest at some UK venues, Bob had not again set foot in Britain, except for his appearance as a white-suited crooner at the Isle of Wight Festival in 1969. Until, that is, 1978. Without warning, in about January of that year, I was absolutely stunned to see a concert advertisement, placed by promoter Harvey Goldsmith, in one of the Sunday broadsheets. It was illustrated by a photo of Bob, sliding a pair of sunglasses from his unmistakable nose. Bloody hell, he was coming!

The ad announced Dylan would be playing a series of concerts at Earls Court in London in June. A list of ticket outlets was printed. My nearest was an obscure record shop in Manchester city centre. It revealed a date in February when they would go on sale. The cheapest seat, and the only one in my price range, cost five pounds.

It was bone-chillingly cold, camping out on the streets of Manchester. I got there around 6pm on the evening before tickets were due to go on sale. Already there were hundreds in the queue ahead of me. For them, it was quite the social occasion – bottles of wine, guitars and Dylan sing-alongs. Everyone else was much older and among friends. I was on my own.

In the late evening, word ripped along the queue that the shop would open and tickets would go on sale just after midnight. That turned out to be the case, although that line ahead of me moved very slowly. Agonisingly so. As I was alone, and too shy to talk to those around me, there was no one even to keep my place in the queue, no escape from the sheer tedium by taking a stroll around the city's streets. For something like three or four hours my face was squashed up against the window of a wine shop, with no hope of varying my view.

I reached the counter at just gone 6am. 'A five pound ticket for 20th June,' I squeaked. I got it (and still have my stub), bright pink, with confirmation of the impossible in red lettering: Bob Dylan, Earls Court, 20th June 1978.

Within a couple of weeks, the timetable for my A-level exams was published. To my horror, my Economics exam upon which, along with those for Spanish and History, my future at Leeds University depended, had been scheduled for the afternoon of 20th June. Not even the ruddy morning of that day. What the hell was I going to do?

Bob Smith was a nice lad, a generous sort, and an incongruous chum in his cavalry twills. But the thing I liked most about Bob, on 20th June 1978, was that he wasn't sitting Economics. He also had a car, a snazzy Mini. At eighteen, he was very much the young man about town.

We got it all worked out. I bought a ticket for a late afternoon train from Manchester Piccadilly to London Euston which was to get me into the capital for about 7pm. Piccadilly was about five miles from our school in Oldham. Working backwards, Bob – engine revving at the school gates – was going to have to pick me up at about 3.30pm. This meant I would have time to sit only half of the three-hour exam.

I went in there and knocked out three essays – about what, I can't for the life of me remember – writing, not for the last time, as a journalist on a disappearing deadline, making sure to chuck in all the jargon and clichés so admired by the academics of this pseudo-science, the disciples of this mystification of the blindingly obvious.

After an hour and a half, I legged it, the senior Economics teacher – a man known as Snippy – in bewildered pursuit of me down the corridor. For Snippy, this was Kershaw's come-uppance. After all, for the last two years, I'd dared to ridicule the subject to which he'd devoted his professional life. Now, I'd blown it, spectacularly, and could kiss goodbye to Leeds University. Bob The Wheels was waiting. For as long as he'd had the car, he'd been looking for an excuse, I suspected, to squeal its tyres. We roared off through the early summer sunshine towards Manchester.

I reached Earls Court just as Dylan and the band were taking the stage. I heard an enormous roar as I passed through the turnstiles. Comparing my seat and block number with the signs, I went racing up a moving escalator three steps at a time. Dylan, behind me, all around me in this concrete cavern, was wailing *Baby, Stop Crying*, his questionable new single.

An usherette held back, obligingly, a thick black curtain and I plunged into the darkness of the auditorium. To my dismay, my £5 had bought me a seat somewhere in the vicinity of, I think, Nottingham. That was only the start of the indignities.

After a couple of songs, and the initial thrill of telling myself that the tiny speck in the middle, way over yonder, was indeed Bob Dylan, *in person*, I had to confront a terrible reality: Bob was bloody awful. And the band – better suited to backing up Neil Diamond at a Las Vegas supper-club residency – was even worse. I wanted the Hawks (later The Band) of 1966. But these guys had neither the menace nor majesty of Robbie Robertson and his buddies. This was what is often termed 'a revue orchestra'. And, from the £5 seats, there seemed to be dozens of the buggers.

Dylan, meanwhile, appeared to be disregarding, quite wilfully, the tunes of his own songs. Some were completely unrecognisable, unless a key word or two could be caught in the competing echoes of Earls Court. It got worse: there was the matter of the trousers.

This icon of cool was standing before us, in mid 1978, in flares, if you please. And no ordinary flares. Some years later, I was able to consult, in the strictest confidence, a fellow Dylanologist – *Whistle Test* co-presenter and friend, Mark Ellen – on the delicate question of Bob's Earls Court leg-coverings. Mark, it turned out, had been there on the same night as me, although seated not far from the stage. Yes, Mark was able to confirm, that *was* a red, metallic zig-zag stripe down the seams of Bob's white flares. And – Mark had me sit down for this bit – it was clear to him, the trousers were in Crimplene.

When Bob lurched into *Forever Young* (he was thirty-seven at the time), a phenomenon I had never seen before spread across the auditorium. Small jewels of light appeared everywhere as people held up cigarette lighters to greet the set-piece sentimental number.

A chap in front of me, clearly swept away by the emotion of it all, set fire to his copy of the *Evening Standard* and I spent the final couple of verses slapping the sparks and embers off my school uniform.

A shameful *Like A Rolling Stone,* contemptuous of the original, sealed a thoroughly demoralising evening. I caught a very slow train home – feeling utterly betrayed and lamenting a lost university future – which dumped me in Manchester around dawn, with hours to wait in the cold for a bus to Rochdale.

The A-level results were to be published one morning in early August. I shambled along to school to pick them up, steeled for the failure in Economics I so richly deserved. Snippy had propped himself up against the wall outside the school office, grinning at my discomfort as I came down the corridor. I went in, picked up the envelope and ripped it open. Spanish and History, no problem, as expected.

Economics? Grade A.

8

A BRUTAL INITIATION –
RORY, LIVE AND LOUD

IF, TO ALL INTENTS AND PURPOSES, I married Bob Dylan as a teenager, then I had a pre-nuptial fling with Rory Gallagher.

At my mother's caravan, around 1973, I became friendly with a lad who was a couple of years older than me – a big difference at that age. Andrew Clay, known as Cass, was bright, funny, fearless, charming and cocky. He embodied only those public schoolboy qualities (Pocklington, in the East Riding) which are attractive and admirable. Girls regarded him as a bounder but, possibly because of that, found him irresistible. And they went into meltdown about his tall, beach bum physique, mop-top good looks, his infantile sense of humour and his puppyish cheek. Cass just didn't give a bugger.

Why on earth he was hanging around with me must have been a mystery to many. Maybe they assumed I was his nephew. But we were, despite our age gap, simply on the same wavelength, bonded by a dedication to irreverence.

Our horizons beyond Ulrome Seaside Caravan Park opened up, thrillingly and noisily, once Cass passed his driving test. Over a couple of delirious summers, he had a series of souped-up bangers and a parade of impossibly gorgeous girlfriends.

There was a scruffy MGB GT – a sparkling new one wouldn't have suited him – and an ancient, purple Ford Anglia, so rusty that most of the floor at the passenger's feet had completely rotted away. I had to sit with my sneakers up on the dashboard as the road surface rushed, visibly, beneath me. Few of these cars had any qualities which would have impressed an MOT examiner and their routinely shattered silencers announced our approach, across the flat farmlands of East Yorkshire, from several miles distance.

Had we had that Bruce Springsteen with us in the back, The Boss could have got a double album's worth of inspiration and material from our pointless runs out to Scarborough and Bridlington or, on a last-chance power-drive, possibly to Driffield and some distant, sleepy village pub.

Most vehicles in Cass's fleet were equipped with a stereo cassette system of state-of-the-art 1970s tinniness. It was on one of these, and on one of our pell-mell dashes around the country lanes, that I first heard Rory Gallagher. The album was *Live In Europe*. Cass was already a big fan of the Irish guitarist. Immediately, I warmed to Rory and his no-nonsense blues and boogie. I admired his totally unpretentious, reluctant rock star style or, rather – in an age of ludicrously-costumed contemporaries – his lack of it. Rory, for goodness sakes, dressed like *me*, in a check work shirt and a pair of jeans. He played a trusty, battered old Fender which he regarded, rightly, as the tool of his trade. And there was never any danger with Rory that he might unleash upon us a rock opera. On ice.

The key track for me on *Live In Europe* was an old blues number, for which Rory put aside his electric Fender and picked up the acoustic. This pretty guitar rag he introduced with, 'Here's a song written back in 1920-something-or-other, by Blind Boy Fuller, and it's called *Pistol Slapper Blues*.'

Blind Boy Fuller, eh? The name alone was exotic enough to tempt further exploration. And so I did. Rory's blues roots and enthusiasms, allied to those behind much of Dylan's music, meant Bradley's Records of Rochdale soon had a bit of a run on the obscure reissues of visually-impaired, pre-war country bluesmen. (I could not have anticipated back then, howling *Pistol Slapper*

Blues out of the open window, that, in 1985 I would meet and interview in North Carolina, Blind Boy Fuller's very elderly widow.)

FOR MUSIC FANS too young to go to pubs, in which the only entertainment anyway was that species of crooner and ballad-eer whose non-microphone-holding hand appears to be constantly adjusting a car wing mirror, there was no live music in Rochdale. None whatsoever. Real bands played in Manches-ter, ten miles away.

Pop and rock music was simply not reflected much back then in the mainstream media. It was largely ignored by newspapers which were run, still, like all other media, by those of the pre-rock & roll generation. It wasn't yet a routine component of television adverts. Only within the previous decade had it been grudgingly recognised by the BBC and institutionalised with the creation of Radio 1 in 1967. On the television, it was repre-sented only by *Top Of The Pops* and the late-night, esoteric *Whistle Test*.

If a gig by a top group was to take place in Manchester, there would not even be a poster for it in nearby Rochdale. The only way of learning who might be about to descend on the Free Trade Hall was to examine a discreet panel of classified adverts, once a week in the *Manchester Evening News*, tucked away with equally coy small-ads for 'Family Planning Requisites' (the purchase of which was, startlingly, by the gross and for delivery 'in a plain wrapper').

I'd scan the concert notices routinely and fantasise that I was old enough, and had the seventy-five pence to buy a ticket for, perhaps, The Faces or Mott The Hoople. Then one afternoon, when I was fourteen, there was an ad in the paper: 'Free Trade Hall Manchester – Rory Gallagher.' The date was some time in the autumn of 1974. I decided I would be there.

The Free Trade Hall was the home of the Hallé Orchestra and a Victorian auditorium of considerable dignity and civic pride, built on the site of the Peterloo massacre of protesting working people in 1819. When I got there, and squeezed through the throngs of greatcoats and loons, I felt like a lost toddler. Everyone else seemed to know each other. To a man – and woman – they were drinking bottles of Newcastle Brown.

I found my seat, quite near the front in the stalls. If there was a support band it was truly unmemorable. Suddenly, without any fuss, Rory was there, with his faithful sidemen. Yep, the shirt was of a soft cotton, washed-out tartan. The jeans were veterans of a number of tours. And the battered Fender was as pleasingly shabby as it appeared on the cover of *Live In Europe*. After some diffident words of greeting, Rory plugged in.

What happened next was truly shocking. Why had no one ever hinted to me that bands played at this volume? For me, the live music virgin, the blast was genuinely frightening. My seat was just in front of the right-hand speaker stack. When Rory hit the opening chord, I swear I felt the skin on my face stretch back. What the fuck was *this*?

I looked up. There were two packed balconies towering above me. I was certain that the volume, so physical was its assault, would bring down both upper and lower circle onto my head. The massive onslaught of Rory's amplification induced in me a feeling of real panic. I actually considered running but held my ground, one part of me insisting to the other that I'd be okay. ('Look, everyone else is fine...')

After a few numbers, I must have settled down. But it was a tremendous shock and an experience which I didn't fully appreciate, nor enjoy the excitement of, until I woke up the next morning, safely at home, with my whistling ears bearing witness to my brutal rock & roll initiation.

Within the decade, I'd be the Entertainments Secretary of Leeds University Union and dear Rory would be a perennial and popular fixture on my programme of gigs. Those early impressions were borne out entirely when I had face to face dealings with him. Other bands' contracts would insist on all manner of dressing-room pamperings. They'd demand a spread be laid on worthy of a state occasion. The drinks requirements would often specify certain expensive wines, served at just the right temperature. Rory, on the other hand, would turn up with his three veteran band members and his brother, Donal, who was his manager and tour manager. Their dressing room requirements were a crate of Guinness and a big plate of cheese sandwiches. After enjoying a couple of these, and leaving the rest for later, Rory would pick up his Fender and amble, almost shyly, to the stage and, for the next hour and a half, play his arse off.

IN THE SUMMER HOLIDAYS, Cass was old enough to be left to his own devices by his mum and dad, when they went back to work during the week. His caravan, therefore, became the Youth Centre. A few of us would 'crash' there – as it was then known – scattering our sleeping bags around the lounge, nourished entirely by cheese on toast and breakfast cereals. Long into the night, we'd lie awake listening to Rory. If it wasn't *Live In Europe*, it was *Blueprint* or *Tattoo*. For variety, another big favourite was Pink Floyd's *Meddle*, particularly *One Of These Days*, the opening track with the galloping tum-tee-tum-tee-tum-tee-tum rhythm, which I shall forever associate with the agonies of appendicitis. Later, in the summer of 1978, The Band's star-studded, live concert farewell, *The Last Waltz* was our constant soundtrack. And there was, always, *Monty Python's Flying Circus*.

The impact, cultural and psychological, made then by this one television programme – and its spin-off records and films – would be unattainable today. In the pre multi-channel cable and satellite age, television was a shared, national experience: much of the population tended to be watching the same thing. That was certainly true of *Monty Python* from 1969 to 1974.

Python's impact arose not from the surrealism and absurdity of the humour, although that was itself revolutionary, but for those it lampooned and the certainties it subverted. Nothing at all was sacred. And, crucially, its habitual figures of fun were those individuals and institutions towards whom the nation had been previously, automatically, deferential.

I am chuckling now at the merchant banker who has on his payroll two pantomime horses; the judge who brings a trial to a conclusion by calling in a roller-skating vicar; an attempt on Everest by the National Hairdressers' Federation; and a television gameshow in which the contestants, in an allotted fifteen

The beach boy I could never be – without drowning. Andrew Clay (Cass), waterskiing, Ulrome, East Yorkshire coast, 1978. *AK*

seconds, have to summarise all seven volumes of Marcel Proust's *À La Recherche du Temps Perdu*, once in a swimsuit and once in evening dress.

To the neighbours, Cass's caravan may have been rocking and screeching unaccountably into the early hours. Behind the curtains, a handful of pals would be in a state of seizure, listening to *Monty Python's Matching Tie And Handkerchief* LP and its football-style commentary to *Novel Writing From Dorchester*, in which Thomas Hardy – 'confident, relaxed, very much the man on form' – settles down at a desk, in the centre of a stadium, to write *The Return of the Native*, 'before a very good-natured bank holiday crowd...'

Monty Python was one of two formative late-night pro- grammes for which I would linger downstairs to watch, secretly, once my mum or dad had gone to bed. The other was *The Old Grey Whistle Test*.

In later years, the *Whistle Test* of the Seventies, presented for most of that decade by Bob Harris, was ridiculed for its cosiness and its gentle hippy values. But lazy critics missed the point: those were its strengths. And its biggest asset was Whispering Bob, who became, and remains, an icon. (Few recall its first presenter was Richard Williams, who went on to become a fine sports journalist.) *Whistle Test* was simply of its age and for the period before punk it was perfect. Its mistake, until its shake-up in the mid-1980s, was to ignore punk altogether – even the valuable bits – in the hope the new fad would quickly fade away and we could all get back to our Allman Brothers records.

As a kid with uncommon music tastes, I loved *The Old Grey Whistle Test*, not just for the artists it prioritised but for the programme's intimacy and that sense that one was a member of a private late-night club. Through the kind introductions of Bob Harris, I made life-long relationships with Little Feat, Ry Cooder, Bob Marley and The Wailers, Joni Mitchell, Bruce Springsteen and The E Street Band, Richard Thompson and many others. (Little did I imagine I would one day find myself presenting it.)

Over on the radio, meanwhile, I discovered an even more important fraternity, if not secret society, and one which, while overlapping with *Whistle Test* on some shared tastes, went much, much further – to the apogee of the esoteric. This peculiar programme was hosted not by some dreamy apostle of 1970s languor but – gloriously – by a tubby, often incompetent, balding little bloke in a comfortable pullover.

GRANDMA NORAH BUYS
A HARLEY-DAVIDSON

THE FIRST I KNEW of it was the roar of an angry engine. And it wasn't that of my granddad's Austin 1100.

It was over my right shoulder. Our Elizabeth and I were on the back seat, my granddad at the wheel and my grandma beside him. On our way to some restaurant for Sunday lunch, we were tootling down Whitworth Road, a main route in and out of Rochdale. It was November 1973.

Even louder now, the revving car was right at my rear passenger window, overtaking – or trying to – with another car coming straight towards us and only two hundred yards away. My granddad began to yell in shock and anger. My grandma let out a long wail. Our Elizabeth's screams joined a crescendo of panic.

First, there was a bump. Our car pitched to the left. The overtaking driver had tried to force his way to safety, bashing into our front right wing, pushing us towards the kerb.

A tremendous bang followed. I remember thinking to myself, calmly and gently, 'You're having a car crash. This is what it's like.'

Most deafening was the sudden, total silence. Then came the

wails and moans. I was squashed down into the space behind the driver's seat. I know this because I was, for a couple of seconds, looking at myself from ten or twelve feet above. It was the classic out-of-body experience. Something was wrong with my mouth. I could taste the metallic tang of blood. My right shin felt as if it were on fire. Already there were voices and anxious faces around the car. Someone opened my door and I crawled out. I was in a chemist's shop. What the fuck was *this*?

Ambulances seemed to be there immediately. And police and fire engines. I walked out through the shattered shop front and propped myself up against the wall. There was much to take in. I watched my grandparents and Elizabeth being lifted from the wreckage and stretchered into the ambulances. Grandma and Granddad looked bad: still, silent, eyes closed and blood-drenched. There were people, uniforms and flashing vehicles everywhere. A crowd of spectators joined them. Soon enough, the ambulances raced away and the onlookers began to thin.

It was when only a couple of blokes remained, sweeping up the glass, that I thought I'd better make my way to hospital. Giving their full and urgent attentions to Our Elizabeth and my grandparents, the emergency services had completely overlooked me. And for my part, I'd been too preoccupied, or too stunned, watching the activity, to tell anyone I'd also been in the crash.

The chemist's we'd almost demolished – luckily, closed and empty on a Sunday – wasn't more than 400 yards from Rochdale Infirmary. I set off there on foot, a little sore and still bleeding from my shin. It had been rammed by the impact under my granddad's seat. My jaw had smashed into the top of his head. Otherwise, I was perfectly okay.

I arrived at a reception desk and told the lady there that I'd just been in a car crash on Whitworth Road. She craned to look out of the window, presumably for my ambulance and its crew. From some emergency room not far away, I heard Our Elizabeth wail, 'No! No!' It was horrific. She sounded very distressed.

'Eh?' said the receptionist. 'How did you get here?'

'I walked,' I told her.

A doctor soon checked me over and told me that Elizabeth and my grandparents would be okay. The bang to my chin had lifted a couple of my front teeth out of line. There was a gouge to my shin which, being right on the bone, couldn't be stitched. There was no skin to stitch in any case. I was bandaged up and, before long, my dad – ashen – arrived to collect me. He'd been at a rugby match at Rochdale Hornets and had had that numbing experience – which, of course, only happens to others – of hearing his name called over the public address system, telling him to go immediately to Rochdale Infirmary.

Elizabeth had some cuts to her bum from flopping back, after the impact, onto broken glass. That, amazingly, was all. My granddad and grandma, however, were in hospital for weeks. On top of all his other problems, my granddad never fully recovered. But Grandma Norah, as soon as she was on her feet again, took charge. There was the court case against the reckless driver – I gave evidence, he was fined – and she still had a pub to run.

GRANDMA NORAH also looked at her little grandson and pitied him. With the car accident on top of troubles brewing at home between my mum and dad, she must have thought I needed, if not a reward, then cheering up with a distraction and some compensation, possibly, for an increasingly absent father.

My motorcycle obsessions did not need bringing to her attention. I was already attending off-road riding lessons at a Sunday morning scheme, with BSA Bantams provided, on the perimeter tracks of Rochdale Sewage Works. The rest of the time, if I wasn't enthusing about some road bike or other then I was evangelising about motorcycle racing, a subject upon which I was already expert – from reading – but a spectacle which, away from television coverage, I still hadn't seen.

Anyone stupid enough to find themselves within earshot of me knew, too, that I reserved particular adulation for the retro stylings and rakish lines of anything made by Harley-Davidson, an American make almost unseen on British roads in those days. In fact, until the mid 1970s, there was only one Harley-Davidson dealer in the UK, the long-established Fred Warr's on the King's Road in London.

Not long after the car crash, I boarded an overnight bus in

Manchester and went to London. It dropped me off at Victoria Coach Station before dawn and, with a little map, I walked to the unfashionable end of the King's Road and to Fred Warr's shop. There, too shy to step inside, I gazed at the gleaming machines in the window. To me, they were creations of immense beauty, from an alien culture and an earlier era. Old fashioned even as brand new, they were just timeless design classics. With one in particular I fell in love – the lean beast that was the v-twin XLH 1000cc Sportster. It was what a proper motorcycle should look like.

That morning, outside Warr's, I promised myself that one day, when I was old enough, and if I were rich enough, I'd buy myself an XLH. In black, of course. (In 1990, I did just that. And I still own and treasure it.)

By the summer of 1974, Harley had opened other dealerships around the UK. These proved to be short-lived but there was one, for a year or two, on Deansgate in Manchester. This certainly saved on my bus fares. The Harley range had also expanded to include a number of lightweight, two-stroke, off-road bikes. Cutest of all of these was the X-90, a mini-bike on ten-inch wheels but in all other respects – perky 90cc engine, four speed box, manual gear change, 55mph – a real motorcycle. And, for a waif like me, just the right size.

I sent off for all the colour brochures. Several times. The photographs I stuck on my bedroom wall and the covers of my school exercise books. The list price of a new X-90 in 1974 was an unattainable £230. Naturally, I never asked. There was no point. And, certainly, I didn't expect.

It was an unbelievable dream come true, then, in July 1974 when my grandma – with no warning – asked me how much were those little motorbikes I liked so much. 'Then go and get him one, then,' she instructed my mum, handing over to her the asking price in cash.

I was in a daze for the next few weeks. We brought it back from Manchester, laid carefully cushioned on its side in the back of a borrowed estate car. On that first night I had it home, I sat up all night with it in the garage, just gawping. A real motorcycle! A real Harley-Davidson! And mine. I could not believe my good fortune, although I could believe Grandma Norah's generosity. (As I write this, the same little X-90 stands just next door, adorning the utility room, restored to immaculate 1974 showroom condition.)

It was shipped again – to the caravan – and in that summer holiday I rode it constantly around the field of a sympathetic farmer. We became inseparable, the X-90 and I. With practice, I became quite a handy rider, able to beat any other kids who brought their motorcycles to this new race-track that the nice farmer never intended to open. And I discovered something else about motorcycles. As the otherwise awkward runt, I felt, on a motorcycle, elegant and graceful.

OFF THE BIKE, I was still a misfit, an obsessive and an outsider. Or so I was convinced. But I was soon to find a soul-rebel comrade and a mentor in someone I didn't actually know – that unlikely bloke on late-night Radio 1.

If I'd heard the John Peel programme before the punk upheaval – and I must have done – then it hadn't made much of an impression on me. Pre-punk, Peel was, most likely, to my ears, a bit of a drip, with an unaccountable fondness for Marc Bolan and attendant beliefs in elves and fairies. Nevertheless, Cass had spoken warmly of Peel's programmes; in fact, he did what turned out to be an unrecognisable impersonation of John's delivery. So I probably tuned in from time to time. And it was at the caravan that I remember first listening to Peel intentionally, probably in the summer of 1976. More than just listening: falling deliriously headlong into this bumbling obsessive's wonky world. It was an absolute revelation.

I was hooked not just by the breadth of the music that John covered. Specifically, it was the juxtaposition of those styles. Already, I was a fan of Annie Nightingale, whose show had become almost completely colonised by correspondents from Leeds University, confirming what the tour advertisements in the music press suggested: Leeds was the higher education repository of rock & roll. Reliably, Annie played all my old faves – Dylan and more Dylan – and my newer ones: Elvis Costello & The Attractions, Ian Dury & The Blockheads, lots of

Wreckless Eric, anything and everything on the gloriously irreverent Stiff label.

Then there was Alexis Korner who hosted a rich Sunday night feast by which I pretended to do my homework. With his smoky, dark-chocolate voice, he introduced blues, real soul, gospel, a splash of Caribbean styles, old R&B and even some African bands. Alexis, playing the South African township jive of the Dark City Sisters on Radio 1, was the first occasion I recall hearing African music.

But John Peel played the lot. And much more – stuff others wouldn't touch with a barge-pole, often with justification. Crucially, John programmed that variety of styles, from all eras, back to back. It was broadcasting in its real sense, as opposed to narrowcasting. In that darkened caravan, I was electrified by adjacent tracks from the likes of Prince Far I, Martin Carthy, The Buzzcocks, Kitty Wells, Kevin Coyne and a hilarious, deadpan Scotsman called Ivor Cutler, intoning some rather unsettling stories, often to harmonium accompaniment, and usually involving herring, a stern grandfather and unremittingly foul weather. What the fuck was *this*?

I received this new radio friend, not just with the excitement of never knowing what Peel would play next, but with a sense of relief. Within the limits of my modest but pick'n'mix record collection, I had been listening by myself to music in this manner at home for some time. The Peel programme's scattershot scheduling told me that this was perfectly okay. I wasn't odd at all. And I wasn't alone any more.

10

HIGH ON CASTROL R

MY DAD, NATURALLY, chose to stay in the car and read the *Daily Telegraph*. I couldn't get out fast enough.

For the last couple of miles, crawling and overheating in a traffic jam on the lanes approaching the circuit, I had been like a bee in a biscuit tin. We clattered across a bridge over the track and parked on the infield. As soon as I tumbled out I heard a sound the like of which I had never heard before. The air was alive with a rushing swarm. It seemed to be coming from all directions, but stronger from here and then there, getting louder and louder, then softening and fading to silence. Then building again. A distant voice on a Tannoy was barking over the clamour. The swarm began to thicken on my left, sweeping invisibly through the trees. I started to run towards it. For years, this was precisely where I'd wanted to be. Truly, literally, here was my calling.

I aimed for the nearest grass bank, a fence and a line of spectators on the crest of a hill. With my face pressed to the wire, I saw for the first time a broad sweep of satin asphalt, bordered by trim green verges, rising from a dip among the trees. The earth banks and barriers were adorned with familiar names and logos of component companies: Shell, Dunlop, Champion. At last, a real race track.

Before I'd had a chance fully to take in this most satisfying panorama, and with no warning, something shattering burst out from the dip and changed my life. With a short, ear-splitting scream and a bark, it shot past my face, only a few feet away, a multi-coloured missile, so fast I had no chance even to confirm a human pilot was on board, let alone note a racing number. I jerked back from the fence, stunned and unable to breathe, the vortex having sucked away the air behind the vanished assailant.

I hadn't yet composed myself, and was fighting to inhale, when another ripped by. Then a third, each detonation followed by a stillness broken only by the crisp yap of throttles as the riders changed down for the corner ahead.

Then came the pack. The unfocused bluster of this squadron, at a distance, condensed into one overpowering hurricane as it closed in. And it was coming right at me. The noise was beyond anything I could have anticipated – dozens of screaming two-strokes and booming four-strokes on an all-out consolidated attack on the senses, four or five abreast, just inches apart, almost within my reach, at 140mph.

I felt something I'd never felt before – an inner quivering and a fleeting, disorientating sense of mild panic; the noise was moving my internal organs. Was that my diaphragm I could feel vibrating? Or my liver? What the fuck was *this*?

It was, of course, insanity. And I fell instantly in love. It just did not seem possible that anything – indeed, anyone – could go so fast in a confined space. All my enthusiasm, my insatiable reading and occasional motorcycle racing coverage on television had not prepared me adequately for this. I knew they were quick. But not this quick. And so close to the trees, the fences, the grass banks and to me. It was more thrilling than I had even dreamed.

A HUGE CROWD had gathered at Oulton Park in Cheshire that August Bank Holiday Monday in 1974. In those days, before the world's top riders became tied up in corporate contracts – with their No Fun clauses and stipulations forbidding factory riders' appearances at non world championship events – major international motorcycle road race meetings at British circuits, for big prize money and appearance fees, drew what were, virtually, Grand Prix grids.

The chief crowd-puller that day was young Barry Sheene, still to win a world title but even then more gifted at self-promotion and media relations than as a motorcycle racer. Sheene was rapidly becoming the first pop star of the sport, the first to plonk himself down into the nation's conciousness. This was achieved not by racing successes but, shrewdly, by squiring beautiful women, hanging out with ex-Beatles, befriending high-profile aristocrats, fronting a television after-shave advertisement and – most importantly – a career-making 175mph crash at Daytona in front of the cameras of a British television documentary crew. A near fatal blow-out of a back tyre and Barry was a household name.

I bought a programme, squeezed in behind the fence at Old Hall Corner, the first after the start, and began to identify, from their bikes, the colours and designs of their helmets and leathers, even their riding styles, my heroes from racing books and magazines.

Sheene wasn't one of them. He struck me as arrogant and, around the paddock, as I began to spend as much time as I could at race meetings, I noticed he treated the fans, their devotion and loyalty, as a barely-tolerable nuisance. He lacked qualities I admired so much in other top riders who, to me, were huge stars and true sportsmen. Modesty and approachability, if not shyness, were characteristics I came to realise were the norm among motorcycle racers. As an adolescent, holding out my autograph book to some famous rider or other as he hastened to the grid to risk his life for my entertainment, I learned a valuable lesson from these brave, noble, unassuming men.

If young Barry swept the board that day and left the circuit with half a dozen models on his arm, I don't remember and the details are unimportant. The enduring legacy was the thrill and spectacle of the experience. It is one that, for the spectator, other sports cannot hope to match. For me, only to be ringside at a great boxing match comes anywhere near motorcycle racing for a sense of theatre, spectacle, sound and drama.

THAT AUGUST BANK HOLIDAY at Oulton Park was the only meeting my dad took me to that year, and over the following autumn and winter I could not get that symphony out of my head. From the vivid memory of that afternoon, I practised noisily the engine battle cries of the Yamahas and Triumphs. At school, in lunch breaks, I would lean my classroom chair through Oulton's picturesque bends and, sandwich in one hand, twist an imaginary throttle with the other while howling through the gear changes. I evangelised to my pals about what I had seen. I tried to articulate the sense of grace and danger, to convey that impression of implausible, unimaginable speed, of cut-and-thrust duelling at impossible angles of lean, often literally shoulder to shoulder, knees sweeping the tarmac, and all carried off with supreme nonchalance, mutual trust, self-belief, and without so much as a scraped fairing.

They thought I was nuts.

Undeterred, I spoke of the true elegance and beauty of the sport, and, nudging my way towards an appearance in Pseuds' Corner, the incongruity of this celebration of speed and technology in the midst of the pastoral and serene. ('Fuck me, there were sheep grazing obliviously in the next field...') I frothed about the overwhelming colours of the bikes, the flashing helmets, the classy, coordinated Italian or Finnish racing leathers. And the smell.

Oh, the smell! Television could convey that no better than it could the true speed. A disappearing racing bike left behind it a sweet, intoxicating aroma of what I would later learn was Castrol R, a vegetable-based racing oil, a tiny proportion of which is burnt during combustion. This perfume hangs in the air, particularly so just after it has rained.

To this day, when I'm watching a race on the television, I like to soak a ball of cotton wool in Castrol R (I keep a modest can in the DVD drawer), light it and let it burn for a few seconds, before blowing it out and allowing the smoke and fragrance to fill the room. One whiff carries me back, evocatively, to some UK circuit, and a distant mid-70s Sunday afternoon. I have ahead of me a long journey home, probably by bicycle. Then train. And bicycle again. I am footsore, dehydrated, sunburned, alone in a crowd, and very happy. The Eagles are in the charts and I haven't finished my homework.

IN APRIL 1975, as a treat for having just had my appendix removed – the experience of the anaesthetic was more horrific than the appendicitis and near septicaemia – my dad drove me to Cadwell Park in the Lincolnshire Wolds, a rival to Oliver's Mount in Scarborough as the most beautiful circuit in the UK. I'd been out of hospital less than a week and, because of the incision wound and the stitches, could still not stand fully upright. To be honest, I was shuffling around bent double. But this was the major domestic international of the spring and I was going. Parental common sense was overridden by recognition that reward was due. More urgently, for the ravenous bike racing fan who'd had only his hors d'oeuvres, it had been a long winter. Even longer since Oulton, the previous August.

For the whole of that delightful spring day, I hobbled up and down Cadwell's daffodil-dotted hills and around the paddock. Again, I watched Sheene on his factory Suzuki do almighty battle with Mick Grant, the down-to-earth Yorkshireman and near-local hero, on his almost unrideable, brutally-overpowered works Kawasaki. Grant prevailed. A huge crowd went wild. I went home happy.

The following Sunday, I was lounging on the carpet at home, half-watching *Weekend World with Brian Walden* on the television, when I felt something warm and wet around my midriff. Pulling away my shirt revealed, to my horror, that my stitches had come undone and the incision had opened. Not many of us can say they have seen their own intestines. But I can.

THERE HAD BEEN a compensatory element to my dad taking me, at last, to a motorcycle race meeting that previous summer. The Oulton international had come less than a year since a split had opened in our domestic unity.

Just before Christmas 1973, my mum, who had become increasingly and visibly depressed and distressed, broke the news to us that my dad was seeing another woman. This came as a huge shock. Not only because all the unshakeable certainty and security of family life was in jeopardy but because my dad was not a man who had appeared to be troubled, previously, by a calling in his trousers. Sure, he'd had a shag, on two occasions that were publicly accountable, but I presumed that was it. Apparently not.

There had, with hindsight, been some odd behaviour. I remember one night when my dad kept playing, over and over again, on the record player downstairs, The Carpenters' *Top Of The World,* a rare, recent purchase by my mother. She was out. From my bedroom above, I was able to make out telephone activity and my dad's voice mumbling in the background to the saccharine siblings. I sensed something was not quite right but the reason behind my dad's apparent sudden conversion to Easy Listening didn't cross my mind. Had his bizarre behaviour not alarmed me, I would have loved to have reversed the roles for once to yell from the top of the stairs, 'Turn that bloody awful din down!'

Occasionally, I'd catch my mum red-eyed. There were muted rows, again filtered through the floorboards. Then my mum escalated hostilities with flying crockery and pots and pans.

My dad left. He came back. He left again. In 1975, things got really weird. Partly, I believe, in retaliation for my dad's philandering, my mum began an affair with a man called Jim, who was about twelve years her junior.

I liked Jim. He shared my sense of humour and was a liberal creature who had come of age in the 1960s. He also liked rock music, particularly the more idiosyncratic operatives of the West Coast variety. I liked them too. He was a keen photographer and encouraged me with my own efforts, helping me out when I was fumbling, ankle-deep, in my own f-stops. But then the bugger moved in. While my dad was still at home.

It worked remarkably well. My dad never discussed it with me but perhaps he tolerated the arrangement because it kept my mother happy and took the pressure off him. When he was at home. For soon he was off again. And in October 1975, my sister Elizabeth departed for Leeds University. Then my mum enrolled, the following year, as a very mature student, for some advanced course in education at a college in Lancaster. Residentially.

That was it. They'd all gone, left home, cleared off. I was

sixteen and on my own. Making another analogy with Michael Palin's *Ripping Yarns*, I would later compare myself to the dreary northern lad and lead character in *The Testing Of Eric Olthwaite*. My folks had all left home, I'd tell people, because, like Eric's, they found their boy too boring.

FOR AN IDYLLIC few months, my mum or dad would appear from time to time, leave me a bit of money, and disappear once again. My dad either felt genuine guilt about this or acted convincingly that he regretted the situation in which his behaviour – and my mother's – had dumped me.

He turned up one afternoon and – insisting I took thirty pounds, which was a small fortune – wept as he instructed me to go and buy some clothes. 'You haven't even got,' he noted correctly, 'a decent pair of trousers.' I looked down at my ragged jeans. Punk had not yet reached Rochdale. Holes in the knees were yet to enter the mainstream of high-street fashion. If mine made a statement, they said urchin.

I was, nevertheless, happy. Happier than I had been amid all the tensions and hostilities of domestic life between warring parents. I pleased myself. I managed to make my own simple meals. I got myself to school. I did my homework. I walked over the moors from Whitworth to my grandparent's pub at Syke. I went fishing. And I listened to Bob.

This wasn't the first time I'd been abandoned. In the summer of 1975, my mum left me alone at her caravan on the Yorkshire coast for much of the summer holiday. This would have been fine by me except she didn't leave me with enough to sustain myself. I was fed by friends' mothers. I can still feel the sting of the humiliation I felt when two older girls I knew, and secretly found very attractive, mocked me one evening outside the local shop, where we tended to gather, in front of everyone else, for always wearing the same clothes. They were right, of course. I was ashamed that my jeans were filthy but I had no others to wear while they were washed.

Living at home on my own for those few months was, with hindsight, not only an instructive experience but beneficial. It taught me to stand on my own two feet and, with all my school pals living almost ten miles away, consolidated – by necessity – my sense of comfort with solitude.

However, within weeks of my seventeenth birthday I passed my driving test, for a car, and could automatically ride a motor-cycle up to 250cc on the road. My years in after-school exile were over. On evenings and at weekends, I would borrow a car from a parent – if one happened to be home – and drive over to Saddleworth, the small collection of Pennine villages above Oldham, where my schoolfriends Jonny Barnes, Paul Taylor and Simon Flynn lived.

Paul's volatility and his stormy relationship with his delight-ful parents didn't always make for an easy visit. More often than not, he'd have a blazing row with them (of his making) and we'd end up tramping the freezing streets of his village until we knocked on the door of some other pal who was happy to host us.

The morning I passed my driving test, I drove over from Rochdale immediately, and in a state of excitement, to see Paul. He'd been taking his test in Oldham the same morning. I found him scowling on the pavement in front of his house. It was clear I had passed. I was alone in my dad's car, beaming and shaking my fist in triumph. Paul approached the car as I pulled up, punched out the front passenger window with his fist, pressed his face to the hole and said, matter of factly, 'I failed. Did you pass, you bastard?'

Paul and I stayed in almost daily contact, by letter, when eventually I went off to university. In my second term at Leeds, one Sunday night in February 1979, I was called to the com-munal payphone on the stairs of our student flats. It was Simon, back at home in Saddleworth. Paul had, he reported, after a row with his girlfriend earlier that evening, jumped into his mother's car and driven at high speed through Greenfield village and head-on into a stone wall, below the station, at the end of the road. I was stunned into silence. There was a long pause before Simon spoke again.

'I'm afraid he's gone, Andy.'

I was devastated. Not only was this my first experience of death but it was the reckless impulsive suicide of a young lad, and my best friend, with so much ahead of him. For days I tramped the streets of Leeds aimlessly, weeping for Paul, his poor mum and dad, and the futility of it all. Still, I think about him, about what he might have achieved. I feel certain we'd have remained soul brothers. In an old leather briefcase, in a cupboard at home, I still have all of Paul's hilarious and wildly illustrated letters.

Simon's home, although more serene than Paul's, seldom seemed to have Simon in it. Instead, he and I spent much of our time, certainly during our earliest drinking days, together in the local pubs. We shared – and still do – the exact same outlook on life. We were both reading *Private Eye* from the age of sixteen. At school, in lunch breaks, we'd howl together over the *Eye*'s spoof news stories, the cartoons and its lampooning of pomposity, authority, arrogance, stupidity, cant, hypocrisy, corruption, greed and power. On those occasions we did hang out at Simon's it was to listen to music, usually lying on his lounge carpet in the dark, his parents out, and our heads swimming with cheap cider. Our rock music tastes were similar. It was Simon who alerted and turned me on to Iggy Pop.

I loved, especially, going over to Jonny Barnes's. His mum, Barbara, had a world-weary, wry, languid air. She affected to tolerate us, although I believe she was actually more fond of us than that. But only on the day she dropped me off on a slip road to the M62, from where I was hitching over to Leeds, and slipped me her packet of Consulate for the journey, did I have it confirmed – aged about twenty by then – that I'd gained Mrs Barnes's approval.

Robert, Jonny's dad, was just plain impish and we regarded him almost as one of us. I really admired him. As well as battling on to squeeze a living from the family's dying cotton mill, he was always doing practical stuff around the house and garden: up on the roof fixing something, turning around internal walls, installing staircases – ambitious jobs for which other dads got a man in.

Jonny's house was for me, given the problems between my parents, a happy, domestic idyll, and an escape. There was there an unmistakeable feeling of love and family. At Jonny's I would instantly relax and we'd always have fun. They had a big garden and a longish driveway. Mr and Mrs Barnes didn't seem to have the slightest problem with me and Jonny, years before the law would let us loose on the road, tearing round the garden and up and down the drive on motorcycles.

Jonny's slightly younger sister, Jane, who was shockingly beautiful but untouchable, kept horses in the midst of this mayhem. Her allure was only enhanced when she passed us, aloof, disdainful, and tightly-jodhpured, in the saddle of some gleaming steed. Jane made me feel small, sweaty, grubby and ugly. And I was.

In many respects, Jonny and I were chalk and cheese. He was cool and cautious. I was impulsive and passionate. Once, during one of our teenage philosophy seminars in his bedroom, he said he thought the devil sat on one of my shoulders, whispering in one ear, and he sat on the other, offering wiser counsel. There may be some truth in this. I would dispute the presence of the devil but I often ask myself, still, in certain situations: what would Jonny do?

Jonny has always been classically handsome – dark-skinned and angular – and striking in the way that I was nondescript and unnoticeable. This had, in our teenage years, glaring advantages and disadvantages. In Jonny's company, beautiful girls were never far away, if not exactly springing from the shrubbery. But when they were in attendance, they didn't seem even to notice me.

This imbalance was most painfully confirmed when Jonny announced one day that he had a girlfriend. We were fifteen. I didn't see this as a betrayal but I did feel he was moving on faster than I was. Or faster than girls were not allowing me so to do.

ANNA JENKINS WENT to the Hulme Grammar School for Girls, Oldham. Yes, we had a girls' school. It was, in strict architectural terms, on the same premises as our own school. It might as well have been on Pitcairn Island.

A broad, heavy oak door at the end of our main corridor led into the secret, forbidden world of the girls' school. The glass

She Belongs To Him – with Jonny Barnes and Anna Jenkins at a party, 1980.
Elizabeth Kershaw

panels in this door were amply curtained on the other side. There was no communication nor any interaction between the two whatsoever. Not even joint concerts or carol services. Our playing fields and playgrounds were also rigidly segregated. Just how on earth, therefore, Jonny had come into contact with Anna is still a mystery to me.

On one of our Saturday nights out in a Saddleworth pub, Jonny walked in with the most divine looking girl I thought I'd ever seen. Anna was totally feline and had the most exquisite almond-shaped eyes. She was also – and this is uncommon, I was to learn, in most women of great beauty – completely unselfconscious of her own staggering good looks. In fact she was meltingly shy but, once engaged in conversation, just an adorable girl. I fell in love with Anna the moment we first spoke to each other. It would be a few years before I dared to let Jonny in on this secret. But then I had to.

Even in Anna's company, and even as she got to know me

better through my close friendship with Jonny, sometimes indicating that she found me amusing, still I had absolutely no confidence with girls.

I believed myself to be physically immature and underdeveloped, and indeed looked three or four years younger than I was. To a seventeen-year-old girl who fancied herself to be five years older than her actual age, and looked and behaved as such, this was, effectively, almost a ten year age gap. I had no grasp of, nor any inclination for, fashion. I couldn't dance and felt silly, clumsy and exposed at discos. By the time most of my friends were dating girls, I'd convinced myself that no female – and certainly not a beauty of the species – was likely even to look at me.

I'd read *Great Expectations* and identified, forlornly, with Pip when, lamenting his awkwardness in the company of the beautiful Estella, with whom he was privately in love, he felt a sharp awareness of his 'coarse hands' and 'thick boots'. In the presence of Anna Jenkins, I *had* those hands and boots. I *was* Pip incarnate. And Anna was Estella. Only better looking. And, unlike the cold, hard Estella, a sweetheart.

My sex drive, meanwhile, had gone nuclear – secretly and without overground tests. But I hadn't a clue how to go about the tricky business of girls. Not many I'd come across wanted to come fishing with me, crouch in our garage fiddling with a motorcycle or lie on my bedroom floor listening to Bob.

Then, against all expectations, I fell into the threshing machine that was Joanna Coop.

11

CAREER OPPORTUNITIES

A DRAB MAN sat behind a drab desk in a drab room. He was wearing, I noticed, a matching drab suit of no particular shade, never mind colour. In front of him was a ring-binder containing, it turned out, rather a lot of drab, black-and-white photographs. Each picture was lovingly protected in a cellophane wallet. They were photographs of machines. Machines, he revealed, which made machines.

He urged me to sit down and began to explain the function and operation of each one. He became quite animated as he turned the leaves. When we arrived at a machine which made machines which made cans for the food industry, I noticed he was salivating. 'There could be a great future with us for a bright lad like you,' he announced as he closed his precious album. I'd said nothing to indicate whether I was bright or stupid. I thanked him and floated out into the school corridor.

This was the annual school Careers Convention, the first I'd been old enough to attend. Representatives of proud local industries – a wave of drab men in drab suits – descended on the school for a day, every spring, to snap up the potential stars of tomorrow in the dizzying world of machines-that-made-machines. Or similar.

The more prominent among these men, especially if they were Hulme Grammar old boys turned top local industrialists, aldermen, magistrates, and leading lights of the Rotary Club, would be invited to address us on Speech Day. After some feeble recollections of 'high spirits' in their own schooldays, intended to establish a bond with an audience of six hundred yawning boys, these monologues would habitually conclude with a reminder that to work hard was a guarantee of success in later life and a passport to the prosperity and respectability embodied in the portly chap then before us. If it wasn't actually articulated, these speeches usually concluded with a flourish implying, '...and that's my Rolls Royce outside!'

Drab Man occupied the first classroom I'd walked into, and one I'd chosen at random. (I was killing time. There were no representatives at the Careers Convention for what I wanted to do. If I even knew.) I didn't walk into another.

Sneaking off early, I caught the bus back to Rochdale in a state of fear and depression. Was that it? Was that what life had to offer? Making or – even worse – selling machines which made machines, from a base in the industrial wilderness between Oldham and Manchester? Was the pinnacle of excitement and aspiration to be the fucking golf club? By the time I got home I was resolved to a couple of career-guiding principles. I was never going to do anything for a living which wasn't stimulating and fun. And I was never going to take a job which required me to wear a ruddy suit. That narrowed things down a bit.

Happily, my enthusiasms were to flourish into what became my career. For that, if for nothing else, I have always considered myself to be the luckiest person I know. I have never done a day's work – aside from university holiday jobs – which I wasn't excited to do.

WITHOUT CONSCIOUSLY DOING SO, I had been amassing, as a schoolboy, the tools and qualifications for my unknown future in the Hacks' Trade, as I would come to know it. English was one of my best subjects at school and I had interests about which to write – and I took photographs pretty well, too.

The remaining requirements came when my mum gave me a portable typewriter when I was sixteen and Jonny Barnes's mother, Barbara, who wrote and published children's stories, gave me her old copy of *The Writers' and Artists' Yearbook*. This contained the contact details of all the national newspapers and magazines in the country. And similar information for many important organisations and institutions. In Our Elizabeth's vacated bedroom at home I set up an office and darkroom and, for some days, made a terrific mess and a lot of exasperated noises as I got to grips with the typewriter.

I warmed up for my career as a writer with a letter of resignation to the Gambian High Commission in London. I found the address in Mrs Barnes's year book. ('Dear Sir, In view of the current situation, I feel I have no alternative other than to offer you my resignation. Yours sincerely, Andrew Kershaw.') This was only one of a number of daft letters I sent off to prominent institutions, individuals and newspapers – at least a year before William Donaldson made a bestseller out of the same ploy with *The Henry Root Letters*. The Gambian High Commissioner – bless him – wrote a most sympathetic reply, although adding that he had so far not been able to find a record of my employment with them.

At the same time, I was getting closer to the motorcycle racing world. Noel Clegg was, at the time, Rochdale's best road racer and an Isle of Man TT competitor, too. He owned a motorcycle shop on Milnrow Road and over a period of months, as a shy lad, I gradually moved from admiring the bikes through the shop window to chatting to Noel at the counter about racing.

From there I was promoted to helping out a bit, informally, around the showroom and workshop. My talents with a duster or a bin-liner earned me a reward more precious than pocket money: Noel and his wife, Pam, would let me ride with them in their van to the international race meetings in which Noel was competing at the weekends. Suddenly, I was an insider of the sport I loved so much. I felt I was part of the team. Noel, however, quickly put a stop to any delusions I had of being his mechanic when I forgot to put any oil in his TZ700 Yamaha at Cadwell Park. I might have killed him.

Soon I had struck up a similar arrangement with a young guy who owned a motorcycle shop near school, Paul Johnson. Paul was huge fun, then only in his mid-twenties, something of a playboy by Oldham's standards and from a family of motorcycle shop owners and racing sponsors. He ran a small team in the domestic internationals. His regular rider was Steve Kibble, a friend of Paul's from Cheshire but, on occasions, one of my racing heroes, the dashing Charles Mortimer, a world-class Grand Prix privateer and multiple TT winner, would pilot Paul's Yamahas.

When a Mortimer ride for Paul was afoot, I'd nip out of school at lunchtime to join them for a sandwich in the cafe next to Paul's shop while arrangements were finalised for the forth-coming weekend. These included details about the back of which transporter I was to travel in. This was the equivalent to a football-mad kid of today darting out of school to hook up for a butty with Wayne Rooney. Except Mortimer had sophistica-tion, class and style. And the appropriate moustache. In an earlier age he'd have been a Spitfire pilot.

ON THESE TRIPS to all the big races, and with the correct accred-itation and documents (my first experience of what would later be the backstage pass), I took photographs and wrote features on the riders. My first published article was about Noel himself, for the *Rochdale Observer.*

I can still recall the thrill of seeing, for the first time, some-thing I had written on the printed page, with my name at the top. Quietly, I glowed with a sense of achievement and the sat-isfaction of knowing people I had never met would be reading what I had written. (This is a thrill which has never diminished. Still, I get the old kick when I see in print words that were formed in my own head, a story that I have told.) Some days after publication, a cheque for £5, from the *Rochdale Observer*, arrived in the post. I couldn't believe it was that easy. I was off. I was a journalist.

I decided to expand my activities when a big anti-Nazi rally took place in Rochdale. this was the late-70s, when the popular-ity of the National Front – or paranoia about its alleged popularity – reached its peak. I trotted along there with my heavy, cheap, Russian Zenith-E camera and got some shots of the marchers. It wasn't Grosvenor Square. I wasn't exposing the atrocities of Kent State. It was barely newsworthy: no counter-demonstration by the NF, no punch-ups, no arrests. But I felt I was working as a proper newsman. And I liked it.

With a couple of rolls of exposed film in my duffle coat pocket, I got straight on the bus to Manchester and headed for the street which was home to the regional offices of all the national newspapers.

At all but one, I didn't get beyond the front desk. But at the *Daily Mail*, a kind receptionist made a phone call to someone upstairs. A chap came down and listened to me squeak an explanation. I held out the rolls of film. He thanked me for the trouble I'd gone to, and, putting an avuncular arm around my shoulder, steered me into the lift and up to the editorial offices. This was a real thrill.

I was treated as a VIP. I'm sure he must have had more urgent things to do. First we called by the darkrooms in which I was introduced to a couple of staff photographers and lab technicians. All congratulated me on my enterprise. My films were handed over for developing and printing. We'd be back to collect them in a few minutes, said my guide.

Then we stopped, it seemed, by every desk in the newsroom as my new friend explained who I was to every hack and how I'd come to be there. 'Good lad,' was the general vibe. 'You're on your way now, old son.'

We collected my prints and negatives – not bad shots – and I was taken in to meet the regional editor. He congratulated me. He thanked me. He admired my photos. And he explained he wouldn't, alas, be able to use them.

'Nothing to do with your photos, young man, but it's not really a news story.' This was my first brush with news values and the notion of what constitutes and doesn't constitute a news story. I reckon it was from this moment that I started to think like a journalist: what's the *story*?

I must have looked heartbroken. The editor asked my new friend to organise a taxi, on the paper, to take me the ten miles home to Rochdale. I couldn't recall having been in a taxi before. A week later, the *Daily Mail* sent me a cheque, just for my trouble. Another five pounds.

My horizons, meanwhile, were expanding to the national motor-cycle magazines. I was getting known around the race track paddocks, not just by riders but by real, professional reporters and writers. And race organisers.

I took a particularly good shot, one year, of Steve Kibble at the September International Gold Cup at Oliver's Mount, Scarborough. With it printed up, I then cycled from my mother's caravan, on a weekend there, to the home of the Scarborough race organiser, Peter Hillaby, in a village some ten miles away.

Nervously, I introduced myself to him on his doorstep and blabbered something about perhaps he'd consider using the photo in the programme of a future meeting. He thanked me, said it was a good shot, and I cycled away, never thinking any more about it. However, when I arrived at the following year's Scarborough Gold Cup (this time on the bus), and approached a chap selling programmes, I got a hell of a shock. My Steve Kibble photo from the year before was on the cover. With a photographer's credit.

A MOMENTUM SEEMED to be building up and a clash between photo-journalism ambitions and the demands of school work, exams and university entry was inevitable. This came, dramatically, one afternoon in the paddock at Oulton Park.

A sports editor I knew from *Motorcycle News* asked me when I was leaving school and what plans, if any, I had for after that. I mumbled something about Leeds University and left it there. A few days later he phoned me at home and asked me if I'd like to be *MCN*'s Grand Prix reporter, starting the following season.

Had I been asked to dream up a career fantasy at that point in my life – I was seventeen – this would have been it. The job would require me to travel all over the world, writing reports on all the Grand Prix world championship motorcycle rounds throughout the year and features on the riders. I'd be in the thick of the action as much as one could be without pulling on a set of racing leathers. I'd be on first name terms with Giacomo Agostini, see all the races close up, visit glamorous circuits such as Spa Francorchamps and Monza (whose layouts I had drawn on the cover of my school rough-book) and get paid for it.

My dad said no.

He was right, of course. But the opportunity at the time seemed too exciting, too rare and too flattering to pass up. Especially when my dad's alternative was to 'do law' at Leeds.

We rowed constantly for days. I took breaks only to sleep and sulk.

Never an impulsive man, my dad argued that if *MCN* really liked my stuff and thought I would make a fine Grand Prix correspondent, they'd still think that in four years when I'd come out of Leeds University with the security of a law degree in the bag.

Too sensible and too boring, I wailed. And, anyway, as I told him, I didn't want to do law at Leeds. Well, what would I study instead? 'I dunno,' I said. 'But I'm sure as hell not going to spend the rest of my life doing ruddy house conveyancing in the Rochdale area.'

Law was never again mentioned. *MCN* gave the Grand Prix job to someone else and I filled in all six choices on my university application form with slightly varying permutations of the same subjects. All at Leeds.

12

LIFE-COACHING WITH
ALBERT HAMMOND

THE LAD STANDING in the queue in front of me was wearing a black leather motorcycle jacket in the classic 1950s style, that variety popularised by Marlon Brando in *The Wild One*. Johnny Strabler, as played by Brando in the film, was another of my rebel anti-heroes. Although if a waitress had asked me, 'Whatcha rebelling against, Andy?' I would, in all likelihood, have replied not with, 'Whaddya got?' but 'Get yourself a pen and a pad of A4, love.'

Clearly, here was a soul mate, a brother, the first I'd encountered in my rebirth at Leeds University. I decided we were going to be pals.

We were lining up in the Great Hall to register as new arrivals. It was the first week of October, 1978. This was my first day at Leeds – the first day of the rest of my life, as those vacuous posters on so many student bedroom walls were soon to remind me – and I was putting my name on the dotted line for a Politics degree. I'd arrived here half-filled with noble intentions, vaguely academic inclinations and ambitions to be a journalist. I'd also arrived determined to reinvent myself, having shed almost everyone who'd known the little drip I'd been on the other side of the Pennines.

But my main reason for signing on at Leeds was to become the Students' Union Entertainments Secretary. Through my obsessive reading of the music papers since the age of twelve, I'd realised that Leeds University was the biggest and most prestigious college venue in the UK. This was explained, I was to learn, not only by the large, 2200 capacity of the hall – the University Refectory, cleared of tables and banished of diners – but by the absence in the city of rival venues of that optimum size. Leeds University was, therefore, a fixture and a flagship gig on the rock & roll national touring circuit. If a major band was playing at Birmingham Odeon, Sheffield City Hall, London's Rainbow and Manchester Apollo or Free Trade Hall, its Leeds gig would automatically be with us, in an early 1950s Festival of Britain-style student dining hall.

Just less than a decade before my arrival, Leeds University's rock & roll reputation had been cemented when The Who's performance in the Refec, as it was known affectionately, on Valentine's Day 1970, was recorded and released as the famous *Live At Leeds* album.

Possibly helped by competition between the early 1970s rock band giants, the pioneering Ents Sec of the day, Simon Brogan (who went on to become a sheep farmer in Orkney), had them queuing up to play: Led Zeppelin had nipped in to pound the plywood stage just three weeks before The Who's famous appearance; Pink Floyd followed The Who only two weeks later; the Rolling Stones, on their 'farewell' tour of the UK before becoming tax exiles in French châteaux, had played in the Refectory on 13 March 1971. And, Led Zeppelin almost upstaged that one too, returning for their second gig in the Refec, just four days before the Stones' historic concert.

It's likely that the Rolling Stones were intending to seal their reputation with a *Live At Leeds* benchmark LP too: their gig that night was professionally recorded; bootlegs exist of what was an outstanding performance by the Stones at the peak of their powers that knocks the spots off *Get Yer Ya-Yas Out,* their official live album of that period.

(Memo to Mick Jagger and Keith Richards: Do yourselves a favour, boys. Release officially the *Rolling Stones – Live At*

Leeds University, if only for that jaw-dropping performance of Robert Johnson's *Love In Vain,* which features, Mick, possibly your finest recorded vocal performance, enhanced – you may remember – by Mick Taylor's exquisite lead guitar. If you no longer have the recording, you can borrow mine.)

Enlightened hard-working Ents Secs had consolidated those early coups. Notably, in that sweltering summer of 1976, Bob Marley and the Wailers had played two Refec concerts on one night that June, the first show at 5pm, followed by another at 8pm. Friends who were there recall the condensation falling as rain from the low ceiling and the marijuana fumes being so thick that skinning up oneself was entirely unnecessary.

Our Elizabeth had gone ahead of me to Leeds University in October 1975. She studied Textiles which she then deployed to great advantage in subsequent jobs with British Telecom and, later, as a Radio 1 DJ. Elizabeth 'didn't bother' to get tickets to see Bob Marley but she did occasionally phone home with accounts, to her wide-eyed little brother, of seeing in the Refec the likes of Roxy Music, The Clash or John Martyn. John performed at the University so regularly – almost weekly, it seemed – that I suspected, during my regime as Ents Sec, the dear old thing was living under the stage.

In the spring of 1978, shortly before Elizabeth finished at Leeds, and just before I was due to start there in the following October, I made one of my occasional visits to see her in her shared Headingley hovel, 16 Norwood Terrace, a squalid student slum I would myself occupy two years later. I liked the idea of student life and sometimes, on these trips over there, I got to play at being a further education drop-out (of medium-length hair) for the weekend. On that particular occasion, we went along to see good-time, singalong Geordie folkies, Lindisfarne, playing to a packed, beery Refec.

'Tell me again how these concerts are organised,' I asked Elizabeth on the way home. 'Who exactly books the bands?'

She explained that there was an Ents Committee within the Students' Union, headed by an Ents Secretary, who was also a full-time student and not a sabbatical officer. Despite Leeds University's stature in the rock & roll scheme of things, the Leeds Ents Sec – unlike sabbatical Social Secs at many tiny colleges of further education or polytechnics with venue capacities nudging 300 – was expected to do his or her course at the same time as running professionally what was a busy, prestigious venue. Poor bugger, I thought. I want his job.

And now here I was. October 1978. Signing on in the Great Hall to let the authorities know I'd managed to turn up.

When the lad in the black leather motorcycle jacket half turned round, I smiled and said, 'What kind of bike have you got?'

He looked at me as though I was an imbecile. 'Bike?' he asked.

'Yes,' I said, prodding his leathered arm. 'I'm a motorcyclist, too. What are you riding?'

'No, no,' he said. 'No bike. I'm not a motorcyclist.' He looked slightly offended. 'I'm a punk.'

'Oh,' I said. 'I see.'

It was one of my earliest brushes with style over substance.

AFTER REGISTRATION, I set off in search of the Students' Union building. As soon as I stepped inside I felt – overwhelmed and nervous though I was – that this was home. There were girls, bookshops, girls, bars, girls, a travel agent's, girls and a record shop, run by a gorgeous, pouting sexbomb I would soon learn was called Helen From The Record Shop and upon whom I was to develop, inevitably, a powerful crush – despite being reflexively timid of her amply-knockered, slightly older woman allures.

'Excuse me, please,' I mumbled at the Porters' Lodge counter. 'Please can you tell me where I will find the office of the Ents Secretary?'

I was directed upstairs to the Executive Office, an area of open-plan chaos, occupied by all the Union officers, from President to Women's Affairs Secretary. What I was doing was completely out of character and to this day I have no explanation of how I managed to shed my shyness and pluck up the courage to act so atypically. It wasn't hard to find the Ents Sec's desk. In the far corner of the office, posters on the wall for earlier gigs, and one for The Ramones, our Freshers' Hop later that week, signalled the way. Below them, at a desk, sat a chap with bog-brush hair and a wonky grin who was joshing with a few lank-haired lads standing around him. All of them radiated self-confidence and easy familiarity with each other. They stopped talking when they spotted me and eyed my approach. I looked about twelve. And I was fucking terrified.

'Excuse me, please,' I began. 'I'm looking for the bloke who books all the bands?'

The guy with the bushy hair smiled his lop-sided smile as the others made loud, lame jokes about their leader's belief that he booked the bands and derogatory remarks about the programme of gigs he'd assembled for the autumn term. He was, noticeably, much older than the others. Good grief, at least in his mid-twenties! Some kind of mature student, I decided, who'd evidently plugged himself into the mains.

He waited until the laddish clamour subsided. 'Er, well, I do,' he said in an almost apologetic, nasal voice.

'Hello,' I said, fidgeting, shuffling and forgetting to extend my hand. 'My name's Andy. Please can I have your job when you've finished?'

The uproar from his acolytes was deafening. He cackled, too. I stood my ground, but turned bright red. I thought I might burst into tears.

He beamed and reached to shake my hand. 'My name's Steve,' he shouted through the din. 'Steve Henderson. Have you just arrived?'

I nodded.

'Well, look: let's get you signed up as an Ents steward first. And then we'll see what we can do from there, eh? Where are you from?'

'Rochdale,' I told him.

'Ha!' said Steve. 'I'm from just next door to you. Bury.'

He produced a form. I filled it in and signed it. I gushed my thanks and ran.

I was so thrilled. For the next ten months, I was to sit at, and safeguard, remote fire-doors around University House, the greater Refectory building – all vantage points from which I would miss seeing some of my favourite bands.

But I was in. I was signed up. I was, from my first day at Leeds University, on the team. I'd met the main man. And he seemed like a nice guy. I'd been accepted. An insider, straight away. A member, no matter how lowly, of the most famous college venue crew in the world. *Me*. I belonged.

I flew back down the broad staircase and out onto the campus. If I had my first Politics lectures scheduled for that afternoon, I don't remember. Certainly, if there were any timetabled, I didn't attend them. In my pocket, I had a ticket for BB King that night at Manchester Free Trade Hall. I ran down the hill to Leeds City Station and caught that westbound train to see the King of the Blues.

I had – and the fact is unavoidable – run away from university on my first day. Without realising it at the time, of course, I was setting a pattern for the next three years of academic life.

As Albert Hammond put it so romantically: 'My parents and my lecturers could never understand, why I gave it up for music and the free electric band...' But Albert only imagined and wrote the bugger. I was about to live it.

13

AN EYEWITNESS TO HISTORY
(IN A POLYTHENE RAIN HOOD)

IT IS ASTONISHING that I made it to Leeds University. Not only had I gambled my future on Bob Dylan by running out of my Economics exam, I'd also absconded during my A-Levels to see another of my heroes in action and to witness, I hoped, history in the making. For in January 1978, an announcement was made of another return – and one even more unlikely than the re-appearance of Bob. Mike Hailwood, after a break of eleven years, and a career in between as a Formula One motor racing driver, was to make an Isle of Man TT comeback at that year's motorcycle races.

News of this was greeted with a mix of incredulity, concern, delight and scorn. Mike The Bike, for goodness sakes, would be thirty-eight years old by the following June (people aged more quickly in those days) and he'd not raced a motorcycle regularly or seriously since the end of the 1967 season when he'd retired as nine times World Champion, twelve times an Isle of Man TT winner and a Honda factory rider.

Mike's status as a living legend of motorcycle racing was undoubtedly justified. If fans took issue, during saloon bar debates, on who was the greatest of all time, they certainly

- 90 -

agreed that Hailwood's name jostled for the top spot only with those of two others – Giacomo Agostini and Jarno Saarinen – as the most naturally gifted motorcycle racer of them all. News of Hailwood's TT intentions was greeted at our house by parental indifference and my private resolve to be there, come hell or high water. Lucky, then, given the inconvenience of the Irish Sea and the imposition of my A-Levels, that I was prepared to face both.

IT SHOULD HAVE COME as no surprise to anyone that I would run away to the Isle of Man, during my A-Level fortnight, to watch Hailwood ride again. I had, after all, gone AWOL to the TT for the previous three years.

My first escape there had been for the races in June 1975. It was also my very first solo adventure. Anywhere. I'd saved up secretly for months, acquiring almost a tenner. In those days, it was possible to catch a boat around midnight from Liverpool which dumped its passengers onto the quayside in Douglas around six the following morning. With a day return ticket, it was then possible to watch a day of racing and catch a boat back to Liverpool around tea time.

For those with money, a passage on those Isle of Man boats of yesteryear was quite an elegant experience. For those of us on a budget, it meant a recreation of the hellish scenes in steerage of *A Night To Remember*, confined to dormitories below the waterline, in the enforced company of emotional, heavy-drinking Scots and over-familiar Scousers.

In theory, and in the idealised adverts of the Isle of Man Steam Packet Company – showing happy daytrippers not being sick and dappled with Manx sunshine – this was a splendid arrangement. But the tempting adverts, travel posters and my dreams did not account for the whimsical Manx weather. Throughout my day trip in 1975, it never stopped bloody lashing down. I tramped along Douglas promenade. From a bucket and spade shop, I bought a plastic rain-hood, the kind favoured by old ladies on coach trips. And I wore it.

In a cafe, I eked out a mug of tea to last an hour or more as I wiped the condensation off the window to monitor a heaving grey sea and the hammering rain. The talk among knots of fellow TT fans, sitting around me and gently steaming, was of racing postponements and a possible cancellation.

From the cafe, I splashed up the hill to look at the start-finish area, the grandstands and the scoreboard, features with which I was already intimate from the photographs in my TT books. I felt a small sense of achievement to be admiring them in reality, and to have got there by myself.

Close to where Victoria Road meets the TT circuit, I found a most accommodating bus shelter and sat down in it. I read my TT programme. Then I read it again.

The gentle hiss of the downpour was disrupted, mid-morning, by the crackle of a two-stroke racing engine. I stuck my head out of the shelter to see a chap on a Yamaha TZ 350 racing bike making his way leisurely, and within the speed limit, up Victoria Road. He turned off towards the paddock, leaving a little trail of froth on the road surface.

And that was it – the only racing bike I saw at my very first TT. By the time I'd eaten my sandwiches, drained my flask of coffee and studied more Manx rainfall, it was time to paddle back to the harbour to catch the ferry home.

But my enthusiasm, if not the rest of me, remained undampened. I was back in 1976. Well, almost.

In those days it was possible to catch a ferry to the Island from a number of UK ports, and so it was that, in the intense heat of that June, I was sprawled on the deck of another Isle of Man steamer at Fleetwood quayside, for a crossing to see that year's Senior TT, the most prestigious race of the fortnight.

On that occasion, I didn't even see the Isle of Man. The boat had engine failure before we'd had chance to cast off. As the sun got hotter, we made the most of it and huddled around someone's transistor on the ship's open deck, riveted to the Manx Radio commentary as a most dramatic race unfolded.

The great John Williams of Cheshire, race leader for all of the six laps, despite the handicaps – almost from the start – of a broken clutch and steering damper, was only 400 yards from home and victory when he stalled his factory Suzuki. Unable to restart it, John pushed his dead machine heroically to the finish line, roared on by a packed grandstand, where he collapsed and fainted from heat exhaustion but still finished seventh.

It was the stuff, again, of *Ripping Yarns*, and my disappointment to miss the TT for a second year running was eased somewhat, as we trudged down the gangplank of our disabled boat for an unexpected afternoon in Fleetwood, by the moral victory of an inspirational, modest, quiet, tough-guy sportsman from the Wirral. Three years later, John was killed at the Ulster Grand Prix.

At last, on my third attempt, in 1977, I saw the TT for real. Playing truant from school for a week, and with only a fiver in spending money, I took with me an old tent in a small rucksack but no sleeping bag. I couldn't afford an open or a weekly-return ferry booking and a sleeping bag would have revealed the true intentions, I calculated, of someone holding only a day-return ticket. (As though anyone really cared.) And I figured, as it was summer, it would be warm enough at night.

It was absolutely fucking bitter. I camped on a site near the bottom of the awesome Bray Hill in Douglas. First thing next morning, I walked down to the town centre and bought some plastic rubbish sacks from the Co-op. What little insulation they offered also retained evaporated body moisture as condensation. For my second sleepless night, I was desperately cold. And wet through.

The days, however, were a dream. Without money even to catch a bus to vantage points around the course, I either walked to sample spectating alternatives or settled for the unbelievable drama of Bray Hill, down which the fast men hurtle between pre-war semis and suburban street furniture in excess of 170mph.

From Mr & Mrs Bradley's corner shop, where Tromode Road meets Bray Hill itself, I bought lumps of cheese and bags of nuts and raisins and washed them down with cartons of milk. I survived. And managed to stretch out the fiver to last the week.

Sitting on the Bradleys' wall, in the warm sunshine, chewing on my cheese, and thrilled by the racing, I decided this was as close to heaven as being alive could get. There and then I made a little promise to myself: one day, I said, I'll live here.

MIKE HAILWOOD, like my other great hero, Bob Dylan, paid scandalously little regard to the Joint Matriculation Board's A-Level timetable when drawing up his plans for 1978.

If Bob had been downright inconsiderate to have one of his Earls Court concerts clash with the Economics exam, then Hailwood was equally cavalier when it came to History. His TT return was scheduled for just a couple of days before the test, which was to be my best chance for a passport to Leeds. There was nothing else for it. I would have to combine both.

Following the reliable strategy of the 1975 and 1976 disasters, I took the overnight day-trip option to see Mike's first comeback race and prayed for good weather. We got it.

Off the boat in Douglas, and again on a budget of small change, I walked the four or five miles, before the road closed for racing, from the quayside up the hill through town and beyond, against race direction, almost to the bend called Kate's Cottage, on the mountain descent of the thirty-eight-mile course. There I settled down for the day with my sandwiches, my race programme and my History exercise books.

The crowds that day were enormous. We were all drawn there for just one reason, just one man. From Kate's Cottage, up the moorland to my right, and down the hill to Creg-ny-Baa, on my left, the grass bank was solid with shoulder to shoulder fans. And that's a long straight.

Before the race began, I boned up on the Causes Of The First World War. I could scarcely concentrate. The sense of anticipation was gnawing, all-consuming. Those around me were reaching a state of near panic. If we weren't entirely fearful for Mike's life, we were dreading disappointment, for him more than us. Fairy tales, I kept telling myself are just that. It won't happen. He's been away eleven years. He's no youngster any more. His familiarity with the TT course will have faded. Modern bikes are vastly more powerful animals than those of Mike's heyday. The best we could hope for was that he wasn't humiliated and that he survived.

Ripping Yarns – John Williams, urged on by his crew, pushes home his factory Suzuki, Isle of Man Senior TT, June 1976. Note approaching rider in the distance and disbelieving official in white coat. *FoTTofinders*

Effortless at 140mph – I took this shot of Mike Hailwood at Donington Park, 9th July 1978, with my crude Zenith E camera, just a month after Mike's historic TT return and victory on this same Ducati. *AK*

Years later, I became great friends with Jim Redman, Hailwood's 1960s Honda team-mate – a six times World Champion and six times TT winner himself. Jim told me that as I was sitting on the grass bank that morning, revising my History, he was arriving on the Island at the last minute and hastening to Hailwood's hotel to try to talk his old pal out of this folly. 'I thought he was crazy,' Jim confided. 'I flew up from South Africa to beg him not to do it. I told him he must be mad and that he was too old. I was also worried because I'd thought for some time Mike was drinking too much.'

Wily old Redman's advice went unheeded and Mike set off in the Formula One race on his big 864cc Ducati twin carrying the number 12 and the adoration and anxieties of thousands. He led from the start and was never seriously challenged.

Mike Hailwood, in tests, shortly before his Isle of Man comeback, 1978. He was just thirty-eight in this photograph. *Unknown*

When Hailwood boomed down the mountain on the final lap, past my perch, just three miles from home – and history – the grass bank from Kate's to the Creg was a washing line of flapping programmes. Grown men around me were in floods of tears, embracing each other. My eyes, too, prickled at the effortless splendour of the spectacle and the romance of his achievement as he roared by to the finish. Children who were unborn the last time Mike raced in the TT were screaming themselves blue. Their dads were yelling even harder. Mike won – from John Williams – by two clear minutes.

Within the hour, I was to learn from Redman years later, Jim and Mike walked into the bar of the Palace Hotel in Douglas where Jim bought Mike a drink with an apology and the reminder that 'There's no fool like an old fool'.

Simultaneously, I was yomping back down the re-opened road to Douglas and to my waiting boat, happy as a village idiot. 'Yes, he really did it,' I was able to tell them at school, 'and I *was there*.'

This was the first occasion I'd been an eyewitness to history. If I recognised the morning after that the buzz from it was strong, I didn't realise immediately that it was also powerfully addictive. Still on that high, I sailed through the History A-Level.

Less than three years after his remarkable return to the TT, Mike Hailwood died, along with his young daughter, after a car crash near Birmingham. A truck driver had made an illegal U-turn right in front of them. The driver was fined £100. Mike was taking his children to buy fish and chips.

◉

14

CONQUERED
IN A CAR SEAT

'PULL OVER HERE,' said Joanna Coop, motioning towards the museum car park on the left.

We were driving through the middle of Uppermill village in Saddleworth. It was in the early hours of a Saturday morning in January 1980. We were on our way back from a party. I had borrowed my mother's Austin Allegro.

'Eh?' I said. 'Here? The car park? What for?'

She showed me what for as soon as I applied the handbrake.

Joanna Coop had much in common with the Royal Canadian Mounted Police. A single-minded girl – very pretty, blonde, elfin and with a wicked, mocking smile – she had a reputation of legendary tenacity and efficiency in apprehending her quarry. Like the Mounties, Joanna always got her man. I just never expected it would be me.

It was all Jonny Barnes's fault. Heading back to his mum and dad's in Saddleworth for the weekend, from Law studies at Hull University, he had phoned me in Leeds during the week to tempt me over to our old patch.

'Diane Fallowes is having a party,' he announced.

Diane was one of our circle and, like Anna Jenkins and

Jonny's sister Jane, had been an Oldham Hulme Grammar pupil in our mysterious female wing. A stunning girl with incredible long legs, Diane was also celebrated for her fabulous flashing eyes which appeared to be in a state of permanent alarm. Jonny didn't have to pile on any more incentives for me to cross the Pennines.

Not that Diane Fallowes was the slightest bit interested in the imp, Kershaw.

During Diane's party, I was descending the stairs after a trip to the toilet. Joanna Coop was halfway down, leaning against the wall. She had that smile locked on to me. I smiled back, uneasily.

'Are you driving back to Rochdale after this?' she asked.

'Yes. I've borrowed my mum's car.'

'Would you be able to drop me off at home in Saddleworth on your way back?' she fluttered.

'Sure. No problem. It's as quick to drive that way, back over the moors, yes.'

And so it was that I swung the Allegro, on Joanna's instruction, into the museum car park in delightful Uppermill and came to a halt just where it backs, most attractively, on to the Huddersfield Narrow Canal. Van Morrison's *Astral Weeks* was playing on the cassette machine. (And that is the only aspect of this adventure which could be categorised as cool.)

I switched off the engine but left Van in full, transcendental flood. If I started to twitter inanities and small talk, Joanna put an abrupt end to that. She grabbed me by the collar and pulled me over on top of her, expertly reclining the passenger seat without missing a beat.

'Crikey,' I thought to myself. 'This is it.'

And it certainly was, despite the trickiness of my chosen party attire: lace-up sneakers and bib and brace overalls, the kind favoured by window cleaners. (I was pioneering at the time, with little impact, a post-punk, proletarian, Hungry 30s look.) It's unlikely Joanna had had much practice with the intricacies of the bib and brace arrangement in her previous conquests but she had them unhooked in a trice and yanked down. Resistance was futile.

'Bloody hell, I'm actually doing it,' I said to myself, as I felt that accommodation for the first time. 'This is what it's really like.' And I went through the motions I'd rehearsed in my head for this moment for the last five years. Nothing too acrobatic, just a modicum of easing backwards and forwards.

I'm not sure what sense of occasion I'd expected, or hoped for, but certainly this wasn't what I'd anticipated. It was oddly undramatic. To start with.

Joanna was clearly deriving more from this caper than I was. Van Morrison was joining in, too – lamenting, in the song, *Cyprus Avenue*, about being 'conquered in a car seat'. I felt a fraternal solidarity.

(This wasn't to be the only occasion I found myself in a three-some with Van Morrison. In the mid 80s, I was entertaining a gorgeous and amusing girl who worked in the press office of a major record company. I was giving it my best – or so I thought – when my companion went into a monologue about Van The Man, who had popped up on the bedroom CD player and with whom she had recently worked.

'Eee! Man! Pet! But!' she squealed in her fluent, melodic Geordie. 'Van Morrison! I can't fucking stick him.'

'Really?' I managed.

'Yeah. He's a pig,' she expanded, her mind now far from the matter at hand. 'And he fucking looks like one, too.'

'Dear me,' I panted, in spirited defence of one of my favourites.

'And I think his new album's crap, don't you?'

'Not his best work, no,' I puffed.

'I had fucking nightmares, working with him the other week,' she went on. 'Real nightmares, that I was being shagged by a pig. And it had Van fucking Morrison's face.')

Affecting a degree of athleticism, with Joanna in the car park, I bobbed up, level with the passenger window. In the sodium glare, I noticed a couple of ducks were standing beside the car. I bobbed up again, a minute or two later. There were more. Next time I had a quick look, there were dozens.

I murmured this news, tenderly, to Joanna. A chorus of soft, muted quacks was now audible.

'They're only after a bit of bread,' she said.

And so they were. By the time the deed was done and Joanna had committed upon me what, in a later, more neurotic age, would have been regarded as a serious sexual assault, there were possibly a hundred or more mallards crowding the car. The activity inside had lured them down off the canal, accustomed as they were to motorists pulling up, more routinely at lunchtimes, to eat a sandwich and then toss out the crusts to the charming little fellows.

WHATEVER PLEASURE I had given Joanna, inexpertly, she was quietly hungry for more. And a swift, unexpected rematch followed.

Two days later, I was back in Leeds and preoccupied with something in the dank kitchen of 16 Norwood Terrace. It was early evening. The doorbell rang. I went to answer it. There stood Joanna, without warning or invitation. But with two suitcases and another girl, a beauty not previously of my acquaintance, who Joanna introduced as Samira.

In real life, people never say – as they always do during door-

The ducks still talk about it – the museum car park, Uppermill, Saddleworth, 2010. No blue plaque, but... *Darren Robinson*

step exchanges in films, television dramas and sitcoms – 'You'd better come in.' I certainly didn't. I was too stunned.

Joanna smiled her impish smile and marched in, pulling Samira behind her.

'Are you stopping for long?' I asked.

Half an hour later we were gathered round the gas fire in what was laughably called the lounge. I was trying to concentrate on the news on a big black-and-white television. The American Embassy hostage crisis in Tehran was gripping the world.

Joanna leaned over to me. Her lips were tight and curled in an expression of pity and resolve. 'You're sleeping with me *and* Samira tonight,' she announced.

This *ménage à trois* did not last. We had a row. Joanna, thirty years later, now tells me our parting came about following a dispute in which I accused her and Samira of having a hand in the death of my freshwater crayfish – an uncommon crumpet-magnet, I know – which I kept in an aquarium in my room. After that, we did not see each other for three decades.

THEN, IN JANUARY 2010, by a spooky coincidence, we were back in touch, great pals again, and tramping the streets of Saddleworth together one January afternoon.

We walked along by the old canal (a little confused, I remember well) before emerging on to Uppermill High Street from a side road. Joanna, a few steps ahead, turned left.

'No, no,' I said. 'Come on, this way. We can't come to the middle of Uppermill and not make a pilgrimage.'

With resignation, and a little smile, Joanna plodded after me, to the right, along the main street.

On the fifty yards or so to the museum, I was turning back towards her and making feeble jokes about the possible installation of a blue plaque to mark the historic event of thirty years ago that very week.

'What, with it being in the car park of a heritage centre, and all that,' I teased.

'Oh, be quiet,' she said. 'Will you never grow up?'

'I can even remember,' I gushed, 'the precise spot on which you made me park my mum's car.'

'So can I,' she sighed.

As we moved through the parked cars and vans towards the grass bank up to the canal Joanna, trailing, noticed me freeze.

When she saw for herself what I was staring at, we both creased over in snorts and giggles.

The local authorities have commemorated the site of my deflowering not with a blue plaque. The very spot is now the museum's only disabled parking space. And marked as such, with a wheelchair symbol.

15

LIVE AT LEEDS – KEEPING
HOWARD MARKS BUSY

THE SHADOWS WERE GATHERING and thickening on the wall. One among them was unmistakeable, even in silhouette, thrown onto the side of the stairwell – an institutional shade of magnolia – by the glare of a bulkhead light down below. It was that of a stooped figure in a floppy cap and swaying on a walking stick.

My palm, pressed against a panel of brass light switches, prickled. The house lights. It was time for action.

The tour manager swung round the corner of the stairwell, looked up, gave me the nod and a wave of his torch. I grinned back, drew a here-we-go breath and wiped my hand up the switches in one sweep. It was as though those switches were hard-wired to a couple of thousand throats. A massive roar went up as the Refec dived into darkness.

Following my torch beam, and emerging from below, the shadows took on human forms and clustered around the gallows steps up to the famous stage. They were just as they had looked on television and in the photos in the music papers, only slightly smaller. Always just that bit smaller. At their centre was the most unlikely rock & roll hero of the age – in his case, middle age – Ian Dury, tense, crabby and grim-faced.

Still in darkness, the band climbed the steps, Dury hobbling and supported by his minder. Positions were taken, the pencils of torchlight drawing the crowd to a crescendo of bellowing. Dury, now at the centre microphone, began to whisper – at several thousand watts. Instantly, the audience hushed and paid breathless attention. No music yet. Still no lights.

It was a saucy little story, pure Dury music hall stuff, of Yer Uncle Ian having illicit leg-over in some girl's bedroom with her oblivious parents in the room below. He mimicked the sound of every creaking floorboard on the landing, the squeak of the opening bedroom door. The Refec stood rigid and airless. In her room, the girl lay down and beckoned Dury to the bed. Two thousand pairs of eyes, locked into night-vision, probed the blackness of the centre stage. Our hero eased himself onto the mattress alongside his companion.

'And then she said...' breathed Dury, hardly daring now even to whisper. He paused. The Refec was silent.

'Fuck me! Fuck me! Fuck me!'

As he screamed her instruction, all the stage lights came on, three huge gantries, all at once – painfully, blindingly. At the corner of the stage, I felt the heat of them.

Suddenly, they were all there: Dury, the Blockheads and even Wilko Johnson, positioned on perches around a stage set of bright red scaffolding. As the stage lit up, and before we could adjust to the spectacle, the intensity and the colour, the band kicked straight in: *Wake Up And Make Love With Me*. The Refec roared back its delight and lifted, as one, from the sprung floor. We were off.

IT WAS ALMOST CHRISTMAS 1980. I'd been Leeds University Union Ents Sec since March, halfway through my second year. Things were going pretty well. With Ian Dury, I was sending the students home for their holidays. Only the night before, I'd given them Dire Straits.

If Steve Henderson had been spooked by the audacious fresher who'd stalked him for his job, he was quick to realise that here was someone sufficiently enthusiastic, knowledgeable, driven and loony enough to dedicate himself totally to the demands of the Ents Sec position. Glamorous and attractive though it seemed to most student observers, it was a full-time commitment to a non-sabbatical office. Amazingly, despite Leeds University Ents's standing and professional rock & roll reputation, Ents was still considered by the University *and* fellow Union officers as a maverick if not disreputable organisation. Consequently, its leader had never been granted the sabbatical status enjoyed by those with other more worthy responsibilities, and few of the necessities to do the job. When, just a decade before me, Simon Brogan, the truly ground-breaking Ents Sec, had booked The Who and the Rolling Stones, he'd done the deals from a Students' Union phone box with a pocket full of loose change. And not much had changed since.

It was, in reality, bloody hard work – long hours and a huge responsibility – and only those who were prepared to flunk their degrees, or, like Henderson, were on some cushy, layabout, post-grad scam, could do it properly. Fleetingly, two came between me and Steve, due to their seniority and lip-service to the task. Both resigned prematurely, to return – disgracefully – to their course work.

When Steve was in his final months in the job, he wangled me onto the Ents Committee. He'd spotted that at the first meeting I attended, as an unknown observer, I'd come straight from a second-hand record shop in Leeds city centre and was carrying a copy of *Muddy Waters – Live At Newport 1960*. 'I don't know much about this waif,' he'd thought, 'but he's clearly hardcore.'

Before Henderson moved on, to enliven academia with a research fellowship in material science at the Open University in Milton Keynes, he hooked me up with Al Thompson, Ents' Stage Manager and boss of the Stage Crew. This was a team of around fifteen supremely dedicated volunteers, girls as well as blokes, who worked the gigs from the arrival of the trucks, first thing in the morning, until they had finished reloading those trucks in the early hours of the following day. In terms of Leeds University Union Ents – itself the most admired college concert team in the country – Stage Crew was the SAS.

Uncle Al, as he was known, had earned his *nom de guerre* by

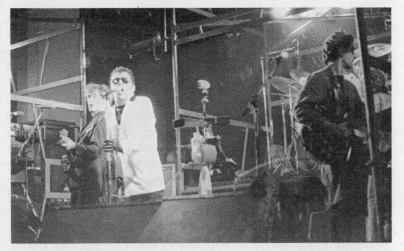

Ian Dury & The Blockheads on stage in the Refec, Leeds University, 14 December 1980. With Wilko Johnson as guest guitarist. Only the night before we'd put on Dire Straits. *AK*

Mentor and protégé: with Dr Steve Henderson, Leeds, 1981. Ents's loss was – ahem – academia's gain. *Unknown*

being a mature sudent in his late-twenties and for having, at the same time, a respectable other life with a wife and family in a nice semi, in an agreeable non-student neighbourhood in north Leeds. He had a more than roadworthy car – very grown-up – thanks to the time he put in, occasionally, at his mother's recruitment agency business in Leeds and Rotherham. When he wasn't being 'that nice Mr Thompson from number 27', Al was second in command of Ents. And simultaneously neglecting a maths degree.

I don't think Al's neighbours had a clue about his rock & roll alter-ego, unless they were twitching the curtains the night he brought Johnny Rotten home to Josie and the kids, briefly and to avoid over-zealous fans, between a Public Image sound-check and gig. And they probably knew nothing of his previous life, almost a decade earlier, in the hedonistic, early-70s rock & roll heyday, when he'd worked as a photographer for Island Records.

I gave Uncle Al something of a problem. Henderson had suggested he draft me onto Stage Crew, all the better, and closer, for me to familiarise myself with, and get experience of, the inside mechanism of running the gigs. But Al wondered to what use on Stage Crew this puny kid could be put.

He needn't have worried. Towards the end of my first year at Leeds, I finally began to grow, eventually just touching six feet in my boots. Loading and unloading the trucks soon toughened me up. I was still famine-thin but, quietly and steadily, I was becoming strong, particularly in the upper body. And, soon enough, Joanna Coop was to fully uncork my testosterone.

STAGE CREW PROVIDED me with a ready-assembled gang of friends, a band of brothers. And sisters. We were bonded by the hard work and the enthusiasm for what we did. We were proud of our Stakhanovite drive, dedication and indispensability, our reputation for that and, above all, our professionalism. No booze was tolerated when we were working. Drinkers and slackers were instantly fired. We thrived on the respect, even awe, with which the professional road crews of top groups regarded us. That would soon begin to pay dividends. At the highest level.

We did, however, smoke quite astonishing quantities of dope. All the time. (It should be noted that the dope we smoked in those days was not the psychosis-inducing, genetically-modified dynamite which is the predominant variety of today. Ours was that pale brown crumbly resin, usually from Morocco or Lebanon, mixed in with tobacco. It was a working dope, gentle and user-friendly which could be chuffed on, reliably, all day. Which is why poor Howard Marks and others had to smuggle it in by the fucking ton.)

My initiation had come, one sunny afternoon, when a few of us from Stage Crew were avoiding lectures by sprawling on the grassy slopes next to the new library. A discreet joint was making the rounds. Initial reluctance – because, back then, I didn't smoke at all – gave way to this ritual of companionship.

After a couple of drags, I lay back on the grass, eyes closed against the sun. I was aware of the warmth and softness of the conversation around me, the close comradeship of my newish pals, the stillness of the spring afternoon, the distant, happy babble of students going about the campus, the busy chatter of sparrows in a nearby bush. My palms, flat to the grass, were tingling. And the slope itself was oscillating pleasantly. This was nice. I was at one with the world. For once, I liked being me. And on a day like this, bugger Aristotle. Sod Political & Social Theory.

Within Stage Crew, I found a few soul mates for whom the music itself was a passion: Uncle Al, Big Dave Lunnun, his house-mate Paul Tracy (who would later become Our Elizabeth's partner and father of her two boys), Gary Grieve, Howard Kew, and two Hulme Grammar pals who also enrolled at Leeds and followed me onto Stage Crew, Jeff Wharfe and Dave Brown. Then there was the most obsessive music fan of them all, Dave Woodhead. Mirroring the priorities of a classic cinema partnership of the day, we too were 'on a mission from God'. Although for most of us on Stage Crew, *The Blues Brothers* wasn't just a movie. It was a way of life.

Woodhead's encyclopaedic knowledge of rock & roll was worrying, even to me. This was a guy whose dedication to those who most embodied the heart and soul of the genre had led him to embroider the logo of Southside Johnny and the Asbury Jukes on the canvas haversack in which he carried around his textbooks or his sandwiches on punishing and bitterly cold walks across the Yorkshire Dales.

Like me, Woodhead worshipped Bruce Springsteen. One day, on Crew, working on a gig, we challenged each other to see who could go the longest without humming a Springsteen song. Dave lost. Before the load-in was complete, he was caught singing to himself the first verse of *Racing In The Street*. When we weren't loading and unloading a couple of articulated trucks – and PA systems were bulkier and much heavier than they are today – Dave and I would spend blissful afternoons combing the second-hand record stalls on the markets of Leeds, trying to outdo each other in the accumulation of obscurities and bargains. Through my introduction, Dave would later become Billy Bragg's regular trumpet player.

PAUL, ALONG WITH ME, Henderson and Dave Lunnun, was a roots reggae connoisseur. In fact, all reggae was roots reggae, back then. This was its golden age, pre-digital, pre-dancehall and before cocaine and its crack variant replaced marijuana as the drug which informed and drove the music. After the Wailers, our favourites were the militant Black Uhuru (before corporate demands, gormless American radio-friendly production values and line-up changes blanded them out), and the mighty Culture, led by a wonky-eyed, dreadlocked spider called Joseph Hill.

Few white people in the UK knew of Culture. But their albums *Cumbolo* and *International Herb* were rarely off the turntable when half of Stage Crew would flop out to drink beer and roll joints at Paul and Big Dave's in the early hours, after finishing a gig in the Refec.

Rastafarianism, like all religions, is mumbo-jumbo, a triumph of belief over reason, an elevation of superstition into a moral framework, regardless of the fact that a moral framework doesn't need superstition, of any stripe, as a justification for, and an expression of, its morality. Lurid, Old Testament nonsense Rastafarianism may be, but its roots reggae medium, nevertheless, gave us some bloody wonderful records.

Bob Marley, the former street tough whose early inspiration had been gun-slinging rude boy culture, had become, more lately, the John the Baptist of Rastafarianism and the apostle of woolly-headed One Love. It was powerfully seductive. I loved the music – and still do – but for the music itself, its soul rebel instincts, and roots reggae's militancy rather than its garbled, herbally-distorted and feeble-minded philosophy. I would later come to realise, for example, that confronted by the reality of their Back To Africa rhetoric, most Rastas would want to scamper straight back to the airport after ten minutes face to face with the continent of their dreams. And few African governments would welcome, with open arms, the Rastas' agricultural business models.

Seldom off the turntable in Leeds – Culture's unambiguous *International Herb* LP.

Paul and I followed Culture around on their occasional UK visits, often finding ourselves to be the only white faces at another shambolically organised gig in some shabby, makeshift nightclub, possibly in Manchester or, on one occasion, in that hotbed of *lickle riddim,* Huddersfield.

Invariably, Culture would not appear on stage until most normal people were thinking of getting out of bed the following day – if they appeared at all. At one gig, I actually fell asleep behind the PA, to be woken by the band, just inches above me, charging into their opening number, *Jah Jah See Them A Come*, real horns and all.

Roots reggae was my first real encounter with what came to be labelled world music. It was an astonishing achievement that the parochial folk and gospel-informed style of a religious minority on a smallish island, in the hands of – pretty much – one man, went on to conquer the world.

WHAT TURNED OUT to be Bob Marley's final UK appearances took place in the summer of 1980. I saw him twice on that tour, once outdoors at the Crystal Palace Bowl and, most memorably, at the Bingley Hall, Stafford – a vast shed which otherwise functioned as an indoor cattle market.

From Marley's UK agent I'd secured enough tickets for us to fill the Students' Union minibus. Jonny Barnes and the adorable Anna Jenkins had split. I took the plunge and invited Anna along, with a girlfriend as a chaperone. When Bob hit that stage, in that atmosphere, I wanted to have only Anna alongside me.

I can't pretend this was something I achieved smoothly. Anna and her friend were to arrive at 16 Norwood Terrace, from Saddleworth, around lunchtime on the day of the gig. Big Dave Lunnun had volunteered to drive the minibus. In our excitement and anticipation of seeing the Wailers, the rest of us – my Stage Crew pals and I – had welcomed in the day with much ingestion of the sacramental herb. And then followed it up with a lot more, during a DJ sound-clash, between competing bedroom hi-fis, across our first floor landing.

Around mid morning, Jeff Wharfe and I went to the corner

shop, just at the end of our street, to get supplies for the trip. The nice Asian shopkeeper, accustomed to the ways of the student ghetto, was unfazed that Jeff and I were crawling around, among his displays, on our hands and knees, unable to recall why we'd gone there in the first place.

Just before Anna showed up, I was in my room, no doubt communing with Selassie-I (Yes, I!), when there was a tremendous blast. My aquarium, quite a big tank, spontaneously blew itself apart, propelling fish, gravel and gallons of water all over the room. And all over me.

It was probably as well I was stoned. With resignation, I gathered up the fish in a bucket, took them round to Big Dave's house and lodged them in his tank. Then Dave and I climbed into the minibus, collected Anna and the others and, with me smelling like the bottom of a pond, set off for Stafford.

'I think we should go as the crow flies,' said Big Dave who, in spiritual preparation for the gig, had also been enjoying a number of exotic lunchtime cheroots of north African origin. 'We'll avoid the motorway, and head over the Peak District.' It seemed to make perfect sense.

Of course, it made no sense at all.

Before we'd breached Leeds's inner city ring road, the rear of the minibus was a joint-rolling industrial unit. On a glorious afternoon, we were soon trundling over hill and dale, then dale and hill, and along twisting lanes, remarking on the scenery, my heels up on the dash, a bammie jammed in the corner of my mouth, *Uprising* on the stereo and the girl I adored dimpling prettily in the back.

Somehow or other we did arrive at the Bingley Hall in time for the concert. The next miracle was that we got right to the front. And it wasn't particularly crushed. At times, I was up against a horizontal scaffolding pole that was the crash barrier, right under Marley, and only fifteen or twenty feet away from him. The air was sweet and thick with the fragrances of marijuana although our happy hand-rolling artisans in the back of the bus had also taken the precaution of bringing in plenty of our own. Just in case.

When, finally, the gracefully ascending doo-be-doo-bedooooo Hammond organ gospel intro to *No Woman No Cry* slipped from the speaker stacks, a great sigh of surrender swept the Bingley Hall. In that moment, as Marley – eyes squeezed shut, right arm raised heavenward – closed in on the microphone, it was possible to believe in anything, especially One Love.

Anna, brushing up against me, was slowly grinding to the intro. With one voice, every throat in that shed took up the response to Marley's call. For no reason, other than emotional overload, tears were rolling down my face. It was the finest, most complete moment of my life so far. And, for the first time in my life, I was truly in love.

Big Dave drove us back to Leeds by another of his trailblazing routes. But time no longer mattered. The mood in the bus was just euphoric. For the return journey, Anna sat up front with me, her cat's eyes flashing as we shared joints.

Dawn wasn't far off when we reached Leeds and piled into the front room of Dave and Paul's tiny terraced house at the grottier end of Headingley. First, for the Union's records, I had to make a note of the minibus's mileage. A conventional drive from Leeds to Stafford is just about 100 miles. Taking Big Dave's short cut over the Derbyshire Peak District – and back – we'd topped 400 miles, round trip.

Black Uhuru hit the turntable, beers were cracked open, more Jazz Woodbines were rolled. Then came a knock at the door.

There was real paranoia in those days about being busted, the authorities not having yet adopted a workable and sensible view of dope smoking. We all froze. I got up and, gingerly, went to the door, which led directly from the front room onto the street. On the pavement were two policemen.

'Fuck,' I thought. 'This is it.' I pulled the door behind me, as far as I could, without forcing myself off the premises and into their arms.

'Hello, sir,' said one of the coppers.

'Good evening, officer,' I replied, although the sun was coming up.

An impressive roller of marijuana smoke was tumbling out of the room behind me and over the two policemen.

'Is this your vehicle?' asked the other, pointing to the Union minibus.

'Er, yes, sort of. The Student Union's, actually.'

'Well, sir. Just thought we'd better let you know that you've left your lights on. Sorry to bother you, sir. Mind how you go.'

16

LIVE AT LEEDS – BONKERS AMATEURISM TURNED PRO

'IT'S LIKE THIS,' explained the coiffured youth. 'We really need the cash. A cheque isn't any use to us. We need cash to pay for our B&B. Tonight. And we haven't got any other money. If you can find it for us, somehow, we'd be really grateful.'

The sum in question was fifty quid. I took pity on them. It wasn't a glamorous life on the road as a support band to a bigger group. The main act didn't necessarily feel any bond with the unknowns on the undercard. They may not even have liked them.

Standard procedure was that when a promoter booked an established band from an agent, the headliner would bring with them their own support, who would be the opening act on all dates of the tour. For the privilege of this second-class status, and in the hope of wider exposure, the support band's record company bought them into that position with a handsome payment to the main band. Local promoters, like me, then paid the support a token fee of £50 per night. This was standard and didn't change for years, regardless of inflation.

Because I had rightly predicted, at the time of what had been a bargain booking, that she would soon go racing up the charts with *Breaking Glass*, Hazel O'Connor was in shrill overdrive just upstairs, before a sell-out Refec.

Meanwhile, down in the dressing room, a defunct kitchen, I was listening, sympathetically, to this tale of penury from the support band's struggling young singer. It was December 3rd 1980. Student Union Finance Office policy forbade Ents to pay groups in cash but I couldn't see these lads humiliated. Nor on the streets. I tore up their cheque and told the singer I'd be back in a moment. I went to the Union's cashpoint machine and took out £50 of my own money (quite a lump for a student then) knowing, with a receipt, I'd be able to claim it back the day after.

I gave the cash to the singer. He and the rest of the band were genuinely grateful and noticeably relieved. They called themselves Duran Duran. And the receipt for fifty quid was signed by a Simon Le Bon.

Nice enough lads to deal with on the night and, earlier in the evening, I'd even caught a bit of their set. On the basis of that, I still feel they were slightly overpaid.

MICK JAGGER, STANDING in that same mothballed kitchen, in March 1971, had remarked to *Leeds Student* newspaper, 'Everybody seems to want to play here.' That may have been so, but under my regime I booked only those groups I liked personally, or those whose immense popularity (and, therefore, their profitability) made them unavoidable.

On an almost daily basis, for most of my two and a half years as Ents Sec, I was pestered by an agent – full marks for his tenacity – to book this group of his called U2. Sadly, for Bono and his pals (all very decent chaps, granted), I'd seen U2 some time in 1980, opening for Talking Heads at the Hammersmith Palais and decided there and then that they were a big bag of wind, an opinion which they have only reinforced in the intervening years.

Only once, in that time, was I asked by the agent of a headliner if I could arrange the support group myself. And I'm afraid I can't recall for which main band it was. I do, however, remember that it gave me the chance to help a spotty little outfit from

Manchester who had released a couple of sparky independent singles, played by John Peel, and for which I'd developed great affection.

You Know What You Told Me by The Frantic Elevators was a couple of minutes of glorious DIY minimalism: a soaring, soulful voice, riding a catchy tune as other band members whacked an electric guitar and what sounded like a tin tray. That was it. An instant classic. The voice belonged to a confident, carrot-haired youth who, on my invitation and the promise of fifty quid, turned up at the University in a tatty van. He introduced himself as Mick. Mick Hucknall.

Once a term – or once a year, if I could get away with it – I felt compelled to keep the loveable heavy metal hordes happy with a token gig featuring the strangulated poodles of current favour. Otherwise, there was always the reliable fall-back of Motörhead, the idea of whom I enjoyed more than their music. It was impossible not to like a band whose leader, Lemmy, when I interviewed him some years later on Radio 1, characterised thus: 'If Motörhead moved in next door to you, your lawn would die.'

I also took the decision to open up Leeds gigs to the public, arguing that a students-only policy at the biggest regular venue in the city wasn't only elitist and bad PR around town for the University but that enlightened self-interest ought to be asking why we were restricting our potential ticket sales to just the student minority of the city's population. The small price I had to pay for this altruism was an occasional grudging concession to mass popularity. Enter Haircut 100.

Nick Heyward and his chums played to a squealing Refec in March 1982. It was like punk never happened. A record was set that night: my Front Stage Security lads lifted out from the audience 131 girls who had fainted clean away at the very idea of *A Blue Hat For A Blue Day* – or were pretending to have fainted in the hope their condition would get them attention backstage. It got them, instead, carried out of a side door and down a fire escape to be revived by a lady in sensible shoes from St John Ambulance in a dingy car park down below.

* * *

ASIDE FROM THESE and one or two other aberrations, I let my own tastes dictate and ran Ents, as Henderson had done before me, as a benign dictatorship. The Ents Committee, which I chaired, was little more than an excuse for me and my generals to get together on a Wednesday evening and for the junta, over a couple of pints, to endorse the deals I'd made and the bands I'd booked already, possibly earlier that afternoon. I knew what had to be done.

Steve Henderson had carried this off with great charm, good humour and, behind his party-animal persona, quiet, meticulous attention to detail. Subconsciously, I learned a lot from watching him operate: how he dealt with strutting tour managers – fairly but firmly, never taking them, or himself, too seriously – and how he always had time even for the most humble Ents volunteer, possibly manning an isolated Refectory basement rat-run, as some legends of rock & roll thundered away upstairs. I was on the brink of discovering a flair for leadership that I didn't realise I had. If it came from anywhere, it came from Henderson. And Uncle Al.

A couple of weeks before becoming Ents Sec, I had taken over as Crew Boss from Uncle Al – who needed to spend time with his family and his differential equations – and for several months I did both jobs simultaneously, starting out with a gig by The Pretenders. They were supported by some unknown Brummies who were soon to have much success playing reggae-lite for audiences who were disinclined to listen to real reggae. And, on that night, they played it for the statutory fifty quid. It was my first encounter with UB40.

If I'd quite fancied Chrissie Hynde before she rolled in for the afternoon soundcheck, I didn't afterwards. Perhaps she thought being stroppy with everyone who was working hard for her convenience was a rock star requirement. It didn't impress us. Good gig, though. And I rebooked them.

We had, in the course of more than a hundred concerts on which I worked at Leeds, surprisingly few incidents of prima donna petulance – or, indeed, crowd problems.

Sadly, reggae concerts were often troublesome. A proportion of the city's population seemed to think it was their birthright to storm through the front doors without tickets – and racist of my stewards to suggest they might care to pay for admission like everyone else.

Black Uhuru's concert – the bits of it I caught – was one of the finest performances I saw in the Refec. But it was a nightmare of a gig to run. There were break-ins all over the building. I spent the evening racing, through blood and broken glass, from one emergency to another, all to the menacing muezzin wail of Michael Rose and the live serpent rhythms of Sly Dunbar and Robbie Shakespeare.

At one point, I was rushing across the Student Union bar, in

Now we're having fun! With Big John Bisbrowne at the 1995 TT Races, Isle of Man. *Unknown*

the building next door to the Refec. There, sitting at a table, enjoying a pint with a few old buddies, was my dear friend Big John Bisbrowne. To call him Big John was, and still is, to diminish him. But, at twenty-four stone, John looked anorexic alongside his pal, Jon Silsby. The pair had been students, and Ents stalwarts, back in the era of The Who and the Stones. Neither had fully detached himself from the old firm.

Hugely likeable, with a plummy, booming voice and a thick black beard, Silsby was still living in Leeds and he had an open invitation to be my guest at all the gigs. Big John had moved to Burton on Trent but frequently came up to his old patch for the weekend. He was dating Our Elizabeth and often stayed with us, especially if I was putting on a band of his liking. Black Uhuru was one of them. John is one of the most naturally funny men I have ever met. And one of the sourest.

Nursing their Tetley's, and no doubt reflecting that Ents wasn't what it used to be, the two veterans were on the point of having just one more pint before catching a bit of the band. When I ran in.

'Ah, great! Boys,' I said, 'bit of trouble at the front door. Could do with your help, if you don't mind.'

Big John raised one eyebrow at Silsby. They put down their beers and, as I hared off to the next crisis, they plodded out of the bar.

About ten minutes later, I was again tearing through the Refec foyer. In the war zone of the front doors, I spotted Big John in the thick of things. He was holding a wriggling invader in one hand, fully off the ground. Hurling the guy clean over the barrier, as you and I might fling a bin bag into a skip, he turned to me, inflating with indignation.

'When you invited me up for the weekend,' he said, 'I was expecting an agreeable couple of days with old friends. And a Black Uhuru concert. Not a re-enactment of Rorke's Drift.'

I WAS SUMMONED, inevitably, on the Monday morning to the University administration building to account for the trouble and damage. This was routine. We, as the Union, hired the Refec from the University. If my cleaning team had as much as overlooked a couple of empty beer cans on a Refec windowsill during our late-night transformation of a legendary rock & roll venue back into a spotless dining hall – an amazing effort and achievement – I would get the call to explain myself, if not face-to-face with the Vice-Chancellor in person, then to one of his lieutenants.

None of these chaps was of the rock generation. None yet appreciated that I was far from unique: that many university applicants were drawn to Leeds because of its rock & roll history, reputation and the quality of its gigs. They hadn't yet grasped that *Live At Leeds* had put the University more emphatically on the map than any academic achievement.

These 'pop concerts' were considered to be a frightful nuisance by the University authorities. Much of my time, as Ents Sec, was spent justifying them to fundamentally decent old coves who were plain bewildered as to why we couldn't just settle instead for an occasional string quartet or a dinner dance. I was regarded much as a talented but irredeemably wayward schoolboy might be looked upon by a kindly deputy headmaster. And I also had a hunch that lurking within the grey flannel and bifocals brigade, I had a secret protector.

The Politics faculty, meanwhile, was ostensibly unimpressed by my rock & roll lifestyle. In my first year at Leeds, I'd been almost a model student, even getting the highest marks in one component of the course. But once I'd joined Stage Crew, and then become Ents Sec, I did not attend another single lecture or tutorial for the next two years.

Letters from the department would arrive from time to time. Occasionally, they hinted they might write to my local education authority, inviting them to cut off my grant. (It never happened.) This seemed to me a little rich. As I saw it, my mum, dad, and grandparents had, in taxation, already paid for my higher education – and, if I wished, the opportunity to be a rock & roll layabout – in advance, and a long time before. Any argy-bargy about how I was spending my time at the Butlin's of academia was surely a family matter and no business of the Men With Beards in the Politics building.

They would also demand to see me. Not that it made a blind

The greatest venue in the world – The Refec, Leeds University, during the load-in for a band, early 1980s. *Steve Saunders*

bit of difference. From time to time, I'd shamble over to these meetings. Once, a particularly pompous tutor broke off from his latest final warning when I removed my leather jacket and he spotted a line of insect bites along the inside of my forearm.

'Are you, Mr Kershaw,' he asked, 'on drugs?'

BACK IN OUR smoky den, my fellow herbalists enjoyed that one. Ents had been moved out of the main Union Executive office, because the President and others said we were too noisy. I believe the truth was they hated seeing us having fun while they tackled the necessary, the worthy and the downright dull.

We were exiled to an office which hadn't been used for years, at the top corner of the building, up a back staircase. While we lost the immediate care and attention of the wonderful Exec secretaries, Gloria Rawle and Edna Wilson (Gloria, especially, had become to me what Aunt Dahlia was to Bertie Wooster), the new office had the advantage of being isolated, with a lockable door, its own bath and toilet, and a private roof terrace. The daft buggers downstairs had given me a penthouse. As a punishment.

It was in here that I spent nearly every waking hour, on the phone to agents and others. Or in conference with my closest comrades. These now included my self-appointed PA, Zillah Kennedy, a girl of about nineteen – twin-set and pearls – going on fifty-nine. I don't ever recall Zillah starting in this job. There hadn't been a job. She just gradually took over the organisation of the office – and of me – making herself indispensable. In an earlier age, she'd have been one of those women at Bomber Command, pushing models of Lancasters across a map of occupied Europe.

The threats from my department bothered me only in that to be kicked off my course would mean I'd have to surrender, as a non-student, the Ents Sec job. On the evidence I saw at many Refec concerts, I decided it was empty bluster. I liked to make a study of the audience as it came in. After giving the instruction to open the front doors, I'd often linger in the foyer. It was quite common for me to spot one or two of the groovier Politics academics, disguised in denim, filtering through. If they weren't complete hypocrites, I figured, they'd probably grasped I was doing something valuable – if not their essays – and not kick me out. And, to their credit, they never did.

The day arrived, though, in early 1981, when I had to make a definitive choice. Either I backed out of Ents and slunk back to my degree before it was too late or I chose the Albert Hammond option.

I'd taken a stroll, as I often did, into the Refectory during the afternoon when, between lunch and evening meal service, it was empty and silent. I found it a peaceful, soothing place in those periods, and I liked to sit on a corner of the stage, round the back, beneath a semi-circle of tall narrow windows through which the afternoon sun would pour. I'd finger the flaking plywood boards and think of the bands who'd strutted upon them. I wished I'd been old enough, or aware enough, to have been in the Refec that night the Rolling Stones played, just ten tantalising years before. Or there to feel the charisma of Bob Marley filling the long, low-ceilinged hall, ringed by that famous balcony and bridge. I'd consider that history and summon those ghosts. 'And I'm running it now,' I'd say to myself. 'Bloody hell. Me.'

The reality of my good fortune was always sharp. The thrill never diminished. And the responsibility was scary. If I was anxious about anything it was not to betray that history and not to fail early pioneers like Simon Brogan. Their vision and energy had made it all possible. Ents was a treasure which I had been immensely lucky to inherit and it was both a joy and a worry to be the custodian of that legend and the guardian of those standards. Ents deserved I give it my best.

If I stuck with my course and passed the exams, I calculated, I would emerge from Leeds University with an unremarkable bit of paper, identical to the one awarded to dozens of other Politics students that year. Then I could start hustling for a job, to start with on a local paper. Perhaps.

Meanwhile, I was running an organisation of around two hundred volunteer helpers: security, caterers, cleaners, stewards, publicists and Stage Crew. That wasn't an experience most twenty-year-olds could put on their CVs. I was booking the bands, haggling with agents, dealing with tour managers, roadies, rock stars, the public, the press, Students' Union officials and University authorities. I was doing okay. Perhaps I'd leave Leeds and, with this experience under my belt, go on to be the next Harvey Goldsmith, then the biggest concert promoter in the country. Anyway, what the hell. I was having a blast. And, on top of that, weren't we doing Siouxsie & The Banshees next weekend?

I made the decision. Bugger a BA in Politics.

IF WE HAD REASON to expect misbehaviour from any visiting rock star, it was Iggy Pop. Less than ten years on from the mayhem in Detroit (caught on his *Metallic KO* bootleg), there were lurid accounts of riots at Stooges gigs, Iggy slashing his own chest on stage, a troubling heroin appetite and a fondness for pulling out his considerable plonker. He was the embodiment of true punk and, allegedly, a genuine Wild Man of Rock.

On the afternoon of the gig, approaching soundcheck time, I saw the familiar huddle that was always the band's arrival making its way down the Refec towards me and my Crew buddies by the stage. I stepped forward to introduce myself. It was Iggy alright and I extended my hand and said hello to him and his band members. He was charm itself.

During the soundcheck we were standing together by the stage, Iggy waiting to try out his vocals.

'Do you still do *Louie Louie*?' I asked him.

It was one of my favourite rock & roll songs, I explained, fail-safe in its simplicity. Iggy laughed when I told him I collected versions of *Louie Louie* and I mentioned how much I'd enjoyed his reading of it on *Metallic KO*.

'Nah, I'm afraid we don't do it anymore,' he said. 'We haven't played that in a long time.'

Cut to seven hours later and the Refec floor is bouncing and booming as thousands of feet pound the parquet for an encore. The band climbs back on stage, the crowd goes wild again and Iggy, now stripped to the waist, leans on the microphone stand and leers at his disciples. There is a hush. He looks across at me, winks, and turns to the band.

'Okay, you guys. How about we give 'em *Louie Louie* and get outta this goddam fucking whorehouse?'

BA-BA-BAM, BA-BAM, BA-BA-BAM...

The Refec goes nuts.

A few minutes later, winding past my position by the house lights, and on his way downstairs to the dressing room, Iggy gave me a hard, friendly punch in the chest. And a big grin. 'Betcha the best fucking gig we ever played, Andy!'

Iggy Pop – Wild Man of Rock. And an absolute poppet.

The same could not be said of Bob Geldof.

17

THE CLASH AND THE RATS

IN ALL MY TIME with Leeds University Union Ents, from junior supervisor of distant fire-doors to concert organiser, the greatest gig I saw in the Refec took place on Thursday 31 January 1980. No other contenders came even close. The Clash were on the *16 Tons Tour*, to promote their new album, *London Calling*, and they were, in that flash of lightning, the last word in rock & roll bands.

For sheer enjoyment, and mindless rock & roll fundamentalism, The Ramones had given the Last Gang in Town something to follow. They'd been with us only the previous Saturday and Al and I, in our usual corner by the stage and the dressing-room stairwell, had counted twenty-one songs in the first half an hour.

Others will recall the night they saw Joy Division open for the Buzzcocks. Or, more likely, they'll pretend they were there. (I prefer to remember the delirium of the shambolic headliners that night.) And that was the quality of the gigs, week in, week out. It was a huge privilege to be booking bands for, and running gigs at, a legendary venue. Simply by maintaining the standards of those before me, we were making history, and adding to that legend, every weekend. I was twenty years old and promoting the best bands in the world at a time when rock music still mattered.

We seemed to enjoy a special relationship with Elvis Costello, dating back to the first Stiff Tour in 1977. Elvis himself, the Attractions, their management, agent, record company and road crew – like those of many others – trusted Leeds University to do the job more professionally than all other venues.

When, in the spring of 1981, Elvis confounded expectations, and confronted most rock fans' prejudices against the genre, by releasing *Almost Blue*, a Nashville-recorded album of pure country music, there was to be no UK tour to promote it. I wasn't having that and phoned, not Elvis's booking agent, but his manager.

Jake Riviera had reservations: one-offs were problematic; it was tricky, for a start, to pull together all the necessary personnel for a single gig; Elvis wasn't around; Elvis already had a busy promotional schedule for the album, but no plans for gigs.

I kept upping the offers.

The normal price for a major band – Siouxsie & The Banshees, for example – at the time was about £1500 to £2000. Ticket prices for that would be around three quid, occasionally nudging £3.50 if a group's fee was slightly more.

'Four thousand pounds?' said Jake, on the phone. 'In cash?'

'In cash,' I confirmed. 'Ticket price four quid.'

We got our Elvis Costello and the Attractions gig – a masterclass – the only concert our greatest living songwriter played at that point in his career, apart from an appearance in a small club in Aberdeen which was set up mainly for a *South Bank Show* television recording.

I had absolutely no authority to promise readies to Jake. The Union Finance Officer, when I told him the terms of the deal, had a fit. A jumpy man at the best of times, he turned up himself on the night of the gig, something he'd never done before, at the dressing room, with the cash in a briefcase, surrounded by a platoon of Securicor men wearing helmets.

Similarly trustworthy of Leeds were Island Records, who chose us to stage the European debut concert of Kid Creole and the Coconuts. With Island seemingly bussing and flying in half the country's media for this showcase, it was flattering they decided we were the ones who could best handle it.

The gig was spectacular, quite unlike anything that we had

staged before. Instead of just four blokes with guitars bass and drums, Kid Creole brought showbiz to the Refec – dancing girls, costumes, colour, performance, a tropical stage set with palm trees, entertainment, a real show.

But, for me, all other gigs were measured against that night in January 1980.

I'd seen The Clash before, of course, and their earlier scratchy fury was itself impressive, if limited. But by the *16 Tons Tour* they had matured into something magnificent. They had rejected their previous tactical but silly Year Zero approach to any music that came before punk. Now, live – just as they had on record with *London Calling*, a radical departure from earlier releases – they were finally allowing their collective musical enthusiasms and their immersion in rock & roll history to enrich, gloriously, their performances on stage. Not just evident now, but cele-brated, were the elements of R&B, roots reggae, Keith Richards, country, soul, rockabilly and dub.

The Clash of January 1980 had also accumulated those almost indefinable qualities necessary for elevation to the status of greatness. To embellish those musical components (and, nat-urally, their playing had only improved over time), they had the look, the charisma, the *élan*. In the Refec that night, they were the fully-rounded, finished article. And utterly riveting. I stood agape. I was not, however, witnessing the future of rock & roll. Nor, strictly speaking, the end. But both. The alpha and the omega.

After that gig, I came to realise, anything that followed, in the name of rock music was, by definition, at best second-rate. And probably pointless.

THE PROGRAMME OF GIGS for my final term as Ents Sec, in the spring of 1982, ran thus: The Pretenders, The Boomtown Rats, Kid Creole & The Coconuts, Rory Gallagher, Black Uhuru and The Clash. Thank you, Leeds, and goodnight.

I was thrilled I'd secured The Clash for my last stand. There could not have been, after what I'd seen of them two years ear-lier, a more appropriate band with which I could finish – a triumphant, maximum rock & roll farewell.

Posters for The Clash's gig – totally unnecessary, but they made great souvenirs – were already up on the Students' Union notice-boards on 30 April, the day we were hosting The Boomtown Rats. No longer as popular as they were, and without a hit for two years, I was jolly satisfied and relieved that The Boomtown Rats gig had just sold out in advance. They weren't personal favourites of mine. I considered them to be pretty much a girls' band – for girls who didn't really have much appreciation of rock & roll but quite liked the idea of shagging the cut-price Mick Jagger who was the singer.

It was getting close to doors-open time and I was making my routine last patrol of the Refec and its connecting basement corridors to the Union Building before heading to the foyer. Striding through that labyrinth I heard, up ahead, a tearing sound and a

The Ice Age is comin'! Joe Strummer and Mick Jones of The Clash, on stage at Leeds University, 31 January 1980. That night, they were the last word in rock & roll bands. *AK*

raised voice. When I turned the corner, there was a bloke ripping down a Clash poster and ranting to himself.

I'd had the posters printed with the words, above The Clash's name, 'The return of the world's greatest rock & roll band...' The guy heard my approach and swung around. It was Bob Geldof.

'What the hell do you think you're doing?' I demanded.

'Focken, focken, fock! World's focken greatest rock and focken roll band, my focken arse,' he explained, scattering drawing pins.

I told him who I was and told him to leave the posters alone. This was met with more Plastic Paddy eloquence from the future spokesman of a voiceless continent, Honorary KBE and candidate for populist canonisation.

'What's your problem?' I asked. 'Calm down. Your gig's sold out. The Clash concert doesn't affect you.'

He strode off towards the dressing rooms, chucking a ball of torn, screwed-up poster on the floor.

'Focken little cunt,' he called over his shoulder.

Later that evening, I wanted to hand over the band's cheque to the tour manager and went looking for him in the dressing room. Geldof, just off stage, where he'd received a rapturous response from a rammed Refec, flew at me again. The same stuff. About The Clash and the posters.

'This is the world's focken greatest focken rock & roll band,' he was snarling, sweeping an arm around the dressing room. His band members looked sheepish and awkward.

Then he was right in my face, eyes bulging, spraying me with spit. 'Focken little cunt!' And he shoved me in the chest.

Instantly, a couple of his band members were on his shoulders, pulling him back.

I thanked them, told Geldof he was a charmless, ungrateful little prick and paid off the tour manager.

Some minutes later, he came upstairs to find me in the hall and apologised for Geldof who was, he revealed, still ranting in the dressing room at no one in particular.

* * *

ALMOST A YEAR before my first run-in with the future Saint Bob, Zillah and I were up in the Ents Office. It was near the end of the spring term, 1981. We had only the Iggy Pop concert left to do before the holidays.

'The results of your Finals come out today, remember?' she trilled. 'I'll go over to your department, if you like, and see what you've got.'

I'd turned up at the exams only so that it couldn't be said I hadn't, mainly in the hope that this would deter Lancashire Education Authority from feeling emboldened to ask for their money back.

Academic failure was an inevitability. As I arrived for one of the exams, held for some reason in the Engineering block, an acquaintance from Ents was waiting at a bus stop, just in front of the building.

'Morning, Andy,' said Stuart as I scurried by. It was Political & Social Theory. As ever. I wrote my name on the top of the paper, studied the questions and looked around at those already scribbling. 'Morning, Stuart,' I said, passing the bus stop on the way out.

I hopped it from another Final when, looking up at the clock, I realised the trucks were due to arrive at the Refec half an hour later for the load-in for the Elvis Costello one-off.

Our Elizabeth, back working in Leeds and sharing a flat with me close to the University, was making breakfast just before I had to leave for a third exam.

'Have you got time for any?' she asked. 'Alas, no,' I said and ambled off to the campus. Within twenty minutes, I'd rejoined her for bacon butties.

In one sense, and for twelve months, my future was secure. In early 1981, I'd stood in a Union election for the office of Treasurer. I had absolutely no interest in the Union's finances. But Treasurer was a sabbatical post and, if I got the job, it meant I could stay on, simultaneously as Ents Sec, for an additional year after my Politics course had ended. I won the election and never did a stroke of work as Treasurer.

Zillah came clicking up the stairs, back to the Ents office.

'Your name's not there,' she said. 'Not on any of the lists.'

'Oh,' I said. 'Not even on the list for those who've got a basic Pass? The one they give just for turning up?'

'No,' she said.

We got on with our work.

Later that afternoon, the phone rang. It was the Vice-Chancellor's office. Would I, they asked, be able to walk over there now? What was this about, I wondered. There'd been no problems I could recall at the Costello gig. Off I went to find out.

'Look, old man,' said the VC. 'Obviously, I've heard the news.'

Hell's teeth. What? Surely he'd not discovered I'd been sleeping, secretly, with one of his secretaries.

'About your exam results.'

That was it. Thank goodness. Not even trouble in the Refec. Instead, my latest achievement – becoming the first student to fail a Politics degree in the history of Leeds University.

'You must be terribly disappointed,' he went on. 'But I want you to know this. You have worked hard here. Not academically, we know. However, I think you've made a valuable contribution to student life. And when you leave us, if you ever need a reference, I want you to know you can always use my name.'

Once I'd composed myself, I leapt up and, beaming, pumped his hand. He was beaming too.

'How very kind,' said Zillah, back at the office, having poured the tea and rolling us a joint. 'That was very decent of him. What a nice man.'

A YEAR LATER, in April 1982, Zillah answered another significant call. I was nearing the end of my extra year. And the end of my time as Ents Sec.

'Andrew Zweck from Harvey Goldsmith's office,' she said, handing me the receiver.

'Andy,' said Andrew, at the other end, 'how do you fancy working for the Rolling Stones? And can you bring the Leeds Uni Stage Crew with you?'

18

THE ROLLING STONES' GUIDE
TO PAINTING & DECORATING

ALREADY THE SIZE of an aircraft carrier, the stage was only partially built when we arrived. Members of Stage Crew, like the remnants of a rebel patrol, were threading their way down through the trees, into the natural bowl of Roundhay Park, and gathering behind the vast scaffolding framework. A couple of dozen articulated lorries, and a similar number of empty flatbeds were parked up in neat lines. More were rumbling into the park.

We squinted up at the riggers, chatting and clanking, swinging and building, climbing higher on their Meccano as they worked. 'Fuck,' said Al. And we all concurred with his expert analysis. It was an impressive erection, even for Mick Jagger. And, at that time, the biggest stage that had ever been built, anywhere in the world. Roundhay, in Leeds, in front of 120,000 fans, was to be the final date on the Rolling Stones European Tour, 1982, which broke records, set standards and established precedents on a scale never seen before.

The logistics alone were mind-boggling. The infrastructure being unloaded before our eyes in Roundhay was extraordinary, but for the Stones to play a handful of consecutive dates in new locations there had to be three of these set-ups on the road, leap-frogging each other: one under construction, a second ready for the gig; and a third being dismantled following the previous performance. We were just a fraction of the total operation.

To meet the backstage requirements at Roundhay, I was to be in charge of those logistics and grandly titled, for the next three weeks, Backstage Labour Co-ordinator. So it was reassuring to find a couple of familiar and friendly faces in the Portakabin offices which had been plonked down overlooking the grassy slope of what would become the backstage area.

Andrew Zweck from Goldsmith's office, and Harvey's earthly representative during the build-up at Leeds, is a bluff, blond Australian with a reputation for getting things done. Uncommonly, for the music business, Andrew is good-humoured and devoid of self-importance. Similarly, Paul Crockford – Andrew's assistant for the gig. Dear old Crockers was about the only bloke in the music industry I considered to be a pal. Just a few years older than me, and a former Ents Sec at Southampton, he was now working in a freelance capacity for Harvey Goldsmith's concert promotion company.

A tour of the Rolling Stones magnitude had required Goldsmith, the UK's biggest promoter, to be co-opted by the enterprise's overall mastermind, legendary hippy impresario and pioneer, Bill Graham. In fact, this Rolling Stones adventure – taking in Europe and the States over two years – was the first time one promoter had staged a whole tour, globally; and Graham's experiment with the Stones tour would become the model for the industry in years to come. For the moment, however, in this previously uncharted territory, Graham and Goldsmith were making it up as they went along.

EVEN WHEN RIPPING me off, selling me bands for the University, Crockers was always huge fun. Like Andrew Zweck, he doesn't know how to be pompous. And like me, he was amused most by the ridiculous and the absurd. This was to be a quality we would find indispensable over the following couple of weeks.

'That's your desk,' said Andrew, pointing to a freshly-acquired bargain, in simulated teak finish, from some second-hand office supplies outlet. My position was in the middle of our HQ, handily by the door, and with a window overlooking the side of the stage and the slope leading down to where the dressing rooms and band's hospitality area hadn't yet been built. I could keep an eye on everything.

Crockers dumped in front of me a telephone, a heavy new ledger and a cash box containing five hundred pounds, before briefly outlining the mysteries of double-entry bookkeeping.

It started to rain.

A stocky, bearded little bloke soon popped up at the door.

'Hey, you,' he said. 'Who's the guy around here in charge of all the purchases?' The accent was American.

'Me,' I said. 'My name's Andy. Who are you?'

'Magruder,' he snapped, as though he was a brand. And one that I should recognise.

'What's your job here?' I asked.

'Site Co-ordinator, Rolling Stones.' It crossed my mind it was unlikely he'd have been there for The Tremeloes. 'Get me fifty pairs of Hunter's boots and fifty waterproof capes,' he snapped. And he was gone.

I'd not heard of this aristocrat among wellingtons before, but I packed Uncle Al off in his car, with a wad of the cash, to go and find fifty pairs of them around Leeds. He returned with a full load of alluring rubberwear. And we stashed it all in one of the shipping containers that became our stores. The shower which had so alarmed Magruder soon passed. And the wellies and capes remained untouched, and forgotten, for the next two and a half weeks.

If it wasn't Magruder himself who appeared at my door, there was a wealth of other petitioners, day and night, appealing for building materials and plumbing supplies. The latter were the requirements of a team of temporary toilet specialists – to a man polite, cheery lads with fruity Somerset accents – marinaded, for a fortnight, in human filth and who we branded the bogtricians. They were proud to tell everyone that, on his recent UK appearances, they 'had just done the bogs for the Pope'.

Crockford's initial float of five hundred quid quickly began to look like a laughably trifling sum of small change. Soon there were thousands crossing my desk, in cash, hurriedly noted in my ledger, handed to runners and enriching, within the hour, the city's economy.

The source of most supplies was an extraordinary hardware store, of Al's discovery, in the Harehills district of Leeds, called Stanton's. Nothing remarkable to look at, mind you. Stanton's exterior – a few plastic buckets, galvanised bins and a range of step ladders out on the pavement – did not suggest it had cellars going down two levels and more stock, no matter how arcane the item, than a B&Q national distribution facility.

If, at the counter of Stanton's, one were to ask, 'Have you a three-quarter inch thrust-grommet, please, for a 60 degree inverter?' Mr Stanton would possibly respond, 'Weldon shank?'

'No. It's the old screw shank model.'

'Not to worry, sir. The screw shank did have its merits. Is that with or without the retaining flange? With, is it? Very good. Do bear with me, sir. I know there's one here somewhere.'

Or, equally, 'I wonder if you have, please, an extended under-cut lay-shaft (coarse-toothed), with drive dogs?'

'Helical gear?'

'Bevel gear.'

'With bushes?'

'Yes, please.'

'Plain or roller?'

'Er, roller, please.'

'Certainly, sir. Just the one, is it? There we are.'

After a few days, it became clear to me and Al that the Stones gig was dependent entirely on Mr Stanton's remarkable little shop. With others, Al had been operating an almost constant shuttle service between Harehills and Roundhay. Work was going on around the site twenty-four hours a day. Stuff was always needed.

'Al,' I said one afternoon, about a week before the gig. 'Stanton's not being open is unthinkable. What's more, with the day of the concert being a Sunday, suppose we need something vital from Stanton's then?'

Al took off again to see Mr Stanton, this time with a business proposal and a bundle of readies.

'No problem,' he reported when he returned. 'Stanton's will be on call, around the clock, until a week on Monday.'

In all seriousness, the Rolling Stones Roundhay mega-concert could not have happened if Mr Stanton, handsomely bunged, had not become the pioneer in Leeds of twenty-four-hour shopping.

'HEY, YOU.' It was my friend Magruder again. Winning hearts and minds did not seem to be his mission in Roundhay. 'About this fence...'

'What about the fence?'

'It's the wrong fucking colour.'

The fence which was offending Magruder was the perimeter fence of the site. Ringing the bowl, forming the arena, it had been built with sheets of heavy plywood, about ten feet tall, bolted to scaffolding pole supports.

'Well,' I said. 'It's plywood colour.'

By now, Magruder and I were standing in the centre of the battleship stage, gazing out at the distant barrier.

'It's gotta be green,' said Magruder.

'Any particular shade of green?' I asked.

'Grass green, of course.'

In the Yellow Pages, I found a paint company in Batley. Not a shop. Not even a trade outlet. A factory which made paint.

A patient chap there listened to my requirements.

'But there's no recognised shade as grass green,' he said.

'Oh, isn't there? Well, never mind. You get the idea. As long as it's green. Like grass.'

'So this fence is ten feet high, you say. And how long is it?'

'About a mile,' I told him.

There was a pause.

'I see,' he said.

The next day a couple of flat-beds arrived, laden with drums of green paint. I got the drivers, with Stage Crew's help, to dot them along the perimeter of the fence. With rollers on long poles my lads set to work. They got it done impressively quickly. I was proud of them.

Magruder was at the door. 'It's the wrong fucking green!'

I swivelled in my chair. Together we marched back to the stage.

'That's not grass green. It's too dark.'

I had nothing to say.

'Do it again. Get the paint guys to add some blue.'

I jumped. 'Eh? That'll make it even darker. You mean add some yellow.'

'Look. I mean what I said. I know what I'm talking about. That's why I've got my job and you've got yours. Add blue.'

I phoned my man in Batley.

'That'll make it even darker,' he said.

'I know. I've told him that. He won't listen. He's insisting on a new batch. With added blue.'

The flat-beds returned. With drums of blue-enriched Magruder Green. Stage Crew got to work.

'It's fucking darker!' Magruder was squawking.

'I know. That's what I told you.'

'Okay, okay. Yellow. Get the yellow.'

'How about I send you one load of yellow?' suggested Batley's new leading fence-camouflage consultant. 'Get your lads to mix it into that last batch of green.'

The yellow arrived. Stage Crew tipped it in and applied the fence's third luxurious coat.

For the next inspection, a top-level site meeting was convened on the stage, now also involving Crockers and Zweck, who had begun to notice the Rolling Stones were spending thousands on emulsion.

Magruder, ever the perfectionist, was not going to compromise. 'That still ain't grass green. It's gotta be done again, until they get it right.'

We were back, pretty much, to the shade of the original offending coat.

Crockers and Zweck, who were newcomers to Magruder's spectrum sensitivities, tried to soothe him with platitudes and deferential assurances that everything would be fine.

I'd been wondering how long it would be before Magruder, in this week-long debate over exterior decoration, invoked a personal relationship with the Rolling Stone in Chief.

'If that fence is still that goddam shade of green when Mick gets out here on Sunday, the Rolling Stones will walk off this stage' he snarled.

'Dear me,' I said. 'And who will explain to 120,000 fans who've bought tickets why there's no Rolling Stones concert? Mick himself? You? Or would you like me to tell them? That it's all about that plywood being the wrong colour.'

THE FENCE WAS not mentioned again. Attention instead switched to the Japanese water garden.

'*What* Japanese water garden?' I asked.

'They want us to build one.' A delegation from my Stage Crew had gathered at the door. 'They want a stream, a bridge, a waterfall, a pond and koi carp.'

'Stop!' I said 'What for? Where, ferfuckssakes? And when?'

'In the Stones dressing room. By Sunday.'

The Rolling Stones dressing room was more of a leisure complex. And what estate agents like to describe as 'executively appointed': individual suites for each band member, over which was flown a big marquee, creating a hidden compound with its own communal area for mingling, fine dining and entertaining. The water garden was to be its centrepiece. We had three days to get it done. After sourcing the components.

I beetled off to Roundhay's Parks Department site office where I found two nice old boys drinking tea and watching the comings and goings out of the window. I explained my predicament.

'Oh, aye?'

There was some discussion about rocks, waterproof linings and pumps. At their suggestion, a few plants in tubs were added to the list. And water-lilies. Yes, they could help. (As I'd been finding, the bundle of free tickets for Sunday's concert, in my pocket, helped to overcome any inertia.) And as for the fish, wasn't there – one of my new friends wondered – still that supplier over Harrogate way? Not to worry, lad. They'd get everything dropped off, probably tomorrow.

Back at the Portakabin, no demands from the Stones representatives – however preposterous – could now faze us.

'Find me someone who can write Japanese.'

'Get Bill Wyman a masseuse for Sunday.'

'We need a ton of dry ice. Now.'

The communal area of the dressing room – now alive with Stage Crew, multi-tasking as hydrologists and landscape gardeners, and working out the plumbing of an artificial stream – was to be dotted with tables, chairs and parasols. On these parasols, someone in the Stones camp had decided, it would be appropriate to have painted, 'Welcome, Rolling Stones.' In Japanese.

I phoned the School of Oriental Studies at the University. Would they have a student who, for a couple of Stones tickets, might be willing to come down and carry out this calligraphy? They called back. Yes, they'd found a girl who'd do it. I sent over a car to pick her up.

'About this masseuse,' I murmured to Crockers in the office. We were gazing out of the window at the efforts of a man called Graham 'Nipper' Dixon, who enjoyed the position of Rolling Stones Balloon Co-ordinator. For some days now, Nipper and his team had been inflating thousands upon thousands of helium balloons and storing them in a couple of giant nets at both ends of the stage.

'If I were to phone a masseuse in the Leeds Yellow Pages, Bill Wyman would be getting more than his back rubbed.'

Then I remembered my friend Maggie. A schoolteacher in Headingley, Maggie was New Age before the syndrome had been identified and classified. She subscribed to all manner of mumbo-jumbo: alternative remedies and other nonsense which, over the centuries, had been tried, dismissed and eliminated as treatments – because they didn't work – leaving us instead with science, medicine and drugs. Maggie burned a lot of joss sticks. She was bound to know someone who did massage. Probably with combined aromatherapy.

And she did. But they were away.

'You can do it, Maggie,' I said.

'No, I can't.'

'Of course you can. Just pummel his back a bit. Squeeze his muscles. Rub him up and down. That sort of thing. He'll never know the difference.'

I promised a bundle of tickets and said I'd send a car on Sunday morning.

'OH, FACKIN' 'ELL!' The man who was addressing us was Harvey Goldsmith himself. He'd arrived to supervise matters, just the day before the show. Now he was occupying the desk at the far end of our office. It was the morning of the gig. And he'd covered his face with his hands. Someone asked what was wrong.

'I've forgotten the fackin' guest passes.'

Looking down the office, I took stock. The world's two biggest promoters were in the same hut: Goldsmith, at the far end and at the desk on my left, in shorts and sandals, suntanned and on the phone, was a genuine living legend – Bill Graham, a man whose initiative and enterprise had shaped the course of rock & roll history. Together, they had a little problem. And I had a solution.

Eighteen months earlier we'd put on Dire Straits at the Refec. My printers had assumed I'd made a spelling mistake on the order for the backstage passes and took it upon themselves to correct this. When they delivered them, I'd explained they'd been too literal and I got them to print a new batch. Consequently, in my drawer in the Ents office, I still had a brick of about two hundred unused, and I thought useless, stick-on passes. It was lucky I hadn't thrown them in the bin.

'They'll do!' said Goldsmith, when I told him.

I sent Al across town to fetch them.

So it was, when the Rolling Stones After Show Guests – not a party, one would imagine, noted for self-deprecation – were floating around the backstage area and in and out of the Japanese hospitality garden, they did so enduring the indignity of having to have slapped on their chests stickers celebrating 'Dire Straights'.

* * *

By MID-MORNING, though, guest passes were the least of Harvey's worries. He'd been on the phone and turned to us as he put down the receiver.

'The Stones are stuck in traffic.'

Traffic? I'd assumed they'd be helicoptered in, possibly from a rented country house in the Yorkshire Dales. But no. Again, it was the consequence of unavoidable inexperience, of staging an event unprecedented on this scale. The Stones had stayed in a Leeds city centre hotel, were coming up from town in a bus, and were now democratically grid-locked along with – and because of – their own fans. Everyone, including the band, was on the way to Roundhay. All at once.

Roundhay Park, Leeds, 25 July 1982, on the morning of the huge Rolling Stones concert. Note perimeter fence, which ought to be invisible, and the immense stage. *Yorkshire Post*

George Thorogood & The Destroyers and The J Geils Band kept the early arrivals distracted, giving the Stones the chance to take in many of Leeds's attractive north-east neighbourhoods.

I could sense the moment they finally arrived on the premises. Magruder and his American colleagues became even more manic and self-important.

Now a man was bellowing over the immense PA system. An ocean of humanity was roaring back. The flaps of the Stones canvas compound were drawn open. A white limo reversed in and then emerged, seconds later. It crawled up the grassy slope, fully fifty yards to the steps of the stage. Out swung Jagger, followed by Charlie Watts, Ron Wood and Bill Wyman. Jagger, in a sky blue lycra jogging suit, began bouncing up and down on the bottom step. Someone was missing.

The announcer's voice was rising. '...ladies and gentlemen, the Rolling Stones!'

A hurricane of euphoria swept the bowl. It said thank you, simply for surviving. Mick Jagger had turned thirty-nine that morning. I heard the deep boom of explosions. Nipper Dixon liberated his balloons all at once, pink and blue, his week's work. They climbed and darkened against the clear afternoon sky, like a swarm of starlings, and floated off to litter much of West Yorkshire. Jagger jogged up the remaining steps, Watts, Wood and Wyman clomping steadily behind.

The flap of the marquee this time snapped back. A tall, angular figure – a black-and-white cartoon – stepped forth, alone. He had implausibly long, thin legs. A fag was jammed in the corner of his mouth. By the neck, he gripped a Fender Telecaster. He grinned at well-wishers. In what seemed just half a dozen long strides he was at the top of the grassy slope and on the stage steps.

Despite the best efforts of the Stones corporation over the previous fortnight, my faith was instantly, warmly restored. By the sight of a humble craftsman going to work.

The shapeless rumble of outdoor rock music solidified into something recognisable.

'Under mah thumb...'

I turned to Crockers and deflated in my swivel chair.

'Thank fuck for that.'

Maggie popped her head in at the door.

'How did it go?' I asked.

'Fine,' she said. 'He said it was great. One of the best he's had.'

I went for a wander and watched a couple of numbers through the side of the stage: Jagger pouting and peacocking on the platform of a cherry-picker; Jagger, high above the crowd, wiggling his bottom from the bucket of a crane. I felt the urge to buy his band members a pint.

'Hey,' said Crockers, 'did you manage to get that Japanese writing done on those umbrellas?'

'Oh, yes.' I said. And smiled my secret smile.

But it wasn't until a couple of years later, over a drink in London, that I told him the full story.

We were standing – the sweet child from Oriental Studies and I – by a chortling brook in the Stones hospitality area. She had a box of brushes and some ink.

'Thank you for helping us out,' I said and handed her a pair of tickets for Sunday's show. 'And there are two more for you here if you wouldn't mind amending slightly the message on the parasols.'

I explained the minor rewording. She dimpled shyly but said she'd do it.

When Jagger and the band were later luxuriating, post performance, in their indoor oriental garden, with their friends perhaps lingering on the delightful bridge to remark on the koi in the pool below, I trust they also admired the parasols. For each was decorated exquisitely with the hand-painted greeting, in Japanese: 'Fuck you, Rolling Stones.'

19

BOOZE, FAGS & LIGHTBULBS:
LIFE WITH OUR ELIZABETH

'GET A PEN, OUR ANDREW,' said Our Elizabeth. 'And a pad of paper.'

It was Christmas 1982 and we were sharing a glamorous flat on the top floor of a mock Tudor mansion in Headingley. Elizabeth had a flair for landing accommodation that did not much hint at our penury, and finding new flats for us had become her hobby. On at least one occasion, I had shambled back home from the Ents office at the end of the working day to discover we had moved. This was not a major operation. Apart from my records and books, I didn't own much. Elizabeth, on the other hand, had an ever-growing collection of black bin-liners stuffed with clothes that she didn't wear. As a dwelling became too small to accommodate these, they were simply chucked in the back of a friend's van and carted to larger premises where, as before, they remained unopened.

Number 33 Shire Oak Road was the most elegant apartment yet – and she had bought it.

That terrible reality, and our lifestyle, incongruously rock & roll for the location, attracted the resentment of the more respectable residents. In the flat immediately below was a middle-aged chap with a piping Scottish Borders voice and an affectation of excessive enunciation. He would make only one form of contact: appearing at our flat door to complain about the level of the music. I looked forward to this routine. He would stand there, cock back his head, regard me from beneath his glasses and along his thin nose, cough lightly, and remark on the volume of 'the high-fidelity equipment'. This terminology he seemed to find not archaic but distasteful and alien, and after he had unloaded himself of it, as though referring to a variety of pornography, he would smack his lips.

'Okay, sorry. We'll turn it down.'

He probably imagined the billowing dope fumes were those of incense. Inevitably, he became known as Hi-Fi.

Hi-Fi's appearances at the door were most predictable just after sex. (Usually mine. Or Elizabeth's. Never his, I assumed.) The lure for this was our routine of running out of our bedrooms into the hallway of the flat, where we kept a hefty 1960s Rock-Ola jukebox, and playing a favourite at full volume, to announce that we had 'just done it'. Elizabeth always chose Cilla Black's nasal *You're My World*, while I preferred the swagger and wallop of Eddie Cochran's *Something Else* – actually, a hell of a compliment to the startled girl left under the duvet.

One day, Al and I returned to Shire Oak Road to be introduced by Our Elizabeth to her new beau.

'This,' she said, 'is Constable Truscott.'

About three weeks later, Al and I tiptoed back into the flat to check if the coast was clear. I had stayed with Al, his wife Josie and the kids until Elizabeth's love-life had taken a more promising turn. And before long it did, Constable Truscott having been told to 'mind how you go' after he'd asked Elizabeth if he could 'do it' while wearing his helmet.

Life soon returned to normal and, to Hi-Fi's dismay, our flat re-opened as an all-hours drop-in centre for those with a rock & roll lifestyle dependency.

The parties often seemed to flow seamlessly from one into another. And even when a party had not been formally declared, there were always pals in the flat joining me and Elizabeth for a bottle of her favoured drink of those years, Lambrusco. This cheap, gassy, sweet Italian wine also happened to be very weak – thank goodness – for we drank it in pint pots.

We lived on Elizabeth's meagre income from British Telecom. When she had money, we ate well and fed anyone who happened to drop by. But there were other occasions when we could barely afford to nourish ourselves. Most memorable was the morning she made a sandwich, cut it in half, took her portion to work and left me the other for my lunch. But only once were we so pushed that I was forced to choose a few albums from my collection and take them down to the second-hand record stall at the Merrion Centre indoor market to swap them for small change. This was the same record stall at which Woodhead and I were usually eager buyers. Walking home I vowed, 'Never again.'

33 Shire Oak Road, Headingley. Our Elizabeth and I shared a flat (and rock & roll drop-in centre) here, much to the irritation of our more staid and respectable neighbours. Worst for them was, she'd bought it. *Elizabeth Kershaw*

As instructed, I fetched the pen and a pad of paper, long accustomed as I was to being treated by Elizabeth as the butler and footman. (To formalise this role, she named me Treadwell.) She was, she declared, about to dictate our Christmas shopping list.

We sat opposite each other, on facing sofas. Elizabeth began. After twenty minutes, I looked down and examined my notes. It was a list which read, in full, *Booze, Fags & Lightbulbs*. Being a stickler for these things, I feel sure I must have made a good case for bogrolls too. But that was it. She handed me some money and her car keys and off I went. Festively.

AFTER SHE LEFT Leeds University, just before my arrival there in 1978, Elizabeth had taken up a job with some boring corporate in Liverpool on one of their graduate recruitment schemes. Naturally, she found this fast-track to respectability dull. Aside from crashing her car into a petrol pump on the day she passed her driving test there, her stay in Liverpool was unremarkable and brief. Within a couple of years she had found a job with British Telecom in Leeds and – against all sensible advice – had moved back into the moist familiarity and cheery uproar of 16 Norwood Terrace with me and all my dreadful pals. In a trice, we'd got her smoking and hooked for life on Bruce Springsteen, a habit which would later take her on Lourdes-like pilgrimages to New Jersey.

Bruce moved among us quite a bit around this time. We Springsteen obsessives were – until he hit mega-stardom with the misunderstood *Born In The USA* and the execrable *Dancing In The Dark* – a relatively small gang. With the release of *The River* in 1980, I actually saw him and the E Street Band in the conventional 3000-seater surroundings of Manchester Apollo. I went over from Leeds with Helen From The Record Shop. We were sitting very close up. Along with The Clash in the Refec at the time of *London Calling* and Bob Marley at Stafford and, later, any number of Bhundu Boys gigs, Bruce at the Apollo was one of the greatest concerts I have ever seen. His performance was one of contagious concentrated exuberance. It was also – for Bruce was just thirty – tirelessly physical.

In this respect, allied to his appeal as an incurable romantic, Bruce was, for Helen, the pinnacle of manhood. But in the meantime, I would have to do. And so it was, in Helen's Renault 5, that we chugged back, elated, over to Leeds on a highway jammed with broken heroes (we were on the M62, just passing Halifax), inevitably to shag each other with the ferocity of stray dogs, on my bedroom floor, tearing off each other's clothes even before we got inside Norwood Terrace.

In Roundhay Park, five years later, I would get an even closer look at Springsteen. By now presenting *Whistle Test* and long gone from Leeds, I nevertheless agreed to Andrew Zweck's request that I rejoin him as Backstage Labour Co-ordinator for Bruce and the E Street Band, just as I had done for the Rolling Stones.

Just before the Boss came back on at Roundhay for the encores, which can, of course, be a performance as long as the main set, Harvey Goldsmith turned to me in our makeshift back-stage office. 'Andy,' he said. 'I want to head off home now, before the traffic. Would you mind going up there and doing my usual announcement about please take your litter home with you, thanks for coming and drive home safely?' (The latter being advice notably absent from the Springsteen songbook.)

Within moments I was *in* the E Street band, leaning on a stack of side-fill speakers, just a few feet from Bruce and Clarence Clemons. It was a revelation. That close, it was obvious what elevated Bruce to greatness, and why he had, bouncing and bobbing, 120,000 people in a municipal park – which, for that moment, had the community and the intimacy of the steamy confines of the Stone Pony, Asbury Park. It was his enthusiasm. Like his soul brother Willie Nelson, he was able to play three-week sets because he clearly loved what he was doing.

His exhilaration was absolutely genuine. At one point, as the last chord of one song was still raising the roar of the crowd, he swung round in my direction and, without a pause, hammered out a count of four with the heel of his engineer's boot, beaming and yelling to Clarence and Max Weinberg, 'Twist and Shout!' *Bah-ba-ba-bam, ba-ba-bah-bam...* And the roar swelled stronger to recognise he was yanking us through the history of rock & roll. For the sheer fun of it.

THERE IS A HANDFUL of performers whose songs and careers are so intimately entangled in my own development that I regard them almost as family. Springsteen is one. But chief among them is Loudon Wainwright. In the summer of 1980, when I wasn't in the Ents office, trying to book up the autumn term, I spent dreamy afternoons by my open window in Norwood Terrace and, to the background murmur of the crowd at the nearby Test cricket ground, smoked joints and listened in rotation to five albums: Bob Marley's new one, *Uprising*, Mississippi John Hurt's sublime and soporific *1928 Sessions* (with a sleeve that begged to be framed), *London Calling*, Springsteen's *Darkness On The Edge Of Town* and Loudon Wainwright's *A Live One*.

Cass had introduced me to Loudon's songs some years before, at his parents' caravan, but only now did my relationship with Loudon flourish into something extraordinary and life-long. I had become a mirror of the character in *School Days*: 'Blaspheming, booted blue-jean baby boy – oh, how I made them turn their heads. The townie, brownie girls they jumped for joy, and begged me bless them in their beds.' In the fullness of time, I noticed that Loudon, the old sage, always had a song spookily appropriate to every twist and turn in my life, from *Motel Blues* to *Being A Dad*. (In 2007, *One Man Guy* was among my eight Desert Island Discs.) Later, the thrill of having Loudon come on to my radio programmes to play regular live sessions never diminished. I never did quite get used to the idea that I really could, on a whim, get Loudon to appear, and that he would want to do it.

The Bob Marley expedition to Stafford and the trans-Pennine trek to see Springsteen were not the only adventures from Leeds to remarkable gigs further afield. In the summer of 1979, I hopped on a train to London for the Capital Jazz Festival on the grassy slopes in front of the Alexandra Palace. Doing my best to block out the unlistenable, fire-in-a-pet-shop modern jazz, and with the whole of London as a backdrop to the stage, I saw, in the space of one glorious, sunny afternoon, Muddy Waters, BB King and Chuck Berry.

For the performance of the latter, an appalling human being but, truly, the greatest American poet of the twentieth century, I simply walked down to the front. Perhaps the pompous jazz bores were offended by the presence at a high-brow gathering of the man who gave us such populist triflings as *Promised Land*, because I found there was plenty of room to leap around right in front of the stage. At one point, I turned and glanced at

Blaspheming booted blue-jean baby boy – and that's just the photographer. Loudon Wainwright on stage at Cropredy, 1998. *AK*

the woman who had been twisting vigorously, and alone, right next to me for half an hour. It was Princess Margaret.

In my first year at Leeds, George Thorogood & the Destroyers' first two albums, were constantly disappearing from my room. Soon, George had a fan base of six of us in the Headingley area. We noticed he was to play a gig at Sheffield Polytechnic. Only one of our number had a car. It was a cramped Opel Kadett. No matter: a couple of pals, Daves Hall and Brown, volunteered to travel the thirty miles down the M1 in the boot. And back.

George and the band were tremendous that night and played a blinder, to an audience of which our merry party made up precisely half. We formed a thin, grinning line, right along the crash-barrier and George even addressed us individually.

Back in Leeds, both Daves remarked on the bruises and stiffness they'd acquired on the journey. We sat down, straight away, around the kitchen table and, in the name of one of the stowaways, wrote a letter to Opel, complaining about the discomfort: 'Dear Sir, Last Friday evening I had occasion to travel from Leeds to Sheffield in the boot of one of your Opel Kadett models. It is no exaggeration to say it was the most uncomfortable boot of any car in which I have ridden...' I was proud particularly of the final line: 'A colleague, who was travelling in the boot with me, will confirm this.' Opel, alas, did not extend to us the courtesy of a reply.

SOME WEEKS OF those Ents Sec summers and beyond were spent with Al at his mother's family holiday home in Trearddur Bay, Anglesey. Usually, we would drive down when we knew we'd have the place to ourselves, sometimes just for one night. This was an excuse for a mini road trip in the latest of Al's posh cars, a perk of his minimal input to his mother's firm – hardly Kerouacian, and through Colwyn Bay. But with the music wound up, and chain-smoking joints, my latest squeeze in the back and the prospect of dawn on the cliff tops, it was, as my grandma always described utterly aimless car journeys in the novelty days of Rochdale post-war motoring, 'a run out.'

The squeeze on one of these breaks in Trearddur was the incredible Melanie Tanner, the most beautiful creature at the

Hulme Grammar School for Girls, Oldham, and a stunningly gorgeous girl by any measure. We had, implausibly and to my complete surprise, got it together in the summer of 1981, at the party of an old school friend in Rochdale. Neither of us having money for a taxi, Melanie had walked with me afterwards the three miles back to my mother's house where, without a word being said, she slipped alongside me, into my old bed, like a soft mist. Happily, my mum was away. By the time we got round to getting up, it was to learn Ronald Reagan had been shot. Quite a day.

I treated Melanie, the sweetest and most loving of girlfriends, disgracefully, of course. She would traipse over to Leeds, devotedly, on the train to see me every weekend, and during these visits I would pay her scant attention. I deserved to lose her. And I did. The pattern was set for relationships with one or two other wonderful women who I would, through downright self-ishness, neglect and drive away.

20

FIRST, WE TAKE NORTHAMPTON

AFTER CLEARING ROUNDHAY PARK of any evidence of the Rolling Stones, Stage Crew and I – already exhausted – had gone straight to the University, and our home turf of the Refec, to run a concert by The Clash. It was to be my swansong as Ents Sec and there wasn't a finer flourish with which I could finish.

The gig had been postponed from the spring and pushed back into the summer holidays because Joe Strummer, it later transpired, had undergone a temporary nervous breakdown and vanished to lie low in Paris. With Joe's return and recovery our gig was rescheduled for July and I was able to announce that tickets bought for the June gig would be honoured.

As we were directing the trucks up to the front steps of the hall, a pal on Crew held out his hand and dropped a couple of little white pills into mine. 'You look all in, Andy. I reckon you could do with these to get through today.'

Later that evening, half a dozen Andy Kershaws were spotted simultaneously in different parts of the building, tirelessly performing all manner of duties as well as catching much of The Clash's set.

In the early hours of the following morning, I flopped down

and fell asleep in front of the gas fire back at the flat I shared with Our Elizabeth and, save for necessary trips to the toilet, didn't move for three days. Speed, I decided, was amazing. But I could sense, if I took it regularly, speed would like me too much. I never did it again.

When I climbed up off the carpet, I was no longer Ents Sec. I had no degree, no job and no offers from London to become the next Harvey Goldsmith. For more than two years, I'd felt what it was like to be famous, albeit within the limited, artificial city of the campus. I sat at the lounge table and watched busy people beetle across Woodhouse Moor, to and from the University. Suddenly, I had nothing to do. Even before my ears had stopped ringing from The Clash, I was a nobody once more. Life, I told myself – for I had to face up to this – will never be as exciting or as much fun again.

There were, as a rule, for kids of my generation, three key events in the process of transition from adolescence to adulthood: passing one's driving test; losing one's virginity and getting one's own place to live. That was as true for me as the next lad but I was lucky enough to have had another component to that metamorphosis. Everything I have done or achieved since has flowed from that inexplicable moment, and that uncharacteristic impulse, when I walked up to Steve Henderson's desk in Leeds University Union in October 1978. And the thought of that frightens me to this day.

OUR ELIZABETH SORTED me out. She'd been listening to Radio Aire, a new local commercial station in Leeds. Its studios were just at the bottom of our road and I'd already been in them a couple of times. For Radio Aire's launch, DJs from other cities and stations had, necessarily, to be imported to fill the air time. One of these was a bloke with whom I bonded instinctively and immediately. Martin Kelner had been brought in from Radio Hallam in Sheffield to do what the industry insists on calling a drive-time show in the late afternoon and early evening. Martin was very bright, funny and healthily contemptuous of local radio broadcasting conventions, blockhead DJs and the self-important, quick-buck spivs who, not out of any love for the medium, tend to own and run commercial radio stations. (He still has all of these qualities, although latterly he has become a very funny columnist for the *Guardian*.)

As a newcomer to Leeds, Martin did not at first know much about local bands, gigs and venues. So he phoned me up, in my latter days as Ents Sec, and invited me on to his show, once a week, to give a run-down of the notable forthcoming concerts. And so it was, muttering into a crumpled bit of paper, that I made my broadcasting debut.

As the weeks went by, and my confidence grew, I began to spark and spar with Martin on air, honing with him a routine which we radio insiders recognise as 'matey DJ chat'. Although, being Martin, we were straight away subverting the form.

Then Our Elizabeth heard the on-air ad: Radio Aire was looking for a promotions manager. 'You could do that,' she said and pushed me into phoning up.

I got an interview, the only formal job interview I have had in my life. Radio Aire management did not agree with Elizabeth and I didn't get the gig.

But then the person who did, Martin reported to us one evening round at the flat, possibly over two or three pints of Lambrusco, had walked off the job after only a couple of weeks. I wrote an insolent letter to the managing director – a nice man called Derek Gorman, who wasn't to last much longer – pointing out the inadequacy of his previous appointment and that he should have given me the job in the first place. He phoned to summon me for a chat, at which he told me he admired my cheek and asked me to start as soon as I could.

I WAS GIVEN a desk in an open plan office, occupied by Martin and all the other more conventional DJs, and a wage of £40 a week. There was no budget for promotion. Nothing at all. So there was nothing effective that I could do except to write the Radio Aire page in a local free newspaper. Martin and I used this to lampoon ruthlessly the station, its management, its programmes and its DJs, yet in a manner which none of our targets seemed to notice.

Mark Mardell, now North American editor of the BBC, then just a fat youngster in the newsroom, I described as 'swashbuckling'.

He was, and still is, anything but. And, on his encounters with celebrities, I reported thus: '"I was once beaten up by Jean-Jacques Burnel of the Stranglers and earlier this year stood very close to Princess Diana," quipped the vivacious blonde bombshell.' Helen Boaden, then another newsroom junior but later Controller of BBC Radio 4, also got the Kershaw PR treatment: 'A converted Northerner, addicted to beer, she has become a vital part of Radio Aire's newsroom. (It's alleged – Ed).'

James Whale, who then passed for a Radio Aire late-night shock-jock, I revealed – in the station's official James Whale hand-out – was 'pompous, arrogant, self-opinionated, bombastic, egotistical, dogmatic, stubborn and bald'. No change there, then. And Martin Kelner did not escape, either. Of him, I wrote, 'Martin is interested in camping and one day hopes to visit Northampton.'

The latter was, absurdly, true.

A seven-inch promotional single had been sent out to radio stations by the Northampton Development Corporation. *Sixty Miles By Road And Rail* by Linda Jardim, a session singer, was a couple of minutes of optimistic froth to promote Northampton as a dormitory town for London. ('It's a feeling I can't explain,' trilled Linda. 'I just can't wait to be in Northampton.')

Martin, being Martin, decided that instead of chucking the single in the bin, he would give it heavy airplay. His audience, already purged of those who expected rotation Lionel Ritchie by Martin's unconventional sense of humour and his choice of music (Tommy Makem & The Clancy Brothers' banjo-driven *Holy Moly! My Father Loves Nikita Kruschev* was an evergreen Kelner commuter favourite) couldn't get enough of Ms Jardim's musical endorsement of Northampton.

By telephone, Martin interviewed the chairman of the town's Development Corporation, live on his programme. It was perfectly clear to me: a momentum for everything Northampton was building. And I decided we'd better organise a listeners' coach-trip and day-out there.

Radio Aire's management couldn't understand what the hell was going on but, as all the tickets were instantly snapped up, necessitating a second coach be booked, the suits stood back and let me and Martin get on with it – whatever it was.

On the morning of our great expedition, Yorkshire Television's regional news programme came to cover our departure. The reporter struggled gamely to explain the caper to himself as much as to the viewers. To each passenger that climbed aboard Martin and I handed a kazoo and a packet of Spangles. And off we went. More than a hundred of us.

On arrival (in the UK's third-largest town without official city status, I'll have you know), we were taken on our coaches for a guided tour, before being given at a civic reception, a warm, welcoming speech by our new friend, the chairman of the NDC, followed by lunch at some local golf club.

ANOTHER PROMOTIONAL TRIUMPH – which did little to promote Radio Aire but did wonders, years later, for the circulation of the *Daily Telegraph* among male readers of a certain age – was to help, unintentionally, the propulsion of Carol Vorderman into media orbit.

Geoff Sargieson, Radio Aire's amiable Programme Controller, asked me one morning to organise a competition among the listeners called *A Song For Leeds*. My heart sank. I anticipated a deluge of lamentable bedroom-recorded dirges and ditties. We got just two. The clear winner, only marginally less excruciating than the runner-up, was written and performed by the shrill mother and daughter duo of Jean and Carol Vorderman, with Jean at the front room piano.

The Vordermans lived, it turned out, in the next street to me and Elizabeth. Soon enough, Carol was a regular round at our flat. And for a period of about three weeks in the summer of 1983, we were romantically attached – although I wasn't very good at the romance bit. Soon, though, Carol returned to the allures of some rugby-playing specimen. (And Rugby Union, at that.) We remained pals, despite this clear lack of judgement, and during that summer Carol was, briefly, one third of our Elizabeth's vocal group, Dawn Chorus & The Bluetits, the other third being Lindsay Burrows, a model, the new Miss Radio Aire and my latest recipient of Eddie Cochran on the jukebox.

That Carol Vorderman quit the Bluetits in a huff, just before they recorded their one and only John Peel session (with me as guest whistler on a number called *Lucky Lips*), was a setback from which I feel her media career has never fully recovered.

I had, in the meantime, introduced her to the host of Radio Aire's mid-morning programme, Peter Levy. In a trice, Carol was a regular guest on Peter's show, baffling West Yorkshire with numerical puzzles of her own concoction. And before too long, she was joining us less frequently at the scruffy pub behind Radio Aire and spending time at the bar of Yorkshire Television, next door to our studios. Within a few months, I watched her, with avuncular pride, presenting something on television called *Countdown* and she has since, I gather, gone on to appear in pantomime and to launch her own range of power tools and a DIY colonic irrigation video.

MY OWN MEDIA CAREER, meanwhile, was gathering pace. Geoff, the Programme Controller, had noticed I was a music obsessive with unconventional tastes. To secure a licence, it was the custom of new commercial radio stations to make promises to the franchising authorities about the range of their music output. This was lip-service and a promise which they had no intention of keeping once the money got tight, their listeners were falling away and it was safer, commercially, to retreat to the lowest common denominator. (Which is how a nation ends up anaesthetised on rotation airplay of *In The Air Tonight*.)

Before Radio Aire reverted to this position, Geoff stuck me on the air once a week, presenting a late night 'alternative' show, with some emphasis on local bands. Then he gave me a weekly one hour blues programme. I was useless but enthusiastic. And cheap. I got nothing over and above my forty quid.

The idea of being on the radio as a presenter had never crossed my mind before. But now I'd been shoved into it, I loved it. Geoff had let a genie out of a bottle. And one that only he and Martin Kelner had spotted.

Meanwhile, a nice lad called John who worked on the station's radio commercials decided my future lay elsewhere.

'You ought to go into advertising,' he said one day. 'You've got the imagination for it.'

Certainly, I would sit in front of the television and be astonished by the utter gormlessness or pretentiousness of the ads and I had no doubts I could come up with better. Television commercials are, essentially, a bore and an interruption. So they might as well be amusing or entertaining, I figured.

'I've got lots of pals in ad agencies in Leeds,' said John. 'Why don't I fix up a meeting with some of them? Something informal. Just to let them meet you. A bit of a chat. You never know...' I agreed to the exploratory meeting.

In an office in the middle of town, about a week later, I was, with nothing to lose, all crap and confidence.

In which ways, the chap from the ad agency was asking, did I think television and radio commercials could be improved?

'The viewers and listeners,' I told him, making a bold opening pitch, 'would surely welcome a little more honesty.'

'Give me an example,' he said.

'Well, take Andrex,' I said, warming to my theme. 'Instead of all this nonsense of a labrador puppy running up and down stairs with bogroll in its mouth, the viewers would rejoice if the ads were to just tell it like it is.'

'How do you mean?'

'Their slogan ought to be, *Andrex – really gets the shit off your bottom.*'

They didn't ask to see me again.

I WAS SOON to get the career boost I genuinely needed by getting the sack. In another round of cost slashing, Radio Aire, in November 1983, showed me the door. Martin was fired that same afternoon, along with our good friend, Dave Silver, a local club DJ who seemed to live, endearingly, under the permanent delusion that he was a member of Earth Wind & Fire. Dave and I had become great pals, a double act of two over-sexed single lads being rightly rebuffed by every beautiful waitress in every diner in Leeds. Poor Dave was also living proof that the talents of the club DJ certainly do not transfer automatically to the radio, a lesson unlearned to this day by Radio 1.

As station dogsbody – that was the reality of my job – I had been underpaid and overworked and now told I wasn't worth forty quid a week. But, over fourteen months, I'd got from Radio Aire more than just my first broadcasting experience and the basics of radio from Martin. In another of those moments of pure chance, I'd come away, without realising it at the time, with my next life-changing break.

At lunchtimes, when most of the Radio Aire staff melted away to the pub (and I was usually too poor to join them), I had the run of the record library. In a corner of this room, also the office of the woman who was known, laughably, as the station's Head of Music and Record Librarian, stood a huge cardboard box which had once protected a washing machine. Into this, the Head of Music chucked, in accordance with what I understood to be the music policy, every new release she was sent that wasn't recorded by Elton John.

It was from this box that I used to put together my spotty

Martin Kelner and I celebrate our sacking from Radio Aire, Leeds, November 1983, with the report in the *Yorkshire Evening Post*. *Elizabeth Kershaw*

little radio programme, taking home and listening through anything that looked interesting.

One afternoon, in the early summer of 1983, I had pulled out
a 12-inch EP with an orange and white sleeve, a parody of a
Penguin paperback cover. This was illustrated with a photo of
an inspection lamp. I was curious. The record also had a title
which, alone, merited further investigation. And it had been
recorded by a then unknown singer and guitarist: *Life's A Riot
With Spy Vs Spy* by Billy Bragg.

21

TEN DAYS IN LONDON

'DO YOU PLAY CARDS, BOYS?'

We were being addressed, Billy Bragg and I, by a gable-end of a man – a sweetheart as it turned out – but one with the presence and demeanour of a gangland enforcer. This was Kenny Wheeler, veteran minder and tour manager of Paul Weller. That we were being interrogated by him in a car park behind some warehouses in Camden Town did not diminish our unease, nor the feeling that we had stepped into an episode of *Minder*.

It was the early spring of 1984. Life for Billy, and for me, was in acceleration at a rate too dizzying even from which to stand back, take stock and be amazed. I had been Billy's driver, tour manager and roadie for only two months. Almost every day, something fantastic and unpredictable was occurring.

Now, Billy's manager, Peter Jenner, had got the call from John Weller, father and manager of Paul. Would Billy like to open for The Style Council on their UK spring tour? We had deliberated over this in the office for, ooh... a good four seconds.

'They're at a rehearsal studios today in Camden,' said Pete. 'Why don't you and Billy drive over there, Kersh, just to introduce yourselves?'

In a huddle across the car park was the instantly recognisable sharp-suited figure of the former Jam front man, with his silver-haired, barrow-boy dad – both seemingly under the shelter of Kenny's armpits.

We'd begun with some pleasantries before the talk turned to the routine of being on tour and pastimes on the tour bus.

'Cards?' I gulped. 'Er, yes, we can play cards, I think, can't we Billy? But,' I added, affecting a worldly-wise nonchalance, 'only for matchsticks.'

Kenny eyed me from on high, before bending slowly forward to put his nose to mine. 'Well, young man, then you'd better bring Epping fucking Forest with you, hadn't you?'

BACK IN LEEDS, the previous summer, my first hearing of *Life's A Riot* had so impressed me, right from the rumbling guitar introduction to *A New England*, that I wrote that same night the only fan letter I have ever written. I posted it to Billy care of Charisma Records, his label. I may have mentioned something about 'a one-man Clash' but, certainly, I signed off with the words, 'more power to your plectrum!'

Within a few days the phone rang.

''Ello. Is that Andy? This is Billy Bragg.'

We hit it off straight away and arranged to meet in London during a trip to the capital I had planned already with Our Elizabeth.

The historic encounter took place in a cafe called Sandwich Scene on Wardour Street. That night, with my old university pal, Dave Woodhead, we trooped along to a pub in King's Cross in which Billy played to about ten of us. It was the first time I saw him live and I was elated: his performance matched the thrill of the record, and his on-stage patter was as sharp as his songwriting.

Although I hadn't remotely been looking for anyone, I came away from the gig with an overpowering sense of *I've found him!* Billy embodied my deep attachment to protest and to the duty of us all to question authority and power. But he wasn't American. He wasn't protesting still about 1960s issues. Although he upheld those same values and principles, he was of *now*. Billy was a protest singer for the post-punk era. And he was from, of all places, Essex.

For the remainder of the year, Billy, criss-crossing the UK by train and carrying his electric guitar, a hold-all of drab clothes (none of which were the correct size), and a small amplifier, became a regular guest at our Shire Oak Road flat. Through my live music contacts in Leeds, I fixed him up with a couple of gigs in the city and at these I could see that I was far from unique and alone in my reaction. Billy was received by an almost instant sense of relief: someone, in this cultural vacuum, in a new age of glam and a Thatcherite climate of preening self-satisfaction, was saying something awkward and something that mattered. And he seemed not to have noticed that his trousers didn't fit. We liked that. Billy was *ours*.

More particularly, he was mine. And would be pretty much full time from the following January, 1984.

In November 1983, when I was made redundant by Radio Aire, I had decided it was time to pitch assertively for that job in the music business. I made dozens of photocopies of my CV and created at the bottom of the page a slip for recipients to cut away and send back, marked by a dotted line and a scissors symbol. On that slip, I put a passport-size photo of my face, glowering in the centre of a hand-drawn star, from the like of which pools winners used to beam in adverts on the sides of buses, with their eyes blanked out ('Mrs B, Kettering, £100,000'). Below that, alongside a box that may be ticked, and above a few lines for the respondent's name and address it read, 'Yes, I would like to know more about this exciting youth...' To booking agents, concert promoters, artists' management companies and record labels, I sent out nearly two hundred of these.

I got one reply. It was from Peter Jenner.

I HAD KNOWN Pete from Leeds Ents days. He'd been manager of The Clash at the time of *London Calling* and had accompanied the band, uncommonly for a manager, when they came to the University on that tour. He'd also visited the Refec as manager of Ian Dury & The Blockheads when I'd put them on just before Christmas 1980. On both occasions I'd found him to be that rare creature, a gentleman within the music business and one with a most atypical manner for the industry – that of a bookish and pleasingly dotty vicar's son. Which is precisely what he was. And still is.

As an amateur rock & roll and social historian, I already knew of and admired Pete for his activities in the 1960s: groovy young leftie LSE academic begins to manage unknown psychedelic band who call themselves The Pink Floyd; becomes *éminence grise* and intellectual voice of London counter-culture, scene-maker of psychedelic happenings and stages, among other historic events, the Rolling Stones 1969 free concert in Hyde Park.

Blackhill, Pete's management company, had gone bust following his period of guiding the careers of Ian Dury and The Clash, in both cases thankless activities described to me by one observer as 'managing the unmanageable'. To support his family, he had taken an A&R job with Charisma and it was to Pete that Billy Bragg was steered when he walked through Charisma's door with a demo tape. Pete stuck Billy in a little studio to

The manager counts the money, the artist has beautiful thoughts and the driver and roadie multi-tasks as photographer. Billy Bragg and Peter Jenner, Brussels, July 1984. *AK*

bang down a few more tracks. Those rough and ready recordings became *Life's A Riot*...

Seeing Billy's potential, Jenner – ever the maverick – jumped from Charisma to manage his new discovery. A Greater Force was at work. Simultaneously, I fell upon that first EP, sent the fan letter and received Billy's phone call. I remember feeling relieved that Billy had stumbled accidentally upon Pete. He was in good hands. Meanwhile, Pete was telling Billy of his positive dealings with me at Leeds University.

Soon after my November 1983 redundancy from Radio Aire, Billy called again. 'Kersh, can you drive?'

Then Pete phoned. He was, he explained, getting too busy on Bragg business in his office at home to drive Billy (a defiant non-motorist) around an increasingly busy schedule of gigs. Did I want to come down and help out?

And so, one drab, damp morning, in January 1984, Our Elizabeth put me on a National coach at Wellington Street bus station in Leeds. I really didn't want to have to go to London. The capital, viewed from two hundred miles north, was not welcoming. To go there meant uncertainty and loneliness and to leave behind everyone and everything that was comfortable and familiar. But it also spelled opportunity and, at last, my professional entry to the music business.

And it wasn't some piss-pot insecure job with a grasping record company of questionable taste. I was going to become Pete Jenner's right-hand man, and Billy Bragg's driver, tour manager and roadie – all rolled into one. In Pete's battered Volvo estate car, Billy and I would be *The Blues Brothers*. I was, again, as a committed atheist, 'on a mission from God'.

'I'm going for ten days,' I told Elizabeth as I stepped up onto the bus to London. 'And if I don't like it by then, I'm coming home.'

I stayed for more than twenty-two years.

22

LIFE'S A RIOT –
IN A VOLVO ESTATE

TO MY COST, I have never been money-driven. And money was not a component of my contract of employment with Pete Jenner – and, therefore, Billy Bragg. Pete and his delightful Japanese-Canadian wife, Sumi, didn't yet have any. Billy, when I joined the team, was picking up – for club gigs – only a couple of hundred pounds a night.

My package, as these things are nowadays termed, with Sincere Management (slogan: *It's in the post*) was to be fed, given a roof over my head, twenty cigarettes a day and the opportunity to watch *Newsnight*. I put this in writing before Pete and he added his signature. Sincere's slogan I soon changed to *Another day, another three quid*.

I loved life at the Jenners' Maida Vale home on Bravington Road. They took me in as part of the family. Our office was in a ground floor front room. I slept in a box-room surrounded by Pete and Sumi's impressive collection of books. We went out only to gigs and, occasionally, to see art films. Pete and Sumi didn't drink. And, at that point, neither did I. As part of the family Jenner – they had two children, Kaya, a boy of about ten and his younger sister, Mushi – I felt valued, loved, secure and deliriously happy. At night I would fall asleep in my little room, having read another 1960s classic. (Richard Fariña's *Been Down So Long It Looks Like Up To Me* made a major impression. A biography of Willie Nelson, one of my music heroes, taught me that no one ever achieves anything remarkable nor makes any valuable or lasting contribution by adherence to conventions. The lesson was, Break the Rules). And I would wake up energised by the possibilities of the day. If I didn't have to collect Billy and drive him, say, to Frankfurt, then it was a ten yard walk along the hallway to work and another day in the office, scheming with my hero and mentor, Pete, on how best to subvert the corrupt, lazy, stupid, smug and shallow music industry.

Our secret weapon was living at the time in a newly built one-room flat, a few miles west, in Acton. A routine day was a morning spent in the office before picking up Billy to drive him to increasingly rammed gigs for which he paid me a tenner per show.

For me, Pete and Sumi, working days started early on a breakfast of enthusiasm, gallons of real coffee, the *Today* programme, the obligatory reading of the *Guardian* and the first of many joints. Just as we'd done in the Ents office in Leeds, at Sincere we chain-smoked mild marijuana all day, a pleasant, soothing variety I had long before designated as 'working dope'.

My particular talent, as the instinctive journalist, was handling Billy's press relations and much of this stuff I would hand deliver to the writers themselves on the *New Musical Express, Sounds* and *Melody Maker*, running at full speed from one office to the other across Soho. Quickly, I realised how much they valued the personal contact with Billy's team. It almost guaranteed regular, positive coverage. I also noticed how some of these legends of rock journalism found my Bragg bulletins entertaining. More than one remarked that I was a good writer. Possibilities suddenly seemed to be popping up like meerkats.

AFTER A MONTH or two, I noticed I hadn't gone back to Leeds following that ten day trial. I was loving my new life. And, though I was still slightly intimidated by it, I was beginning to love London too.

To a parochial northern lad, it was thrillingly cosmopolitan. Leeds had been enriched by immigration too, of course, but with nothing like this intensity, colour, noise and bustle. At the end of Pete and Sumi's street was the Harrow Road, a multi-cultural clamour – predominantly and incongruously Caribbean and Irish – of formidable women, street-savvy kids, ranting drunks, dangerous drivers and a riot of shops selling fish and vegetables I'd never encountered before. Most of the Edwardian houses along Bravington Road had been divided into flats. Like Pete and Sumi's they had steep flights of steps leading up to their front doors. On fine evenings in the spring and summer, Bravington Road residents would sit out on these steps and socialise with each other. It felt like I'd moved into Sesame Street.

Within a few minutes' walk was Ladbroke Grove and Portobello. My favourite rock & roll band may have broken apart the year before but I felt the spirit of The Clash still moving among us in this part of London, their old patch. Just to get on the tube to go into town was as to be living in a Clash song.

Only the windows of local estate agents unsettled me. On the odd occasion I'd glance in one, I'd look at the price of houses and flats and come away depressed: I'll never be able to afford my own place here, I decided. That, and the sheer size of London was overwhelming. My old Leeds friend, Dave Woodhead, was then living in south London, and nowhere near a tube station. I seldom saw him. To drop in on Dave would have been easier and much quicker had he lived in, say, Nottingham.

Pete and Sumi's friends, regular callers to Bravington Road, seemed impossibly exotic. Among them was Robin Denselow. I was more excited by Robin dropping by than I was to meet any rock star. For as long as I'd been reading the *Guardian*, for whom Robin was already a veteran music critic, and watching serious BBC news programmes, on which he was a regular foreign reporter, I'd admired his unfailing good taste, sound journalistic judgement and breezy Famous Five courage. Although a generation apart, we shared the same unlikely combination of obsessions: music, particularly of the roots variety, and the bonkers world out there as reflected in foreign news. Robin also turned out to be a lovely man, self-effacing and permanently and boyishly wide-eyed with enthusiasm. My spirits would soar, if I spotted Robin at a gig – and I exaggerate only a little – having just flown in from some civil war or other, his lightly rumpled suit ragged with bullet holes. Perhaps Robin also recognised his younger self in me, for he gave me every encouragement. In matching music with mad countries, and turning those interests into a career, Robin was, more than anyone, my role model.

IN EARLY 1984, Billy was on the cover of the *New Musical Express* for the first time. The *NME* was still the rock journal of record, having recovered somewhat from an aberrant period in the early 80s during which it had employed writers purely, it seemed, for their pretentiousness, impenetrability, an attachment to the dicier aspects of Berlin, allied to a belief that Nick Cave was the future of rock & roll and that a weekly column devoted to cocktails was somehow relevant and valid. (God spare us! What *had* become of music?)

Billy had also just had broadcast his second session for John Peel. He was, suddenly, red hot. And Braggmania coincided with, and was probably helped by, the miners' strike. We did countless benefits.

Billy was not, in those early days, an especially sophisticated young man. In fact, he was what he was – a former squaddie from Essex. His political education came in a brutal crash course on those picket lines and in those mining communities. We were both moved by the resolve and dignity of the miners, their wives and families. Britain for a while became a police state and any faith and trust I may have had previously in the police they squandered by acting as eager, stupid and thuggish agents and enforcers of money and power. But my deepest contempt was directed at other working people who ought to have shown solidarity with the miners but who, to buy into the myth of Thatcher's entrepreneurial individualism (selfishness) sold their loyalties and principles for a pittance. They seemed to have no

Peter and Billy backstage at the Torhout Festival, Belgium, July 1984. *AK*

The tour manager, on his Brussels hotel bed, July 1984. I'm still wearing this shirt.
Billy Bragg

grasp of, nor any concern for, the prospect that they may be next. And any lingering romantic notions I may have had of a working class and its solidarity disappeared there and then. Chavs were born, and were soon to become an invasive species. I sought, and was granted, political asylum among the educated chattering classes.

Over those months in the tatty Volvo estate (The Battlebus), Billy got the benefit of the breadth of my music tastes and, eventually, I came to share some of his enthusiasms. But not to start with. For the first few weeks he seemed to have only one cassette. It was by James Brown, surely one of the most over-rated artists in the history of popular music, and certainly among its more disagreeable. (Had he been white, James Brown would not have been deified by the critics in the manner which is now obligatory. He'd have been recognised as the partially-talented, unpleasant little prick that he was.) James Brown had, essentially, two numbers – *Papa's Got A Brand New Bag* and *It's a Man's Man's Man's World*, both deeply tedious and of which all his other recordings were variants. A rotation C90 of James Brown would, alone, have rendered me irresponsible for my actions as driver, and could have resulted in serious loss of life on the M6, so I retrieved from Leeds more of my own cassettes. If I was playing something Billy didn't like – and, until the AK Audio Re-education Programme sorted him out, he was initially hostile to country music – I just turned up the volume. Billy was strapped in and only I could drive.

Perhaps it grew on him, or perhaps I simply wore him down but a Willie Nelson double album, *Willie & Family Live*, became one of our motoring favourites. I remember driving at dawn, in the summer, through northern France, with Willie singing *Till I Gain Control Again* and Billy asleep in the passenger seat. As I raced along that misty poplar-lined empty road, I felt totally free, unbelievably lucky and life pulsating with potential. It was a perfect moment.

The raw swagger of Juke Boy Bonner's *Houston The Action Town*, a track on one of my blues and r&b compilation tapes, grabbed Billy instantly and he would often adapt it to wherever we were playing that night. ('Now if you're looking for action, man – Hamburg's the town...') Later, our in-car repertoire was enriched considerably when Billy made a trip up to Topic Records, the long-established folk label in north London, where the generous staff loaded him up with a collection of essentials. The Watersons second LP, from 1966, we played constantly, together bellowing along to the travelling songs *Thirty Foot Trailer* and *Jolly Waggoners*. This variety was not, I suspect, what many of Billy's fans and his supporters in the music press imagined we were listening to on the road.

Many years later it was rather satisfying to see Billy reborn as Mr Folk Music, recording with – among others – the great Martin Carthy, by then a member of the Watersons, and also becoming some sort of custodian of Woody Guthrie's legacy in the United States.

As TWO PALS together, on a mission, feeling a Bragg momentum building, and seeing the world for the first time, we had a blast. The early Bragg attitude to foreign travel, however, did require a little polish. If I had seldom been overseas before becoming Billy's tour manager and driver, I don't think Billy had been abroad at all. In the spring of 1984 we were summoned to Amsterdam for the first time. Billy had been booked to play at the legendary Melkweg, first established – or rather squatted – in the 1960s as a hippy arts centre in a defunct dairy. Billy had, at first, a reflex hostility to hippy values and to the cosmopolitan characteristics of our European cousins. These would soften with his experiences around the continent and after endless lectures from me and Pete that hippies and punks actually had a great deal, ideologically, in common.

I adored Amsterdam from the moment of our arrival in the Volvo, one glorious April afternoon. On one of the narrow streets, running along a city centre canal, we got stuck in a traffic jam. There was not, as a reaction to this gridlock, the strutting white-van man response, nor the endearing Cockney cab driver abuse, one would have had to endure in a London snarl-up. I watched, with a stretching smile, as the couple in the VW bus in front of us, got out, stripped off their T-shirts, climbed on their roof, lit cigarettes and laid back in the sunshine – all after turning up Otis Redding on their van's stereo. This, I said to myself, is my kind of town.

The more I saw of the Amsterdam in particular and the Netherlands in general, the stronger I felt a spiritual affinity with what I regarded as the most enlightened country on earth. I marvelled at the reality of even the smallest town having a Melkweg-style culture centre, bringing the civilising activities of music, theatre, cinema and photography and the other visual arts to every community. Why, I wondered, can't *we* live like this? Why can't we have a similar attitude to the popular arts in the UK? It was a real eye-opener.

I also admired the Dutch tolerance of all those human impulses that brought the British frothing to a boil of moral indignation. And, recognising that those activities – such as drugs and prostitution – were going to happen anyway, always had done, and could not be legislated or moralised out of existence, the Dutch had made it possible instead for them to happen under the safest, most civilised circumstances.

The Netherlands was relaxed, freewheeling and instinctively liberal. Moreover, looking around, I could not see there an underclass, nor any obvious poverty or social divide. It was certainly a country uncomplicated and unhindered by any class considerations. Coming, at the time, from and increasingly divided and divisive Britain, I began to regard my own country as peevish, small-minded and selfish. It lacked, by comparison, any generosity of spirit. While 1960s values in the Netherlands had permeated its town halls and beyond, the shower of politicians who later came into government in the UK, as former idealists of the 1960s and 70s, were only too eager and opportunistic to compromise those ideals and principles for power – at any price.

We checked into the hotel behind the Melkweg, which the concert organisers had booked on our behalf. The Quentin was a boutique hotel, years before the species was identified and categorised. It was run by Frank and Philippe a sweet, gay couple, deeply and touchingly in love with each other. They had just opened. Billy and I were among their first guests. After checking in, Frank asked breezily if we would like him to run out to a coffee shop to get us a bit of marijuana. In this place I'd never before set foot, I felt like I'd come home. Billy was absolutely stunned and, at first, jumpy and uncomfortable about our accommodation. I still rate The Quentin back then as one of the most delightful hotels in which I've stayed and, until Frank and Philippe sold it in the late 80s and moved to France, I would bolt there as often as I could.

Naturally, Billy would not set foot in Amsterdam's famous coffee shops – even when confronted with the evidence of how harmless and convivial public dope smoking could be. Marijuana was for hippies. So was exotic food. On that first trip, the Melkweg promoters had paid for us to eat at a nearby Indonesian restaurant between soundcheck and gig. Billy was suspicious. So we ended up eating chips from a vending machine on the street. I was, quietly, bloody furious. And hungry.

Billy was, like many people who are making it for the first time, rather careful about money and its whereabouts. We were staying over with Our Elizabeth at the Shire Oak Road flat in Leeds when, one morning, I counted more than a thousand pounds in cash – gig takings – in my holdall. I told Billy I was nipping down the street to pay it into his account via Barclay's in Headingley. He wasn't too sure about this and was reluctant to lose sight of the readies. Elizabeth had to reassure him that his money paid in there would – he could be confident of this – eventually appear at his own bank in Barking.

Being on the road with Billy guaranteed plenty of rock & roll, but no drugs for him and scandalously little sex for either of us. Unusually, for two blokes in their mid-twenties, ostensibly living out the rock & roll dream, matters of the sub-navel region were seldom discussed in the privacy of the flying Volvo during the dark nights of the autobahn, never mind exercised in the hotel rooms.

I did have a brief relationship with Elise, a lovely Dutch girl (which, naturally, I mishandled), but exasperation does not begin to describe my reaction to what was, otherwise, a sexual famine. In the Billy Bragg tour itinerary, there wasn't even time for leg-over. Our schedules were not only intense, our routings were often insanely haphazard, sometimes requiring me to drive all night, halfway across Europe.

Although I knew straight away that I was chaperoning the wrong rock star to have any backstage expectations of gorgeous girls, squealing to get to Billy's handsome young roadie, there were nights when I returned from the stage with the guitars, and lost the will to live as I found the dressing room crowded yet again with intense youths engaging Billy in another discussion on revolutionary socialism. Only these brow-furrowing little buggers, I would point out cheerily, would not be catching just a couple of hours sleep before having to chauffeur Chairman Bragg to northern Finland the following morning.

THE PHONE RANG. It was Billy, over in Acton. Again, in that dramatic April of 1984.

'Kersh, I've been given a couple of tickets to see BB King at the Hammersmith Odeon next week. Fancy going?'

For some reason I can't now recall, I didn't on the night of the gig collect Billy in the Volvo from his flat. We both travelled on the tube and met outside the Odeon's front doors. It is a terrifying thought but had I picked him up that night in the car I might not have done any of the things I have done over the last twenty-five years.

We took our seats in the front stalls. Clearly, it was a row which had been block-booked by the record company for press and special guests. Few of these freebies had been taken up although, just before show time, I was delighted that Robin Denselow arrived to occupy the seat two places along from mine on my right. As Billy and I were greeting Robin, another chap began to squeeze through into the seat between us. I recognised him as Trevor Dann, producer of BBC 2 TV's rock programme, *Whistle Test*. Trevor and I had met only the week before when I had driven Billy over to TV Centre to make his first appearance on the programme. It is in the nature of television that much of one's time is spent standing around while a man up a ladder adjusts the gate on a studio light for hours on end. Another technician, looking up, holds the ladder and says, 'left a bit'. This had been true of my experience, tending to Billy that afternoon and evening. Trevor and I had whiled away much of it chatting and leaning against the studio wall.

Perhaps I had unintentionally flattered Trevor at that first encounter by remembering his name as that of the producer of my favourite Ivor Cutler session for John Peel, back in the summer of 1979. Whatever the reason, he seemed delighted to see me again in the third row at BB King.

At the end of the gig, Trevor asked where I was living and if I needed a lift home. I reminded him I was staying with the Jenners in Maida Vale.

'Of course you are. I'm going that way myself,' he said. 'I'll drop you off.'

Just where the north end of Scrubs Lane meets the Harrow Road, there is a bus lay-by on the left. Perhaps you know it. Trevor, without explanation or warning, suddenly swerved into that lay-by and switched off the engine.

'Oh, hell,' I thought. 'Here we go. I've heard about these television types.' I was a younger and prettier lad in those days.

'Er... I wonder,' Trevor began, 'if you've ever thought of being on television?'

I turned to look at him, scornfully, thinking this was some kind of joke. Or come-on.

'No,' I said. Which was true.

'Well,' said Trevor. 'I'd like you to be one of the presenters of the next series of *Whistle Test*.'

23

WHISTLE TEST – A TERRIBLE
CHILD IN THE COMFY AREA

THERE IS BAPTISM BY FIRE and there is standing up in a field packed with thousands of jeering, boozy heavy metal fans to make one's television debut.

Still, it could have been worse. Had it been a tribal gathering of adherents to the pious concept of 'indie rock', the grey misguided youths in charity shop chic might have taken me as seriously as they took themselves.

On the other hand, heavy metal fans are – for nothing ever changes in heavy metal – a docile, amiable, undemanding bunch with a fairly reliable line in humour. (There is too, I have noticed, a surprising number of off-duty bank managers in the ranks of the embroidered.) Consequently, delivering my very first words to a television camera, at the Castle Donington Monsters of Rock Festival, in August 1984, I was encouraged to get my tits out as two-litre plastic cider bottles, refilled amusingly with hot piss, were hurled in my direction, spinning away, off target, like liquid Catherine wheels to detonate, amid much cheering, among fellow connoisseurs of these time-honoured merry rituals.

To complete this package for the first programme of the new

autumn series of *Whistle Test*, I interviewed David Lee Roth, Ozzy Osbourne, AC/DC and Mötley Crüe. If I could cope with that, I reflected on the way home, I can cope with anything. That nothing I have done since has felt like doing a proper day's work may stem from this experience. I more than coped with it, even as someone who dislikes heavy metal, because it was nevertheless a good story, so I treated it as a piece of journalism. And one which was ripe with absurdity and humorous potential.

MY FIRST STUDIO PROGRAMME, however, introduced me to previously unknown levels of both terror and exhilaration, as well as the shock of realising just how impoverished the programme was. The studio programmes were live but there was no Autocue. *Whistle Test* didn't have the budget for that essential television presenters' safety net.

I had never done live television before and my on-camera introduction for that first programme was quite long and necessarily detailed. After assembling this menu, I spent much of the afternoon in my dressing room learning it verbatim. Mark Ellen, my co-presenter, burst in to rescue me. He was carrying a huge sheet of white card and a marker pen.

'Andy! Andy! What we do is this: you write the essentials of your link out on this and I'll stand next to the camera and hold it for you as you do it.' I looked at him in disbelief. There was more. 'Then when I'm on camera, you do the same for me.'

As the titles and music rolled, bang on 7pm on a Tuesday evening, I was at that point where fear fades into the serenity of fatalism and is shored up by the certainty that it's too late to pull out now. The floor manager was counting me in. A red light on the nearest camera lit up. My tongue felt like a man-hole cover. I went for it.

The sensation I had at the end of the one hour transmission, buzzing with neat adrenalin and lukewarm Kestrel lager (that programme budget again), was akin to the rush I've had described to me by junkies. Bloody hell, I did it. That was live television! I didn't fuck up. Wow, I've presented the *Whistle*

Test! And it had felt like we'd been on air for perhaps ten minutes. I loved it. I wanted more.

From the off, I had taken to being on television. The record producer Joe Boyd, a man of unerring good judgement in most things, later remarked, 'There are those who take naturally to being on television. And there is you, Andy, who grabs the camera by the lapels.' It was probably also to my advantage that I had never had ambitions to be there. In that sense, I hadn't worked up an act or television persona. I could only be myself. And it seemed to work. This became my only guiding principle throughout what passed for a television career and, more importantly, one I would carry with me into my truly natural habitat, radio.

In that first summer, I couldn't believe my good luck. (And still I can't.) I was suddenly presenting the flagship – and only – BBC television rock music programme, the very programme which had been so formative in my teenage years. One afternoon, I was with Trevor Dann in Covent Garden. He beckoned me over to meet a man fiddling with a cashpoint machine. It was Bob Harris. Bob was delightful, just as gentle as he had been on screen, and he wished me well. I felt, right then, as if I'd really arrived. I had Whispering Bob's blessing. Generously, he had handed the torch to a new generation. While trying to remember his PIN number.

Dedication to doing a good job bonded me with the *Whistle Test* team – in the office, the studios and with the crews out on a shoot. Again, I felt we were on a mission. And in Mark Ellen, particularly, I found my television soul mate, someone boyishly funny who found the interaction of the ludicrous worlds of the music industry and television endlessly amusing.

WHISTLE TEST HAD a major rival at the time in *The Tube*, whch was produced at Tyne Tees in Newcastle, for the newish Channel 4. It was fronted by Paula Yates and Jools Holland, a presentation partnership of the utter shallowness of one, the smugness of the other, and of joint incompetence. It was, of course, hugely successful and in its studied carelessness, calculated offhandedness and vacuity, it was hailed – by those elsewhere in the media who were terrified of being labelled fuddy-duddies – as ground-breakingly hip.

Down at Television Centre, we on the *Whistle Test* – the rock programme with A-levels – didn't give a toss about being hip. We were driven not by fashion but journalism; by substance not style. We were impressed by what we thought was good music deserving of a wider audience or a good story about a band, even if they happened to be terrible, told well. *The Tube*, however, was mesmerised by showbiz and celebrity. These opposing priorities made an editorial difference. Although no music television programme has ever been made without the support of record companies, we, as music journalists and obsessives – and ones who were prepared to trailblaze, to evangelise and to pioneer the remarkable, even if obscure – felt it was also our job to set the agenda rather than to be spoon-fed by the major labels and to jump into bed with them routinely and uncritically. If we felt a big label's new priority band was lousy and there was no journalistic justification for having them on the show, they'd be directed instead to Newcastle.

The Tube was considered to embody fashion. We were defiantly anti-fashion. *Whistle Test* was a programme presented by men in check cotton work shirts for what we imagined were similarly-attired viewers, who probably also liked bands that dressed as they did. And we weren't afraid to lead. Years before the category of Americana was identified, we made on-location films about a new breed of literate American country singers of whom no one else in the UK had then heard – Lyle Lovett, Dwight Yoakam, Nanci Griffith and Steve Earle. We had a themed programme about surf music. We put Zimbabwe's Bhundu Boys in the studio for their first British television appearance, not because they were on Columbia or Polygram Records, far from it, but because we thought they were outstanding.

An enthusiast called Godfrey Cheshire walked into the office one afternoon, having flown from Raleigh, North Carolina, to deliver to us a compilation he had put together of bands from that region, and, liking what we heard, we went almost immediately to make a film about them. My old friend Dave Woodhead passed to me a copy of the first and newly self-released album by Barrence Whitfield and the Savages, an R&B band from Boston. Impressed, I nipped over to catch them one weekend in Massachusetts, at my own expense, and was astonished. We were back, as *Whistle Test*, in Boston within a fortnight to film them. On a shoot in Los Angeles, I persuaded Trevor to use up the remaining film stock, following a Eurythmics interview, on a then unknown black street singer of my discovery called Ted Hawkins. That *Whistle Test* was Ted's first television appearance anywhere.

ALL THE *WHISTLE TEST* TEAM – presenters Mark Ellen, David Hepworth and myself, Trevor Dann, and the lovely and often bewildered *Whistle Test* editor, Mike Appleton – were essentially fans who had been let loose on television. Mark had a worrying fixation with the Incredible String Band and David Hepworth alerted the medical world to a condition in which the patient

Unwinding with Barrence Whitfield after a Savages gig in The Hague, 1986.
Anna Jenkins

genuinely believes himself to be a member of Bruce Springsteen's E Street Band.

It was huge fun, like a rock music programme put together by occupants of the sixth-form common room. (But only David Hepworth had been made a prefect.) On some of our all-night *Rock Around the Clock* specials, when we were pretty convinced no one was watching, things could get very silly. In the early hours of one, while a pre-recorded item was going out, I went wandering the corridors of Television Centre and found a well-known but lonely weatherman in his studio. 'Come and join us,' I said. To the bewilderment of anyone watching, I brought him back with me onto our live programme. For no reason, except the poor chap was in need of some company.

We were never deferential to rock stardom and I was predisposed to be deeply suspicious of it. In fact, for major rock stars, an appearance on *Whistle Test* could be a disorientating leveller. Our set was a desk, an unremarkable black leather sofa with a chromed frame, a couple of matching easy chairs and a coffee table. Mark and I, obeying a floor manager one day, to take our places in 'the comfy area', picked up on this and milked it for all it was worth. It was delightfully, incongruously non-rock & roll. Mark, in particular, was fond of suddenly asking some self-important rock star or other, mid-interview and as a *non sequitur*, 'What do you think of the Comfy Area, then?' And he would pat the upholstery rapidly, beaming at the humourless interviewee. 'Great to have you in it! And, you've got to agree, luxuriously comfy, isn't it? Go on! You can admit it. Just to us.'

Often the budgets wouldn't stretch to cover the all night marathons with enough live bands or filmed reports. Towards the end of one such shoe-string transmission, Mark and I filled in a couple of minutes of empty live air time with some juggling.

Neither was *Whistle Test* noted for its rock & roll excess. On a New Year's Eve special, Trevor had come running down from the gallery just before we went on air, to remind us that we mustn't drink any alcohol, not even around midnight. In the run-up to Big Ben, Mark shot off to hospitality and lifted a bottle of cheap red wine. Then he got a slip of paper, sticky tape and a marker pen. Come midnight, there was, on the table between the two of us, a very visible bottle of red wine, which he had crudely but boldly re-labelled, Harmless Fizzy Pop.

'Hello, again!' Mark breezed to the camera as we came out of a filmed item. 'I guess you're all enjoying a drink or two at home as you watch tonight's programme, and no harm in that. But spare a thought for your hard-working *Whistle Test* pals here who are forbidden to touch a drop until we come off the air at 3am.' Then he seized the bottle and waved it next to his face, in a parody of a commercial.

'So, at about this point in the evening, Andy and I like to unwind with a glass or two of Harmless Fizzy Pop, don't we, old boy?' And with that, he poured us a couple of large paper cups of the stuff. If I was supposed to pick up from him and introduce

Live from the Comfy Area! With the arrival of the Boy Kershaw on *Whistle Test*, Mark Ellen pulls his socks up. BBC Television Centre, 1985. *BBC*

the next item, I was probably incapable of doing so, seized solid with the giggles.

I am convinced that the *Whistle Test* of that era became the model for *Top Gear* of recent years – three blokes having a whale of a time while sharing irreverently their enthusiasms with the nation.

IN THE YEARS BEFORE I was recruited, *Whistle Test* had suffered from one significant mistake: when punk happened, dear old Mike Appleton, Bob Harris and the production team at the time, decided the best way to deal with this revolution was to ignore it and hope it would go away. Mike, pioneer that he was, had developed *The Old Grey Whistle Test* in 1971 out of *Late Night Line Up*, where he had worked as a young producer. Unavoidably, he created the programme to reflect his own music tastes, which were predominantly West Coast. That was absolutely perfect and what was needed at the time. But with punk, the programme needed to embrace the best of the new while retaining a place for what was still good of the old.

To shake things up, Trevor Dann was brought in from a producer's job at Radio 1 – where he'd been regarded as far too bright, awkward and visionary to rise within the ranks of the Nation's Favourite – and as part of that revamp, he set about looking for a new presenter. 'They wanted a girl,' Trevor told me at the distance of early 2010. 'But they got you.'

Over the intervening twenty-five years I had often wondered what on earth had prompted Trevor to yank me off the street or, more accurately, the road, with Billy, to join the *Whistle Test* team. But, improbable though this sounds, I had never before got round to asking him.

'We needed an *enfant terrible*,' he explained. 'And there was no more terrible a child than you. In fact, meeting you was a revelation. You broke the rules in every respect. Okay, you weren't a girl but you were from the north when all other television presenters were metropolitan. You were brusque and you always looked people in the eye. And you also had that musical heritage. Most people at that time were busily disavowing the past. Although you were young, you were happy to say "I like some of the new and quite a bit of the old." Your manner may have been immature but your tastes were very mature.

'It was a combination as unlikely as meeting someone who wore a swimsuit to play the grand piano. So, while we might have been looking for a Mariella Frostrup, we ended up with an educated urchin with a Lightnin' Hopkins habit.

'The point at which you really got the job was when we brought you in for an audition. You were so focused and driven, I thought you were on something. We had the music journalist, David Sinclair, playing the part of a rock star and you had to interview him. David was wearing an old, battered red leather jacket. And you got him to talk about that rather than himself. It was when you said to David, "I bet that jacket could tell a tale or two," that I yelled in the control room, "That's him! Sign him up!"'

A NATIONAL INSTITUTION it may have been but *Whistle Test* was always a low priority for the BBC2 schedulers. If something else considered more important cropped up, our live transmission time would be shoved around to suit. Wimbledon fortnight was the worst. Frequently, we had to loaf around the studios, chain-smoking, perhaps with a couple of live bands primed to perform, while we waited until 9.30 at night for Jimmy Connors to finish a tie-breaker on Court Number One.

The programme was a low priority for the financiers, too. Our trademark bare studio walls were not some designer's idea of a fashionably utilitarian look: we just couldn't afford to cover them up. Likewise our fees were those of highly-respected but penniless BBC flagship programmes – a quaint phenomenon with which, over the next quarter of a century, I would become sorely familiar. My weekly fee for a *Whistle Test* was £200. Presenters of *The Tube* were said to be on £3000 a programme.

Soon there were to be other consequences of being on the *Whistle Test*. Within a few months of my debut, I was enjoying the routine ego boost of performing on live television with, upon me, in the dark shadows of the studio beyond the camera, the flashing eyes of Anna Jenkins, the beautiful Anna of school days, former girlfriend of my best buddy, Jonny Barnes.

Less welcome was the reappearance in my life of Bob Geldof. In the autumn of 1984, Geldof had been on the programme plugging a charity single he and some of his flimsy pop pals had recorded to raise money for the biblical famine in Ethiopia. Beyond that, I didn't pay a great deal of attention and barely noticed over the next few months the Band Aid momentum building, until, one day the following spring, Trevor greeted me in the *Whistle Test* office.

'Ah, Andy! I wonder if you can make yourself available for a special programme in July. There's going to be a concert at Wembley for Ethiopia... Geldof's thing, you know... *Whistle Test* is involved and I'd like you to be one of the presenters.'

◉

24

LIVE AID – AIR-CONDITIONING MAN'S BIG BREAK

'ANDY! ANDY! WAKE UP!'

I'd been driving up the M1, at the wheel of a speedboat, of course, with popular mid-1960s Irish vocal trio, The Bachelors, across the back seat, delivering – as we rushed by the turn-off for Dunstable – their evergreen hit, *I Believe*. In my rear-view mirror their faces, contorted with sincerity, had begun to look menacing. Things, I could sense, were about to turn ugly.

Many years later – I digress for a moment – my old friend, Big John, when I told him that two-thirds of The Bachelors were about to perform in my home town on the Isle of Man, was incredulous.

'What is it?' he snapped down the phone, 'A gig or a fucking séance?'

I awoke with my cheek on a deep, soft, red carpet. I had fallen asleep under a spiral staircase. Somewhere. All around me were smart heels, of shoes male and female, and the babble and easy laughter of a cocktail party.

'Come on, Andy. Wake up, old boy. Time to interview Cliff Richard.'

It was my friend, Trevor Dann, *Whistle Test* producer and, on this day of particular madness, a producer of *Live Aid*.

THE REALITY to which Trevor had brought me round was only slightly less grotesque than my motorway skippering of Con, Dec, and the other one whose name no one could ever remember. As I got to my feet, there in front of me, sitting on a stool, nursing an acoustic guitar and looking repellently wholesome for a national monument to the mortician's art was every mum's favourite other Bachelor Boy.

It had been a long day.

Our coverage had moved, after the concert at Wembley, to this celebrity-stuffed nightclub and impromptu television studio in what is always described on these occasions as 'London's glittering West End'.

Trevor, or a floor manager, must have counted me in and I proceeded to conduct – in my dishevelled, semi-conscious state – what passed for a live television interview with Cliff. (I have not, during my meagre research for this book, sought out, in the interests of historical accuracy, archive video evidence of this encounter. And neither should you. Believe me, you have better things to do.)

It is unlikely, however, that I – ever the diplomat – revealed to Cliff that he had been at number one in the charts, worryingly, on the day I was born with *Travellin' Light*. It is just one of those little crosses, quietly, I have had to bear.

We were in, Cliff and I, one of those discreet and expensive basement nightclubs in Mayfair, the kind in which, on regular evenings, middle-aged aristocrats charm girls a third of their age, called Tamara, when they are not swapping stories about their part in getting 'Lucky' Lucan out of the country. And I suppose I asked Cliff to share with us – for it was that sort of day – his thoughts on *Live Aid* before inviting him to refresh us of one of his many carefree hits.

My memories of the day are patchy. I was, possibly, and medically, in a state of shock. I can think of no other explanation, aside from reflex self-preservation shut-down, for why I should have kept so calm and held it together throughout.

* * *

THE TWENTY-FIFTH ANNIVERSARY of the concert, in July 2010, and the broadcast of a Live Aid television documentary, was the first time I had watched any of the coverage. At that distance, and with my children with me on the sofa, then old enough to appreciate the significance of the event, I was secretly proud of my achievement. So were they. On 13 July 1985, I had been on television for less than a year. But the biggest surprise of the documentary was to notice that I was, in the mid 1980s, a girl. And a rather attractive one too.

'And you did not want to do it,' Trevor Dann reminded me a quarter of a century later. 'You were very uncomfortable with it and sceptical of its motives.'

This I did recall. Although I was not, at that stage, yet an evangelist for Africa – and hadn't already set foot there, never mind developed a love and obsession for the continent – I could sense something was not quite right. I did not, however, take the position of some, that it was just a cynical career move by Bob Geldof, to keep himself in the public eye after the Boomtown Rats stopped having hits. Although the revelations in the twenty-five years documentary about Geldof's ruthless treatment of his Band Aid partner, Midge Ure, added weight to those accusations of personal ambition.

I did feel that Band Aid, of which *Live Aid* was the climax, was aptly named: a sticking plaster, being slapped over a horrendous, deep wound. Not only did it fail to confront the fundamental causes of the Ethiopian famine, it never bothered to recognise there were any. And it was, as a gesture, however beneficial its goal, smug in its assumption that a bunch of largely lamentable rock and pop floozies was capable of making a difference, without tackling simultaneously underlying problems. Sure, there was an urgency to get Ethiopians fed but I felt that *Live Aid*, like Band Aid, was dealing only with symptoms and not even interested in the disease. That unwillingness to understand was to trivialise Ethiopia's misery – a disaster from the pages of the Old Testament that needed nothing more than relief by a modern miracle and a sprinkle of pop music magic. That I found irritating, shallow, sanctimonious and self-satisfied.

* * *

MUSICALLY, *LIVE AID* was to be entirely predictable and boring. As they were wheeled out – or, rather bullied by Geldof into playing – it became clear that this was another parade of the same old rock aristocracy in a concert for Africa, organised by someone who, while advertising his concern for, and sympathy with, the continent didn't see fit to celebrate or dignify the place by including on the *Live Aid* bill a single African performer. There were, meanwhile, hundreds of guitarists in the beer halls of Zimbabwe or Zaire, and dozens of others dotted along the Niger, who could wipe the floor with Eric Clapton.

In this respect, Geldof didn't learn. Or, more likely, didn't care. Twenty years later, at the time of *Live 8*, he again invited no African stars to share the stage in Hyde Park with their European and American counterparts – and on equal terms. When he faced an outcry over that, he made the fiasco worse by announcing a concert at the Eden Project to accommodate African artists. In an op-ed piece for the *Independent*, I was compelled to write:

> I thought apartheid was dead... The *Africa Calling* concert at the Eden Project compounds the insult to the continent Geldof purports to help... tossing Africans the crumbs from the table of Europe's rock aristocracy... I am coming, reluctantly, to the conclusion that *Live 8* is as much to do with Geldof showing off his ability to push around presidents and prime ministers as with pointing out the potential of Africa. Indeed, Geldof appears not to be interested in Africa's strengths, only an Africa on its knees... He might as well put up signs around the lanes leading to the Eden Project saying 'Grateful Darkies This Way...'

In the lead-up to the 1985 concert, Trevor and I debated my position in the Television Centre bar. My moral dilemma was another headache he didn't need. Geldof's relationship with the BBC, and *Whistle Test* in particular, had persuaded him to entrust us with the *Live Aid* television coverage. The period between announcement and concert was only eight weeks. Trevor and the production team already had enough on their plates.

I was not in much of a position to argue. I was the new boy. I'd not been at *Whistle Test* long enough to dig in my heels and if I didn't come on board, I'd have been increasing the burden on Mark Ellen and David Hepworth.

'If you say I have to do it, I'll do it,' I told Trevor over that drink – morally irresponsible, and seeking to be given a way out.

'You have to do it,' he said.

A BBC CAR first picked up Mark and then called round to collect me. We lived close to each other in Chiswick. It was early, and one of those beautiful summer mornings that hums and crackles with promise. Except I hadn't slept and nature's optimism was lost on me. All the way to Wembley, Mark twittered with observations, predictions and schoolboyish gags, trying to buck me up. Unresponsive, I stared out of the window. I was looking but seeing nothing. My eyes had gone into a kind of tunnel vision. I felt sick. I managed a small smile when he slightly dropped his guard.

'Andy! Andy! I'm wearing the brown trousers today. Do you know why, old boy? I'm fucking terrified!' And he threw back his head and roared with laughter. I did feel better. If one is about to be hanged, there is no one more entertaining with whom to stroll to the gallows than Mark.

Not until I saw the crowds around the stadium, did I grasp just how big an occasion this was. It was very big. Oddly, that lifted me: I summoned up the Right Stuff, the spirit of my astronaut heroes of childhood. The eyes of the world, literally, would soon be on me. Now I was going to do it.

That decided, I was ready. The rest would be a breeze.

Up at the commentary box, our TV studio for the day, and on the walkway outside, just under the roof above the terraces, I thought of Anna, my newish girlfriend, who I loved so much. She, like all our partners, had not been allowed to come along for the day. It broke my heart when I had to tell her the news. As the scale of *Live Aid* became more apparent, and anticipation of it reached the level of global hysteria, Anna had been so proud that her Andy would be one of the television presenters. She'd gone up to her mum's in Yorkshire for the big day. I missed her hugely. I thought, too, of Our Elizabeth and other friends who'd be enjoying carefree *Live Aid* barbecues that afternoon and of everyone's complaints that they couldn't properly see, in the bright sunshine, the picture on the televisions inexpertly set up in a million gardens.

As with all live broadcasts, the scariest part is the wait. Once we were on air, I enjoyed myself enormously, particularly when I found myself having to interview Phil Collins, Sting and Howard Jones at a table in the backstage area. I'd got fed up already of hearing all morning that Phil Collins would be performing both in London and then Philadelphia by jetting supersonically on Concorde to the States after his Wembley appearance. Just how this would improve matters for the skeletal kids of Tigray wasn't immediately apparent and the stunt, I felt, was an emblematic exposure of the true priorities of many on the day – self-satisfaction if not self-promotion.

'What are you doing here, anyway?' I turned to ask Collins, a man who I already held responsible for bringing Assistant Branch Manager excitement to rock & roll. 'Because I thought you were supposed to be on Concorde and heading for America. Will you shove off?'

He glanced at his watch and I barged him out of shot, screen left. 'Go on! Don't forget your barley sugars!'

To his credit, he played along with this and disappeared.

THOSE WERE, PERHAPS, the most valuable words I uttered throughout the marathon broadcast. Certainly, a stream of gibberish was otherwise the order of the day, especially during some of the long unforeseen delays between bands. There was a truly gruelling one just before my hero, Elvis Costello, was to perform. I had no idea of the problem, and neither did the director, talking constantly in my earpiece, as I was speaking to millions around the world, filling desperately for several minutes.

'Right, he's in the wings now, Andy,' at last I heard him say. 'Go for it!'

'...thank god for that,' I sighed to the viewers – or something along those lines – 'and here he is: four eyes, one vision, Elvis Costello!' And an unshaven Elvis shambled on.

That was not the worst moment. Not by a long chalk. The worst moment was the arrival of a nice man called John Hurt.

'ANDY! GREAT NEWS! We've got John Hurt!'

I was in position on the presenters' sofa, the Live Aid stage and a third of Wembley Stadium visible over my shoulder. Our studio was then off air, for the duration of some video clip that was going out, possibly the feed from Soviet state television in Moscow which, in a mix up of their tapes, resulted in around nine minutes of a documentary about cherry farming in Georgia being broadcast all around the world, instead of a video made specially for *Live Aid* by some state-approved Soviet singer.

'Who's John Hurt?' I shouted over the clamour. I have never been much of a theatre or cinema-goer.

No one answered. Walkie-talkies were screaming.

I was prepared for chaos. Just as well: it was chaos all day. Nothing in television or concert promotion as ambitious – or as last-minute – as this had been attempted before. There were no precedents on which to build preparation. Everyone was making it up as they went along, and doing so on live television around the world.

A couple of days before the concert, I was summoned to what passed for a planning meeting at Television Centre. I came away from it more bewildered than I had been when I left home. Even by the time we went on air our role, as BBC presenters, hadn't been defined – whether we were to be participants in the event or detached reporters of it. And the running order for our Live Aid broadcast, handed to me soon after I arrived at Wembley, was useful only as an improvised fan later that sweltering afternoon.

'He's coming now! Yep, John Hurt,' someone else confirmed. 'Yes. Up the stairs. Now.'

There was great excitement. You see, John Hurt was coming.

We had teams of runners backstage, bringing anyone famous they could find on the long haul through the crowds and up a steel spiral staircase to our studio for interviews. Frankly, we were desperate for anyone to talk to and fill in the gaps between performances. Trevor Dann recalls that when a contractor finally arrived to fix the air-conditioning in that furnace of a studio, he was assumed to be a famous guest, immediately wired for sound and, before he could explain or object, plonked down on the sofa to be interviewed on global TV. He extricated himself at the last moment. But the startled repair man could have convinced me that he was John Hurt.

'Trevor,' I was yelling over the top of the camera, 'who is John Hurt?' But Trevor was entangled in some other matter.

'Thirty seconds, studio,' a floor manager was barking. In less than half a minute, I would have to be again chatting easily with the whole world. About John Hurt. With John Hurt. But who the fuck was he?

'Fifteen seconds, studio.'

'Ferchrissakes, Trevor, who is John Hurt?'

'Ten seconds, studio.'

'Actor,' Trevor mouthed, now paying attention. '*Elephant Man*.'

This meant absolutely nothing to me. I'd have been more comfortable making small talk about air-conditioning. A man in the doorway was having a lapel mic clipped on. He looked over to me and smiled. This was, I assumed correctly, my new friend John.

'...and five, four, three, two, one, cue Andy...'

John was settling next to me as I gushed how nice it was to have him with us. Then I asked some very bland question about whether, in his view, as an actor – for that was all I knew of the blighter – the acting profession might follow the example of musicians and hold some sort of fund raiser for Ethiopia itself.

He was a sweetheart and pretty much interviewed himself for a few minutes until, brusquely, I had to shut him up to introduce the next band. Had he been a monosyllabic grump, I'd have been sunk. In front of one and a half billion people.

Years later, I was at some BBC cheese and wine reception at which I ran into John for the first time since *Live Aid*. After reminding him of how and when we'd met before, I came clean.

'I don't know if you got any inkling at the time,' I said, 'but did you realise in that studio that I had absolutely no idea who you were?'

'I did suspect that, yes,' he smiled. 'But I wasn't going to give you away.'

I gave him a huge hug. I could have kissed him.

'Thank you,' was all I said, and all I needed to say. He understood.

I AWOKE THE DAY AFTER *Live Aid* alone in my little flat in Chiswick. It was another get-up-and-go morning. Before I did, I savoured the sun streaming between the curtains which Our Elizabeth had run up for me, for the first home of my own, and which didn't meet in the middle. I enjoyed too, for a few minutes, the dawn chorus. Did I really do that yesterday? Did it really happen?

When I came to step outdoors, I got the confirmation that it did. For around ten days, I learned what it was like to be truly famous. Not just well-known but in that bracket of public recognition alongside mainstream television personalities, pop idols, film stars and mass murderers. Everywhere I went, carrying out the most routine activities, I was conscious of people staring, openly pointing or asking for autographs.

But within a fortnight normality was restored. And, reassuringly, the bloke on the tube, or the girl in the pub, was again insisting I was John Noakes.

25

JAMMING WITH
BOB DYLAN

IT WAS DECISION TIME in Amsterdam – an unhelpful place to be decisive. At the side of the stage in the Melkweg, just before Christmas 1984, the conflicting loyalties and competing demands of *Whistle Test* and Billy Bragg had reached breaking point. For the previous four months I had just managed to juggle both but now faced burn-out and risked letting one or both down.

In Finland, shortly before, the madness of my sudden good fortune had been underlined when I'd had to leave Billy in Jyvaskyla, where he'd just done a gig, and make my way to Helsinki. There I jumped on a plane to London on a Tuesday morning, to arrive at TV Centre in time for *Whistle Test* rehearsals in the afternoon, before presenting the programme live that night and then hopping on a flight back to Helsinki the following morning and from there north to Jyvaskyla.

Billy could see my life was taking off on a trajectory parallel to his own and, while he may have been dismayed that the attentions of his operative were being diluted, he never once moaned about my accidental media career. He was pleased for me and, I suspect, quietly proud too.

Pete Jenner was also impressed but my sudden sideways lurch into television alarmed him. We were a great team. I was good. Pete, Sumi and Billy valued me. We seemed destined to work together and, understandably, Pete did not want to lose me.

'Oh, but you don't want to be associated with *Whistle Test*' he argued, unconvincingly. 'It's too long in the tooth and completely boring. It's become a joke, Kersh, and probably won't last another series.'

Trevor Dann, alert to my turmoil, felt compelled to intervene and told Pete he was holding me back. But I felt that to defect immediately would be a betrayal of Billy and the Jenners. Pete and Sumi had put a roof over my head for the past twelve months.

Just as she was skilled and ruthless in dismissing those she regarded as unsuited to be my girlfriends, Our Elizabeth handled this dilemma.

At the Melkweg, where she'd joined us for some Christmas shopping in Amsterdam, Elizabeth could see I was worn out, not just from the travelling, the physical effort and the lack of sleep, but the anxiety over the career paths and the unavoidable repetition of listening to the same Bragg songs and identical stage patter, night after night.

'Chuck it in,' she advised. 'Throw yourself into *Whistle Test*. You're killing yourself. Look at you. You can't carry on doing both. And you don't want to be a bloody roadie for the rest of your life. I don't know why you're agonising about it.'

I left.

BILLY AND I had had a ball. To this day I still feel a pang of guilt (a smallish one) about leaving him, matched only by a gratitude for my twelve months at his side. I couldn't have had a better letter of introduction to working in music, radio and television than having been Billy's right-hand man. At that time, it would have been impossible to come through with better credentials.

By now I was out of the Jenners' box room and into my own rented flat, a cute two-bedroomed place in Chiswick, just one street back from the River Thames. I was in awe of my own small achievement. For the first time in my life I had my own home, without Our Elizabeth, parents or flatmates. I furnished and equipped it with the basics from Habitat – simple but stylish and cheap. I looked around. I'd got here myself on my *Whistle Test* wages.

It was as if I was living in some belated 1960s Swinging London film and, as a post-punk David Hemmings, was out every night at gigs, enjoying my ability to walk into any venue and be recognised, welcomed and respected. But I savoured most the power a position on *Whistle Test* gave me to make things happen.

When the first albums from the Los Angeles country and psychedelic rock movement known as the Paisley Underground were released in the UK – with The Rain Parade, Green On Red and The Long Ryders in its vanguard – my enthusiasm for those bands was able to get them national television coverage. The same would happen with Ted Hawkins, The Bhundu Boys and a whole generation of talented young country music bucks. Those musical enthusiasms, begun in adolescence, were now, to some extent, leading and shaping tastes nationally.

At this point I had – at the risk of invoking a drippy recording duo of the day – everything but the girl. I was successful, going places, young, independent and very lonely. Chiswick was delightful, and genteel by London standards, but its popularity with the professionals in their thirties and forties meant that it was not a neighbourhood brimming with young singles looking for a fun time and new friends. The pushing of buggies appeared to be mandatory on its streets.

Mark Ellen and his lovely wife, Clare, lived close by but they had two babies to keep them busy and, in any case, would not have wanted me troubling them every evening with my latest under-the-counter import of Long Ryders out-takes. I would often come home from a live *Whistle Test* transmission, pick up a Chinese or Indian take-away on the walk from Gunnersbury tube and sit alone for the rest of the evening listening to my records or to John Peel on Radio 1. To my astonishment, I began to get mentioned on the programme. John would occasionally say something dismissive of the bands I so publicly endorsed on television: '...as recommended by Andy Kershaw. That's *television's* Andy Kershaw, listeners. Yummy Andy Kershaw off the *Whistle Test*.'

On this matter of romance – or the lack of it – the sharp eyed among you will have spotted in the accounts of the *Live Aid* pantomime and *Whistle Test* fumblings, a small walk-on part for Anna Jenkins, the divine but unattainable beauty of my later school years and at that time the girlfriend of my closest pal, Jonny Barnes. Anna came back into my life in another of those moments of remarkable coincidence and good fortune which, again, I had done nothing to deserve.

BILLY HAD BEEN booked, in early 1984, to play a gig at the London School of Economics. It was, already for me, just another Bragg concert for which I occupied my habitual position at the side of the stage with spare guitar, strings and tuner. Until I saw her.

Eh? That girl down near the front, shifting in and out of the shadows of the stage lights looked just like Anna Jenkins. But what would she be doing there? Good grief, it *was* her! We'd not seen each other since, I think, our delirious Babylon by Bus trip (Bingley Hall, Stafford) to see Bob Marley & The Wailers four years earlier.

Anna, I learned in our hurried chat after the gig, had enrolled at the LSE to study anthropology. Yes, she was living in London, in a place called Crouch End, which I had always imagined, for some reason, was on the Essex coast. (It would soon become my north London home for twenty-one years.) We started to meet up for delightfully innocent days out together in that heady spring, most memorably doing nothing but lying together in the sun and chatting all afternoon on the grass in Regent's Park. We'd write to each other, across London, several times a week. Anna would make the long trek down to Television Centre to watch from the shadows of the studio as I presented *Whistle Test*. Then I would ride with her back on the tube to Finsbury Park and kiss her gently goodnight before striking out alone again for Chiswick. One unforgettable night, she came with me back to the flat. We were in love. That night, I had everything.

IN THE SUMMER of 1985, the landlord of my Chiswick flat terminated the tenancy and I surrendered comfortable surroundings and moved in with Anna in her semi-derelict shared house in Tivoli Road, Crouch End. We slept on a mattress on the floor. It was cold, damp and Anna's house mates were no better and no more domesticated than any other slovenly student tenants. I was on national television, a semi-famous figure, earning more than most kids my age, and every night I was having a bath – there was no shower – in an inch of lukewarm water in a squalid bathroom from which I could see the Alexandra Palace through a hole in the wall.

It was while I was dozing in front of Anna's gas fire one morning that it came to me – in my semi-conscious state – that Bob Dylan was in our midst. I had flown back to London, overnight from Boston. I was shattered and jet-lagged. On the plane I had noted a news-in-brief item in the latest issue of *Spin* magazine: '...Bob Dylan recording with Dave Stewart in London.'

Only the following day, on Anna's hearth rug, did the reality of that hit me. Dave Stewart's studio was in a converted church in Crouch End. I was on nodding terms with Dave. Hell's teeth! Bob was, *right now,* at the end of the ruddy street. There was no time to lose.

I got up off the floor and tumbled out of the house. On Crouch End Broadway, yards from Dave Stewart's Church Studios, I was possessed by an urge to buy Bob a small gift, a token of my thanks for all he'd given to me over the years. I was passing a wholefood shop. So I nipped in and bought my life-long inspiration a jar of jam.

After I'd thoroughly bewildered the receptionist with my convolutions over the entryphone, Dave Stewart had appeared himself at the studio's front door.

'Hello, Dave,' I began. 'I'd like to see Bob, please. Is he in there with you?'

Dave admitted he was. I was shown in.

Bob was playing the electric guitar in an upstairs studio, behind some hessian screens on wheels. Dave Stewart, over the din, urged me to help him wheel them aside. Annie Lennox, lurking in the shadows, smiled and gave me a little wave. We drew back the screens to reveal Dylan, looking whiskered and wrinkled, wearing black jeans, a white motorcycle jacket and cowboy boots. He was giving a Telecaster a frightful and rather tuneless walloping. There was no singing.

Soon we were sitting on the edge of a drum riser, Bob, Dave and I. Bob was turning the jar of jam in his hand and staring at it. It was as if I had handed a mobile phone to a chimpanzee.

'It's hedgerow jam, Bob,' I was explaining. 'Made with... er, real hedgerows.'

To my horror, Dylan had just agreed to my flippant request for an interview for *Whistle Test*. I'd called the office from the studio control room. Editor Mike Appleton was alone at *Whistle Test* HQ. Once I'd convinced him I wasn't making this up and that, yes, Dylan had just agreed to give his first ever interview to British television, poor Mike had to admit that no *Whistle Test* producer or film crew was available to dart up immediately to Crouch End. I persuaded him to get a BBC news crew up to N8 pretty smartly.

What followed, largely because I was in a state of shock and awe, and had no time for preparation, was the worst interview I have ever conducted in my media career and a waste of the journalistic scoop of a lifetime. The fault for that was mostly, but not entirely, mine. To this day I wonder why, having agreed to talk on camera, Dylan, who had been almost chatty, then dropped into monosyllables and grumpiness once the television crew turned up. If he didn't really want to do it, he should have said no. And we could have simply continued with an agreeable afternoon chatting, privately, about jam.

'GO AND FIND US a nice flat in Crouch End,' I instructed Anna one morning. (I'd grown to like the neighbourhood a lot.)

And she did. So we moved together, into a bright one-bedroomed flat, my first property purchase, and for ten months lived and loved in a perfect little world of Anna's most tasteful creation. Then, naturally, I went and fucked it up.

I was twenty-six, permanently randy and, if not particularly physically attractive, more than ready to exploit whatever appeal my status as the poor man's David Jacobs held to lure a legion of women into bed.

For Anna, there was one humiliation too many and, coming home from my first trip to Africa at the end of 1986, I returned to the huge shock of an empty flat. Anna had packed her belongings – all the feminine touches around our little home had gone – and left for a new life with a less selfish bloke. I was back on the John Peel-with-a-takeaway regime and quietly heartbroken for at least two years.

As a survival mechanism, I did have the distraction and compensation of constant work, a dream job and an Olympian quantity of shallow but instantly gratifying sex, if not love and companionship. I was also beginning to move in some unexpected circles. Towards the end of my time with Billy Bragg and Peter Jenner, the three of us were invited – with others – to the House of Commons by the then Leader of her Majesty's Opposition, Neil Kinnock.

'What should be done about young people?' Kinnock was asking us, assembled as we were in an oak-panelled room, around an oval table, dotted with bottles of red wine and bowls of crisps. 'What do young people want?'

'By Christ,' I thought to myself. 'Do these buggers live so much in isolation from the real world that they have to hold a conference to establish that?' It wasn't just bizarre: it was sad.

And who were we to help him? There was dear old fifty-something Pete, although a father of two youngsters; a twenty-eight-year-old ex-army rock star who lived as a hermit in Acton; and me, a rock & roll TV presenter, temporarily holed up in a rancid squat in Crouch End, but hardly representative of mid-80s youth. I looked around the table – poets, journalists, academics, authors, other musicians – and none of us present was an ordinary young person leading a normal life.

As my mind wandered, an intervention from Pete broke into

a dreary discussion about the Labour Party and the youth vote. It brought me sharply to attention and enlivened proceedings no end.

'What,' asked Pete, 'is the party's position, Neil, on the legalisation of cannabis?'

There was much tut-tutting from the more right-on delegates, notably some humourless feminists, around the table who protested that the question was trivial.

'You fucking silly old hippy!' Billy – wordsmith of renown – barked at his manager.

Kinnock jumped at this chance to avoid the question and handed round the crisps.

'What could be done,' one of the feminists asked, 'to make Labour more relevant to women?'

'Just take existing Labour publicity material,' I suggested, 'and have it over-printed, across the top, with "Hey, Girls!"'

I was telling this tale to Mark Ellen during *Whistle Test* rehearsals in the Comfy Area a week later. 'Actually, I've got a mate who's now a Labour MP,' whispered Mark. 'Got elected at the last election. Used to be in a band with me at Oxford. Nice bloke. You heard of him? Called Tony Blair.'

WORKING WITH BILLY, I had missed my first opportunity to visit the United States, cradle of so much of my favourite music, when I had refused to side with him in an argument over the release of a single. Billy did not want to put out a 45. Pete Jenner and I thought he should. It was Billy's belief – not too dissimilar to The Clash's daft elevation into a political philosophy their refusal to appear on *Top of the Pops* – that to release a single would damage his 'credibility' and appear 'too commercial' in its modest ambition.

'Right,' I said, 'you can go to the States on your own.' Pete accompanied him instead for that first American tour.

Soon after *Live Aid*, I finally made it across the Atlantic, thanks to the requirements of *Whistle Test*. And the manner of my arrival there, in New York City, could not have been more dramatically arranged. Trevor Dann, my pal and producer on the trip, and Bill Fowler a lovely old rough-diamond promotions man from WEA Records in London who was along with us, had conspired secretly that after landing at JFK, we would fly into Manhattan by helicopter. My first proper sight, then, of the USA was to sweep around the twin towers of the World Trade Center with lesser skyscrapers poking up at us like pencils.

We stayed in a rented apartment, next door to one owned by Keith Richards. I woke the next day to the rush-hour racket of New York City, and the aromas of fresh coffee and donuts floating up from the street. I'd arrived! But, more excitingly, I was leaving – to drive that day to see perform and to interview Neil Young, in Philadelphia. I was nervous, inexperienced and over-anxious not to fuck it up. I would be in the presence of one of my great heroes – and the man who had done more than any other to inspire my wardrobe.

Neil turned out to be shy. Worryingly, he was also going through a pro-Ronald Reagan period. The interview came to life only when I played him, on a portable cassette machine, a snatch of Green On Red's album, *Gas Food and Lodging*. He cocked his head on one side and listened like a dog catching an ultra-sonic whistle. 'I think I've heard this before somewhere,' he said.

Trevtours to the States – as we came to call them – were always huge fun and, if we had time or a genuine excuse, Trevor was happy to accommodate my eagerness to visit locations where my kind of music was made, or where its historical origins were to be found. And it was gratifying to watch, on these quietly educational Kershaw pilgrimages, Trevor's own enthusiasm for those styles develop.

In Nashville, we stood open-mouthed in the Ryman Auditorium, a former church that had been the venue of the Grand Ole Opry between 1942 and 1974. I regaled Trevor with tales of historic triumphs and infamous tragedies on that stage. Across the alleyway, out the back of the Ryman, where Hank Williams had to be held upright between shows, we downed beers in Tootsie's Orchid Lounge in which Willie Nelson, as a struggling songwriter, had sold *Hello Walls* to Faron Young for fifty dollars. In Tootsie's, I found myself sitting next to a chap I recognised

High Fidelity, pre Nick Hornby. Shopping for rare records in New Orleans, 1988.
My purchases here are Buck Owens ex-jukebox EPs. I gave them to Elvis Costello.
Paul Rider

from a recent American television documentary I had on video called *The Other Side of Nashville*. In the film, my new drinking buddy was also trying to make it as a songwriter, while living in his battered old car on the parking lots of Music City. On an acoustic guitar he was strumming, to anyone who would listen, a lovely little song he had written called *Mine Was The First Heart She Broke*.

'I hope your luck has changed,' I said.

'Sure has,' he beamed. 'Lost the car.'

I've often wondered what became of him. And the song.

Trevor and I bought old country albums in Ernest Tubb's Records, visited the former home of Hank Williams and found his daughter, Lycretia, collecting the money on the door. In the nearby family museum we admired 'the car in which my daddy died'. We paid our respects, too, at Nashville's Columbia Studios where, in 1966, Bob had recorded *Blonde on Blonde* and in a second-hand record shop in New Orleans I looked up from the browser to recognise the man facing me as Bob Johnston, producer of that Dylan masterpiece. We hit it off instantly and adjourned to a nearby bar to drink beer and talk music for the rest of the day.

In Texas, I interviewed ZZ Top across the bench seat of a space shuttle at the Lyndon B Johnson Space Museum. Although I was no great fan of the band's take on blues, Billy Gibbons and I discovered we shared a passion for the pre-war country blues variant. By the time I arrived at my next destination, a C90 cassette of early obscure recordings was waiting for me, which Gibbons had kindly compiled for me himself and sent on by courier. It is worth noting that he was, at the time, the leading member of one of the world's most in-demand groups, in the middle of a huge tour and with a gruelling publicity schedule to fill simultaneously. Nice bloke.

On the morning I landed in London from the ZZ Top trip, it was to the news that the Challenger shuttle had just blown up, killing all of its crew. Our film, made on a sister ship, naturally, had to be scrapped and I was soon back talking about old bluesmen with Billy Gibbons as we shot the interview again in the more conventional surroundings of an Atlanta hotel.

A later *Trevtour to the States* was a pilgrimage to Austin, Texas – always the hotbed of anti-establishment country music and spiritual home of Willie Nelson and the Outlaw movement. There, I found myself sitting in a coffee shop, wondering what had become of Jimmie Dale Gilmore, a Texan singer of rare purity. In the early 1970s, Jimmie had been in a band called The Flatlanders with Butch Hancock and Joe Ely. Legend had it that after just one exquisite Flatlanders album, Jimmie had drifted away from music and into Eastern mysticism.

As I lamented his loss, I was idling through a local listings magazine and turned a page to read: 'For one night only... Cactus Cafe, University of Texas, Austin, Butch Hancock and Jimmie Dale Gilmore.' Fuck me, the gig was that night, the only night I was in town. It was the stuff of dreams. Jimmie had not been back performing for long. But he was *back*.

Hank Williams wannabe. In the alley between the stage door of the Ryman Auditorium – home of the Grand Ole Opry in its heyday – and the back door of Tootsie's Orchid Lounge, Nashville, 1986. Note faded greeting: 'Welcome Opry Boys'. *Trevor Dann*

He and Butch still had true greatness. And I was well placed to do something about it, becoming that night their friend as well as unofficial unpaid agent. Within a year or so, they were on a UK tour, and the launch of those dates was a gig in the kitchen of my tiny Crouch End flat which was rammed with around a hundred pals and media notables. (I have a recording. One day, it would make a fine live album.)

ALTHOUGH THE *WHISTLE TEST* STUDIO could not match the richness of the American south for the historical context of rock & roll, some minor moments of history were made there. Quite early in my first series as a presenter I found I was interviewing on live television – and dealing with them remarkably well, I have to say – a very drunk UB40. On another show, the most unlikely person to be faultlessly charming, generous with his compliments, amusing and with whom I sparked instantly in hospitality after a Smiths performance, was Morrissey – generally assumed to be a gloomy fellow. Far from it, I thought, after a couple of room temperature Piat d'Ors.

The night the Ramones were with us the broadcast went into black-and-white for their opening number. Trevor had given the inspired order to turn off the colour for dramatic, cartoon impact. I was almost uncontrollably excited during rehearsals and as I introduced them. The forerunners of today's self-serving Health & Safety professional killjoys – BBC fun police armed with noise meters – were teeming around the studio all afternoon, mouthing complaints to Trevor over the din. Meanwhile, I was keeping a check that the amps were returned to maximum and, as they plunged into that first live number of the transmission, the Ramones were bloody loud: loud enough to blow the noise meter men into the nearest tea bar.

But perhaps my proudest moment came with my on-screen introduction to the performer and songwriter who I most admired. Elvis Costello and the Attractions had just released their *King of America* album. Elvis had brought into *Whistle Test* with him, as a motif, the crown he was pictured wearing on the album sleeve. Just before they were due to close the show with their final song, I was sitting, to deliver my last link, on the edge of the low platform, just in front of the band.

'Thanks very much for watching,' I was twittering. 'One final number from Elvis and the Attractions in just a moment... Next week...' and as I ran through the line-up for the following show, I felt something being lowered onto my skull. I cocked my head backwards. I was being crowned on live television by a smiling Elvis Costello.

THEN IN THE SPRING OF 1987, Mark Ellen, David Hepworth and I were invited by Mike Appleton, *Whistle Test* editor, to a posh Chinese restaurant on Hallam Street in central London. We sat picking at the prawn crackers, wondering what could possibly lay behind this unexpected largesse.

'I'm sorry to have to tell you,' said poor old Mike, 'that *Whistle Test* is to be scrapped.'

Butch Hancock (left) and Jimmie Dale Gilmore play their first British gig in the kitchen of my tiny flat in Elder Avenue, Crouch End, north London, 13th July 1988. Similar kitchen concerts featured Baaba Maal, cajuns DL Menard & Eddie Lejeune, and Ali Farka Toure. *AK*

Eh? Scrap *Whistle Test*? It would be like scrapping the weather forecast.

'Janet Street-Porter, who has been appointed head of Youth Programmes,' explained Mike, 'thinks *Whistle Test* has had its day.'

Absurdly, *Whistle Test* had recently been shifted into the phoney and faddish department of Youth Programmes. It had never been a programme whose audience was defined by chronology. Our viewers, we felt, were those of any age who enjoyed good music and good music-related journalism. However, Ms Street-Porter, a woman already in her forties and as desperate as the proverbial disco-dancing uncle at a wedding reception to be 'down with the kids', had made a career from this particular indignity.

'Cutting edge', a phrase much favoured at the time by evangelists of what they perceived to be youth culture, was flung around the media promiscuously although its adherents seemed incapable of defining it except in the production of instantly forgettable programmes presented by incompetent inarticulate children, who the producer had evidently met that morning on the underground. If these tedious brats spent their time on screen gibbering and running away backwards from the camera, with their baseball caps worn reversed, that was as close a definition as we would get for 'cutting edge'. It is what the rest of us recognise as 'crap'.

And Ms Street-Porter, who had already brought the nation the unlamented *Network 7* in her previous position at Channel 4, replaced the much-loved *Whistle Test* with the now long-forgotten *DEF II* – before moving on to become managing director of *L!VE TV*, an ill-fated channel which was defiantly cutting edge in its pioneering of all that was low-brow, notably topless darts, and the financial news presented by a stripper.

Bravo, Janet!

IT IS SOME MEASURE of the affection and nostalgia for *Whistle Test* that I am still asked regularly if it will ever be brought back. But it was, to all intents and purposes, many years ago, disguised as *Later With Jools Holland*, the host of which has reminded us on this *Whistle Test* derivative of all the talent for television presentation and the flair for self-effacement that he brought to *The Tube*.

The demise of *Whistle Test*, while a tragedy for quality music television, a kick in the teeth for thousands of loyal viewers, and a capricious professional scalp for the parvenue Street-Porter, did not mean the end of my infant media career. In July 1985, a safety net had opened unexpectedly to deny the danger of that free-fall. Without even trying – the only presenter in the station's history who can claim that distinction – I had become a Radio 1 DJ.

26

A BLUEBOTTLE
AT RADIO 1

I WALKED IN to find my new Radio 1 producer standing on our secretary's desk – she was on the phone – wearing a sombrero, a huge rubber ear, and playing the trumpet. Around him, in the third floor typing pool of the Nation's Favourite – unable, given the din of The Peanut Vendor, to mew to one another comparisons of train journeys to and from East Croydon – secretaries were varnishing their nails or even typing programme running orders.

Down the corridor in our office – Room 318 of Egton House, a hideous 1960s office block, next door to Broadcasting House, and the home of Radio 1 – the world's most admired broadcaster was having another anxiety attack about something trivial, opening his post, imagining he'd got cancer (again) and disappearing beneath a swelling pile of brown 12-inch cardboard mailers.

It was ten o'clock in the morning, just another day at work. But it hadn't always been like this.

There I was, happily trundling along as the hot young gunslinger of *Whistle Test*, when Trevor Dann, himself a former Radio 1 producer, was approached by an executive of the station.

'That young lad you've got doing the *Whistle Test* these days, has he ever done any radio?'

'Get together a box of your favourite records,' said Trevor, 'and we'll go into a studio and make a tape.'

If I ever had a list of those records, it is long lost. No doubt there were in there representatives of all my favourite styles from R&B to roots reggae and, I daresay, the Paisley Underground was more than quorate. But the only track I clearly recall playing was Loretta Lynn's *Don't Come Home A Drinkin' With Lovin' On Your Mind*. That the appearance of an old honky-tonk country record on my Radio 1 demo didn't alert the management into pulling up the Egton House drawbridge suggests they either regarded it as an amusing novelty number or didn't listen that far into the tape. Because their intentions soon became clear, if unspoken: I was being sounded out as a young replacement for John Peel. And one who would perhaps be persuaded to play a less coltish variety of rock than old Fatty was pumping out. Disregarding the fact that John was the most influential figure in the history of rock music in the UK – Radio 1 management had a track record of not recognising the station's assets, however meagre – by 1985 Peel had reached, my goodness me, the un-poptastic age of 45. (Yes, you're right: and I've never been able to explain the phenomenon of Jimmy Savile either...)

Trevor decided our demo had to be made out of sight and earshot of others at Radio 1. I was to be tested instead, like some secret weapon, in the relative anonymity of the studios of BBC Radio Cambridgeshire, on which Trevor himself presented a rock show at the weekends. We drove up there together one night, in early 1985. Trevor had borrowed a studio and in it we met John Leonard, a Radio 1 producer based at the BBC's regional centre in Manchester and also a popular performer on the British folk circuit. It had been John's idea, which he had voiced to Stuart Grundy, a Radio 1 executive, that I should be auditioned.

I sat in a studio and gushed between my selections about their life-enriching properties. Trevor then drove me home and John took the tape back up to Manchester to edit out all my fluffs and most of my gobbledegook before putting it in front of Radio 1 bosses.

Over the next couple of weeks, I thought little more of our clandestine caper in Cambridge. Then one morning, a fortnight or so later, as I walked into the *Whistle Test* office, Trevor looked up from his desk.

'Congratulations,' he beamed. 'You're a Radio 1 DJ.'

BETWEEN RECORDING THE DEMO and presenting for the first time my own programme on Radio 1, I had already deputised for John Peel on a couple of occasions. One of those was when John had gone to watch Liverpool Football Club play a match at the Heysel Stadium in Belgium and where he was a witness to the deaths of thirty-nine spectators. On the other, most likely, he was having one of his 24-hour nervous breakdowns for which I was yanked in at the last minute to cover while the old boy was having a bit of a lie down. More significantly, these substitutions were to be my earliest encounters with the wonderfully preposterous figure of John Walters.

My first Radio 1 programme was pre-recorded and produced, like those of my first two months for the network, by John Leonard in Manchester. It was necessarily pre-recorded because on 6 July 1985, the day it was transmitted, in the early evening of a Saturday, I was again working in Roundhay Park in Leeds, doing the same Backstage Labour Co-ordinator job for Bruce Springsteen & the E Street Band as I had done in 1982 for the Rolling Stones.

I lay on the grass outside our Portakabin office to listen to it and, from what I heard through the roar of fork-lift trucks and the testing of Springsteen's PA, I was quite pleased with my efforts. The job in hand, however, denied any celebrations and I was preoccupied with the immense gig taking place the day after.

John Leonard and I carried on making these agreeable little programmes out of Manchester for another few weeks, largely unnoticed it seemed both by audiences and critics. I liked John very much. He too had very broad tastes and grasped, even before he put me on the air, that the AK catholicism and enthusiasm – as opposed to a narrow musical tribalism and any self-conscious regard for what may be considered cool – was a strength not a weakness.

I would have been more than happy to work with John indefinitely and hoped I might do so until the afternoon I drove over the M62, following one of our recordings in Manchester, to stay overnight with Our Elizabeth, who was still living at the Shire Oak Road flat in Leeds. Elizabeth was out when I let myself in. But on the telephone table in the hall, she'd left a message scribbled on a blue Post-It note. 'Stuart Grundy of Radio 1 phoned,' it read. 'You are being sent to John Walters.'

THOSE SUBSTITUTIONS for Peel had already steeled me for the state of the office and prepared me to cope with Walters. Over the fifteen years I was a Radio 1 DJ the question I was asked most frequently about the producer I shared with John Peel was routinely prefaced with the questioner's own analysis: 'So, you and Peel both choose your own records. And the session artists. So... what exactly does John Walters do for your programmes?'

My stock answer was to say 'I don't know.' It was just too tricky to attempt to explain, to someone who in their line of work had not enjoyed the benefits of their boss bellowing Ethel Merman impressions up the corporate stairwell, the incalculable contribution that this – or one of Walters' hour-long monologues concerning the weekend antics of Algy, his homosexual cockerel, made to general job satisfaction around the Radio 1 building. It was even harder, for the illumination of outsiders, and as an asset to life in the world's most admired broadcasting organisation, to quantify. Walters, I explained to myself, very early on, was employed by the BBC – although they didn't know it – to be Walters. And that contribution was immense.

To best understand, perhaps, the value of Walters, my own experience speaks volumes. I would go down into central London, even on days on which I had no programme to prepare for Radio 1, simply to sit in the office with Walters. Facing each other across the old desk and the heaps of detritus, we'd chew the fat, sort out the world and, as his protégé, I would bathe in

Walters takes charge. A very rare appearance by my producer, in the Radio 1 studios, during a programme. Minutes before my first live Radio 1 broadcast, in 1985, and after taking me for a pizza, Walters went home. *Unknown*

his wisdom and wit. Walters needed an audience. I was delighted to provide one. And if Peel wasn't in a sulk with his old friend, he was usually there too, chucking droll pebbles into the Walters flow.

Walters made it great fun to go to work. And, in my own case, the work was enriched by those days spent hanging around the office, playing through new releases, dissecting with Walters popular culture and social history, deciding which artists should be booked for sessions and getting the post answered. Simultaneously, Walters – like those early TV variety show performers who could spin a number of plates on the ends of wobbly poles – kept a dozen or more tales running while fielding phone calls and brushing aside irritably the appearances at the door of Room 318 of oily record company pluggers and twitching Radio 1 managers.

'What has it been like,' Walters was asked by Gillian Reynolds, venerable radio critic of the *Daily Telegraph*, soon after my arrival in Room 318, 'after all the years of just you and Peel, now to have Andy with you as well?'

'It's as though someone walked in and let a bluebottle out of a jar,' said Walters.

To another writer, he modified this analysis.

'It was as if an elderly couple,' he reflected, 'in the twilight of their lives, armchairs on either side of the hearth, suddenly and against all medical probability, had a child.'

From where the child stood – or, rather, sat, on an upturned steel waste-paper basket because there was no third chair, nor any room for one in 318 – I saw my new parents played by a couple of pantomime dames – the Hinge and Bracket of Radio 1.

Another observer drew a strikingly accurate literary analogy, identifying Room 318 as a reflection of *The House at Pooh Corner*.

'Walters,' they said, 'is Pooh Bear because he is rather tubby, lugubrious, world weary and a bit pompous. Peel is Eeyore, full of self-pity and miserable, but happiest being so, especially when he's standing in the corner of his field in the drizzle and there are no thistles left to eat. Janice [our programme secretary at the time] is Piglet because, like Piglet, she is tiny, nervous, pink and she squeaks. And Andy, with boundless energy, leaping around a lot, trying to lick your face, is Tigger.'

But, even as a bit of an AA Milne student myself, I do not recall – try as I might – Christopher Robin's house being filled to bursting point with shite. And if you will bear with me, I will now go and compose myself for five minutes with a cup of coffee, a cigarette and a walk around the back yard before we embark – many years after it was bulldozed, although the horror of it refuses to die – on a guided tour of Room 318...

27

IN WHICH ROOM 318 IS RULED A RADIO 1 FIRE HAZARD

NEVER MIND THOSE of our Radio 1 colleagues we regarded with ridicule and contempt, even for us – the three occupants of Room 318 – gaining entry to the office could be a hit and miss endeavour. Putting one's weight firmly against the door, resistance was always to be expected from a bulging accumulation of jackets and coats hung on the inside. None of these actually belonged to me, Walters or Peel. They had been abandoned there long ago by visitors who, I assumed, had left either in haste or in a state of bewilderment. These were reinforced by a number of Peel's tatty pullovers which he always defended as 'comfortable.'

'From time to time we boil one up and it makes a very nourishing soup,' I once overheard him tell someone who remarked on a dress sense that in later years often had me mistake him in the street for a *Big Issue* sales executive.

Pushing open the door against our spongy autumn collection yielded enough room even for Walters and Peel – each addressed the other as 'Tubs' – to ease their way in without lubrication. Should there also have piled up behind the door several weeks of unopened Jiffy bags, containing John's latest unlistenable demo tapes, then several shoves usually snowploughed the unsolicited horrors tightly into the corner beside one of the many filing cabinets. (In thirteen years in Room 318, six of those with Walters at the helm, I never once saw anyone file away or retrieve anything from these. I have no idea what was in them.)

Those entering the room by this technique were thereby presented with the opportunity to twist an ankle by putting a foot straight into the bin – or The Boy Kershaw's seat, as it also was – once righted and returned to the function for which it was designed.

The fearless explorer was then confronted by a scene of utter devastation. A big old oak table sat in the middle of the room which itself was only about nine by twelve feet. It is not uncommon for the desks of some people to be described as 'untidy' or 'piled with paperwork'. It was, however, the norm for Walters' desk – for it was his and certainly not mine nor John's desk – to resemble a scale model of the Matterhorn, fashioned from unopened post, cardboard mailers, tape boxes containing unarchived sessions both valuable and regrettable, newspapers, back copies of *New Statesman* and *Private Eye*, items of clothing and footwear, the trumpet, the sombrero, the rubber ear, teetering piles of singles, record company promotional flotsam, bottles of booze (again, major label largesse from Christmases past) and any other ephemera Walters had happened to amass that week.

In his drawer ('Don't go in *there*!') for years was a partly-smoked packet of ten Benson & Hedges and a copy of *Spick & Span*, a publication considered dangerously erotic, if not pornographic, in the 1950s, displaying – as it often did – black-and-white photos of, perhaps, a tightly-bloused librarian on a step ladder, reaching for an upper shelf while cocking an arousing ankle.

The floor was similarly adorned. A thin, grubby, green carpet was sometimes visible when Peel, occasionally overcome with guilt at the quantity of neglected demo tapes, would shovel a couple of hundred of them into a garden refuse sack, put them into the boot of his car and drive them out to Peel Acres in Suffolk where they would be transferred to a sea container, which, John claimed, he'd buried in the garden, as an underground demos vault.

Against the left wall, after breaking and entering, was a record player, a cassette machine and a reel to reel tape deck. Next to that was a chair, Peel's seat – also mine when he wasn't around or when it was my turn to listen to records. Over on the far side, sometimes visible over the detritus on the desk, and below a length of dirty string from which hung at least five years of Christmas cards, sat Walters with his back to the window. This gave us an uninterrupted view of a brick wall belonging to All Soul's Church. The windowsill, being a flat surface, was also piled with clutter. It was on here that Walters once filed all the entries, sent in by listeners, to some BB King competition I had held on my programme. One hot summer afternoon, just before I was to announce the result, he decided on impulse to open the

The occupants of Room 318. Walters, me and Peel at some BBC function, 1990. *BBC*

window and, within a heartbeat, we were both standing silently watching all the entries flutter away down Portland Place towards Oxford Circus.

'Ah, well. Never mind,' sighed Walters. 'You'll just have to make up the name of the winner.'

It was from this office, it is worth noting, that the most important and influential radio programme in the history of rock music was – somehow – produced.

'MR WALTERS?' A stern-looking middle-aged gent had put his head round the door without knocking. I was already at the record player, going through new releases. He had a clipboard.

'No,' I said. 'He's not in yet. Doesn't usually get in until ten.'

'Please see he gets this,' snapped the intruder and, with a flourish, yanked a sheet from his clipboard and waved it in front of me. I took it.

It was a final notice from some arcane BBC regulatory body with responsibility for fire hazards and for upholding the Health and Safety at Work Act around the corporation's many premises. Room 318, it said, was a fire risk endangering the whole of the Radio 1 building.

'Good news for music fans, then,' I quipped.

'Is it always like this?' asked the inspector.

'It gets sightseers,' I said. 'A Taiwanese coach party last week.'

To support his attempt fully to gain entry, he extended an arm towards some shelves.

'No!' I yelled. 'Don't touch anything, for heaven's sakes! The lot could go over at once.'

He jumped back.

'And Walters says he knows just where everything is,' I explained, catching my breath. 'He has a system, you see.'

The man, still with only his torso into the room, gaped.

'*You* think it's bad,' I continued. 'You ought to try working in here.'

'Yes, yes,' he murmured.

'I tell you what,' I said. 'Why don't you and I just have it bricked up? Before he gets in.'

After he'd gone, I put the final notice on Walters' desk where, naturally, it went ignored before disappearing beneath shifting tectonic plates of vinyl and fresh alluvial deposits of demos. The inspector fellow was never seen again.

'I DON'T KNOW ABOUT YOU...' began Walters, eyeing his watch.

I knew what was coming.

'...but I might just stroll around the corner. Glass of wine, piece of cheese.'

He would never say, 'Shall we go to the pub?' Going for a drink would be presented, although a daily ritual, as if it was a spontaneous, only half-formed idea for an activity we had never before undertaken. I have no idea why. (Just as I have no idea to this day why all of our secretaries had to be renamed as males. Many listeners will recall Peel's grateful references on air to Our Brian who was, in fact, a most capable woman called, not unreasonably, Sue Foster.) Within ten minutes the three of us would be tucking into a substantial lunch at a local wine bar, a nearby pub or the BBC Club.

That 'glass of wine' would, on some days, extend to a couple of bottles or more. And our consumption, by the standards of the Radio 1 drinking culture in those days, was nothing remarkable. We were, in fact, at the sober end of the spectrum. There were some Radio 1 producers who would come into work at 10.30am and be collected by a record company plugger to be taken for lunch by 12 noon. If they were back in their offices by 4pm, that was noteworthy and they would be in a state then suited only to programming the same familiar handful of 'golden oldies' for the following day's show before tottering back to the pub for five o'clock.

Later, after his retirement, and on his trips from his home in Surrey 'up to town' to bother me and Peel (he had nothing better to do), during which he'd behave as if he was still in charge, Walters would lament the changes he'd noticed the conspiring evils of Birtism and yuppiedom had brought down on the BBC: 'I walk in here these days,' he once blustered, 'and the place is overrun with children, *reeking* of Perrier.'

These post-retirement visits became the highlight of my week. I suspect they were also eagerly anticipated back at home by

Helen, Walters' wife, 'surely,' according to Peel, 'a candidate for canonisation.'

Showing cavalier disregard for medical advice – no one knew better than Walters, certainly not doctors – he did not let his diabetes get in the way of his sense of fun. Leaving a record company party together late one night, I noticed there was something odd about his appearance and gait. He seemed to be doing an impression of Frankenstein, with his arms held high and hanging in a forward position. Clearly, he had not noticed anything untoward himself, delivering, as usual, an unstoppable monologue. There was also something strange soaring up, two or three feet, from his shoulders. Under the next street light, I got a better look: he'd put his raincoat on upside down.

On another occasion, he was so busy talking to someone at the cloakroom of a club, he pulled on – and set off for home wearing – not one but three jackets, two of which were not his.

WALTERS, ALTHOUGH a consummate performer under all circumstances, was a supreme pubs man. It is one of the many tragedies of his premature death in 2001 that no fellow radio producer had the imagination to make a series of Walters programmes simply by clipping a microphone on his lapel in licensed premises and rolling a tape as his monologues and the dry white flowed. A thousand sardonic observations were uttered just the once and never recorded. A few survive hazy, unreliable memory. Twentieth century society, he decided unforgettably, during one of our 'walks around the corner', could be divided into two epochs: 'pre and post avocado.'

He was particularly good at bringing colour to that most drab and overlooked decade, the 1950s, and seemed genuinely nostalgic for the simplicities, austerity and imperilled innocence of those years. He would chuckle as he recalled that, as an art student in Newcastle, it was possible to seduce a young lady by revealing that one had something as wildly bohemian and exotic as a jar of instant coffee back at one's digs.

And I never tired of his tales of being guardian and gate-keeper to Peel ('a minor princeling of hippiedom') during the early years of Radio 1, in the late 1960s, casting himself, authentically, as a rather sceptical and bemused witness to a lot of dope-infused nonsense, dismissive in particular – and most witheringly – of the dreamy Aquarian age affectations of his young charge.

'I think the point at which I thought enough's enough was when Peel was closing an edition of *Top Gear* and in the control room I heard him say on the air, "Well, everyone, thank you for listening. I'm now going to go and watch clouds paint poems in the sky over Regent's Park." I stuck my finger on the talk-back button and said, "Oh, for fuck's sakes, cut that out!" He was also, of course, writing a lot of middle-earth drivel at the time for something called *Gandalf's Garden*. Punk *had* to happen after that.'

Indeed, it was Walters before Peel who spotted the cultural significance of punk, was first excited by its revolutionary potential and momentum, attended first the early gigs and encouraged the other Tubs to run with it on his radio programmes.

WALTERS, LIKE PEEL in his later incarnations, revelled in being a square peg in the music business round hole. And his capacity to send himself up was best revealed with the tale of producer and presenter attending Cream's farewell concert at the Royal Albert Hall in 1968:

'A couple of weeks before the gig, Peel and I were in the Speakeasy club and Jack Bruce came over. "Are you coming to our farewell concert?" he asked. "I should think so," I said. "Great," said Jack. "You'll probably want to take these..." And into my palm he dropped these little pink pills, four of them. Now, as you know, I've never been much of a drugs type, but I took them home nevertheless and put them on the mantelpiece. Every now and then, in the run-up to the concert, I'd go over to them, pick them up, have a close look, sniff them, roll them round in my fingers and put them back. Then I forgot all about them. The missus was dusting round them for months. Well, about five years later, I saw Jack Bruce again at some other music business party. "Did you and John come to our farewell gig in the end?" he asked. "Oh, yes," I said, "and very much enjoyed it. Thank you." "Well, I hope you took those things I gave you," said Jack. "Hmm, no," I said. "Course not. Ha, ha! You know Peel and I aren't big enthusiasts for drugs." "Drugs?" said Jack. "Drugs? They were earplugs".'

Walters' incessant outpouring of anecdote, home-brewed philosophy and random musings was a nightmare on those occasions when I was about to go on some foreign adventure and, in preparation, for a whole day beforehand Walters and I would be together in the studio, pre-recording two or three weeks of Kershaw programmes. Blithely oblivious to my need to concentrate, Walters, through the glass, sitting with the sound engineer, would keep his finger jammed pretty much permanently on the talk-back button to bring me – while I was ostensibly addressing the nation – the farcical minute by minute

'As I say, as I say...' Walters, unstoppable as ever, at a barbecue at his home in Oxted, 1988. I seem to have devised a coping mechanism. *Elizabeth Kershaw*

details of, perhaps, a visit he had endured the previous weekend by his Aunty Doris from Newcastle.

On one such foreign trip, some pals flew out to join me in Mali. 'Crikey,' they said when they arrived. 'You should have heard your programme go out last week. It was full of mistakes and retakes.' Walters, if he'd noticed during the recording that editing would be needed before broadcast (and it's likely he didn't), had forgotten to tidy up the tapes in his haste to get us all out of the studio and into the pub.

And on those licensed premises, it was striking that Walters' most eager admirers were always women who, despite his overt chauvinism and a tendency to categorise all females as 'girlies', gathered in packs to dimple adoringly at his hilarious stories and easy charm.

Walters the radio producer, the raconteur and the great broadcaster in his own right was always, in truth, what he had been long before he infiltrated Broadcasting House and before he had been trumpet player in the Alan Price Set in the 1960s. ('I spent most of the decade just going, "Parp-parp, a diddle-it"'.) Professionally, he'd first been an art teacher in Newcastle and, simply swapping the schoolroom for the radio studio, he remained a teacher. But he was, magically, one of those teachers so gifted that his pupils – in the uproar that was his classroom – did not realise they were learning.

'I told them *again*,' he harrumphed to us, having just come downstairs to 318 from a Radio 1 management meeting where he had performed once more as our fearless protector. Peel and I blinked at him in silence from across the table. Evidently the suits had been grumbling, as usual, that Peel was broadcasting a frightful old racket four nights a week and The Boy Kershaw was playing too much music from Bongo Bongo Land.

'I said to them: *We're not here to give the public what it wants. We're here to give the public what it didn't know it wanted.* Anyway, that was the end of that. Right, on we go...'

I have not heard anywhere a better definition of the BBC's role as a public service broadcaster than this. And I don't think there is one.

Over the years, I have often found myself telling people that

I am the luckiest person I have ever met, stumbling – so it has felt – from one accidental success into another moment of huge good fortune. In that process, the one aspect of my broadcasting career about which I feel luckiest was to have been posted, within weeks of being recruited by Radio 1, to Room 318 to work with John Peel and John Walters.

What better induction could I have had into BBC radio and public service broadcasting? What better teachers?

CAPTIVATED BY
A CONTINENT

'YOU'RE THE ONE who plays all that weird stuff, aren't you?' was the manner in which, frequently, I was greeted and identified during my residence on the Radio 1 airwaves.

The equivalent would be if I were to say to someone to whom I had just been introduced, 'Nominated for the Turner Prize, eh? For how long have you been a talentless fraud and a phoney?'

And this assessment often came, surprisingly, from educated and otherwise sophisticated people.

'Some of these groups that you play on your programme, have got rather funny names, haven't they?' observed the presenter of a Radio 4 chat show, smirking around the table at the other guests, when I appeared on it in the late 1980s.

For me, this type of reaction to my musical enthusiasms became a reliable badge of the dickhead, and of a parochialism best not advertised.

'It's not considered weird, and the names aren't thought to be funny, where it's made,' I'd point out politely.

If the hostility persisted, I'd mention that those making this 'weird stuff' have a similar view, where they're standing, of UK music and find 'weird' the phenomenon of, let us say, Simple Minds.

I have not singled out the Scottish stadium rockers here just because singer, Jim Kerr, for a while told anyone who would listen that he was 'going to kill Andy Kershaw'. Jim's intent to murder was, to be fair, in the interests of balance – to correct remarks I made about the band on *Whistle Test*. Memory is unreliable, but I'd possibly expressed my view, on national television, that hearing a Simple Minds record always gave me the feeling that someone had left a window open. Or did I categorise their histrionic output as pomp rock (like that of U2) for people who didn't honestly like rock music and certainly wouldn't like, nor would recognise, the authentic and righteous stuff even if it were to jump up and rip off their ears?

Whichever it was, young Jim and his chums – like Bono and his – found a niche with late 1980s yuppies who, having acquired the semi-detached and the new car, both equipped with these advanced CD player thingies, then realised they didn't have any music to play on them. Moreover, it dawned on these poor lambs that their non-ownership of any music was because they didn't actually like music, didn't have any previous appetite for it and now hadn't a clue what to buy.

Into this void raced the commandos of lifestyle marketing and before the decade was out we had a whole generation buying up, in their millions, albums by Simple Minds, U2 and Queen (for driving the VW Golf), Sting, Phil Collins, the MOR variant of Eric Clapton, Simply Red, Alison Moyet and Hall & Oates (for after the consumption of a Sainsbury's ready-meal in front of *Dynasty*) and Sade (once they brought the Bailey's out). This, with the addition of *Thriller* and a Dire Straits album or two, was the extent of nearly everyone's record collection at the time.

It was the sheer tedium and mediocrity of these artists, their suffocating tyranny over popular tastes, their smug assumption of a position of rock aristocracy, helped by the consensus of a mesmerised media which hadn't the imagination to look elsewhere, and the simultaneous absorption into the mainstream of any remnants of post-punk individuality that had me boost my audio radar to scan the horizons for something stimulating, something imaginative, something fresh. What I found was later explained by Joe Boyd as 'new sounds for a bored culture'. And to a large extent, it was my boredom, and the self-satisfaction of Anglo-American rock and pop in the mid 1980s, which created and necessitated the category of world music.

I HAD BEEN HIRED by Radio 1 as a rock DJ. But within just a few months it became clear to the management that the young face of rock music from the *Whistle Test* had found his radio voice with an internationalism they had not anticipated.

Neither had I, for that matter. When I joined Radio 1, I had no knowledge of, nor any particular interest in, music from other countries, except for Jamaican reggae and American rock and roots styles. The African music of which I was aware at the time, I didn't particularly like, usually that by long-winded Nigerians or Francophone releases given production and marketing gloss in Paris as lifestyle accessories for coffee-table display.

A further deterrent was an attitude among certain elements of the African music cognoscenti that one must not trifle with this stuff, that it had to be solemnly received and that expert knowledge was a prerequisite to listening to it. It was as though many enthusiasts did not want the music to gain a wider audience, preferring to keep it to themselves in a spirit of cultural one-upmanship if not brow-furrowing, humourless academia. Bugger that.

I saw the light with the earliest releases from a couple of British labels, Globestyle and Earthworks, particularly the latter's compilations of South African township jive and Zimbabwean guitar-driven pop. These revealed the music for what it was: pop music and dance music but that of a different hemisphere. It was – bloody hell – exciting and fun. And I began to play it, mixed in with everything else.

Those other elements I harvested from American styles both contemporary and historic: country, cajun, blues, R&B, zydeco, Tex-Mex and vintage gospel. I wasn't shy of introducing the best British folk music into the mix, which, perhaps due to an image problem, had been disregarded even by Peel since the 1970s and I topped it off with what little stimulating contemporary rock I could find, and the more imaginative and enlightened new rap and reggae releases.

My Radio 1 show was, to a large extent, an expansion and an amplification of those components I enjoyed most of the Peel programmes, when John relaxed for a few minutes and played, for example, some old blues or country record which he might introduce with a tale of his misadventures in the Texas of his late teens. I wasn't tight-arsed either about revisiting the best rock music from previous periods. John may have felt queasy about banging out regularly a wonderful old Little Feat or Neil Young track (artists he still loved privately) when his priority was to play the new, for novelty's sake, or for what the equally absurd consensus of 'alternative' demanded.

That anxiety didn't trouble me. I took the view that if John had not occasionally played Little Feat and Neil Young – or

Putting together my Radio 1 programme, on my bed, Elder Avenue, 1991. Note poster for Haiti presidential inauguration, map of Middle East and 10,000 Maniacs T-shirt. *Mark Begovich*

Elmore James or George Jones or whoever – when I was listening as a youth (and beyond), I would not have had the opportunity to hear and enjoy them. The current generation should also have, I thought, that enjoyment, that illumination and historical perspective. The past was just too rich to ignore, especially during a depressingly barren rock present. If I was shouting 'Yes!' at home when John allowed himself a little occasional audio archaeology, so, I figured, were many other listeners. Why, then, didn't he do it more frequently? When I got the chance, I just got on with it.

THE POSITION JOHN occupied at the time, while sharing with me a hostility to the smug rock mainstream consensus, seemed to me little more valid, musically, than that of the enemy. Much of what John was playing, although making an admirable two-fingered gesture to conformity, was actually just as unlistenable.

I had, perversely, an advantage over John in that I had only two hours a week on air (and in all my time on Radio 1, I never had nor asked for any more) while he had eight. That meant there was no need nor room for fat or filler in my weekly show. And I had the time – not available to John with his four programmes a week to assemble – to take extra care over compiling my single show. In other words, it was the records or tracks that I had the luxury of rejecting for my programmes that guaranteed the consistent excellence of the music.

The mechanism of putting together a programme was no science and certainly it was not an art. If I were able to listen as thoroughly to new releases as I liked to do, between shopping expeditions around the specialist stores and by burrowing back into my own collection, then to assemble that two hour programme took four days. Listening to music carefully is not a process that can be shortened. It was hard work, going through piles of often dreary new albums, from morning until late at night, until some small bright nuggets were panned from the pebbles. Dope-smoking helped considerably. Mild marijuana not only enhanced my reception but working dope's stimulation of tangential thought inspired endless musical connections and ideas. I would get immense satisfaction from putting together a sequence of tracks, each one possibly in a different musical style, but with some kind of relationship, especially if the listeners, when I pulled it off on the air, couldn't spot the joins (or the joints) in between.

Seated at my desk or cross-legged on my bed, I'd have a Manhattan of new releases spread around me and a pad of A4 and a pen. As I found tracks worthy of inclusion, these would be timed and added to what I called my master list. This could run to three or four pages. From that, when I thought I had sufficient to put together a colourful programme, I would hand-write the running order of the show, carefully sequencing the tracks so that one thing either led beautifully into another, or to give the listener a jolting sense of surprise. (A real strength of John Peel's programmes, at their best, was never to be able to anticipate, as a listener, what might be coming next.)

The most important track in the whole programme was the opener, which I would never introduce first. On its own, it announced the show and with that in mind, it had to be arresting. When, for example, I carried back from Barbados to London a copy of Grynner's *Get Out De Way*, the triumphant calypso of the island's Cropover carnival of 1990, I fantasised, straining as I was to get on the air and play it, that when it kicked off my next programme, thousands of people, up and down the country, would be asking themselves, 'What's this? It's unbelievable! Where can I get a copy?' My mail over the following week or two suggested that was the case.

Equally, when my old chum Dave Woodhead came back from Nashville in 1986 with an obscure 45 he'd picked up in Ernest Tubb's records – *Harlan County* by Jim Ford – I was in a state of agitation for days, anticipating how dramatic this obscure masterpiece of impassioned southern soul, a cry of despair conveyed through a kitchen-sink production, was going to sound when I let it fly without warning at the top of the next show. The letters flooded in: *Harlan County* finally found its fans, seventeen years after Jim Ford recorded it. Opening the post from the new *Harlan County* converts was as if to uncork a collective sigh of surprise and satisfaction.

Throughout my time on Radio 1, and thereafter on Radio 3,

I never forgot, when putting together my programmes, one piece of advice Trevor Dann gave me when I started. 'Always,' he said, 'lead them by the hand.' No matter how unfamiliar or obscure the music is that you are going to play, ran Trevor's wisdom, it was possible to carry the listeners with you if they were lured by a bit of the familiar in the mix and if you could convince them, simultaneously, that they would like the unfamiliar. He was dead right.

I could not in any case have presented a show that was specialist to the point of being a programme of just one style of music. What listeners got from me was, simply, a reflection and a summary of what I had been enjoying that week at home. And, like many people – although this is never grasped by narrowcasters, as opposed to broadcasters – I tend to pull from the shelves an assortment of different types of music when I am either enjoying a few things alone or playing music for friends. In essence, the latter activity, on the air rather than round the kitchen table, *is* my radio show.

COINCIDING WITH THE SHIFT of my own tastes, soon after joining Radio 1, the activities of other agitators and pioneers was reaching a small critical mass. Peter Gabriel had long before gone public with his own internationalism, most publicly expressed through the increasingly popular WOMAD Festival. In 1986, Paul Simon, with his *Graceland* album, had brought South African township jive and the harmonies of Ladysmith Black Mambazo into the most conservative record collections. *Folk Roots* magazine was expanding its own horizons to feature music from all over the world. More and more small British record companies – Joe Boyd's own Hannibal label, for example – were releasing revelatory albums from overseas artists. Charlie Gillett, with Oval Records, had already been doing that for years, while hosting a programme on local BBC Radio London which had trailblazed African music long before I tumbled into doing it on the radio nationally.

With a momentum building – and now with a programme sympathetic to those tastes on a national BBC pop station – a few of these labels got together for a meeting in a room above a pub in Islington, in June 1987, and came up with the term 'world music', chiefly to help record shops categorise, market and display non Anglo-American albums. These could be as varied as rousing Bulgarian sheet-metal workers' choral ensembles or unsung guitar heroes from Guinea Bissau.

Charlie Gillett turned up one morning at Room 318, in my earliest days at Radio 1. He was an old friend and ally of Peel and Walters. I was meeting him for the first time.

'You've never been to Stern's?' he said, referring to the African record shop over on Whitfield Street, just a ten-minute stroll from Broadcasting House. Like a kindly old uncle, he walked me over there and introduced me to all the staff. They were equally lovely and helpful. Soon I was spending much of my income over the Stern's counter on African imports, mainly from Paris, the capital of the African music industry. It was a turning point for my programme.

So was meeting Lucy Duran. Now a fellow Radio 3 presenter, then working at the Commonwealth Institute, Lucy was more than an academic and musicologist. She was a fan – of west African music in particular – and her enthusiasm was contagious. She also happened to be a fabulous and tireless hostess. At Lucy's Camden home I was soon being invited to very informal soirées at which she would cook wonderful west African food and have play in her living room whichever notable African musicians were passing through London. Slumped on one of Lucy's sofas, surrounded by sparkling companions, I have been lucky enough to be personally entertained by, among others, Youssou N'Dour and the Malian kora maestro, Toumani Diabate.

But it was two specific events which tipped me irretrievably into an obsession with Africa. The first came on an otherwise unremarkable day in Room 318.

Peel and I were sitting in our positions, opening our post, mainly drab cardboard mailers containing drab new LPs. But we'd both been sent, we noticed, a yellow and white 12-inch EP, on Discafrique, a label then unknown to us, by a group from Zimbabwe called the Bhundu Boys. John put it on.

Suddenly, it was as if the room was being sprayed with a

fountain of jewelled guitar notes. Then the whole band kicked in. It bounced. It chimed. It popped. The melodies and harmonies instantly lifted and brightened the spirits. The guitars wound around each other, capturing and tossing back and forth the prettiest of tunes, yet always engaging with sublime simplicity. Peel and I looked at each other, frozen and open-mouthed. For the duration of the first song, neither of us said a word. By the end, I was grinning. John had put his hands over his face in what I took to be disbelief.

'What the fuck is *this*?' I said. 'Who are *these* guys?'

When finally he spoke, the gist of what John said – I wasn't taking notes – was that he'd presumed these moments didn't happen any more. The Bhundus EP became the Room 318 Record of the Week for the next few months.

THE BHUNDUS' FIRST UK GIG – or the first one we could get to – was at a college in Chelsea. It was modestly attended. Peel and I stood in the body of the hall. Five blokes plodded on and plugged in. The singer, a beaming round-faced chap, wearing a straw boater, ululated his soon-to-be familiar call-sign, the lead guitar chimed in and we were off. The first couple of numbers were just delightful but then I witnessed an extraordinary consolidation, which I would see again and again, always during the third song, at dozens of Bhundus gigs. Something between audience and band clicked and was sealed on that third number, but the song needn't necessarily be the same as at previous gigs. Nevertheless, the room as a whole, audience and structure, seemed to lift as one and bounce to the Bhundus' beat. Band and crowd were united, performers and participants together.

I have never seen a bond like it. And I have never seen at any other gig such instant happiness brought on by a group. A Bhundus gig was a shared, joyous experience. And like those who are truly great in any field – guerrilla warfare, motorcycle racing, diplomacy, cake decoration, tax avoidance – the Bhundus pulled it off so effortlessly.

By the end, everyone in the hall was in a state of delirium, not least the band members who looked astonished by the reception. I turned to check on Peel. Fat tears were rolling down fat cheeks, as he blinked at the stage. A music obsessive of almost forty years, a first generation veteran of the rock & roll cultural earthquake, John did not expect to be so moved by music again in his life. But here was something new under the sun. I dragged him, in a trance, backstage.

There we met a most unassuming bunch of Zimbabwean lads, the cheery front man of which introduced himself as Biggie Tembo. Immediately, I adored him. Biggie was always grinning and giggling. And he seemed to take an instant shine to me. We were to become the best of friends. Phone numbers were swapped. The Bhundus were basing themselves in London for a few months. When was the next gig? I would be there.

As it turned out, I was there for as many Bhundus shows as I could get to. It soon became obvious that they were surviving, from digs in Kensal Green, on very little money. I noticed, too, at one gig, that when Rise Kagona, the lead guitarist, broke a string there was no back-up guitar.

'Ah, comrade, comrade,' said Biggie sheepishly when I asked him about this, 'we do not have a spare guitar.'

Earlier in the year, Chuck Prophet of Green On Red had presented me with one of his Fender Telecasters as a thank-you for all I'd done as an evangelist for the band. I arrived at the next Bhundus gig with it in my hand, to loan it to them. And I stepped in, very happily, as their guitar roadie for that performance and all others I managed to attend subsequently.

Meanwhile listeners' letters to the Peel and Kershaw programmes indicated something was going on and that John and I had not lost our marbles over these five lads from Harare. The Bhundus had achieved that rare, and at the time, unique breakthrough – an African band, in their case singing in Shona, reaching and delighting those who didn't think they liked African music and didn't comprehend a word of the songs. It didn't matter. Even my mother was won over by the Bhundus.

Their ability to bridge those cultural divides confirmed for me what I'd suspected all along about thrilling non mainstream music in general and of outstanding African music in particular: that all that was needed was for people to have the opportunity to hear it, possibly having been led there by the hand, and many would like it. With the evidence of the Bhundus working their magic on my mum, I had the mission of my programmes justified and sealed. It boiled down to audience access to this music and, to the extent that I could bring it about with one programme a week, my demystification of it.

Radio 1, within a year of hiring me to present a rock show, had got itself, without asking for one, what was acclaimed as a world music programme. By accident and stealth.

'IF YOU CARRY ON as you are,' warned Trevor Dann, in a moment of uncharacteristic misjudgement, 'you won't last six months on Radio 1.' For once, I ignored his advice.

Trevor had reckoned without the enthusiasm among many listeners for the music I was playing, the delight and support of the critics and the robust defence of the programme's philosophy, internally, by Walters.

At the 1987 Sony Radio Awards, in recognition of my first full year of broadcasting on Radio 1, I won Best Specialist Music Programme. (Given my aversion to the suit, I allowed Walters to suggest my attire for the ceremony. And so it was that I found myself on stage dressed, to everyone's bewilderment, including mine, as a cowboy, and one being snogged by the gorgeous, pouting actress, Rula Lenska – who, for some reason, was presenting my trophy.)

I have, for the record, never used the term 'world music' and I don't recognise it as a generic category beyond its usefulness to record labels and shops who, admirably, release and sell a huge variety of styles from around the world. To me, Sardinian polyphony or Algerian rai, for argument's sake, are not components of 'world music' but examples of Sardinian and Algerian music. That geographical identification does not, when all's said and done, demand much effort. When I am occasionally pressed to categorise my programmes these days for Radio 3, and after I have rejected the world music label, pointing out that I still play much American and British stuff, I have to say the programme is about good music, from wherever it comes.

* * *

MY ROMANCE WITH a continent was consummated by a second life-changing event of that first year or so on Radio 1. Lucy Duran organised every December a music trip to the Gambia where she had once lived and was still good friends with the kora virtuosos Dembo Konte and Kausu Kouyate. For months, throughout 1986, Lucy had been trying to persuade me to join her Gambia-bound party that Christmas. But like many people who have never set foot in Africa, I was a bit nervous of going.

About a week before Lucy was due to depart, I was lying on my bed in a Nashville hotel room, about to complete a filming assignment for *Whistle Test* and recovering from the shock of having just seen Kenny Rogers at the adjacent breakfast table. The phone rang. It was Lucy in London, making one last pitch to press-gang me into the Gambian caper. This time, I agreed.

The tour group was departing a couple of days before I was to return to the UK. I would have to follow on alone and, because of flight complications, get there via Dakar, in neighbouring Senegal. There wasn't time even for me to call in at home after landing in London. Our Elizabeth came out to Heathrow to meet me from the States with a bag of clean clothes and the necessary equipment and medicines. She took home my washing and I boarded a plane for Paris and then on to Dakar. There I would have to stay overnight to catch a connection the following morning to Banjul, Gambia.

While my apprehension about Africa hadn't fully persuaded me that I would be eaten by a lion upon landing, I did take the precaution against the certainty, as I saw it, of dysentery, by swallowing half my supply of Immodium tablets on the flight down to Dakar. The next time I went to the toilet, I was back in Crouch End – fully a fortnight later.

It would be an understatement to say it was love at first sight when the passenger door was opened on Senegal. That does not do justice to the overload on all the senses and, in any case, it was dark. The fragrance of Africa got me first, a comforting blend of wood smoke, damp vegetation, paraffin lamps, sweat, sewage and cooking aromas. In one whiff, all human life was there.

For reasons I did not wish to discover, the arrivals area at Dakar airport was in uproar, a state of civil unrest. As soon as I got through, I fell into the care of the first man who said 'Taxi?' and after I'd bump-started his car we rattled off towards town. When my passenger door fell off, the driver didn't flinch but pulled over without a word, got out, picked it up from the middle of the road, wearily threw it in the boot and we continued, with me clinging to the door frame. That night, I ended up sharing, unintentionally, a double bed with the one-eyed elderly male owner of the guest house I had booked (on Charlie Gillett's recommendation) and left for the airport again the following morning. There I was parted from almost all of my money and I arrived at Banjul, to be met by Lucy, penniless, exhausted and bewildered. That was Africa, Day One.

From then on, with Lucy's protection and guidance, I thought I'd found heaven. After one night in the hotel booked for Lucy's party I moved out, and moved in, at Dembo's invitation, to his home and the compound of his extended family in the nearby

Teaching the kids of Segou, Mali, how to play Frisbee, 1988. They thought it was white man's magic. Their headmaster was not so captivated. I completely emptied his school of children. *Simon Broughton*

village of Brikama. Lucy was also billeted there. It was indeed a privilege to sample compound living on my first trip to Africa. I was especially lucky to have as my host, a musician and a man as outstanding as Dembo, and one so kind. At night, Lucy and I would sit out in the compound's sandy yard and, under a billion stars, be swept away by the hurtling kora duets of Dembo and Kausu. It was at these sessions that I made my first proper field recordings, using a borrowed Sony Walkman Professional cassette recorder, the AK47 of recording devices, as I would come to regard the machines once I bought, treasured and carried everywhere my own.

This amazing music, seldom heard outside of musicology circles, I took home and played on my programme, so that the listeners – I hoped – could enjoy it just as I had: spontaneous and in its natural environment.

I returned from Gambia constipated, captivated by a continent, and driven now to seek out, hunt down and collect music myself.

29

NO THISTLES FOR EEYORE: LIFE WITH JOHN PEEL

JUST AS THERE could never be a New Bob Dylan – despite a history of undignified marketing campaigns for such – neither could there be a new John Peel. That glaring reality did not, however, deter Radio 1 in 1985 from drafting me in as a barely-disguised successor to the most important British figure in the history of rock music and, irrespective of genres, one of the greatest broadcasters ever to mumble into a microphone.

More bewilderingly, John, at the time, wasn't considering retirement and certainly wasn't approaching the point at which there may have been mutterings that the old boy (at forty-five) was past it. He was broadcasting as beautifully as ever. Nevertheless, my arrival as heir apparent was an open secret around Radio 1. It was a status I had not sought and with which I felt deeply uncomfortable. Along with Alan Whicker, John Noakes and Ray Gosling, Peel was one of my broadcasting heroes and the most influential of that quartet. I also resented the implication that, to be following in Peel's footsteps, or even hanging on to his coat-tails, I did not have an identity and musical tastes of my own. This invidious position suggested a lack of depth and integrity.

John's own unease, not only with the danger I embodied as the press-ganged new pretender, but as one who had also been shoved into the established routines and relationship of Room 318, was entirely understandable. (And there was – my goodness me! – to be no question of a punk-style revolution when it came to this particular rock veteran's position.) So John devised a couple of strategies to cope with this: swinging between loudly-advertised affection when he, maintaining his role as king, was embracing me, as crown prince; and being a sulky, resentful old Eeyore, around the office, when jealousy got the better of him, as it often did.

Within weeks, a few realities began to sink in – for Peel, Walters and for Radio 1's management. John was astonished that this brash kid was something more than a post-punk chancer. His cautious probing of my credentials, as we sat in the shambles of 318, revealed I was already something of a rock & roll veteran. Without doubt, I was bang up to the minute on new music. But Peel and Walters were amazed and, I think, quietly proud that their precocious child could enthuse with them, as an equal, an expert and a fellow connoisseur, about – let's say – Big Joe Turner's Atlantic sides or the terrifying cadences of the recorded sermons of the Reverend CL Franklin (Aretha's dad). Occasionally, when privileged visitors were admitted into the office, I was wheeled out to perform.

Many of our tastes did overlap, although I certainly did not share John's apparent unquestioning faith in white rock music, which was particularly unshakeable if a band's records were released on an independent label. I was not in the slightest bit interested in the corporate status of the record company and did not see that business arrangement as a justification for an identifiable category of music. I was interested only in whether the music was any good or not. 'Indie', for goodness sakes, did not guarantee quality. I mean, are you still playing your Woodentops records or those singles by The Pastels? Precisely. And, the truth is, they were bloody awful back then, too.

Conversely, Peel was wilfully dismissive of, for example, Bruce Springsteen – even though Bruce embodied the integrity and so many of the rock & roll credentials John admired and considered essential for his endorsement – simply because Bruce was popular and on a major label.

These contradictions and concern for these spurious values indicated to me that John was not the maverick he liked others to believe he was. He paid far too much attention, I always felt, to what others – chiefly the music press – thought of this record or that band and, crucially, to what others thought of him. This anxiety and ambiguity created the Peel programmes we knew and loved: a mixture of the unlistenable, the fabulous and the unpredictable. But they were always essential radio: partly for the occasional record or session; fully for the lugubrious blighter who intoned the bits in between.

For my part, I didn't give a bugger for what the *NME*'s opinion was of anything or anyone. I cared even less about what was thought to be fashionable, cool or uncool. I trusted only my own judgement, in which I have always had complete confidence. I may have no talent to play musical instruments but I do have good ears.

John's own defence of his public music policy – for, certainly, he did not reach for the Bogshed albums in private, when we were relaxing around the table at my flat or at Peel Acres with a glass or two of red – was that he had a mission and a duty to play this stuff because if he didn't no one else would.

To an extent, that did justify his public service broadcasting role. It also explained the consequent huge amount of chaff from which we, as Peel listeners, had to pick out the wheat. Equally, music considered by Radio 1 bosses to be intolerably experimental on John's programmes in the early days – Pink Floyd, for example – was, by the time I arrived, regarded as so uncontroversial and mainstream it was kept in an emergency cupboard just outside the studios for immediate airplay if it were announced that the Queen Mother had died. (I wasn't listening on the day. Did she really go out with *The Great Gig In The Sky*?)

Pink Floyd were, of course, among the first to benefit from Peel's patronage on *The Perfumed Garden* and for the next four decades John, we like to remember, broke new bands and trailblazed emerging styles. But with four two-hour programmes a week for much of that time, on national radio, playing – almost entirely – bands which hadn't yet made it and of which few others had then heard, it would have been an astonishing achievement if new styles and groups had *not* been discovered and pioneered by such a presenter.

The feeling, which Trevor Dann confirmed to me years later had been widespread, that 'they've finally found the new John Peel' was a serious misjudgement on a couple of counts: to the surprise of Radio 1 management, they soon realised they had, in fact, found the new Andy Kershaw; and instead of becoming rivals, Peel and I became allies and crusaders against conformity. Within that campaign, we had specific targets: mine was, and still is, a *jihad* against mediocrity; Peel's, it became clear, was less concerned with mediocrity but an attack on the broader front of mainstream popularity. What other explanation could there be for John's eagerness to jettison artistes – Rod Stewart and Marc Bolan spring to mind – who he'd championed tirelessly as underdogs, once they achieved wider success?

Radio 1 bosses didn't see it coming, but putting me in the same office as Peel and Walters almost guaranteed we became brothers-in-arms. Not only did my posting to 318 reinforce the position of Peel, until then seen as that of a one-man awkward squad; it created in Walters' office a radio station within a radio station.

IN NO TIME at all, we set about erecting the barricades. Few of our Radio 1 colleagues were allowed across the threshold. Fellow DJs given rare access were Paul Gambaccini (whom we considered our intellectual equal and a fellow music obsessive), Annie Nightingale (battle-hardened survivor), Alan Freeman (lovely old cove), Janice Long (our scally mate) and Kid Jensen (nice lad). The others knew their place and kept well away, possibly sharing Steve Wright In The Afternoon's view that the occupants of 318 were 'from another planet'.

Such was Walters' contempt for the daytime specimen of Radio 1 DJ, that he invented a fantasy presenter for the network, long before Harry Enfield and Paul Whitehouse dreamed up Smashy and Nicey. This character was a composite of all the clichés, whose name, likewise, was a glorious reduction of those traditional Radio 1 values – Dave Dave. And once I began to moonlight across the street, in Broadcasting House, making programmes for Radio 4, Walters – slightly wounded that I was working with another programme-maker and to trivialise that new attachment – also invented a fantasy Radio 4 producer. His name embodied Walters' vision of a slightly effete, bookish, bespectacled bloke in baggy corduroys. 'Well,' he'd say, looking at the clock, 'I suppose you'd better be running along to see Blair Lawnmower.'

Walters – have you noticed how, in this book just as in life, Walters is taking over and occupying all available space? – also granted Room 318 passports to a number of fellow producers who, while certainly not regarding them as his equal, he was prepared to tolerate for brief visits, consultations and the dispensation of his wisdom and ridicule. These were men, like Jeff Griffin and Mike Hawkes, whose motivation to work in music radio was – astonishingly – music. And there was our pal Chris Lycett, considered management material but simultaneously an *ex officio* member of 318. Had Radio 1 been a secondary modern, Lycett – a Senior Producer – was the rebel from the lower-fifth much given to showing his bottom at the rear window of the coach on school outings.

An almost blanket ban was imposed on record pluggers. I can think of only two who were welcomed. Others would push an arm around the door and wave a copy of their company's latest release. This was generally met with a booming, 'No, thank you!'

One afternoon, some over-familiar representative of a major label proffered, in this manner, a new CD to me and Peel.

'Andy! John! Eric Clapton's *Unplugged*,' the promotions man shouted around the door.

'Not before time,' grunted Peel. And the arm darted back, CD undelivered.

UNDER THE REGIME of Radio 1 Controller Johnny Beerling, the management's attitude to 318, and the programmes which flowed from it, was often contradictory. While their values were, in every other respect, very much those of a light entertainment end-of-the-pier variety – most publicly advertised with the horrors of the Radio 1 Roadshow – they were, when all was said and done, quite smart in their handling of me and Peel. They may not have understood what it was that John and I were doing on the air but they did have some grasp that it was highly-regarded, that it somehow upheld Radio 1's obligation to public service broadcasting, enshrined BBC values and reaped an annual harvest of prestigious awards. Walters, naturally, steered them towards this position and defended us robustly. (Whenever Peel and I picked up another Sony Radio Award, Walters would tell others, dismissively, that we had again won, 'The Silver Sea Slug of Dubrovnik'.)

The danger of later regimes, under Matthew Bannister and Andy Parfitt, was their smugness and a self-importance that drove them to meddle. To the credit of the end-of-the-pier boys, they were tawdry but they knew they were tawdry. They were, at least, unpretentious, and we had, on that basis, an understanding. But Parfitt and Bannister thought that they knew best, that they were clever. They couldn't stand back and leave alone something that was already successful. They had to interfere. It was to the arrival of these Birtists, following the loss of our protector, Walters, to retirement in 1991, that we can pinpoint the marginalisation of Peel and Kershaw on Radio 1, in my case eventually into exile as a refugee on Radio 3, and in John's, devalued into a dead of night slot, and having much of his enthusiasm purged in the process.

But in the cheery old Radio 1 climate of enforced jollity we lived, nevertheless, in a permanent state of dread. There was always the danger that lurking in the next memo from upstairs would be the words 'fun' and 'Radio 1' in the same sentence. Reliably, these were warnings of anything but. Chastened and forewarned by the experiences Peel had endured at such gatherings – ten years after the trauma, John was still having anxiety attacks about his escape from Bay City Rollers fans in a speedboat piloted by a Womble – I managed to work for fifteen years at Radio 1 without getting entangled in the atrocities of the

Roadshow, *Top of the Pops* or, most terrifying of all, something called a Radio 1 Fun Day Out.

BEHIND THE DOOR of 318, Peel was a mass, if not a mess, of contradictions. Once he had grasped that our programmes were not in competition but complementary, I became less of a threat and he returned happily and comfortably to his default Eeyore character – grumpy, wary and slightly resentful. I was by now, very publicly and musically, my own man.

Those John embraced fully were those who he considered no threat at all, who had no identity of their own and offered up to him only deference. As with most self-obsessed people, there was, underlying John, a fundamental insecurity. It was always noticeable that he resented the company of some of my more amusing friends and their capacity to hold an audience. Despite his reputation for modesty, and in his role of reluctant celebrity, he sulked if he were not the centre of attention. For someone so secure in his position, so admired and even regarded as a

Just before take-off, about to fly stunts over the 1993 British Motorcycle Grand Prix at Donington Park. Somehow this foolishness benefited Save the Children and Riders For Health. It didn't benefit me. It was terrifying. And I missed the 125cc race. *Unknown*

national institution, John needed, absurdly, constant reassurance if not flattery.

'The Pig saved me from myself,' he once sighed, over a drink, referring to Sheila, his adorable, one-in-a-million, down to earth wife and an indefatigable counterbalance of common sense to John's neurosis. 'God knows where I'd be or what I'd be like without her.' Walters and I just raised our eyebrows to each other. Indeed.

At the same time, John and I frequently had huge fun together. We would tramp around the specialist record shops of central London, often spending more, in my case, than I earned from doing my programme. 'You're not still dancing the *kwassa-kwassa*, are you?' he once remarked at the counter of Stern's African Records, as he thumbed through my new Congolese purchases. 'Don't you know we dance-floor trend-setters moved on from all that simply *weeks* ago?'

On another occasion, sitting in 318 late one night, I heard him tell his listeners, 'The Boy Kershaw is up in the office at the moment, going through the exciting new imports we bought this afternoon around London's glamorous West End. I've warned him time and again, but the impetuous child won't listen: he'll never get anywhere at Radio 1 doing that, my goodness me... Here's another one from The Fall...'

In those glory days when our programmes were on the air adjacent to each other – until a later regime, the one that thought it was clever, split us up like naughty schoolboys – we refined and pared down my handover to John, as a parody of those programme junctions of our daytime colleagues, into an exchange in which all we would say to each other for a few seconds was, 'matey DJ chat, matey DJ chat' until John banged in his first record.

Some of my happiest memories are of our holidays together, away from the competition for listeners' approval, at the TT motorcycle races on the Isle of Man. For six consecutive years – with a bunch of other agreeable pals – we lay in a lot of delightful Manx fields with, as John described it, 'a fattening picnic and much strong drink spread around us, watching midget Irishmen fling themselves around the island for our entertainment.' Of all

John's writings – and he was a most elegant and hilarious writer, borrowing heavily from the styles of an earlier age – the funniest piece I believe he ever wrote was an essay for *Bike* magazine, reprinted in his compendium *The Olivetti Chronicles,* on our works outing to the TT in 1992.

Another adventure, to see our much-detested Radio 1 colleague, Simon Bates, appearing in pantomime in High Wycombe, playing the villain in *Aladdin*, still gets talked about on Peel-related website forums. We had gone, of course, to seize the legitimate opportunity to boo the scoundrel – which we did, heartily – and, to that end, we'd booked the best part of a whole row near the front to stuff with our mates, John's wife Sheila included, all vetted for their reliability as Bates tormentors. Towards the end, as Aladdin held a dagger to Bates's throat, we were out of our seats, baying genuinely for blood. 'Oh, for God's sakes, just do it!' I bellowed over the screaming.

WITH JOHN'S SUDDEN and premature death in Peru on 26 October 2004, there was, naturally, a clamour to pay tribute to a great broadcaster and one who had forever shaped so many listeners' lives. I, possibly alone, in that outpouring of national grief, heard another voice. It was that of Walters, from beyond his own grave, blustering sympathetically, 'Peru? Peru? *Peel?* What in the name of God was he doing in Peru? A man who used to get anxiety attacks about family motoring holidays around Brittany? Weeks before they set off. *Peru?*'

In that clamour, over the years since and, in fact, long before John's death, there has been created a consensus, a mythologising and a deification of John, usually by those who didn't actually know him, which has relied on clichés, caricatures and hearsay. Peel was a far more nuanced, complex and contradictory character than the one of those assumptions.

I can think of no other broadcaster who publicly and audaciously changed his on-air personality and radio voice at least twice to take advantage of social change and prevailing trends – from minor member of the royal family on the radio in Dallas and Oklahoma City when Beatlemania and an appetite for everything English was sweeping the States, to gentle apostle of all that was flower-strewn and lovely in late 1960s London, to the clipped, sardonic, no-nonsense avuncular figure – borrowed directly from Walters, with whom his voice became almost interchangeable – which arrived overnight on Radio 1 with the first Ramones album. Any other DJ would have been fingered as a phoney and an opportunist even to contemplate trying to pull this off. With Peel, no one even remarked on it.

Similarly his attempts – largely successful – to reinvent himself as a Liverpudlian, emphasised by an attachment to Liverpool Football Club and the companionship of its terraces, was to disguise a guilt about coming not from Liverpool at all, and certainly not from the humble origins he would have preferred to advertise, but from a very privileged upbringing on the Wirral, one of the many posh parts of Cheshire, and across the Mersey from the city he hugely over-romanticised.

But the greatest Peel myth of all which, if he did not originate himself he did little to disabuse others from propagating, was that he was a rebel. In reality, he was anything but. He reveals

Peel in Peel, Isle of Man, 1993. When Juliette bought a family holiday cottage here, John said he and Sheila were considering a little weekend place in Kershaw, South Carolina. *AK*

as much himself in his autobiography, concerning a small difficulty we were having with Radio 1's management. Johnny Beerling, the amiable Controller, wanted us to play in the first half hours of our programmes music not too dissimilar from that in the preceding shows. Johnny's idea was that this technique would ease listeners into our sequences or, more accurately we thought, lure them into our traps. In John's case, this required him to avoid walloping those who'd just been bathing in the blandness of, perhaps, China Crisis with, say, Piss, his favoured – for about ten minutes – thrash metal band.

Peel walked upstairs at Egton House to see Johnny: 'Whereas someone like Andy Kershaw, a great but combative broadcaster would have put himself on an immediate war footing, issued an ultimatum and breathed fire in all directions,' John wrote, 'I smiled winningly, promised instant cooperation and continued to programme as before.' And to John's credit, he didn't change his music policy one jot. But he had no stomach whatsoever for a fight when it was truly needed and his recognition of my real and natural predisposition to rebellion terrified the life out of him.

With the mid 1990s infestation of the Birtists, the meagre production back-up we got, the shocking standard of those allocated to work on our programmes – incompetent but cheap – reached levels which even Peel described as 'piss-taking'. My programme was treated with particular contempt and constantly criticised, molested, sometimes openly ridiculed by the self-satisfied arrivistes. In 1997, an announcement that I was to be moved to a midnight till 2am slot caused a listeners' revolt and Matthew Bannister, then Controller, in a rare gesture of sensitivity to licence payers' views, and to his credit, climbed down. But the year after, under Andy Parfitt, those persistent hostilities and the incompetence and carelessness of those assigned to work with me had become so intolerable I went on strike for a few months until Radio 1 came up with a supportive producer who could actually meet my meagre requirements.

More than once during this long fiasco, I pleaded for John's help and solidarity, often predicting that if they were prepared to do this to me they would come for him next. He refused. Worse still, I felt he distanced himself from me to avoid being damned by association. And so, while I did lay down fire all around me, winning that battle solo, but ultimately losing the war, Peel kept his head down, safely below the parapet. My prediction turned out to be accurate: it took them a few more years to summon up the bottle but, eventually, they did come for John too, just before he died.

But that instinct for self-preservation was the secret to Peel's survival for so long in the fickle, shifting world of Radio 1. John was the supreme survivor, the skilled politician. In truth, he was one of the most establishment creatures to inhabit the BBC. He was also a dad who, not unreasonably, wanted to support his family and, to that end, survival and continuity for John was all.

'HAVE YOU HEARD it?' snapped Walters. My phone had rung at precisely 2.15pm, just as *The Archers* was finishing, and just as it had done every day since our preposterous friend retired.

'Have I heard what?'

'This new programme Peel's doing on Radio 4.'

'Yes,' I said. *Home Truths* had, at the time, been running for a couple of weeks.

'Well, what do *you* make of it?' Walters heaved.

'Inconsequential, smug, neurotic suburban nonsense, as you ask,' I told him.

'What is he *doing*, for goodness sakes? How has he got himself mixed up in something as *awful* as this?' he gasped. 'I mean, I'm frankly not one bit interested if some ghastly, silly woman in Chalfont St Peter has decided to name her deep freeze Derek. Are you?'

'No.'

'You know what's happened, don't you?' Walters was approaching the triumphant conclusion of some analysis, formulated while waiting for the goings-on in Ambridge. 'You realise what he's become? Peel, I mean.'

'No. Tell me.'

'He's become the Queen Mother.'

THERE WILL NEVER, alas, be a John Walters autobiography. (Some of you, without room on your shelves for a seven or eight volume stroll through his life, may be comforted by that reality.) And without, so far, a biography of the great man, let it instead be recorded here: John Peel was a true one-off, a wonky giant of broadcasting – as flawed as the rest of us – and someone who, over five decades, did more publicly to shape the course of contemporary music in the UK than The Beatles and the Rolling Stones combined.

But the true genius of Room 318, the philosopher, the creative force, the cultural prism, the inspiration, the social historian and agitator, and the genuine soul rebel behind that achievement, was John Walters. The frequently quoted line about their relationship, for which Peel and Walters both claimed credit (of course), that it was 'one of man and dog, each believing the other to be the dog,' is a decoy, albeit a wry one, from the reality: without Walters, the national treasure that Peel became could not have existed.

Equally, without their adoption of this novice radio presenter and without the values and programming foundations that this odd couple together laid down, and upon which I built and modelled unashamedly my own programmes, I would have had a radio career both short-lived and unnoticed.

30

LOOKING UP
OLD BLACK MEN

KILLING TIME IN MEMPHIS – not a bad title for a Jerry Lee Lewis country song – I did not expect to have an adventure during a stay at the Airport Hilton of that city.

It was the tenth anniversary of Elvis Presley's death, August 1987, and Radio 1 had despatched me to Memphis, specifically to Graceland, to cover the maudlin ceremonies, the tribal tribute gatherings and a city-wide shopping frenzy for truly shocking souvenir tat. Elvis fans must be the easiest consumers upon whom to unload tawdry, sentimental baubles: being an Elvis true believer is itself a measure of abysmal taste and poor judgement. It is significant, too, that merchandise most in demand by Elvis fans celebrates a particularly gruesome period of a grotesque career, the Las Vegas years.

My sympathies incline more to fellow Memphis resident Jerry Lee, who, in November 1976, and just ten hours after being released from jail, had been arrested on the front lawn of Graceland at 3am, waving around a pistol. 'Tell him the Killer's here!' the heart and soul of rock & roll was shouting at Graceland security guards, before he was handcuffed and bundled away by the police.

So it was with some relief, having survived the necrophilia, that I checked into the bland surroundings of the airport hotel. The following day I'd be flying over to Raleigh, North Carolina, to stay with my dear friend Godfrey Cheshire. At Godfrey's, I would also hook up with Our Elizabeth, Jonny Barnes and another pal, Chris Heath, to follow, approximately, the coast to coast route across the United States of Chuck Berry's 'poor boy' in his masterpiece *Promised Land*. Much of this road trip is through the American south, and the heartlands of the continent's great music. (Route 66, on the other hand, romanticised by the songwriter Bobby Troup, steers the traveller – as it winds, you'll recall, from Chicago to LA, more than two thousand miles all the way – through the dullest regions of the United States. I've always suspected Bobby selected that road only because its name rhymed with 'kicks'. If he ever did drive it, then it is unlikely he'd have been moved to celebrate it in song.)

That morning in Memphis, for something to do, I took a taxi to the old Sun Studios and from there headed to Beale Street. But, finding the old blues quarter corporately heritage-themed and touristy (and aimed at those tourists who believe the blues is Stevie Ray Vaughan), I went strolling aimlessly about the surrounding neighbourhoods. Although the streets were pretty deserted and I encountered no hostility, I began to get that creeping feeling that I was in a part of town not often walked by many whites. I stopped to get my bearings and, looking up, found I was right under the shabby sign for an equally tatty motel: the Lorraine Motel – the name made me jump – where Martin Luther King had been assassinated in 1968. And just *there* was the very balcony on which he'd been shot, the one in the famous photo with Andrew Young, Jesse Jackson and Ralph Abernathy pointing together in the direction of the gunfire. It was all so quiet that sunny morning of my accidental pilgrimage, so terribly banal.

'Yes, sir, this is it,' said the woman at the front desk. 'Though I'm not sure you should be walking around here on your own.'

A few minutes later I was loitering on a busy road bridge over the Mississippi. Could this be the same one that Chuck Berry had in mind in *Memphis* – just half a mile from Marie's home, on the south side, high upon the ridge? And there, indeed, when I looked, was a ridge, on the south side.

Later that afternoon, I was lounging in the sunshine on the front steps of the hotel, listening on my Walkman to James Carr, the greatest of southern country soul singers. Country soul was a type of soul music which occurred at that point where black gospel and white country music met and overlapped. The finest stuff was recorded in Memphis, Nashville and Muscle Shoals, Alabama, in the mid- to late-1960s. Its best known voice, although nothing anywhere near as powerful and as dramatic as James Carr's, was that of Otis Redding.

I'd been alerted to James Carr's stupendous talent by my friend and fellow music obsessive, Barrence Whitfield, the Boston R&B singer. On a recent trip to stay with me in London, Barrence had presented me with a James Carr *'Best of...'* reissue. It was – and still is – unbelievable. The sleevenotes told me all Carr's great recordings had been made for the obscure Goldwax label of Memphis and that Carr, a troubled man – that much was clear from his on-the-edge delivery – had been overcome by stage fright on a tour of Japan in the 1970s, had subsequently suffered a nervous breakdown and had not been seen nor heard of since.

Back in my hotel room, with nothing better to do, I picked up the Memphis phone book. I turned to the page on which the Carrs were listed. I wondered. There was no James Carr but, I reckoned, if the great man were still with us, one of these other Carrs may know him. I started at the top of the list.

'Hello there, I'm sorry to bother you,' began my pitch to those who answered, 'but my name's Andy, from BBC radio in London, England, and I'm wondering if you would perhaps know the where-abouts of a James Carr who recorded *You Got My Mind Messed Up* for Goldwax Records here in Memphis in 1966?'

'I'm sorry, but I'm afraid I don't,' said the first dozen or so voices.

I made the same little speech to a woman who answered and identified herself as Rose.

'I sure do,' she said. 'He's my brother.'

'Good God!' I yelped. 'And do you know where he is these days?'

'Yes, sir. He's asleep on the sofa in the next room.'

I asked Rose if she'd mind, with my apologies, giving the greatest soul singer of all time a gentle shake and ask him if he'd come to the phone. 'Hello,' a hoarse voice whispered a few moments later. 'Yes, this is James Carr.'

I explained who I was, where I was, why I was anxious to track him down and that I was in Memphis only until the following morning. Could we meet? Where did he live? I'd get in a taxi and come right over if that was okay.

'You a white boy?' he asked. I confirmed I was.

'You probably shouldn't come over this way,' he advised.

Would he, instead, be willing to come over to the Airport Hilton?

'I ain't got no money,' he said.

'Don't worry. Just get a taxi over here and I'll pay the fare both ways. I'll wait for you at the hotel entrance.'

About an hour later a cab drew up and out got a tall, emaciated, bewildered-looking black guy in his late forties – the mighty James Carr in person. I guided him into the foyer bar, we sat down and I rolled my Sony Walkman Pro.

Not much of what he said made a great deal of sense, alas. He seemed very confused, shy, disorientated and not quite with it. I learned later that his psychological problems had not been helped by his fondness for smoking copious quantities of strong weed. Little of what passed for this interview was broadcastable. In the semi-coherent bits, all James revealed was that he couldn't remember much about the previous twenty years.

After he'd left, I was making my way across the foyer when I noticed a poster by the reception desk, advertising a concert in the hotel's basement ballroom. This was turning into some kind of stop-over. Playing that same night, and just a ride down in the lift, three floors from my room, was Carl Perkins and, opening for him, the black-voiced southern soul singer, Tony Joe White.

'*Dixie Fried!*' I yelled at Carl later that evening, although I didn't need to shout. Standing alone, right at the front of the low stage, in a gig attended by me, a handful of lonely, out of town businessmen and a huddle of airline cabin crew, I might have leaned over and whispered softly my request to the rock & roll originator.

Carl had not, I was thrilled to discover, slipped like so many of his generation into a supper club self-tribute cabaret routine. Fronting a tough little band, he was belting out no-frills rock & roll, without concession to showbiz embellishment. Which probably explained why the place was empty.

'You got it!' he said. And fired off, without a pause, the rabble-rousing, jumping guitar intro.

I caught the lift to my room an hour later, still buzzing on the events of an extraordinary day, and with Carl Perkins having serenaded me personally into insomnia: *'Rave on, children, I'm with ya! Rave on, cats,'* he cried. *'It's almost dawn and the cops are gone, let's all get Dixie fried!'*

I fell on my bed and wrote up an account of the whole mad day in a letter to Peel. In it, I'm sure I echoed what the incom-

'Missing' for years, I found him at his sister's. The mighty James Carr with me at the Airport Hilton, Memphis. August 1987, listening to his own 1960s recordings on my Walkman. *Unknown*

My dad, Jack, aged around twenty, wearing his sitting-in-the-back-garden suit, Rochdale, late 1940s. *Unknown*

My mum, Eileen, in an election photo as a Labour Party candidate for Rochdale council, 1964. She won. *Unknown*

The fat, giggling, cross-dressing infant on the right is the future poor man's Keith Fordyce. Me with Our Elizabeth on the sofa at home in Rochdale, 1960. *Unknown*

Pushing a lighting case through the Refectory foyer during the load-in for a band at Leeds University, 1980. Joanna Coop had just uncorked my testosterone. *Al Thompson*

Mild Man of Rock – Iggy Pop on stage in the Refec, Leeds University, 2 July 1981. *AK*

Booking the bands, as Ents Sec, in my Students' Union penthouse office (with roof terrace and private bathroom), Leeds University, 1981. Note poster for Elvis Costello's one-off country music concert behind me. *Al Thompson*

Dawn Chorus & The Bluetits, Leeds,1983. L–R: April Showers (Lindsay Burrows), January Sales (Liz Kershaw) and May Bank-Holiday (Carol Vorderman). I was attempting – simultaneously and unsuccessfully – to style myself, 'Johnny Angel'. The only Bluetit I didn't date was Our Elizabeth. *Unknown*

Who needs acid? Billy Bragg and I stepped out of our hotel in Hamburg one morning, turned the street corner and a camel was coming along the pavement. By itself. *AK*

The Driver and the Battlebus. Peter Jenner's elderly Volvo estate, in which I drove Billy all over Europe throughout 1984. It never once let us down. *Billy Bragg*

Right behind my boy. Billy on stage at the Pink Pop Festival, Holland, 11 June 1984. *AK*

Interviewing my old hero, Rory Gallagher, for *Whistle Test*, Dingwalls, Camden Town, 1985. *Maxwell Ferguson*

Lyle Lovett's first brush with the British media. *Whistle Test* producer, Trevor Dann, on location in Texas, in 1986, where we were filming a special about a bunch of talented but then unknown young country singers. *AK*

Another young hopeful in that *Whistle Test* country music special. And Dwight Yoakam, left. *Trevor Dann*

No idea what was going on. With my friend and co-host, Mark Ellen (of the Lower 6th), in our makeshift studio – the football commentary box – presenting makeshift television to an audience of more than a billion. *Live Aid*, Wembley Stadium, 13 July 1985. *BBC*

With my first real love, Anna Jenkins, at the Elder Avenue flat, Crouch End, February 1986. The sofa bed was our one item of furniture. *Unknown*

Thrilled to bits and wet through. Biggie Tembo and I reach Victoria Falls at the end of our Zimbabwe adventure, January 1988. It was Biggie's first sight of the Falls, too. *Unknown*

John Walters, oblivious to a Radio 1 calendar photographer, tucks into a Greek meal at our favourite restaurant, Jimmy's in Soho. Other Radio 1 DJs had their publicity photos taken with sports cars. And without their producers. *BBC*

Masterclass for a witless and sluggish pupil. My friend Jim Redman, six times motorcycle racing world champion, as a Honda factory Grand Prix rider in the 1960s, tries to teach me the techniques, Donington Park, Derbyshire, 1996. *Steve White/CameraSport*

Standing under the engines of a Saturn V rocket at the Lyndon B Johnson Space Centre, Houston, Texas, 1987. My awe at the bravery and achievement of the pioneers of manned space flight remains undiminished. Imagine this bugger going off underneath you...
Jonny Barnes

Not much evidence of food. The kitchen cum office of an unmarried broadcaster and journalist. Elder Avenue, Crouch End, 1993. *Steve Benbow*

Photo evidence here of an undignified return to skateboarding, August 2011, after a 33-year break. I'm on a board I made myself in 1977 from solid mahogany. It weighs a ton. Gull Wing trucks and soft wheels still worked a treat. Pilot less so. *Peter Greste*

We'd made it! And there wasn't a lot there. With Ali Farka Toure on our first morning in Timbuktu, December 1988, recording *Now That's What I Call Mali. Chris Heath*

With Ted Hawkins in his yard in Los Angeles, 1986, at our first meeting. I flew out there unannounced and knocked on his door. *Unknown*

Look out, mamma, there's a white bloke comin' up the river … with Simon Broughton, my friend and Radio 4 producer, on the Niger River, in the Sahara, Mali, December 1988 *Chris Heath*

Trackside at the TT races with John Peel and Juliette, my partner at the time, Isle of Man, 1992. John seems to have brought on holiday the contents of Room 318. *John Bisbrowne*

With Rwandan Patriotic Front rebels on the Nyaborongo Bridge, Rwanda, 17 May 1994, at the height of the genocide. Innocent Kabandana is on the far left; Little Derek is third from left. Ten minutes after this photo was taken, we were ambushed. *Geoff Spink*

For each unharmful, gentle soul misplaced inside a jail... Interviewing wrongfully-detained prisoners in Haiti, for Radio 4's *Crossing Continents*, December 2000. *Lucy Ash*

Bikes and broadcasting, two of my defining passions. On my XLH 883 – I still own it – below the transmitter at the Alexandra Palace, 1991. *Unknown*

At work but completely at home. On the air, BBC Radio 1 studios, 1986. Note hand-written running orders. *Ian Anderson*

Trust me, I'm a doctor. Twice over. With my mum after receiving my Honorary Doctorate from Leeds University, 2005. The citation noted I still owed the politics department 'at least five essays'. Tie courtesy of the Jon Snow Collection. *Unknown*

Getting ready to follow the firefighting teams of Red Adair and Boots Hansen to the burning well-heads of Kuwait, for Channel 4's *As It Happens*, 1991. *Unknown*

"WE SEEM TO BE PICKING UP STRANGE SIGNALS, SIR. I FEAR IT MAY BE THAT KERSHAW AGAIN!"

Illustration by the great Glen Baxter for the cover of my 2004 compilation CD of obscurities, *More Great Moments Of Vinyl History*, on Wrasse Records. *Reproduced with Glen's kind permission*

'Andy Kershaw, without you we wouldn't know nothin'!' With Joe Strummer at a Radio 3 party, not long before his sudden death in 2002. It was at this event that Joe and I, with Brian Eno, began plotting a reunion gig by The Clash in Baghdad, to show support for ordinary Iraqis. It never happened. *Tim Anderson/BBC*

Citizen of the world – Sonny aged 6 months on my shoulders in South Africa, 1998

In Algeria, against Foreign Office advice, for a Radio 3 documentary, 2006. *James Parkin*

Not a bad start in life. Sonny, just nine months old and in the arms of Willie Nelson, at the recording of Willie's session for my Radio 1 programme, May 1998. *Paul Sherratt*

Dolly meets Dolly, Hammersmith Odeon, 2003. Ms Parton, to my daughter: 'Oh, my, Dolly! That's such a pretty dress.' *Unknown*

Live At Leeds again! Before The Who's return gig, 17 June 2006, Pete Townshend and Roger Daltrey unveiled a blue plaque with Leeds University Vice Chancellor Michael Arthur. *John Bull*

Live At Leeds Again – The Who on stage in the Refectory, Leeds University, 17 June 2006. *Richard Hanson/University of Leeds*

Together again. The photo which ought to shame the Isle of Man authorities. Reunited with Sonny and Dolly, Autumn 2009.

' 'Cos baby I'm just a scared and lonely rider, but I gotta know how it feels ...' Before my debut ride on a thoroughbred racing motorcycle (1979 T23500cc Yamaha), at the Festival of a Thousand Bikes, Mallory Park, 7th July 2012. (Bike kindly loaned to me by Dean Want). *Bill Saner*

Old sea-dog. And Buster, our adorable schnauzer, Peel harbour, 2009. *Vic Bates*

parable James Carr screams, just before going over the precipice in *That's The Way Love Turned Out For Me*: 'Say it one more time for Memphis, Tennessee!' Years later, when I asked John if he still had my dispatch from the Memphis front-line, and if I might have a photocopy for my scrapbook, he confessed to not having kept it.

ALTHOUGH THE MONEY I earned at Radio 1 was meagre, and some weeks I spent more than I was paid on records, being a semi-famous figure had other financial spin-offs. I began to get regular voice-over work for radio and television commercials. The money for this was easy and, compared to my BBC earnings, given the work I put into my programmes, obscene. But I wasn't going to argue. I would walk into a commercial production studio in Soho, say something like 'Monster Munch, from Walkers,' be pelted with hundreds of pounds and be out of the door again within five minutes.

This income financed almost all of my trips. Only twice in fifteen years, to Memphis in 1987 and South Africa in 1995, was I sent anywhere, or had a trip paid for, by Radio 1. And only later, by and on behalf of Radios 3 and 4, were my broadcast adventures bankrolled by the BBC. To that extent, I became a patron of the arts, subsidising the corporation by enriching my Radio 1 programmes, which frequently won awards, with music collected on my self-funded travels.

It wasn't my duty to be the explorer but my passion. When I realised I had enough money to go and hear, for example, cajun music played in cajun country, I took myself off to south-west Louisiana to sit in bars to meet and record fiddlers and accordionists. Then, in that quest for soul music in all its varieties, and for the need to recapture that sense of *what-the-fuck-is-this?*, that search expanded to Africa and eventually the rest of the world. My job abroad – just as it was at home, sitting and listening for days on end, acting as a filter and a funnel on behalf of the listeners – took on, when I could afford it, a global reach. I was, as ever, driven by plain nosiness: I wanted to see and hear for myself. In fact, I couldn't imagine why anyone in my fortunate position and with these enthusiasms wouldn't also go seeking remarkable music. It was astonishing that I, in the twenty year history of Radio 1, was the first broadcaster with the inclination and curiosity to do so.

For my efforts on these field trips and adventures, and because of the non mainstream music featured on my programmes, I was acclaimed, frequently and flatteringly, as an expert, sometimes even a musicologist. I wasn't anything of the kind. Evangelist, maybe – and how lucky I was, as a professional fan, to be in that position – but no expert and certainly not a musicologist. In fact, an immensely exciting aspect of my activities on Radio 1 was that I was exploring and learning as I went along, and taking my audience with me, whether that knowledge was gathered at the counter of Stern's Records, in the swamps of Louisiana or the townships of Zimbabwe.

The listeners, I felt, deserved to be on board for these discoveries. From what I knew of them – by their letters and encounters at gigs – they were even more enthusiastic than me. I seemed to have found a constituency which was bright, sophisticated, curious, educated and open-minded. (And a puzzling number of them seemed to be self-employed potters in the west country.) Apart from the Peel programme – and although they adored John as a broadcaster, they disliked much of his music – they had nowhere else to go. Few other presenters treated them as non-imbeciles with interests more sophisticated than those of the lowest common denominator. Radio 2, meanwhile, had still to realise that this audience was not yet ready for *The Organist Entertains*.

Broadcasting to fellow enthusiasts, I was completely at ease. I came to regard them as soul mates and with a few I did develop personal friendships, often meeting up at gigs. It was because of their reception for what I did that I found, after starting in television, my true home in radio. Radio has an intimacy that television can never attain. Listening to it is also largely a solitary activity. For that reason, the best radio broadcasters are those who make their listeners feel that they are being addressed not as a mob but individually.

The bulk of my Radio 1 colleagues, by contrast, saw radio as an inconvenient but necessary stepping-stone to getting a Saturday evening light entertainment television variety or chat show. One presenter, for example, used to spend much of his afternoon programme discussing what had been on television the night before and previewing the television schedules for the evening ahead. This spoke volumes about his regard for the medium in which he worked.

I had a rapport with the listeners based on mutual admiration. Their often superior knowledge informed the programme and I heeded their suggestions for music I should play. They didn't just have the radio on: they were actively listening, participants in the programme. One regular and entertaining correspondent, Jon Carr of Lincolnshire, had some unspecified chronic illness. The radio was his lifeline and my programmes seemed to lighten his load. His letters certainly used to lighten mine. 'I've not been very good at all,' Jon wrote in one update. 'But I refuse to die before Crosby, Stills and Nash.'

OUR *PROMISED LAND* TRIP detoured to Nashville, naturally, and again slightly off-piste to take in Hank Williams' grave in Montgomery, Alabama. We also paid a courtesy call on REM in Athens, Georgia. This was before I had been obliged to roll up my sleeves to Michael Stipe to extract from him an apology to Our Elizabeth in the bar of the Mean Fiddler in London.

A bunch of us, including Stipe and the likeable REM guitarist, Peter Buck, were out together at some gig. Our Elizabeth was in the middle of an anecdote in the bar afterwards. Stipe was not, at that moment, the centre of attention. And the rest of us were not finding, unanimously, Michael as moodily magnificent and as fascinating as he found himself.

'Shut the fuck up!' he snapped at Elizabeth as she was in mid-sentence.

I invited him to apologise or to step outside. He did say sorry, eventually, and I was not obliged to give the rightly-admired singer and songwriter the horse-whipping, on that night, he so richly deserved.

Beyond Athens, and approximately ninety miles out of

Atlanta by sundown, rolling cross the Georgia state, as Chuck put it in *Promised Land*, I went looking for the grave of my favourite pre-war bluesman and ragtime 12-string guitarist, Blind Willie McTell. In an academic paper on Blind Willie, given to me by my old friend and fellow blues enthusiast, Dave Foster, in Leeds, I learned that Blind Willie, on his death in 1959, had been buried with his beloved 12-string in the graveyard of Jones Grove Baptist Church in his birthplace, a little town called Thomson, Georgia. If finding Thomson was difficult, tracking down a church – not something easy to hide, you'd imagine – was even harder. Eventually, and almost at sunset, we were directed up a narrow road between fields of maize, some distance from Thomson. A mile or two along there, and set down from the road, was a neglected clapboard church standing in the middle of an overgrown graveyard. Jonny, Chris, Elizabeth and I jumped down and began pulling the weeds and creepers from the headstones. The academic paper told me Blind Willie had been buried under his real name of Eddie McTeer.

Get your kicks on, erm, Route 35. In Austin, Texas, on our Promised Land Tour across the American south, 1987. L-R Jonny Barnes, Chris Heath, me, Our Elizabeth. Route 66 is for the clueless. *Unknown*

After some scraping around, we found him. Flat to the ground was a sad grey slab of cement and a matching headstone with the name Eddie McTeer, and the dates of his birth and death, nothing more, impressed in it. I snapped some blossom off a nearby tree, placed the bough on the cement and sang tunelessly a few bars of Blind Willie's *Lay Some Flowers On My Grave*.

The solemnity was broken by a yell.

'Hey, you!'

From a small house across the road, a white woman was approaching, picking her way through the weeds and grave-stones. She had a hard, pinched face and in her arms was a sticky baby.

'Whaddayall doin' in here?' she demanded. 'Dontcha know this is a blaaack cemetery?'

On this balmy early evening, a chill shot up my spine. She put about three syllables into 'black'.

'Of course. And don't you know who's buried here?' I asked.

Silence. She didn't. This was long before Blind Willie McTell had become more famous than his own recordings had ever made him through an eponymous dirge by another of his fans, Bob Dylan. Not that she'd have heard of Bob either.

'Blind Willie McTell,' I told her.

She squinted at me hard. Not only a nigger but a blind one, too.

In the heart of Louisiana cajun country, little had changed, due to poverty and isolation, in years. It still felt like a United States of the 1950s.

We met Johnnie Allan, a full-time headteacher and part-time singer, whose swamp pop version of *Promised Land*, with its belching accordion break by Belton Richard, is one of those rare cover versions which equals, if not betters, the original. We dined on crawfish and alligator, drank cold beers and, in Fred's Lounge in the tiny town of Mamou, we danced cajun waltzes and two-steps. It was from Fred's on a Saturday morning, start-ing at 9am, that a weekly cajun dance, with a live band, was broadcast over the local radio station KVPI. The announcer, JD Fontenot, standing at the microphone in the centre of Fred's one small room, introduced the tunes and read the ads for local businesses, such as animal feed suppliers. A notice above the unplugged jukebox requested us, as patrons, not to dance on top of it.

Outside, I took a few minutes' breather, leaning up against the wall. I was joined by the guitarist from the band.

'You from England?' he asked.

I confirmed that I was.

'Do you know The Beatles?'

Smiling, I told him I didn't.

Not yet mid-morning, it was already oppressively hot. The street was silent and empty, except for the pair of us and a dog asleep in the middle of the dusty road. My new friend looked up and down the pavement. 'Man, let me tell you,' he said. 'The Beatles stood this place on its head.'

It was from cajun country, a year later, that I received an invitation to attend a worldwide convention of people called Kershaw. 'Hmm,' Peel reflected, as I read aloud to him the invitation in Room 318. 'If they were to hold a gathering of the Ravenscrofts,' his real name, 'you could bet it would take place in Solihull, West Midlands.'

Happily, the international get-together of the Kershaw clan, to which I signed up, was held in south-west Louisiana, where a couple of thousand of us converged in a swamp for a crawfish boil and cajun music festival.

AT THE END of the *Promised Land* trip, I went looking for, and found, in Oakland, next door to San Francisco, an elderly ex-pat singer and guitarist from Sierra Leone, SE Rogie, upon whose 1960s recordings of palm wine music in Freetown my listeners and I had become terribly keen. Within months, Rogie had a UK record deal and a British tour arranged, along with a session on my radio show. Into the bargain, I also put him up for a couple of weeks – somehow – in my one-bedroomed flat in Crouch End.

My love of Trinidadian calypso, particularly the first glorious flowering of that style in the hands of its earliest recording and broadcasting masters, took me to Port of Spain in 1990, on the hunt for the last survivors of that generation. The reception desk had pushed a couple of messages under my hotel room

Lay Some Flowers On My Grave – Finding Blind Willie McTell in Thomson, Georgia, 1987. The great man, buried under his real name of Eddie McTeer, has since been recognised and dignified with a proper memorial. *Jonny Barnes*

door when I got back from an afternoon poking around town: 'While you were out... The Roaring Lion telephoned.' And, 'The Mighty Terror called in person.'

The Lion, who was admired by Bing Crosby, had sung for Roosevelt and Churchill. Now, at eighty-two, he was selling lottery tickets on the steps of the Republic Bank in Port of Spain. I found him there, gold-topped cane in hand and dressed in his trademark pink suit and Panama hat. Although he was still revered by Trinidadians as the elder statesman of calypso, his particular style, that of singing the news – and doing so spontaneously – had long ago been overtaken by the popular appetite for soca (soul-calypso), with its emphasis on beefed-up dance rhythms and the partying priorities of its subject matter.

We spent a most agreeable afternoon together in The Lion's favourite rum bar, where I recorded with him a lengthy interview. Age had not diminished his legendary sharpness, nor his recall. There wasn't a significant event of the twentieth century that I could mention which The Lion had not chronicled at the time in song, from the abdication of King Edward to the first moon landing. Not even Italy's invasion of Abyssinia escaped The Lion's attention and in 1935 he was straight out with a calypso warning to Mussolini about the aggression.

This kind of activity, in search of favourite musicians alive or dead, Walters came to characterize indelicately and, of course, dismissively. 'Yes, yes,' I overheard him telling someone on the phone one morning. 'I'm in the studio, pre-recording with Andy all afternoon. He's off again on his travels next week. Hmm, yes, Oven Chips, Missouri, or somewhere like that. You know what he's like. Yes, yes, the usual Andy stuff: Looking Up Old Black Men.'

TWO OF THESE made a dramatic impact. Neither was particularly old but both, although coming from worlds apart, had extraordinary talent built on the common foundations of blues.

In the autumn of 1985, I'd nipped over for the weekend to

One of Trinidadian calypso's 1930s originals and greats, still singing the news in his eighties. (And selling lottery tickets.) The Roaring Lion, Port of Spain, 1990. *David Corio*

Boston, Massachusetts to see again, in action, Barrence Whitfield & the Savages, my favourite group of the time. Through a contact at North West Orient airlines, I found myself the only passenger on a free flight to Boston, the real mission of which was to deliver, as a promotional stunt, *Beaujolais nouveau* to New England.

After scouring the second-hand record stores of Boston, Barrence and I called in at the headquarters of Rounder Records, the eminent American roots music label, based in nearby Cambridge. Bill Nowlin, the founder, was generous enough to load me up with free Rounder samples. One of the LPs I pulled off Bill's warehouse shelves had an intriguing cover on which a burly black guy, holding an acoustic guitar, was photographed in what looked like a prison yard. The album was *Watch Your Step* by Ted Hawkins.

Back in London, when stylus touched vinyl, I felt that familiar and favourite shock once again. From Ted's opening rasp of 'Watch your step!' it was clear this was something very special. In fact, the whole album was outstanding: a solo country soul voice, coming over like an unpolished Sam Cooke. I couldn't wait to get on the radio with it. And when I unleashed the title track for the first time over the air, I flopped back in my studio chair tingling, and sensing that everyone listening would be scrambling for a pen. They were. I got letters even from drivers who had pulled over on to the hard shoulder of the motorway to fumble in the glove box for writing materials. The reaction was astonishing.

The album had been recorded, I noted, in 1971. What since? And where was Ted now? Bill Nowlin, who seemed to have forgotten or overlooked the obscure classic in his catalogue, gave me the last address he had for Ted. It was in Inglewood, near Los Angeles airport.

A couple of weeks later, after finishing a *Whistle Test* job in the States, I was due to fly home from Atlanta. At the airport, and on impulse, I put a credit card down on the counter and bought a ticket to LA. A short taxi ride brought me to a modest wooden house in a black neighbourhood. The door was answered by a giant, who I recognised as the guy on the album sleeve. At this point, Ted was fifty years old and since having been first sent to a young offenders' institute at the age of thirteen in his birthplace of Biloxi, Mississippi, he had spent much of his adult life behind bars, mainly for theft and vagrancy. In the American south of Ted's youth, being black was barely legal. Black, poor and homeless amounted almost to a guarantee of incarceration. It was in prison that Ted had learned to play the guitar and had been encouraged to sing by the governor's wife.

Although a little taken aback by this cold-calling white kid, Ted was happy to sit down there and then with his guitar and record, in his living room, four songs into my Sony Pro. Within the week, we put these out as Ted's first Radio 1 session and to what seemed like national euphoria.

Until I turned up, Ted was earning a meagre living as a busker at Venice Beach, the closest approximation Los Angeles offered to a bohemian hang-out. He'd recorded a cassette, *The Venice Beach Tapes*, which he sold to passers-by. I was blown away: he had on it more amazing self-compositions and well-chosen covers, enough for a double album.

Just a few months later, Ted was with us in London. He played live on my programme. The studio was filled with his admirers and newly-recruited media supporters. Even Walters was excited and revealed a sense of occasion I didn't know he had by going out to buy a couple of bottles of hospitality wine, a few beers and some bags of crisps.

Ted's first British gig was at the 100 Club on Oxford Street. When I came round the corner and saw a queue outside a hundred yards long, I had to blink back the tears. This was what being on the radio was about. 'I'm ready,' said Ted in the dressing room, grinning at me and wide-eyed. In that smile was a child-like eagerness and a recognition of some achievement after decades of denial. For Ted, this was it.

Beyond the dressing room door, we could hear the crackle of anticipation. Ted put a white towel over his head and followed me, bouncing on the balls of his feet and shadow-boxing, as I cleared a path through the throng. From the dressing room to the stage, Ted's new fans clasped his hand, slapped his shoulders and roared him to the rafters. At the microphone, his ring walk left me with only one thing to say.

'Ladies and gentlemen, the heavyweight champion of the world, Ted Hawkins!'

He plunged immediately into *Watch Your Step*. Apart from Ted's opening cry, much of the rest was lost to me in the deafening reception. It was, truly, one of those I-was-there evenings.

IN PARIS, it turned out to be one of those I-was-there afternoons. Which was fortunate for an unknown and, by then, retired blues guitarist who was sitting, that day, with not much to do, in his village on the banks of the Niger river in the Sahara desert of Mali, west Africa.

I had brought my record shopping, as was the requirement for most things back then, into line with the rest of Europe. The record shops around Barbès, a vigorous immigrant neighbourhood of central Paris, had albums I hadn't seen even in Stern's. As the shopkeeper of one was totting up my purchases – Congolese, Malian, Guinean and Senegalese LPs – I was flicking through a bargain bin. I stopped at an album with a bright red sleeve. In the middle of the cover was an out-of-focus photograph, taken at some distance, of a long-fingered wiry man in blue Muslim robes and a yellow skull cap. He was partly obscured by a shrub and sitting on the baked earth with other adults in what I took to be a family compound, somewhere in west Africa. A number of children were milling around. No guitar, nor any other instrument was in the picture. In white lettering above the photo it said Ali Farka Toure. Nothing more. There was no album title.

'What's this?' I asked the guy.

He wasn't certain but said it had been in the bargain rack for a long time. Having calculated my reckless spending on the other records he was bagging up, the shopkeeper let me have the intriguing red album for next to nothing.

Back at home, with the first notes of the rolling acoustic guitar melody that introduced the opening track *La Drogue,* I froze up. Then I was out of my seat and pacing around the kitchen. Here we go again. Who the hell is *this*?

It was blues but it was also deeply west African, very Saharan.

Ali's guitar picking and fingering and his choice of blues scales was, at the same time, spookily similar to those of two American bluesmen: JB Lenoir and Lightnin' Hopkins. (Ali would later be compared constantly to John Lee Hooker by those who didn't know of any other blues musician.)

Ali, it turned out had been a musician for many years but, despite some trips to Soviet bloc countries when Mali was patronised by Moscow, had remained unknown outside of Mali. He hadn't made a lasting impression at home either and had, a year or two before my Parisian shopping trip, and just after recording the red album in 1984, decided to pack in music and perhaps return to his old day job as a sound engineer at Radio Mali in Bamako.

He had no idea until an envoy, acting on my behalf, tracked him down in his vast, sandy homeland, that, in the UK, late night Radio 1 audiences were beginning to worship him as the most significant blues discovery since Robert Johnson, jumping to the conclusion that he was some kind of lost link between American blues and its African origins (a coelacanth of the flattened seventh), and crashing their cars whenever I played one of his tracks. Like the Bhundus, Ali had that indefinable quality which gave him appeal to those who did not ordinarily listen to or enjoy African music.

Ali was a blues musician of true greatness but he was no living and missing link. Since his youth, he'd been a big fan of American blues and R&B and had, over the years, accumulated quite a collection of cassettes. Some he'd picked up on his travels outside Mali. Others had been passed on to him at home by travellers and ex-pats. He did, however, recognise, he told me, similarities between the American styles and the traditions of Mali. 'This music was taken from here,' he once said. Ali's achievement was to bring the two back together.

Somehow or other I established that Ali was Malian – although there was nothing on the sleeve to indicate that, no information at all – that the record had not been a big seller and that no one was sure of his whereabouts.

Anne Hunt worked for World Circuit, then a little London-based booking agency specialising in overseas artists. It would soon reinvent itself as a label, releasing Ali's records and, later, those of Cuba's Buena Vista Social Club. I bumped into Anne at an African gig at London's Town & Country, soon after my discovery of the bargain-bin bluesman.

'I'm going to Mali next week,' said Anne. No one went to Mali in those days. We were, even as African music fans in the UK, only just familiar with Salif Keita.

I almost jumped on her.

'Please!' I implored. 'You've got to find this guy called Ali Farka Toure. Ask in Bamako if anyone knows where he is. We've got to bring him to the UK.'

Anne, bless her, ended up trotting along to Radio Mali and put out an appeal for Ali's whereabouts over the air. He showed up. By chance he was visiting Bamako from his home village of Niafunke, far to the north.

A few months later, Anne and World Circuit did bring him to the UK. I threw a little party to mark his arrival in my tiny flat in Crouch End and invited a few pals and sympathetic media friends to hear him play. Ali performed sitting on his guitar amp in the kitchen. The Sony Pro was deployed and the recording was later broadcast on my programme. He made his UK debut, to a large and ecstatic crowd, at that same Town & Country Club in London, where I'd historically accosted Anne Hunt.

In 1988 Ali and I travelled along the Niger together, to Timbuktu and back, for a BBC radio documentary, *Now That's What I Call Mali*, which was broadcast simultaneously on Radios 1 and 4 – an unprecedented arrangement and one which has never been repeated. It was at the start of this trip that Ali, as *le grand patron*, honouring his *petit frère* (as he always called me), presented me with a live sheep on a bit of string. Some of this animal, lugged around by me in a couple of plastic shopping bags, was still with us, and maturing richly, long after we reached our destination.

By the mid-1990s, Ali had made a Grammy Award winning record with Ry Cooder and I was having to sit up straight in the formal surroundings of the Barbican or the Royal Festival Hall to see my old pal play.

But Ali never forgot. Back in his Niger village of Niafunke, where he became mayor, he used his wealth to benefit the community, paying for the installation of, among other amenities,

Of royal descent in his native Mali, soon to become king of the African blues worldwide. Ali Farka Toure coming down a staircase in the compound of his home in Niafunke, December 1988. *AK*

sanitation and electricity. And in January 2005, he summoned me to Brussels and the beautiful Art Deco Theatre Des Beaux Arts for his first European gig in years. It would also be among his last. The hiatus had been due to serious illness. Ali was dying. He knew it and I knew it. By now working for Radio 3, I made a little documentary about this triumphant comeback, knowing privately that it would be short-lived. Away from the microphones, Ali and I had a final chat in his hotel room. I was still his *petit frère*. We said our *au revoirs* but our goodbyes went unspoken. We knew we'd never see each other again. Ali died from bone cancer, at just 66, on 7 March 2006.

ANDY & BIGGIE
IN ZIMBABWE

BIGGIE TEMBO AND I were propping up the bar of the Mean Fiddler, at the time London's premier live roots music venue, located unhelpfully in Harlesden. Biggie's band, the Bhundu Boys, had just finished another delirious gig. A lava flow of fans was pouring out of the venue, to stand smiling, chattering and steaming in the taxi queues. Typically, for Bhundus disciples, they seemed, by the end of the evening, to have been hosed down.

'Comrade, comrade, I really don't understand,' Biggie was saying. It was 1987 and Zimbabweans were still in post-independence euphoria and on an indefinite honeymoon with their liberator from the apartheid-in-all-but-name of Ian Smith's Rhodesia. Robert Mugabe had not yet fully revealed the extent of his madness and his avowed Marxism had lent to Zimbabweans' everyday conversation smatterings of communist nomenclature. Personally, as a leftie myself, although of the militantly woolly-minded variety, I quite liked comrade as a form of address, it being classless, genderless, chummy (but respectfully so) and assuming, however optimistically, a universal solidarity. It is certainly preferable to the modern infestation – Australian in origin, I suspect, but now the *lingua franca* of white-van men everywhere – of an assumption on the part of strangers that they can call you 'mate'.

Where were we? Oh, yes. At the Mean Fiddler with Biggie...

'Don't understand what?' I asked him.

'Ah, all this fuss, comrade, here in Britain, about the Bhundu Boys.'

'Well, I do, Biggie,' I said. 'It's because you've got an absolutely wonderful band.'

I'll never forget his answer. And his lumpy syntax.

'Maybe, comrade. But in Zimbabwe, there are three hundred groups which are much more better than us.'

I looked at my friend. He had his sheepish face on, always a sign that he was being honest.

'You are joking, aren't you, Biggie?' If true, this was serious stuff.

'Oh, no,' he said. 'They are everywhere. When I next go back home, you should come and see.'

IN THE ARRIVALS QUEUE at Harare airport, I found myself standing behind a breathtaking young woman. She was a local girl, although of Asian descent: tall, slender, a smile as wide as a continent, teeth which could be safely admired only through a welder's mask, a soft tumble of rich dark hair over caramel skin and the bones of her face and limbs an arrangement of long, fine, geometrically-pleasing lines and angles. Welcome to Zimbabwe, comrade.

I hadn't got through immigration yet, never mind to the music. And I'd had no confirmation from my Bhundu buddy that he had received my letter to say that I was flying down. Reliability was never one of Biggie's many endearing characteristics. I had no confidence that he'd be waiting to meet me.

'Ha, comrade!' he squealed. 'You hadn't properly arrived in the country and already you've fallen in love with a Zimbabwean girl!' We were driving into town from the airport, Biggie at the wheel of his little car, an elderly model of uncertain Eastern European provenance, which looked as though he'd borrowed it from Noddy.

'Did you talk to her?' he asked.

'Yes.'

'And who is she?'

'She's called Nidhi. She's from here but lives and works in London. And she's come back to host a women's conference.'

For a while, silence descended in our Toytown taxi.

'When is it? Where?' he finally asked.

'Oh, I dunno. Anyway, Biggie, even I wouldn't have the nerve to gatecrash a symposium of feminists in an attempt to seduce the organiser.'

We'd arrived at Biggie's family home, a modest bungalow in a former whites-only and Home-Counties-in-the-Fifties suburb of the capital, which Biggie rented with the meagre money he got from the Bhundus success. I was introduced to Ratidzai, Biggie's partner, and his three little boys. Proudly, he showed me my room and around the house and garden, including a swimming pool alive with tadpoles. He'd been away in Europe for a long time.

I'd not been in Zimbabwe for a full day before I realised that Biggie's Mean Fiddler assessment wasn't much of an exaggeration. On the first of our many trips into the townships around Harare, notably Highfield, live music was being played everywhere. It was pouring out of bars and beer gardens and, on a Saturday, even the nightclubs were open in the daytime and advertising afternoon residencies by Zimbabwe's top bands. Street musicians were commonplace – I recorded blind, strolling gospel groups – and from every record bar sparkled the guitar melodies of the latest local hits.

These were not dedicated record shops but grocery stores which, among the cans of corned beef, condensed milk, sacks of sugar and maize meal, also stocked bundles of gritty 45s, on one of the two local labels, Gramma or ZMC, and dusty LPs the sleeves of which, as soon as they were released, looked faded and ten years old – instant classics. I brought as many as I could carry back to the UK and pretty smartly the Radio 1 airwaves were ringing every Thursday night with the casual inventiveness of hitherto unknown Zimbabwean gods of the electric guitar.

In the beer gardens, vast open-air compounds laid out with

tables and chairs and a stage at one end, it was possible to see, at the weekends, world-class bands then unknown outside of Zimbabwe. Among those playing within a couple of miles drive of each other, and at the same time, could be John Chibadura & the Tembo Brothers, the Jairos Jiri Band (all handicapped in some way and the flagship of a disabled foundation), the Marxist Brothers, Thomas Mapfumo & the Blacks Unlimited, Oliver Mtukudzi, or the Four Brothers.

Patrons got themselves in a dancing mood on Chibuku maize beer. This alcoholic drinking yoghurt with added bran, also known as *shake-shake*, was sold – no exaggeration – by the bucketful, intended for sharing, and was marketed as 'The Beer of Good Cheer'. It seemed to live up to its name. Not once did I encounter, on my many trips to Zimbabwe, any hostility or resentment in the townships – except when I was briefly detained while deejaying at the Saratoga Club in Highfield by plain-clothes CIO secret service officers, who presumed I was, being white in a black beer joint, a South African spy. And, frequently, I was roaming around as a sore-thumb of a white guy, on my own, often at night. The CIO agents finally had to agree: if I were an agent for BOSS (the South African secret service), working to destabilise Zimbabwe, it's unlikely that collapse could be guaranteed through spinning a few records. And secrecy was not best achieved using the cover of white-bloke-poncing-prominently-around-stage-of-township-club.

One afternoon, I spotted an advertisement for a John Chibadura gig which was to take place the following Saturday in Mbare township's beer garden. The poster announced a 9am start. Surely, a mistake, I thought. It must mean 9pm. I drove by there anyway, around ten on the Saturday morning, just in case. Bugger me – the band was indeed already in full swing, coaxing astonishing music out of cheap electric guitars, shattered amps and cobbled-together drum kits with cracked cymbals. I returned later with Biggie. We stayed all day. And all night. By tea time, I'd volunteered as a roadie, changing and tuning the hot-shot guitarist's strings. By 10pm, I was turning cartwheels across the width of the stage, to the amusement of the crowd and band, neither of which was accustomed to seeing a white guy react to their music with abandon, nor moved to make such an undignified plonker of himself in public.

'Ah, Comrade Kershaw,' Biggie was squealing after this spectacle, 'you have a European skin but an African heart.'

John Chibadura left the stage for the last time around one o'clock on the Sunday morning. Constant performance explained why Zimbabwean guitar bands were musically outstanding. Wage slaves to the venue owners though they were, they did not – rather like The Beatles undergoing their apprenticeship in Hamburg – lack practice.

This approach to performance was the norm. Some months later, when we first got the Four Brothers to the UK, they went into BBC Maida Vale studios, the regular recording facility for Peel and Kershaw sessions. A standard session was four numbers. Producer, Dale Griffin, once he'd sound-checked the band and set the levels for the recording, spoke to the group from the control room over the talk-back.

'Okay boys, if you can give us four, then, please...'

And off they went, trundling effortlessly through a quartet of effervescent tunes. Then they rolled into a fifth. And non stop into a sixth. With a session and a half now in the can and the Four Brothers conferring on a seventh offering, Dale hit the talk-back once more.

'Thanks, boys. That's great. More than enough. In fact, we only needed the four.'

The musicians blinked back at Dale through the glass, puzzled. Never Mutare, Four Brothers' bassist and bandleader then spoke up for them all.

'Oh, you meant you wanted four *songs*. We thought you wanted four hours.'

WITH HINDSIGHT, but not at much distance, it became clear that the equivalent to my first couple of Zimbabwean adventures would have been to have stumbled unwittingly into something called roots reggae in Jamaica in the early-1970s and returned to the UK foaming at the mouth with reports of the indigenous wonders, then unknown in Europe, that were Bob Marley &

the Wailers, Burning Spear, Culture, Black Uhuru and Prince Far I. The only difference was that this southern African phenomenon had received little previous outside attention. Zimbabwean jit, unlike Jamaican roots reggae, had not had the benefit of a forerunner to trailblaze international success, even in a novelty record capacity.

Although thriving in splendid isolation, until the Bhundus breakthrough, Zimbabwean guitar pop in the 1980s was, like that Jamaican creativity of the previous decade, at the peak of its powers. Its development from *chimurenga* rebel music of the 1972–79 liberation war, and the transfer of that style's *mbira* (thumb piano) accompaniment to the electric guitar, had been relatively recent and rapid. It was all still very fresh and terribly exciting, even for local musicians and audiences.

The environment in which that blossom burst open, and did so *because* of that climate, was one still of post-independence optimism, reconciliation and euphoria. Despite the horrors of the

Biggie Tembo with his Sony Radio Award (Best Specialist Music Programme) for *Andy & Biggie In Zimbabwe*, on the roof of Radio 1, 1989. *BBC*

1983 Matabeleland massacres, the convenient death of one of Robert Mugabe's more imaginative and popular potential rivals, Josiah Tongagara, and the detention and torture of his own air force top-brass, which ought to have alerted his cheerleaders of the time (I admit I was one) to what lay ahead, the overriding spirit within the country was incredibly positive both among blacks – who'd won the war, against all predictions – and the more liberal or phlegmatic whites who'd chosen not to scarper, as many did, to the remaining fools' paradise of South Africa. The soundtrack to that transformation was music that was the product of a particular history in a particular period. I count myself extremely lucky to have found myself accidentally in the thick of it, in what turned out to be its golden age, with, as my guide, Comrade Tembo, one of its chief protagonists and my great friend.

It wasn't to last for ever. Robert Mugabe became increasingly paranoid and authoritarian, and his cynical and strategic encouragement of racial hostilities – largely absent before he whipped them up for political advantage – brought about economic collapse and almost total unemployment. With it, that first dazzling eruption of a new music from a new country was snuffed out. Without money even for food, Zimbabweans did not have spare cash for the frivolities of buying records and packing beer gardens to drink and dance to live bands. Aids also took a terrible toll. By the turn of the millennium, there was hardly a Zimbabwean musician friend of mine still alive.

'OH. THIS IS A SURPRISE,' said Nidhi, the beauty from airport arrivals. 'Fancy seeing you here.'

We'd arrived at a hotel in the eastern highlands, a handsome stone lodge in the mountains close to the border with Mozambique. Nidhi, trailed by a glum straggle of her Women in Africa delegates, was crossing the reception area, where she found me and Biggie fumbling to check in.

'Yes, fancy!' I coughed, feigning astonishment. I introduced her to Biggie.

'What brings you here?' she asked brightly, and not unreasonably.

Biggie, rushing to explain why we'd rocked up, against all

odds, at this particular hotel of all the ones available to us in the country, began to blabber some convoluted, implausible nonsense – albeit it with great charm – about our interest in women's affairs. I stepped in.

'Biggie and I are on a tour of Zimbabwe,' I explained, truthfully. 'Biggie hasn't seen most of his own country before.' Also true.

'How lovely,' said Nidhi, that huge smile making me feel slightly drunk.

Although I hadn't lied, not even a little bit, I did spare the girl the full truth behind this remarkable coincidence.

Biggie had been stretched on the sofa, back at home in Harare, reading a local newspaper. Already we'd resolved I'd hire a car, more suited than Biggie's clockwork vehicle to bush driving, and we'd set off around the country, our goal being Victoria Falls, which neither of us had seen. The eastern highlands, although beautiful and tempting to the visitor, were in the direction opposite to our intended destination.

'Comrade!' shouted Biggie, flapping the *Harare Herald*. 'There is a story here about a women's conference which is taking place at a hotel near Mutare. Do you think it's the same one?'

Later that day, with me at the wheel and Biggie in the passenger seat (he was a better chatterbox than a driver), and resembling that famous illustration of *Tintin au Congo,* we were gone in a cloud of highway dust on the scenic route to Victoria Falls, out west. Via the eastern highlands. And a feminist conference.

To allay any suspicions Nidhi undoubtedly held, Biggie and I sat in, without fidgeting, on a couple of workshops. But there were limits to the lengths to which even I'd go for my overactive glands, and we were on the road again next morning.

Poor Nidhi, however, was not yet off the hook. Checking in for her flight back to London, a fortnight later, she found trainee metrosexual man again in the same ruddy queue. We sat together all the way home. Nidhi was not only beautiful but sparklingly intellectual and a delightful person – a totally adorable girl. In London we dated for a few weeks. I took her to the premiere of

Hail! Hail! Rock'n'Roll, the made-for-cinema documentary about Chuck Berry. With Nidhi on my arm, I was, at this glamorous gala do, aware of others staring and asking themselves who the great beauty with that twerp Kershaw might be. I felt, for a night, like one of those movie star husbands, seen on news reports, shuffling along the edge of the red carpet at the Oscars. True to form, at the after-screening party, Chuck Berry made a shameless attempt to pick Nidhi up, knowing full well she was with me. But I was no better in my treatment of her, simultaneously dating a gorgeous and angelic college girl, aptly named Amanda Sweet, who wrote her dissertation on the phenomenon of the Bhundu Boys in Britain. Later, I lamented the loss of both Nidhi and Amanda, cursing myself – again – as a selfish dickhead.

(In the summer of 2010, I was friends once again with Nidhi, reunited through the internet. Our first contact in more than two decades came about when I was fiddling around on my laptop in the Hotel Intercontinental in Kinshasa and she was at home in Canada, where she's lived for many years. Marvellous, isn't it, what they can do these days?)

IN A CAFE facing Bulawayo railway station, I got an indication of the power of radio. For a couple of years, at that stage, I'd been doing a programme for the BBC World Service. *Andy Kershaw's World of Music* was, before it was extended to half an hour, only fifteen minutes long, thus giving me the opportunity to inflict on the rest of the world no more than four records a week. This generated some post, usually from Nigerians who seem to labour under the misapprehension, as many still do, that theirs is the only country on the African continent. Aside from that, I'd resigned myself to the idea that, enjoyable little programme though it was, not many people were paying much attention globally. Walters felt the same.

'Come on, then,' he'd say, as he led us down to the studio for the weekly World Service recording. 'Let's get it over with. Mind you, I don't know why they bother broadcasting it. You may as well just open the window and shout.'

Back in the Bulawayo cafe, I spoke just eight words to the local lad behind the counter.

'Could I get the chicken and potatoes, please?'

'Are you,' he asked shyly, 'Andy Kershaw?'

I was absolutely astonished, almost as much as Zondiwe Nyasulu (I'll never forget his name). Young Zondiwe was, he revealed, a big BBC World Service listener and a fan of my weekly fifteen minutes of music from anywhere.

The reach of the World Service, I came to learn, could be humbling and slightly scary. The former hostage John McCarthy once told me that my programmes had been something he came to look forward to in the otherwise uneventful five-year stretch he spent chained by Islamic Jihad to a radiator in Beirut. And on a trip to Timbuktu, the police chief was fascinated by my BBC identity card.

I'd presented myself at the police station there because travellers can get their passports stamped by the police as proof of having reached that Saharan town, synonymous as it is with remoteness and isolation. After examining my passport, the police chief twirled my BBC card in his fingers.

'BBC?' he asked.

'Yes,' I said.

'World Service?'

'Actually, yes. I do present programmes on the World Service as well as domestic BBC.'

'Hmm,' said the chief, smiling and still fondling the card. He looked up.

'Do you, then, know Dave Lee Travis?'

I was able to report to him that I'd stood next to the Hairy Cornflake, presenter of the World Service's *Jolly Good Show*, at the Bush House urinals only a fortnight before. My passport was stamped 'Vu au passage au Tombouctou' immediately and amid much handshaking, backslapping and general bonhomie.

ON OUR LAP of Zimbabwe, without a producer or a sound engineer, I recorded enough material on my Sony Pro to fill eight C90 cassettes and all with the single hand-held stereo microphone, as supplied with these extraordinary machines. When I returned to London, I played some of the recordings to Roger Lewis, a Radio 1 manager. He was impressed by what he heard and stepped in as a producer. I was delighted and reassured that he drafted in, too, Brian Thompson, a meticulous, veteran BBC senior sound engineer and a lovely man. It was a tribute chiefly to Biggie, Brian, the exhilarating music of a new nation and the unbeatable little Sony that the resulting documentary *Andy & Biggie in Zimbabwe* won Best Specialist Music Programme at the 1989 Sony Radio Awards.

Radio 1 had got itself a documentary on Zimbabwean music without asking for one. (I'd put a couple of weekly shows on tape and flown off to Harare without telling Radio 1 bosses where I was going 'on my holidays'.) And now they had the industry's highest award for it. My old supporter, *Daily Telegraph* radio critic Gillian Reynolds, was also chairwoman of the Sony Awards Committee that year. In time for Biggie's next trip to the UK, Gillian ordered up for him a duplicate of our trophy. He was thrilled and proud. Rightly so.

The climax of the documentary and of our road trip was to arrive at the Victoria Falls. There was then absolutely no commercial exploitation of the most dramatic natural wonder in the world. Not even a sign, pointing through the trees, saying 'Falls this way'. Given that, and the humility of Victoria Falls village, Biggie and I first overshot the attraction – and the town – and arrived at the Zambian border, at the iron bridge over the river gorge, before we realised we'd driven too far.

I treated us both to a few nights stay at the splendid old colonial Victoria Falls Hotel, one of the world's most elegant and understated. It was on the terrace here, during a later trip with me, that Our Elizabeth would flag down a chap in a crisp white shirt, black trousers and tie, moving briskly between the tables. 'Oh, excuse me,' she said. 'Please could we get another jug of Pimm's?'

The man smiled most solicitously.

'I'll see what I can do for you, madam,' he said. 'Let me find you a waiter. For I am the Zimbabwean Minister of Education.'

Nothing can prepare you for that first confrontation with the falls. There is nothing in the realm of human experience to rival their immensity, power, magnificence and majesty. For me and Biggie it was an emotional end to a life-affirming trip. We wrapped up our recordings, with an embrace under the statue of David Livingstone above the Devil's Cataract and in a down-pour of warm spray.

OUR DOUBLE ACT – my straight man to Biggie's clown – our friendship and our adventures didn't end there, however. Memorably, among those capers, was Christmas with my mother in Rochdale. Sometime in December 1989, I asked Biggie when he'd be flying back to Harare for Christmas with his family.

'Ah, comrade, when I went to book a ticket, all the flights were full.' Typical Tembo personal organisation.

To her credit, my mum, therefore, found herself hosting a seasonal UN summit. With me, Biggie, and Our Elizabeth was Marta, my girlfriend of the time, who I had met in her home town of Novi Sad, Yugoslavia a few months before. Walters had dragged me there to keep him company at a European Broad-casting Union conference. I'd met Marta at a pavement cafe when I'd managed to slip away from what are always referred to, for some reason, as 'keynote speeches'. We got talking over a couple of beers.

'There is civil war coming here,' she said, flatly. It was during our chat that I first heard the name Slobodan Milosevic. Just about everything Marta feared and predicted that afternoon came true two years later. The next day, at Belgrade airport, I bought her a one-way ticket to fly with me to London. Marta settled eventually in New York City where for many years she has run her own travel agency. She, like every other woman to whom I introduced him, adored Biggie, mainly for his boyish-ness and a sunny disposition allied to a vulnerability. Yes, they all wanted to mother him.

My own mother had booked for our merry party to go out to a restaurant for lunch on Christmas day. Biggie was sitting across the table from me, next to my grandma, then eighty-three. She and Biggie had been chatting and laughing for some time. Suddenly, Grandma Norah leaned forward.

'Where's he from again?'

'Who?'

'Your friend.'

'You mean Biggie?'

'*What's* he called?'

'Biggie. And he's from Zimbabwe. You might remember it as Rhodesia, Grandma.'

She took all this in. Biggie was chuckling. And for a minute or two we carried on eating. Then...

'Eee!' she announced along the length of the table. 'He's a proper nice lad for a darkie, isn't he?'

Biggie yelped and flopped forward over his plate, coughing and snorting, choking on his food, convulsed with the giggles. He understood there was no malice intended. It was a generational thing.

APRIL 1990 was the tenth anniversary of Zimbabwe's independence. It was also to be Biggie's wedding to Ratidzai and he asked me to be his best man. Only for Biggie, in this role, would I have led – and danced at the head of it, with Oliver Mtukudzi as my partner – a parade through the streets of Harare from church to wedding reception. In a suit. I forgot, as soon as we set off, all the steps Oliver and I had rehearsed for days. And it was a pitilessly long way.

For the official independence anniversary celebrations, our seats were right up at the top of Harare's massive new stadium. I noticed, during the military displays and parades down on the pitch, a gate in the perimeter fence, leading from the terraces and on to the running track. The journalist in me decided to give it a go.

The gate was manned by a hefty CIO man, with a bulge in his jacket. As an unaccredited journalist, I decided to wing it, clutching a spiral bound notepad and with my camera case swinging from my shoulder. I smiled at the secret service man and he opened the gate. Perversely, I suspect he let me through without a question, and without a search, because I was white.

I loitered on the edge of the pitch, trying to blend in with just three other reporters. Dark suits were emerging from the players' tunnel. As they drew closer, there among them was Julius Nyerere, former president of Tanzania, Dr Hastings Banda of Malawi, and Kenya's Daniel arap Moi. Then right next to me was Kenneth Kaunda, ageless president of Zambia since independence in 1964. I said hello. Dr Kaunda said hello. We shook hands. All the leaders of what we called the front-line states were now milling around me: Eduardo dos Santos of Angola, Sam Nujoma of Namibia, Mozambique's Joaquim Chissano, genial host Mugabe himself and even that old monster, Mengistu of Ethiopia.

It was massively exciting. And terrifying. If I'd been a renegade agent of South Africa, on a suicide mission with a pistol in my bag and not a camera, I could have taken out the lot in a trice. I was spinning this way and that. And when I swung to my right there, from nowhere, was Nelson Mandela. It was only two months since he'd walked out of jail. And he was just back from London and a musical celebration of his freedom at Wembley Stadium only two days before.

I stuck out my hand. It was reflex.

'Mr Mandela!' I yelled. 'Nice to see you.'

Christmas comrades in Rochdale, 1989 – Grandma Norah and Biggie Tembo. This is one of my most treasured photos. *Elizabeth Kershaw*

'And very nice to see you,' smiled the conscience of the world, taking and squeezing my hand.

The stadium crowd was roaring, louder now as more spectators realised who – unadvertised – had walked out of the tunnel, on to the pitch, and was at last among them.

'Please may I take your photo?' I asked.

'Of course,' he said with a sweep of his hand, inviting me to stand in front of him. He straightened up, pulled back his shoulders and adjusted his tie. His attention was all mine.

'Ready?' he asked, grinning.

I could barely hold the viewfinder to my eye.

'Ready,' I piped. And fired off a couple of shots.

'Thank you,' I said.

'No, thank *you*,' said Mandela.

'Did you enjoy London?' I asked.

'Very much,' said the world's most famous man. Still, amazingly, we had not been interrupted, although a bossy-looking lady in a white frock was now striding towards us.

'I dunno, though, Mr Mandela...' began my final words to him, '...you spend twenty-seven years in prison, they let you out and they give you a Simple Minds concert, eh?'

'Who are you?' barked the bossy lady.

'My name's Andy,' I said. 'What's yours?' Mandela was shuffling away, now waving to the crowd.

'May I see your accreditation, please?' she asked.

'I haven't got any,' said I.

'Where are you sitting?'

'Right up there,' pointing to where I'd left Biggie.

'Then I suggest you go back to your seat.'

'No problem.' I'd got more than I could have dreamed of.

The eyes of every spectator, naturally, had been on Mandela from the moment he'd appeared. On my climb back to our perch, there was a scrum of people, all the way up the steps, reaching and groping to shake my hand – the hand they'd seen shake the hand of Mandela. I found Biggie, still saving our seats, weeping with laughter.

I would never see him so happy again.

* * *

THE DEMISE OF the Bhundu Boys and the eventual tragedy of Biggie was a parable of the stupidity and greed of a predatory corporate music industry meeting the gullibility and ambition of the naïve.

The Bhundus' appeal, beyond the circle of African music aficionados, was noted by the major labels and the boys signed with WEA. At the personal request of Madonna, who'd not previously shown any interest in Africa, and twenty years before she started helping herself to Malawian toddlers, the Bhundus opened for her at three Wembley Stadium shows in front of 240,000 people.

The first two Bhundus albums, released in the UK on Discafrique, and assembled from the recordings the band had made in producer Steve Roskilly's Shed Studios in Harare, are as close to perfection as music can get. So, WEA, smug and contemptuous of if-it-ain't-broke-don't-fix-it realities decided to draft in, for the Bhundus first major label release, *True Jit*, Robin Millar, the producer of Sade. Naturally. The assumption was that anything made in Africa had to be inferior and could be improved upon in Europe. Yet there was absolutely nothing in Millar's productions for Sade which suggested there were benefits he, and WEA's budget, could bring to the Bhundu Boys.

Producer and record company should have paid heed to what Steve Roskilly told me in the *Andy & Biggie in Zimbabwe* documentary, a lesson he'd been taught early on by another Zimbabwean producer: 'If you listen to this through white ears, you're never going to have hits.'

True Jit was a disaster. It won the Bhundus no new fans and alienated many of their core supporters. I shudder to recall it now: a soothing bland-out, bleating with skittish keyboards and stripped of all the spontaneity, simplicity and vivacity that made the Bhundus great. *True Jit* was the embodiment of the vision of someone who didn't like African music or how African music should sound: as non-African as possible. That the Bhundus went along with it indicated the extent to which they had been mesmerised by promises of riches untold if only they'd swap their kingdom for a handful of shiny glass beads.

Twenty-seven years in jail and they gave him a Simple Minds concert. I took this photo of Nelson Mandela (just back from that Wembley Stadium tribute), the surprise guest at Zimbabwe's Tenth Anniversary celebrations, Harare, April 1990. *AK*

The album's failure was the beginning of the end. Biggie was ousted in an internal power struggle in 1990. He told me that the other members were envious of his individual popularity and his gifts as the band's communicator. Stunned by the dismissal, for a while Biggie struggled on gamely. There was a misguided attempt at stand-up comedy and collaborations with useless British groups who were eager to capitalise on the affection in which he was held. All failed.

His behaviour became increasingly erratic and he was drinking excessively. Alcohol was something for which he never had much capacity. He'd appear in London unannounced and I'd put him up. He talked of being possessed by demons and for a while fell back on religion. He was, by the autumn of 1994 when last I saw him, severely depressed and off the rails. Everything he had achieved, against all the expectations of a poor, rural African kid, he felt had been snatched from under him. Back in Zimbabwe, he was no longer keeping in touch. I had no idea how he was nor what was going on. I should have gone down there and I didn't.

On 29 July 1995, Biggie broke out of a strait jacket in a psychiatric hospital in Harare and hanged himself.

32

A TOUR OF THE CAGES

THE WINDOWS OF THE GOVERNORS' Dining Room in Broadcasting House were flung open, allowing those moving below around Portland Place to be stirred by our carol singing, fortified as it was by a few preparatory mulled wines. It was an uncommonly warm afternoon, even for late summer in the city.

The Radio 1 DJs' Christmas Lunch, a conceit recorded routinely in September, for broadcast on Christmas Day, was intended to give the nation the impression that we DJs all lived together, rather like The Beatles in *Help!*, as one big happy family. Beyond that, one cannot imagine why the Radio 1 management thought the whole country would want to tune in to listen to us eating a meal.

Even if that domestic arrangement had been true, then the traditional family squabbles and brawling, inevitable at these festivities after the intake of much drink, should not – in the interests of authenticity – have been edited out of the seasonal special as broadcast. Particularly in the case of the eventful Christmas lunch of the summer of 1985.

'Now then, now then, double knockout, as it happens, guys and gals... uuh-uuh-uuh... yes indeedy, because, you see, what I have got here... uuh-uuh-uuh...'

Crashing through the swing doors from the kitchen into the dining room, robed and hooded in a Father Christmas costume and pushing on a trolley a mutantly-proportioned roast turkey, was none other than Sir Jimmy Savile, veteran Radio 1 DJ, tireless charity worker and another national institution, much recognised for his interest in young people.

'What would be the point,' I asked Walters, as we surveyed the scene, 'of taking acid?'

MY RADIO 1 COLLEAGUES could be categorised into three species. There were those who, by the measures of most people, would be considered unfit to be released into the community, never mind set loose on national radio; others had absolutely no personality whatsoever, and even less interest in music, rendering their presence in the broadcasting game, and on a music radio station at that, unfathomable; and just a handful were quite normal, engaging individuals. How the latter bunch ever got over the threshold is, in the light of evident recruitment priorities, perhaps the biggest mystery.

There was also, in the 1980s, a temporary flurry of Adrians. Finding oneself in the lift back then with a DJ colleague to whose face one could not immediately put a name, Adrian was a reliable bet. One of our many Adrians had gravitated to Radio 1 from a previous career as a speedway rider and another left us to take up bus driving.

Simon Bates divided the country. One part of the population couldn't get enough of his booming actor-manager voice and the centrepiece of his mid-morning programme, the maudlin *Our Tune*. ('What Mark hadn't told Kathy, because he wasn't the kinda fella who liked to put all his problems out on the table, was that a few years back he'd been a very different kinda person. In fact, he'd been Marcia, a hotel receptionist in Worksop. Which, I kinda guess, made his love for Kathy kinda complicated...' Tune: *Every Man Must Have A Dream* by Liverpool Express.) The rest of the nation would have cheerily had Bates shot. In public.

Over the four or five courses of our jolly Christmas lunch, Bates, sitting directly across from me, Walters, Peel and Chris Lycett, offered us his tabloid analysis of the miners' strike. During the soup, and into the main event, I had tried to debate

Doing my best to hide at the back, with Peel, in this 1987 Radio 1 DJs 'fun' group photo. Back row, L-R: Bruno Brookes, Robbie Vincent, Mike Read, Dave Lee Travis, Mike Smith, me, John Peel, Gary Davies, Simon Bates, Our Elizabeth, Miss P, Andy Peebles. Middle row: Peter Powell, Janice Long, Adrian Juste, Steve Wright, Adrian John, Simon Mayo. Front row: Annie Nightingale, Jeff Young, Nicky Campbell, Ro Newton. *BBC*

this with him reasonably, deploying my experience of the encounters Billy and I had had with the miners and their families to challenge the reflex inhumanity of his position, a view gathered from the vantage point of his Radio 1 office where, when I'd last checked, little mining had taken place for years.

'Don't rise to it,' muttered Walters between mouthfuls.

'Keep your cool. Just ignore him,' cautioned Peel, anxious as ever to avoid confrontation.

I did neither. At some point, late into the feast, Bates made another boorish, ill-informed remark about the miners that caused me to snap and I lunged across the table, intending to seize him by his ample self-satisfied chops. In mid-flight, and wearing a pirate's hat, I was yanked backwards by the grip of Lycett, Peel and Walters on my shoulders, upper arms and collar. Chris single-handedly frog-marched me out of the room, down the staircase, across the street into Egton House and delivered me safely to 318, thus depriving me of the instant accolade of national hero.

'Don't bother,' he panted when we got there. 'Everyone knows what Bates is like.'

BATES WAS NOT the only noteworthy figure of the daytime schedules.

Mike Read was a genuine music fan and a perfectly agreeable chap in all respects except for his apparent and startling belief that he was also Cliff Richard. Similarly, Gary Davies was a pleasant enough young man with whom to find oneself in the lift, although he bore an alarming resemblance to Frankie Vaughan and was always an inexplicable shade of fluorescent orange. Gary, not anticipating the unavoidable expiry date of his chosen slogan, styled himself as Young, Free and Single. (I wonder if he is trading somewhere today, with the passing of twenty-five years, as Middle-aged, Done and Dusted.) He was fond of playing an immodest jingle on his lunchtime show in which some admiring female purred 'Ooooh, Gary Davies...' Gary, you see, was regarded by Radio 1 bosses, if by no one else, as a bit of a heart-throb. This jingle was stored on a rack in the studios and I used to love firing it in, on my programme, whenever, and just before, I played a track by the Reverend Gary Davies, a blind, black and long-dead American ragtime guitarist and gravel-voiced gospel singer.

The allures of Gary's programme included *Willie On The Plonker*, in which Gary's producer, Paul Williams, a very eccentric man and a gifted musician who always looked as if he had been freshly run over by a truck, interpreted a current chart hit by banging it out, pub-style, on a piano. (Don't even ask why.) This gave rise to the famous 'Dear Mr Madigan' letter of Walters' exquisite discovery.

Evidently, a Mr Madigan had written to complain to Radio 1 that he found the name of Gary's pub pianist feature offensive. His complaint had been handled by Doreen Davies, a veteran Radio 1 executive, who'd been in the job since the network was called the Light Programme and Portland Place was still all open fields.

Doreen's reply to Mr Madigan had been photocopied by her secretary and the original left accidentally in the machine along the corridor from Room 318. Of all the people who might have been next to use the copier it had to be – gloriously – Walters.

'Dear Mr Madigan,' it began, promisingly. 'I am so sorry you find the piano character "Willie on the Plonker" offensive. I can assure you it is meant as pure fun, and our programmes are not in any way planned to aggravate, offend or outrage any of our audience. I wonder if children really do think it is "garbage" as you suggest. I do think in this case the suggestion of a smutty phrase is in the mind. It may surprise you to know that we literally get hundreds of letters each week asking Willie to play a particular tune on the piano.

'The piano is situated just outside Gary Davies's studio and his producer, Paul Williams, to whom he refers, plays the piano each day. Paul Williams is a Cambridge University music graduate, and has three children, two daughters and a young son. You can believe me that in no way would Gary Davies or indeed Paul Williams set out to present the listener with any more than a bit of harmless fun. Radio 1 policy, generally speaking, is to make the audience feel a bit better, look at life lightheartedly and enjoy themselves whenever they switch on. Yours is the first letter of complaint I have received.

'I completely go along with you when you suggest that the next stage generally and socially might be public copulation, but I don't think that Radio 1 can ever be blamed for contributing to this social trend, if it ever happens!

'May I just close by saying that Gary refers to "Willie on the Plonker", he does not refer to "Willie and the Plonker, nor "Willie and his Plonker". Willy has always been a nickname not only for male private parts but also for people with the surname Williams, and I believe that if you start examining every common or garden nickname and look for further implications, the fun would really go from One.

'It might further interest you to know that at the end of this month Gary Davies's producer is going on to another commitment, and Gary Davies's new producer's name is Martin Cox, and his name does not lend itself to any fun phrase, nor does Martin Cox play the piano...'

'THAT BRUNO BROOKES seems a nice little lad,' Peel announced one afternoon, squeezing around the door of Room 318. Bruno had recently joined us at Radio 1 and, out in the corridor, John had just been greeted eagerly by him again.

'Oh, really?' murmured Walters.

'Yes,' said John. 'Terribly enthusiastic. Every time he bumps into me I want to pat him on the head and press a sovereign into his hand.'

Young Bruno, we learned, as a small boy had dreamed of becoming, and played at being, a Radio 1 DJ. (Couldn't someone have given him a cowboy hat?) By 1989, he had graduated to the position of sidekick to Our Elizabeth on the weekend breakfast shows they jointly presented for three years. It was a stormy professional relationship and their programmes were often enlivened by on-air quarrels and at least one fight.

My dad went to his grave – more accurately, into the incinerator of Fleetwood Crematorium – in July 2009 wondering, given our upbringing and his hostility to rock and pop music, just how he had managed to produce not one but *two* Radio 1 DJs.

It has always been assumed that I, already on Radio 1, had played some hand in getting Our Elizabeth on there too. But I am innocent as charged. It was also a common assumption, and one propagated by those in the media who actually knew nothing of the reality, that Radio 1 had only two female DJs before Our Elizabeth joined (Annie Nightingale and Janice Long) because the network was 'sexist' and 'anti-women'.

The truth was that Radio 1 had very few female presenters because few females bothered to approach the station to become one. Our Elizabeth got her gig with the Nation's Favourite by going into a studio in Leeds, where in 1987 she was still living and working for British Telecom, to make a demo tape, which she then sent in, without telling me what she was doing, to Radio 1 executive, Stuart Grundy. And Stuart offered her a job. So, some glass ceiling, that.

Elizabeth had been watching me, from two hundred miles distance, having a whale of a time in London, working for *Whistle Test* and Radio 1 and – good for her – instead of whinge-ing and blaming everyone else for her isolation, decided that she wanted to be in on the action too and was going to do some-thing about it. And so, with her new job in radio, she moved down to London, to a flat just around the corner from mine in Crouch End, in which she relocated from Headingley her drop-in centre for those of a rock & roll lifestyle.

Bruno, meanwhile, had bought himself a huge and rather lovely old merchant's house in the renovated London Dock-lands. Among its fixtures and fittings, were a lot of built-in bookshelves. Bruno was a canny businessman but not a noted reader. Elizabeth and I, like most Radio 1 DJs, earned BBC fees which, had they been public knowledge, would have horrified our listeners. Bruno, however, to travel between his Edwardian domestic riverside splendour and Radio 1, somehow employed a chauffeur. It was to this driver, one day, after surveying the bare shelving, that Bruno gave the instruction to go into town and buy 'a few yards of books.'

For Bruno's house-warming, a marquee was erected on the lawn, in which pop stars of the day schmoozed with Radio 1's finest. Bruno had very kindly invited me too. I walked into the tent, nodded to a few colleagues, and picked up a beer from a bucket of bottles on ice.

'That'll be three quid,' said one of Bruno's staff.

'That'll be my bus home,' I said.

WITH HER ARRIVAL, my previous reticence to socialise, born of a desire to be incorruptible, was brushed aside rudely by Our Elizabeth ('Don't be so bloody miserable!') and she soon organ-ised our own partying rat pack. This comprised a floating membership of me, Elizabeth, Janice Long and a few of Janice's Liverpudlian-in-London pals, notably Pete Wylie (the singer of Wah!) and Janice's plugger friend, Taryn, a stunning yet foul-mouthed young woman, who fascinated and terrified Peel, and who would dress for our nights out at record company parties, gigs or clubs in what appeared to be just her lingerie.

Reinforcement later came with another scally, Jane Buchanan, who I'd first known as a teenage Billy Bragg fan, one of those who was likely to turn up at Billy's gigs anywhere in the UK. Jane – very bright, jolly, street-wise and down-to-earth – had reappeared as a producer at Radio 1. (Even though she has lived in New York City for almost twenty years, Jane and I have remained good pals.) We were code-named Hattie and Eric, after Hattie Jacques and Eric Sykes. The similarities were striking. There was also our friend Alex Radvanyi, a plugger for WEA. Alex and I looked so similar we were routinely taken for brothers, sometimes twins.

Alex once agreed to keep me company on a trip to Guernsey, where I'd been booked to do a Saturday evening gig. On the Friday night, the great and the good of the Channel island with, one presumes, no more prestigious VIPs on the horizon for a while, were laying on some kind of reception and dinner at which I was to be guest of honour. On my way to Heathrow, my tube train became laid up in a tunnel, due to signal failure, and I missed the flight on the Friday afternoon. But Alex caught it. Delayed twenty-four hours, I also missed the civic reception, but still managed to make the gig by catching the corresponding flight on the Saturday. Eventually, arriving at the venue, I went in search of the organiser and found him with a group of other local notables.

'Who are you?' he said.

'Me? Well, I'm Andy Kershaw,' I replied, slightly baffled and a little miffed. Some warm reception, this.

'*You're* Andy Kershaw,' said the man who had booked me and flown me in. 'So who's this bloke, then?' he asked, jerking his thumb at grinning Alex.

'I knew you'd be on the flight this afternoon,' Alex explained later, 'so I knew you'd make it for the gig. I didn't see any point in letting them down last night over the posh meal. They didn't know you were bringing a friend so it was easy: I was you.'

It was entirely possible, in the music business of the late-

1980s, awash as it was with money, to go out to lavish parties nearly every night. I recall arriving at one, in a film studios in west London, to find, when the bouncer held open the door for me, an entire fun-fair had been built within. One didn't really have to buy food or keep any at home. That was certainly true of booze. Similarly, my wardrobe of check shirts was lent the variety of endless freebie T-shirts, sometimes even 501s and sneakers. If only the record industry had been minded also to provide beds at these dos, one wouldn't have been troubled with the need to rent or own a home.

None of this largesse, of course, influenced what I played on the radio. And the record company promotions folks soon understood that. After their initial dismay at discovering I was not a DJ of the mainstream variety, they were a good-natured enough bunch to invite me to parties anyway and would even manage to smile when I'd remind them, over another bottle of designer beer (whatever that was), that their generosity did not mean I would now be playing tracks from the shitty new album we had been invited to celebrate.

'WE'RE GOING TO SEE Motörhead on Friday,' said Janice. 'All of us. You included. They're on at Hammersmith Odeon. There's a backstage party afterwards and I've got you on a blind date.'

We trooped along, mob-handed, to Hammersmith.

Janice introduced me to my date, a blonde American girl, scruffy but not unattractive and who, I thought, would probably scrub up quite presentably. At the after-show party, she showed that irritating tendency to look constantly over my shoulder, to see if anyone more famous or attractive was around, all the while talking about herself and not giving any indication of hearing anything I said. She was, she revealed, in London hoping to get a part in the next cinema film featuring Joe Strummer, the former front man of The Clash. Only when I remarked that I knew Joe, did she suddenly, miraculously, find me irresistibly gorgeous.

Years later, I was thumbing through a Sunday colour supplement before lobbing it in the bin. The cover story was about some American popinjay, who had become famous, or so it seemed, for having married some sad rock junkie. He had died young and, for that, had been deified despite his meagre talent and insignificant legacy. In the spread of photos, the woman, who was called Courtney Love I noted, looked vaguely familiar. Good grief, it was my blind date at Motörhead.

Details of similar misadventures were occasionally and informally brought to Radio 1 listeners in a spontaneous feature on Janice's programme we styled *Andy Kershaw's Bad Nights Out*. These reports occurred only when Janice could tempt me into her studio and persuade me to reveal on air my inexpert interaction of the night before with celebrity. I may have confessed in these how my dancing, and occupation of the dance-floor, at some record company party at the Roof Gardens Kensington, so offended and distressed Simon Le Bon of Duran Duran that his minders approached Our Elizabeth, advising her to remove me immediately, to make way for Simon to execute his own twirlings, or they would call Security.

At an after-show bash for Prince in Camden Town, I took pity on a forlorn little figure, leaning against a pillar in the shadows. Worse for him, many other revellers were staring at the poor guy from a distance of about ten yards. I went over.

'Hello. Fancy a drink, old chap?' I said in the near darkness. 'My name's Andy. What's yours?'

'Prince,' he said.

He asked for half a lager and lime. I didn't expect him to call roughly for a pint of real ale but, I ask you, *lime*? We got on famously. Prince is, of course, not only very bright but, despite his own stardom, basically still a music fan.

'Fancy *you* chatting away with Prince,' one or two people remarked later.

'Why not?' I said. 'No other bugger was.'

In the late 1980s Janice left Radio 1. Our Elizabeth moved out of London to live in a Northamptonshire village. Jane 'Hattie' Buchanan got a job in New York, never to return. Alex, my twin, went on a holiday to Thailand and didn't come back, deciding instead to live on the beach. My social life withered to nought.

* * *

MEANWHILE, NEW ARRIVALS at the BBC – robotic zealots, true believers and little spivs in designer-label suits, crap-and-confidence modernisers, a corporate Khmer Rouge – towed in behind them hugely overpaid frauds and phoneys known as marketing or management consultants, all focus groups, fads, flip charts and strategy reviews upon whom licence payers' millions was pissed away. There was, suddenly, no instinct, no spontaneity any more. A producer couldn't make a good idea into a programme without it going first before a plenary committee or squirming through a steering group. Everything had to be priced and quantified. The dawning of the digital age was marked by pointless pen-pushing, paperwork and an internal invoicing innovation called Producer Choice. In this Year Zero insanity, knowledge was old hat. Experience was out. Walters, for one, was pensioned off. Cheap kids, who couldn't actually do the job, were in. Imagination was dangerous. Formulae had to be followed. If it wasn't new, it was bad and had to go.

The 1993 purge of Radio 1, to its credit, did cut out a lot of long-dead and rotten old wood. But its flaws were exposed when it became clear that what was to be done after the coup had not been properly planned and much of what was brought in to replace the old regime, although undeniably new, was in many cases, even more risible.

'How's ya shit, man?' The tall dark stranger, who had dived in behind me to catch the Egton House lift was, it later transpired, the son of the Bishop of Peterborough.

Affecting the vernacular and manner of a Brooklyn crack dealer – as appropriate and authentic as it would have been for me to present my programmes in a bogus Congolese accent – my new companion was also making downward arching hand movements as he addressed me, extending his thumbs and both index fingers in an attempt, it seemed, to draw my attention to his shoes.

'My *shit*?'

'Yeah, man. They tell me your shit's pretty good.'

'Who does?'

'My brothers. In fact, they say your shit's *real* good.'

'Well, I can't complain. The same as ever, you know. Ten o'clock every morning. With *Woman's Hour* on.'

'Yeah?'

'Yeah!'

He raised his hand to offer a high-five. I raised mine and we slapped palms.

'Westwood,' he said.

'Andy Kershaw,' I said.

We reached the third floor and the doors opened. I swung out.

'Man,' said Westwood before he was taken away, 'I dig your shit too!'

The new intake had arrived.

33

MY ACCIDENTAL LIFE
IN SHOWBIZ

(Warning – this chapter contains flash photography)

'IT'S GLORIA HUNNIFORD. FOR YOU.' Walters was stage-whispering and cupping his hand over the mouthpiece of the office phone. It was sometime in the late summer of 1987.

Eh? Why was the Queen of Radio 2 wanting to speak to me?

'Never you mind. I'll deal with her. Just you leave it to me. Get on with your work.' He returned to Gloria.

'Yes, yes. I see,' he was smarming, 'Yes, I'll tell him. Of course he will. No, that'll be fine. Don't you worry. Yes, I'll see to it. Jolly good. Thank you. Leave it with me. Not at all. On we go... Bye!'

'What's going on?' I asked.

'Oh nothing, really,' he breezed. 'Just Gloria Hunniford wanting you to date her daughter.'

'*What*?'

'Apparently, she's got a daughter, called Caron, who's just got herself this gig as a new presenter of *Blue Peter*. Lived in Northern Ireland until now but she's moved to London. Dear old Gloria is worried about the gel coming to the big city and thinks you'd be the bloke to look after her. She said, "I think Andy's just the kind of lad who'd keep Caron's feet on the ground".'

Later that same afternoon, Walters and I beetled down to a

vacant Radio 1 studio, which had a television, to catch that day's live transmission of *Blue Peter*. And there, smiling and stroking a dog, was Gloria's daughter. 'Ooh,' said Walters, 'she's a bit of a looker. She won't want to go out with you.'

Keeping young Caron's feet on the ground did not go quite as planned.

I was excited about going to see Tammy Wynette and had blagged two front stalls seats for her gig at the Royal Festival Hall, thinking Caron would be impressed that she was not only to be squired by a dashing young man about town but also to a concert by a living legend.

'We're going to see *who*?' she said, when we rendezvoused outside Broadcasting House.

She didn't, it seemed, recognise Tammy's true standing – a position way above the bad soft-rock norms of what passed for contemporary Nashville country. True country music, even in its finest expression, has always suffered in the UK from a lot of ill-informed, lazy stereotyping and clichéd criticism, lumping the good in with the bad, by those who, were they anatomists, would have identification difficulties with arse and elbow. I made a preliminary and rather pretty speech along these lines to Caron, outside Broadcasting House and then, on public transport, off we went.

I decided it best not to reveal to Caron – not on our first date, anyway – that when I had interviewed Tammy at the Wembley Country Festival, she had concluded that I was 'real cute' and had offered me a job 'taking care of my yard'. Graciously, I'd declined, suspecting this would have involved more than chopping logs and keeping the Wynette woodpile in order.

If Caron, once seated at the RFH, had been mildly troubled that I eagerly joined – and sometimes led – the applause which recognised Ms Wynette's many costume changes, it was when the band strolled into the intro to *I Don't Wanna Play House* that things took a turn for the worst. For the opening scenario – pre-school children at carefree play, oblivious to imminent divorce – set out in song by Tammy, I held it together. But I knew what was coming. And as Tammy downshifted a gear and hit that huge note as she sang of teardrops making her eyes grow dim, I erupted into uncontrollable sobs. Caron looked aghast. And then mortified.

Just to help the evening along, it was bucketing down as we left. We'd sploshed some distance, looking for a vacant taxi, before I managed to flag one to a halt.

'Crouch End, please,' I said. We were due at Our Elizabeth's for some food and drinks. Most of The Long Ryders were to be there, no doubt anxious for an eyewitness report from the frontline of the Queen of Country's gig.

'Nah. I'm not going there,' chirruped the cabbie. It was the era of Loadsamoney and the most vocal cheerleaders of that Thatcherite achievement were London's loveable taxi drivers. Such was the demand then for their services, many were reluctant to drive far from the easy pickings of central London. Others seemed to resent the inconvenience of having to carry passengers at all.

I reminded the driver that it was his obligation to take us a maximum distance of six miles from the point of collection, according to the regulations displayed in every black taxi. And I'd made it my business to be familiar with the perimeter of the six mile radius from London N8. We were just within it.

The rule book aside, the fat oik behind the wheel had no regard whatsoever for the woman who was, during this debate, drowning on the pavement. I told Caron to get in and I hopped aboard behind her. We sat there, the cab stationary, as the driver effed and blinded. He told us to get out. I refused. He threatened to drive to the nearest police station.

'Excellent!' I said. 'Please do. We'll sort this out there.'

By now the glamorous young saviour of *Blue Peter* was sobbing on the back seat.

The first police station our driver's cabbying skills located was in Camden, already halfway home. We paddled in, as a trio. There, an officer behind the desk advised the taxi driver to convey me and my weeping companion to Crouch End immediately. So he did, in silence, before wishing us, at the kerb – regular cock sparrer that he was – a cheery 'fack off.'

My talents and dependability for keeping her feet on the ground were not called upon a second time and I never again saw Caron Keating after our big night out. Nor did I get the chance later to apologise. Cruelly, the poor girl died young, from breast cancer, in 2004.

FIRST AS A *WHISTLE TEST* presenter and then as a Radio 1 DJ – albeit a DJ who'd never had any ambitions to be one – these brushes with celebrity were inevitable. Even with the protection of Walters and Peel and the sanctuary of Room 318, and despite being a specialist music broadcaster as opposed to a regular disc jockey, I was not entirely shielded from what became My Accidental Life In Showbiz.

Try as hard as I might to shut myself away in our office at Egton House with, perhaps, a pile of country blues reissues, or hide in my dressing room at Television Centre, sign-writing the bones of my *Whistle Test* links on a sheet of white card the size of a bedspread, I came up against rock stars, unavoidably, on a daily basis. In most of them – inarticulate, self-obsessed, over-rated mediocrities – I had no interest and couldn't get out of our encounters fast enough. There were, nevertheless, a number of rock & roll confrontations with those who, for me, were living gods. In the case of Little Richard, getting out of there fast enough was not an option he wanted me to have.

Radio 1 had two identical studios adjacent to each other, separated by a large pane of glass and a heavy soundproofed door. For the purposes of matey DJ chat, even off air, the studios were connected by an intercom. I would go downstairs from 318 to occupy my studio, and to set out all my records and bits and pieces, about an hour before going live. For much of my first two years Janice Long was on the air before me and I would go about my preparations listening to Janice's show and nattering to her either over the talk-back or by nipping in to see her next door.

One evening, Janice had Little Richard in as a live interviewee. Now, without wishing to drag you back over old ground, you will know already that I consider Little Richard and Jerry Lee Lewis to be the two most important figures in the history of rock & roll. Chuck Berry comes in a close third, mainly for his lyricism, while Elvis Presley was, in the AK Book of Rock & Roll, hardly deserving of a footnote. Agreed, Elvis's impact was massive. But popularity is no measure of quality. Almost an entire generation mistook a competent easy listening crooner for the King of Rock & Roll.

One can put on today Little Richard's *Rip It Up* or *Keep-A-Knockin'* and – more than fifty years after they were recorded – still they sound violent and shocking. In the case of the latter, one would be hard pushed to come up with a better audio definition of punk rock. God alone knows what the impact of Little Richard and his sound must have had on those first hearing it in the 1950s, although Peel once tried to explain the sensation by describing it as 'hazardous to teenage glands'.

I was, therefore, gawping through the glass into Janice's studio at a genuine legend and one of my living deities. The figure opposite Janice was quite astonishing: tiny, ostensibly female and, apparently, about twenty-three years old. (He was fifty-four.) Paying attention was a mistake. Those impish eyes flashed in my direction.

'Oh, my!' squealed Richard. 'Now, who's that purty young thang through there?'

Just as Janice was giggling that that was her mate Andy, Little Richard was out of his seat and tugging on the lead-lined connecting door. In a trice he was in my studio, his live radio interview forgotten.

'Well, hiiiiii!' he trilled. And lunged at me.

I swerved round the desk. He scampered after me. I made it to the other side. He stopped and I stopped. He feigned to go one way around the consoles and then, laughing, darted the other. Likewise, but to anticipate which way my admirer would jump, I was swinging first this way and then that. After a few seconds of this (I can't avoid the phrase) slippin' and slidin', I had my back to the door into the corridor. I grabbed it and made good my escape while the Queen of Rock & Roll was subdued and steered back to his interview with Janice by an unflappable minder from his record company.

✽ ✽ ✽

AWAY FROM ROCK music, famous figures from other walks of life, I noticed, had a startling habit of strolling through mine.

'It's my birthday today,' said Ned Sherrin one Saturday morning. I was making a guest appearance on Ned's Radio 4 programme *Loose Ends* and, for the broadcast, I'd ridden down to the BBC on my motorcycle.

'I wish I could get into those leather trousers,' the ample Thespian had remarked, as I walked into the studio.

'I wouldn't let you, Ned,' I said.

'We're having a few birthday drinks later at a friend's house in Clapham,' said Ned towards the end of the programme. 'Would you like to come?' He gave me the address and I said I'd follow everyone else down there on my bike.

The door was answered by the hostess. As she was welcoming me in, I heard a familiar – and notorious – mooing noise, swelling along the hallway. Frankie Howerd was barging towards me, hands outstretched, lips puckered.

'Francis! Come here! Do leave him alone,' Ned was shouting from back in the kitchen.

But 'Francis' was unstoppable. Within seconds of arriving, I was being chased along the hall, around the kitchen table and up and down the stairs by the comic genius, national treasure and outrageous old queen.

'Mmnnooowmmm! No. Wait! Yes. Stop him, someone! No! Yes! I *say*! Ooh, stand still! Yes!'

Arriving in tight black leather, from head to toe, I must have looked like Frankie Howerd's fantasy of a kissogram. In someone's possession, there is a priceless photo, taken that morning. I am sitting on my motorcycle, sandwiched between Ned Sherrin, who is astride the petrol tank, and Frankie Howerd, squeezed up behind me on the pillion.

'THE THING IS, DAME BARBARA,' I was yelling at Dame Barbara Cartland (she was quite deaf), 'even I had a moment's hesitation when I arrived at your house just now.'

The prolific romantic novelist and I were sharing a pink upholstered sofa in a pink upholstered room at her pink upholstered home in Hertfordshire. On the floor between our feet was a dozing King Charles spaniel, which had appalling and audible wind. Not that Dame Barbara seemed to notice. I was interviewing the old girl for a Radio 1 series I was making with Trevor Dann about modern Britain and we were round at Barbara's to talk about class and if those social rankings still had any meaning or relevance.

Despite the impact on a class-bound society of the two world wars and the social revolution of the 1960s, I was suggesting to a woman who seemed not to have noticed that decade, never mind been altered by it, that there was still a legacy of deference towards a perceived social hierarchy. Dame Barbara blinked her huge bowls of mascara. The spaniel let rip. I began to smirk and shudder with suppressed giggles. Who would the listeners assume was blowing off? Me or the grand old dame?

I pressed on with making my point. 'Yes, arriving here just now, I was a little uncertain – and I'm not someone who recognises class distinctions – what to do when we reached that fork in the driveway where one sign saying *Visitors* points towards the front of the house and another directs *Tradesmen* to the back. You see, Dame Barbara, I wasn't sure,' I heard myself saying, 'if I should present myself at the front door or come up your tradesman's entrance.'

'Precisely,' she said. 'There you are, dear!'

THERE IS JET-SETTING and there is regular long-haul air travel. Much of the last two and a half decades I have spent cultivating deep vein thrombosis and roughing it in steerage during the latter. Only once have I found myself flying first class. On an assignment to Haiti in the mid-1990s, I arrived at the Virgin Atlantic desk at Heathrow to check in for my flight to Miami, the first stage of the journey to Port-au-Prince.

'Oh,' said the lady on the desk, looking at her screen, 'I see you've been upgraded.'

She had no idea why or from whom this instruction and generosity had come but, within the hour, I was being directed up a spiral staircase in the lumpy bit at the front of a Boeing 747. To my surprise, there was a bar up there. To my even greater surprise, my two companions in first class were Danny La Rue and Dave Gilmour of The Pink Floyd. This must be one of the more unlikely trios to have been thrown together on a transatlantic flight. We bonded readily and convivially nevertheless.

As my new friends Danny and Dave swapped stories, I pitched in to relate the tale of another of my recent trips, when the *Observer* magazine had sent me to Oakland, California to interview and profile Sonny Barger, the world's most infamous Hell's Angel and the veteran outlaw motorcycle gang leader routinely but erroneously credited as the founder of the organisation.

I was apprehensive as I went in search of Barger and his boys at their clubhouse. These were the same guys who had beaten Hunter S. Thompson to within an inch of his death almost thirty years before. Hunter had also been hanging out with them, to research and write *Hell's Angels*, the book which made his name and established his style of gonzo journalism.

'Thompson was a pussy,' Barger told me, soon after he'd welcomed me in and I'd asked what he'd made of the book. I felt a tightening in my throat. In Little Rock, Arkansas, the previous autumn, I'd spent the best part of a week with Hunter, at the bar of the Capital Hotel, as we prepared ourselves to cover Bill Clinton's presidential election night in his home town. Not much I saw of Hunter then suggested feline.

By the end of the week with Barger and his boys I didn't want to go home. I am no subscriber by a long chalk to the Hell's Angel manifesto but there are few experiences as thrillingly pointless as riding out in a squadron of my beloved, booming Harley-Davidsons and to have the freeway traffic part at the approaching menace of this rolling thunder.

As I was taking my leave of Barger and his gang I had to ask him the unavoidable question. 'Sonny, if I wanted to do so, could I join the Oakland Hell's Angels?'

'I'm afraid not, Andy,' he said, putting his hand on my shoulder. 'You see, you're too nice of a guy.'

* * *

IF BARGER HAD once been a contender for Baddest Man on the Planet, that office, by the late 1980s, was occupied by the heavyweight boxing champion of the world, the crude but devastating Mike Tyson. I found myself squaring up to Iron Mike not because of the spurious celebrity status of the Radio 1 DJ but because of my lack of it.

Someone from Hoxton Boys' Club in London's east end had contacted Radio 1 asking for a famous DJ to present the club's annual boxing prizes. Having been directed first to the agents of Gary Davies, Steve Wright and the like – and been told of their fees – the applicant had returned to Radio 1 and the assistance of a nice executive there called Bill Morris. In a nutshell, Bill was asked which Radio 1 DJs came cheap. Below the level of cheap, Bill advised, was Our Man Kershaw and he offered my services. For free.

'Thanks,' he said when he outlined to me this *fait accompli*. 'You're doing us a favour. It'll be dead easy. All you'll have to do is stand there and hand over some trophies.'

At the club on the night, once I pinned down the organiser, I was given a scotch egg and a bag of crisps and made to wait in a side room. One or two sightseers put their heads around the door. 'Is that him?' one asked another. 'I've never heard of him, have you?'

The prize-giving itself was going as smoothly as one could have expected. I was seated at the end of a semi-circle of notables, including the mayor of Hoxton, on the stage and under the scrutiny of several hundred fidgeting small boys and their parents. A thin parade of these youngsters was filing across the stage, to undulating applause, and I began to hand over a lot of cheap cups as an official of the club read from a list of achievements. So far, so good.

Then something made me look up, towards the doors at the back of the hall. There at the end of the centre aisle, stark against the lights of the foyer was an unmistakeable silhouette. What the fuck was Mike Tyson doing here?

I froze, except for distractedly pumping the hand of some child whose trophy I was failing to hand over. Everyone in the hall, save those of us on the stage, had their backs to this apparition, unaware of who had just landed. Slowly, Tyson strode down the aisle, revealing his presence as he went. All hell unfurled.

By the time he reached the apron of the stage, after one of the longest fights of his career, he looked genuinely shaken. I reached down, offered him my hand and pulled him up to safety.

'Thankth,' he lisped. 'Whath going on, man? Whath going on?'

'I wish I knew,' I said.

Mike Tyson, it was later explained to me – under sedation – was in London for some promotional appearances. Earlier in the evening of our historic shared top billing at Hoxton Boys' Club, Tyson had appeared on the *Wogan* show on BBC television and from there, as a favour to Jarvis Astaire, a director of Wembley Stadium, who was also a patron of the Boys' Club, he had agreed to go with Astaire, his UK chaperone, over to Hoxton to give the lads a surprise and a treat. Clearly, no one had first told the Heavyweight Champion of the World that a low-ranking Radio 1 DJ, of whom no one had heard, had already been booked for that excitement.

Once the civil unrest had been quelled, Tyson agreed to take over my prize-giving role. And as Mike assumed his duties, another club official came and whispered to me that they wouldn't mind if I went home.

'IS ANDY THERE, PLEASE?' The phone had rung at my flat in Crouch End. It was answered by Our Elizabeth who, until she found her own place nearby, was sleeping on my sofa bed at 53 Elder Avenue, alongside whichever members of struggling American or African bands I had also invited to stay.

'No. Sorry. He's down in town. At the BBC, I think. Who's that?'

'It's Robert Plant. Please could you tell him I called? About Barrence Whitfield.'

'Pull the other one,' said Our Elizabeth. 'You'll be singing *Stairway To Heaven* next.'

The caller cleared his throat.

'There's a lady who's sure all that glitters is gold...'

'Fuck me,' said Elizabeth when I got back, and she was passing the message on to me. 'It really was Robert Plant.'

Robert had left a number. We'd not spoken before. When I called him back, he revealed himself to be a regular listener to my Thursday night Radio 1 programme and, like many others, had been blown away by an obscure import – the debut album of Boston, Massachusetts R&B hurricanes Barrence Whitfield & The Savages. The former Led Zeppelin front man had, furthermore, followed my excitable reports of my fearless fact-finding missions over to Boston to see Barrence and the Savages live. And now he had heard me announce that I had arranged their first UK dates and that their debut London gig was to be at Dingwall's in Camden Town in a couple of weeks.

Tousle-Haired Rock God Exhausted By Duracell Man. Making arrangements, at my kitchen table, for where Robert Plant and I should watch the next motorcycle race. Isle of Man TT, 2005. *Unknown*

Would I, Robert Plant was asking me, please keep a ticket for his collection on the night?

In what little chance we had to talk at the gig, Robert spoke only of his enthusiasm for Barrence and the band, and other music he had heard on my programmes. But some time soon after, I was waiting for a flight in a departure lounge at Oslo airport when my daydreaming was disrupted by a man with a mane of golden curls, vaulting towards me over rows of nearby empty seats. 'Andy! Andy!' he was shouting and waving a cassette in the air. It was Robert.

'I'm glad I've seen you,' he said, as though Oslo airport was one of my known hang-outs. 'You've got to hear this: a tape of some fabulous musicians I heard in Morocco recently. Take it. Have a listen.' And he was gone.

Years later, in June 2005, I brought Robert and his band over to the Isle of Man for two concerts in Douglas during the TT motorcycle races. Not for him hiding in hotel rooms between shows or scurrying back to the UK once they had performed – and done so triumphantly. He and his young musicians came with me to watch the races, taking shelter when the rain lashed down at the home of friends who lived on the course where we ate our picnic sitting in their kitchen. There, and at other spectating positions on the island, the man who once fronted a band that was a bigger concert draw and sold more albums than the Rolling Stones mucked in and chatted to any TT fan who chatted to him.

What I truly admire and like about Robert – and I was never a particular fan of Led Zeppelin – is that his phenomenal success and superstar status has not diminished his enthusiasm nor his curiosity for music in particular and life in general. And he is, despite the adulation heaped upon him for more than forty years, as down to earth as the next bloke sitting on a dry-stone wall, watching the TT races, with a sandwich in his hand.

34

LAWYERS, GUNS AND MONEY

WE WERE – facts had to be faced – surrounded by UNITA. The brutal right-wing guerrillas of Jonas Savimbi, until recently bankrolled by the United States, had the town of Cuito encircled. The war of terror which Savimbi had waged against the population of Angola and its elected government, for seventeen years on behalf of his former sponsors (who would, of course, later bring us the war *on* terror), had just passed its twentieth birthday. It was April 1996 and I had, literally, dropped in.

The light aircraft which had carried me from Luanda, the Angolan capital, to Cuito, in the dead centre of the country, was circling above the town, according to the altimeter in front of my nose, at 21,000 feet. I didn't realise small planes could reach this altitude, especially one with its passenger window flap pinned open. I was surprised to find I was still breathing.

'Hold tight!' shouted the pilot. The little plane plunged down to the right and my stomach soared up to the left. We were dropping in a tight corkscrew pattern, diving rapidly.

'What the fuck...?'

Not since I'd agreed to stand on the top of a biplane, flying stunts over the 1993 British Motorcycle Grand Prix at Donington Park, which – don't ask me how – was to raise money for charity, had I had such a horrific experience in the air.

'We've got to minimise ourselves as a target,' the pilot was yelling. 'UNITA has surface-to-air missiles.'

I was soon to be on very familiar terms with these.

To report on the heroic efforts of British de-mining teams – the Halo Trust and the Mines Advisory Group, both working closely with Oxfam – I was in Angola for BBC Radio 4's *The World Tonight*. In Cuito, the Halo Trust was kindly putting me up in a house they rented for their engineers, mostly former British army officers. Their main task was to train Angolans to clear mines for themselves. It was thankless, perilous work. Angola was already infested with an estimated twenty million landmines and these experts reckoned they were still being planted by both sides in the conflict faster than they were being removed. When I asked for their estimation as to when Angola would be mine-free, the answer was never.

The revolting consequences of these nasty, indiscriminate and enduring weapons were everywhere, horrors brought down largely upon civilians and a high proportion of those children. Angola, as a nation, was mutilated.

I HAVE BEEN in some fairly unpleasant hospitals in the poor world but the central hospital in Cuito was truly stomach-churning. I forced myself to tour the wards. If I were going to vomit, then so be it: the listeners at home should understand, I decided, how ghastly and massive this inhumanity was. (The UK, at the time, was still making and exporting anti-personnel mines.) In one of my reports, in which I confronted fresh mine injuries, I described the result of an anti-personnel detonation as 'to turn people into stewing steak' for that's what it looked like. This comparison was cut out of my report when it was broadcast on the grounds of 'taste'.

Exhausted doctors and other saintly medical staff were doing what they could to treat terrible injuries with almost nothing. The wards were as clean as the struggling medics could make them but the flies couldn't be kept out by broken windows. Squadrons of giddy bluebottles feasted on the bloodied bandaged stumps of mine victims, many of whom were writhing and screaming in agony.

Outside, the streets of Cuito made one wonder how *any* of its citizens had survived, with or without limbs. Thirty thousand had been killed during the 1993 UNITA offensive to capture the town. The main street had been, not long before my arrival, the front line of a long and vicious battle in which Cuito was recaptured by the MPLA government troops. The wreckage of that once elegant boulevard was almost as shocking as what I saw of the centre of Beirut at the end of the civil war there. In Lebanon, hardly a right-angle on any building left standing remained sharp or square. Such had been the quantity and intensity of flying hot metal over a fifteen year battle for the city, that everything was pitted, rounded, and looked as if it had been chewed by giant mutant wasps. Cuito was similarly gnarled by gunfire and shrapnel. Heavier weapons had been used too. There were many shattered and smashed buildings on the main street, some of several storeys, that had collapsed under bombardment to resemble concrete club sandwiches.

On a lane beside the Halo Trust house, I watched a woman one afternoon, with a mixture of horror and admiration, as she worked a little plot of land. She was swinging a hoe into the red earth, with a baby strapped to her back, and somehow balancing herself and child on her one remaining leg. In all likelihood, she would have been doing just this kind of work, to feed herself and her children, like so many other mine victims, when her other leg was torn off. And, still, she carried on. Because she had to.

Even without the constant terror of mines, survival was a grim and gruelling struggle. In the madhouse of oil-rich Angola, safe drinking water was more expensive than petrol and the curses of malaria and diarrhoea took their share of poor Angolans, as they do still, in a joint annual global death toll of more than three million. These illnesses – both water-related and, where there is the money and political will, easily preventable – do not get the headlines, nor the donations, afforded to AIDS. (Malaria and diarrhoea are not perceived to be sexy issues.) For that, the scale of the slaughter, largely of children, is all the more scandalous.

* * *

I GOT UP one morning, at Halo Trust HQ, to much merriment – not the routine of previous days.

'It's Sunday!' announced one of the team, when I asked which minefield we'd be finding ourselves in today. Sunday was, to my relief, and theirs – especially theirs – a day off. Soon after breakfast, the gin and tonics were handed round, the gin having been dispensed from the empty casing of a 120mm mortar shell, mounted on the wall, with an optic measure fitted to its base.

We filtered out into the garden, amid some talk among my new friends of whether it was more agreeable to see the tennis at the Queen's Club or Wimbledon during leave in London. I found myself a sunny position in which to lie back. It was against a stack of Soviet-made BM-21 Katyusha rockets, which the team had collected from around town, where much of this type of thing was lying on the streets, unused and abandoned. For safety, the Halo Trust boys had piled the rockets against the gable end of the house, along with a lot of other unexploded

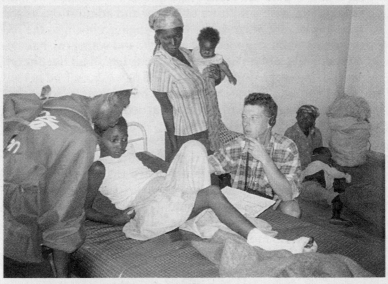

A nation mutilated – for big profits. Interviewing landmine victims in Cuito, Angola, during the civil war, for BBC Radio 4's *The World Tonight*, 1996. *Unknown*

ordnance arranged around the garden. On the other side of the wall from the Katyushas – which have a range of about nineteen miles – was, I realised, my bed.

One of the guys brought a ghetto-blaster out into the garden and a wallet of CDs. I had a leaf through it. Predictably, this collection comprised the usual suspects.

But, hang on! Somehow or other, amid this depressing assortment, was a Warren Zevon *Best Of*. I yelped at this discovery but no one among the de-miners claimed its ownership. ('Warren *who*? Must have been left here by someone else.') I threw myself on the CD player. Seconds later, I was sitting back against enough high explosive to obliterate a small town, gin & tonic in hand, chuffing on a cigarette, considering the real possibility of another UNITA attack and whacking my knee to *Lawyers, Guns and Money*. Would that Warren, the Hunter S. Thompson of rock & roll, were with us now!

> *I went home with a waitress,*
> *The way I always do.*
> *How was I to know,*
> *She was with the Russians too?*
> *I was gambling in Havana.*
> *I took a little risk.*
> *Send lawyers, guns and money.*
> *Get me out of this!*

THE FRONT LINES of the Angolan civil war were not what you'd call overcrowded with Radio 1 DJs doubling up as foreign correspondents. (I was a week in Cuito without even a glimpse of Andy Peebles.) Mine was a parallel career that had begun, as these things do, over a drink.

In the summer of 1989, I'd arranged to meet Gillian Reynolds, my surrogate mother and radio critic of the *Daily Telegraph,* for lunch at the Royal Festival Hall. We settled at a sunny table, outside my favourite London building. Over a couple of reflective beers, I confessed to Gillian that I felt unfulfilled. Not bored: I was enjoying enormously what I was doing and felt very lucky to be in that position. Things, in fact, couldn't have been going any better. But, if anything, it was all too easy. I wasn't stretching myself.

Already I'd made an uncommon jump for a Radio 1 DJ to become a regular contributor to Radio 4.

Out of the blue, in 1986, I'd been phoned by the broadcaster Russell Harty, then the host of Radio 4's *Start the Week*. Russell invited me for breakfast at a hotel near Broadcasting House at which we were joined by Michael Green, then the Radio 4 Controller. Michael, like his successor, David Hatch, was, as occupant of that office, a BBC species soon to become extinct. He had total confidence in his own producers, allowing them to use their imagination and instincts to get on with making outstanding programmes. If there is an opposite of control freak, Michael was it. As captain, he ran a happy Radio 4 ship.

Russell told Michael he thought I should be making and presenting programmes for Radio 4. Michael agreed. That was it. No focus groups or consultants were brought in over the marmalade. I was soon posted to producers Cathy Drysdale, with whom I'd start making archive-based features, and Simon Broughton on the arts magazine programme *Kaleidoscope*. With both Cathy and Simon I became great friends. Simon was producer of *Now That's What I Call Mali*, my radio adventure along the Niger, part of it with Ali Farka Toure. And I was soon a regular guest presenter of *Pick of the Week*, a dream job for me – someone who always had a radio on in every room. Walking through the heavy brass doors of Broadcasting House, I felt awe and real pride to be working for the most admired network of the most respected broadcasting organisation in the world. (Whether it is a job for Radio 3 or 4, that feeling in the foyer is just as strong for me today.) To be valued in those Radio 4 circles, by bright, like-minded friends, committed to excellence in programme making, gave me a sense of belonging beyond Room 318. I would derive enormous satisfaction and happiness, in the late-night solitude of Cathy's or Simon's office, listening through material or editing our tapes to make the best programme possible. It was, and still is, a thrill and a privilege.

As a Radio 4 regular, I would find myself rubbing shoulders

WITH Ker sh AW IN BEIRUT...

" Now here's a likely looking lad who should be able to tell us all about this constant, thumping beat you hear everywhere you go in the Lebanon..."

Cartoon by the much-missed Ray Lowry for the *New Musical Express*, late 1980s. Ray, as always, presented me with the original. *By kind permission of Sam Lowry*

with those whose company I never expected to enjoy, certainly not as an equal. At the network's cheese and wine parties, I would look forward to running into again, for example, the playwright, humourist and fellow radio lover, Peter Tinniswood who I once managed to introduce to his wife. ('Do you,' I asked, feeling sympathy with a shy-looking lady at the edge of our conversation circle, and coaxing her in, 'by any chance, know Peter Tinniswood?' 'Yes,' she said. 'I've been married to him for twenty years.')

At another of these dos I wondered if I was actually in the middle of some mad dream, chatting away merrily, as I was, with that irregular double-act, Alistair Cooke and Barbara Windsor. At some charity function, months later, Babs – as we showbiz insiders know her – made a bee-line for Our Elizabeth: ''Ere! I don't 'arf fancy your bravver!'

Print journalism, which I had not really pursued since my mid-teens, was also opening up to me again. For that, the credit must go to a Crouch End friend and neighbour, Susan Jeffries, who was at the time working on *The Listener*. Susan asked me to write for them a couple of book reviews and then an account of an adventure I'd had in the Dominican Republic. This led to an approach by the *Independent* and, soon after, the *Sunday Correspondent*, the *Observer* and the *Daily Telegraph*. My career was – good grief! – acquiring respectability.

The bulk of my writing and Radio 4 work, though, was music or travel related. But in the late 1980s we were living through extraordinary times. The world was in a spin cycle almost as dramatic as the turbulence of the 1960s. I was impatient to see that history in the making.

'So,' said Gillian as we gazed out along the Thames, 'what else would you like to be doing?'

'I've always fancied being a foreign correspondent,' I said.

This was only a partial bluff. A coward at heart, I may be, but I've always been a news junkie – and I'd probably read too many Graham Greenes for my own good.

'Well, go and be one,' Gillian said. Coming from my most trusted advisor and guardian, that settled that.

There was only one problem. Although I didn't doubt for a second that I could cut it, no news organisation, to begin with, was going to send me, someone with no track record in foreign journalism, and a Radio 1 DJ, off to cover major world events. I was going to have to start as a freelancer, deciding my own stories and destinations, and finance at least the earliest trips of this career move alone. So, I did. And I got lucky again.

My first foreign assignment, Graham Greene could not have better scripted himself.

35

HAITI: *THE COMEDIANS* REVISITED

AT THE FOOT of the aircraft steps were two men in dark suits and dark glasses. One was holding a video camera and filming our descent. The daylight at Port-au-Prince airport was not just intense but painful. I was feeling for the steps with my feet and rather relishing the appearance of the characters with the camcorder. Even without the obligatory pork-pie hats and Thompson sub-machine guns, they looked just like Tonton Macoutes secret police from 1960s newsreels of Papa Doc Duvalier's terror.

We had flown into Haiti from the neighbouring Dominican Republic. Our flight, after putting down briefly in Port-au-Prince, was then continuing to Miami. From the air, and as though studying a political atlas, it had been possible to see the border between the lush, green Dominican Republic and parched, brown, dusty Haiti. Poverty, brought on by decades of brutal misrule in the former richest colony on earth, had compelled the Haitians to cut down all the trees for firewood and charcoal. And that had triggered erosion. Also from the air, in the mouths of Haiti's rivers, the country's missing soil was clearly visible, washed away and deposited in the sea.

Once our plane had parked in front of the arrivals terminal, I stood up to reach down my BBC box from the overhead locker. A stewardess put a steadying hand on my arm.

'Sir, this is not Miami.'

'I know,' I said, thanked her and walked down the aisle.

Three of us got off.

I had persuaded Jonny Barnes and my friend Chris Heath, a writer on – of all things – *Smash Hits,* to join me on this adventure. To the most troubled of countries, Chris brought an unrivalled intimacy with the Pet Shop Boys. Both Jonny and Chris were veterans of our *Promised Land* odyssey a couple of years earlier. The deal with my pals was that after a week or so in the poorest and most wretched outpost of the western hemisphere we would then regroup and relax on St Barthelemy, described in the Caribbean Islands Handbook as 'young, French and sophisticated.' (For that, read 'smug, snobbish and shallow.' Trapped for a few mind-numbing days on St Barts, I decided enough was enough when, sitting at a pavement cafe one evening, I noticed that the show-off roaring up in a Jeep, wearing sunglasses after dark, and with a luxurious companion pouting in the passenger seat was Billy Joel.)

At the bottom of the steps at Port-au-Prince airport, I heard a military band strike up and, shielding my eyes, I watched a red carpet rolling toward us. Muscling along it was a hefty chap in military uniform, a peaked hat and bristling with brocade. Gathered about him were a number of soldiers, swinging automatic weapons. They barged straight for us. We had to swerve out of their way. The big guy plodded up the steps of the plane.

I recognised him from press photos. This was General Prosper Avril, Haiti's latest military dictator and the second army goon to grab the presidency since the Duvalier dynasty had fallen three years earlier. It had been from this same shabby terminal in February 1986 that Jean-Claude 'Baby Doc' Duvalier and his extravagant wife, Michelle, flew into exile. The first couple were collected by the Americans in a US Air Force transport plane – along with their closest cronies and crates of stolen cash – and, in a gesture of spectacular US generosity to the French, evacuated to Paris. This was the same pair to whom, when she visited Haiti in 1981, 'Mother' Teresa had remarked that she had 'never seen poor people being so familiar with their head of state'. The accomplished Albanian self-publicist and PR genius was in Port-au-Prince to accept the Haitian *Légion d'Honneur* and a substantial donation from the thieving dictatorship. Five years later, the poor brave Haitians – finally having lost their fear, and sick of Duvalier terror and misery – were at their most familiar with their slow-witted president and his grasping first lady the night they chased them all the way to this very airport.

Avril, we learned later, was flying first to Miami and then on to Taiwan to beg for foreign aid. For my first night in Haiti, the country was without its strongman. And in Haiti, as anywhere else, when the cat's away the mice will play. But as I was to discover just a few hours later, many of the mice in Haiti had guns.

A NUMBER OF FACTORS had decided Haiti as my destination for this first of more than twenty trips to the island. I had looked along my record shelves and noticed I had music from every Caribbean island except Haiti. I wondered why it was, apparently, a musical black hole. The republic's recent history was still alive and still unfolding. The radio news reports of Baby Doc's departure remained vivid. Haiti seemed to be a country in constant turmoil. Just to mention I was thinking of going there caused friends, even journalists among them, to recoil. Everyone was frightened of Haiti. Especially me. My in-at-the-deep-end instincts were stirring.

Also, I'd just read *The Comedians* by Graham Greene. Much of the action in Greene's not-so-fictional mid 1960s novel about Haiti under Papa Doc takes place in an eccentric colonial hotel in Port-au-Prince called the Trianon. Over a curry in London, Joe Boyd told me the hotel actually existed but its real name was the Oloffson, a filigreed wooden mansion built in the late nineteenth century in the style known as gingerbread. Joe had been one of those who in the mid 1970s – before the regime of Baby Doc revealed itself to be as brutal as that of his father, Papa Doc

– went down to Haiti when it was enjoying that bogus *belle époque*. Among many celebrities who were then seduced by Haiti as a chi-chi hideaway were Mick Jagger and Jacqueline Onassis. It was Oloffson legend that Jagger had written, or had been inspired to write, much of the Rolling Stones album, *Emotional Rescue* on the hotel's veranda.

Then, on the caper to Guernsey, where I found my friend Alex had impersonated me for twenty-four hours, I picked up a copy of *National Geographic*, left by a previous passenger in the aeroplane's seat pocket. In it was a long feature on Haiti. Prominent in that was the remarkable character of Jean-Bertrand Aristide, a liberation theologian Catholic priest who, according to the report, had been the only public figure in Port-au-Prince to have had the bravery to stand up to Duvalier and the military thugs. From his little church of St Jean Bosco, in the city's slums, Aristide preached fearlessly every Sunday against the injustices and the cruelties of the regime.

The measure of his effectiveness and the threat he presented to those with power and money was recognised in the most audacious attempt on his life. In September 1988, the Tonton Macoutes had stormed the church during his Sunday morning mass, machine-gunned and macheted the congregation and opened fire on Aristide as he stood on the altar. Miraculously, he wasn't killed but around a hundred of his congregation were butchered. Policemen and soldiers stood across the street and watched as the killers arrived in vehicles laid on by the mayor of Port-au-Prince, Franck Romain, a big Macoute himself. Municipal rubbish trucks came to cart away the bodies. The Macoutes' parting violation was to burn down the church. Aristide's survival only enhanced the divine status already conferred upon him by Haiti's downtrodden. At the insistence of his supporters, he went to ground. I wanted to meet him. He was still in hiding when I first arrived in Haiti in December 1989.

JONNY, CHRIS AND I checked in to the peeling, raffish romance of the Oloffson Hotel. And for the next ten years, it would be my home-from-home.

The Oloffson is the centre of Port-au-Prince social life – and not just because there is nowhere else to go. On the veranda every evening would gather local politicians, foreign embassy staff, journalists, aid workers, shadowy 'art dealers', wealthy bohemian American women of a certain age looking for exoticism and liaisons, Tonton Macoutes, adventurers, mercenaries, eccentrics-without-portfolio, spies for the current regime, spies for the regime-in-waiting, lobbyists, emissaries of Washington think-tanks both of the left and right, Aristide groupies, Aristide tormentors, CIA officers and tiresome unshaven preening French photographers who regarded themselves more as combatants than chroniclers. Either mingling or eyeing each other with suspicion, these characters would gather to gossip and to plot, eavesdrop and evangelise, drink and dine, and dance to Richard Morse's Haitian roots band, Ram.

Richard, the young, languid Haitian-American owner of the Oloffson, was directing his staff from the veranda. It was breakfast time, our first morning in Haiti. Out on my balcony bed, with only a ragged mosquito net for protection, I'd had little sleep but plenty to occupy my thoughts. Gunfire had been popping all across the city for most of the night. There was one exchange of very loud automatic fire from what seemed to be the street just beyond the Oloffson's garden wall. Who had been shooting at whom wasn't clear. Mad dogs, yelping near and far, had kept up a constant call and response through the darkness. When the sun came up, early, there was an exquisite humming bird, no bigger than my thumb, inside my net.

Richard was unflappable, a characteristic of his I would come to know well and one which would secure his tenure to this day of the world's greatest and wonkiest hotel.

'There's a body at the bottom of the garden,' he shouted down, in Creole, to a couple of Oloffson operatives on the drive. The two men turned without a word and sloped off to pick up and remove the intrusive corpse. (Students of *The Comedians* will recall that, in an early chapter, the body of the Minister of Public Works is found in the hotel swimming pool on a similar morning.)

– 331 –

'Welcome to Haiti,' Richard grinned, adopting his customary breakfast position, his foot up on a vacant chair at our table and dragging on a *Comme Il Faut* Haitian cigarette. Richard always has the look of one who is pleasantly, and possibly necessarily, herbally-refreshed, even at breakfast time.

We carried on with our omelettes.

I LIKE AND ADMIRE Richard a lot. He bought the lease on the Oloffson in 1987 for $20 from a voodoo priest in the back of a taxi. Previously, he'd been in punk rock bands in New York City where he'd grown up, the son of an American academic and a renowned Haitian dancer. Richard figured that, in the near-constant uproar of Haiti, the elegant old hotel would be filled with journalists and, during periods of relative calm, a few tourists would be drawn to the famous veranda. Not many of the latter had troubled the drowsy waiters since Richard and his Haitian wife, Lunise, had taken over. The couple found themselves living out a piece Graham Greene had written for the *New Yorker* in the early 1960s, and which he developed into *The Comedians*. Based on his first visit to the Oloffson, Greene's essay was called *The Mechanics Of Running An Empty Hotel*.

Little had changed. It would not be surprising to see bats flying in and out of the open shutters onto the veranda and the Oloffson of the late 1980s and 1990s still had its own cast of Comedians.

Aside from Richard there was Aubelin Joilcoeur, a real-life character from the book who Greene had portrayed in the novel as Petit Pierre, a slippery though charming socialite and gadfly gossip columnist. Greene gave Aubelin a sinister side, as a spy on the Oloffson veranda for Papa Doc and the Tonton Macoutes. The hotel terrace and bar has always been a magnet and a refuge – the only one in Port-au-Prince – for the city's movers and shakers and visitors of any significance. It was also Aubelin's stage. While he vigorously denounced *The Comedians* and his portrayal in it, he was quietly flattered by the fame and immortality Greene had conferred upon him and he would reminisce fondly of the time the two spent together on the veranda.

I never felt a day in Haiti had properly begun until Aubelin

Richard Morse, owner of the Oloffson in Port-au-Prince, Haiti, on the hotel's front steps, January 1990. Richard is still at the helm, and the hotel survived the earthquake of 2010. *AK*

– miniature, and of burnished chocolate – had arrived for breakfast, clicking up the front steps to the veranda with his gold-topped cane and dressed, to cross the squalour of Port-au-Prince, in an impeccable suit and silk cravat. He was still fond of quoting Wordsworth, speaking in meticulous English, when not in classical French.

'Ah,' he would sigh, staring out over the teeming, stinking city – which offended his refinement – to the bay beyond, 'distance lends enchantment to the view...'

If Aubelin Jolicoeur (translation: Little Dawn Pretty Heart) wasn't actually a spy, then he was, in the land of the midnight knock, certainly the great survivor, bending effortlessly with unpredictable political cyclones. I once asked him if he was or ever had been a spook or a Macoute. He feigned mortal offence, naturally. Then he offered some sharp analysis.

'Everyone in Haiti is a Tonton Macoute. It's in their blood. It's their mentality. You give a man a little power, you give him a gun and he uses that power or that gun to keep above the rest and to keep them down.'

The Tonton Macoutes were established in 1958 by Papa Doc Duvalier. He had become president the year before. Following an assassination attempt he did not fully trust his own army – with good reason – and so, as a counterbalance to the military, he set up the Volontaires de la Sécurité Nationale, a para-military of civilian thugs, answerable personally to the President For Life and used by him to eliminate his opponents and to rule by terror. The VSN's popular name was borrowed from a bogeyman of Haitian folklore. Tonton Macoute (Uncle Knapsack), during the night, carried off naughty children in his bag. The Macoutes' only official leader was a woman, the particularly sadistic Madame Max Adolphe. But there were, down the decades, many other *de facto* heads of the Tonton Macoutes. With the demise of the Duvaliers in 1986 the Macoutes were disbanded. But, as Aubelin suggested, Macoutism, as a state of mind and a political method, never disappeared.

Among the other characters Richard had inherited with the hotel was Monsieur Jacques, the masseur. Poor Jacques had not got his hands on anyone for years but that did not deter him from rolling up at the Oloffson every morning where he would settle for the day on a bench on the veranda like a fat bluebottle. When he wasn't napping, Jacques would blink out sadly towards the city through his thick spectacles. His long silences were broken only by memories of those to whom he had given muscular relief. 'Me? I give good massage,' he would insist to all-comers. 'I give good massage to Jacqueline Kennedy.'

The former American first lady was the client Jacques recalled most frequently although he never said any more than this and had probably forgotten he'd told me many times before of his attentions to Jackie O. Then we'd sit there together some more, again in silence, still gazing out over the madhouse of Port-au-Prince. If, during those soporific afternoons, Jacques wasn't daydreaming about rubbing his hands along the alabaster flanks of the most beautiful woman of the age, then I was.

Our reverie on the veranda was often disrupted by an elderly pale-skinned creole man, with brilliantined hair, known as 'Mr Thompson'. He, it was said, lived underneath the hotel, sleeping among the wooden legs of the gently rotting structure. Mr Thompson had only one line of conversation: 'You want to go to the beach today?'

The nearest beach, worthy of the name, is a stretch of white coral sand, among mangroves, about thirty miles from the capital. A beauty spot incongruous to its surroundings, it has no facilities and very few visitors. This did not deter Mr Thompson, who peddled his day trips tirelessly, regardless of the reality that he never had any takers. Even if someone were to sign up, he had no means of getting them there.

A hefty perspiring German, called Rolf, with a moustache that only a German would attempt, and then not outside the context of a 1970s porn film, had appointed himself the redeemer of the Oloffson's whimsical plumbing. For many years Rolf's job was to stride along the veranda, puffing and cursing the mysteries of the hotel's water supply and sanitation, usually with pipes and fittings in hand. Although he was constantly busy, no improvement was ever noticeable for Rolf's efforts and his profanities. It was said he'd arrived in Haiti, not with plumbing qualifications, but with a warrant for his arrest in the Dominican Republic. It was impolite to ask what for. Just as it would have been poor form to ask why my shower in Chambre Onze had never more than dribbled through two dictatorships and as many democracies.

During her long shifts, the gloomy reception desk and the ancient switchboard were the sovereign territory of the formidable Douca, a woman with a heart of gold, a vast bottom, and an unfortunate vulnerability to voodoo possessions (which were particularly inconvenient for me when they took hold of Douca just as I needed her to put me through to London to file copy for the BBC or a newspaper).

BACK OUTSIDE ON the veranda, graduation from intrepid traveller to foreign correspondent came, over repeat trips, with my adoption and schooling by Greg Chamberlain, the most authoritative of reporters in Haiti. For donkey's years Greg had been the *Guardian*'s Caribbean correspondent but he wasted little of his time on less fascinating islands. His first morning in Haiti had been in 1971, when he was woken in some guest house to be told Papa Doc had died during the night. Greg was, and is, spectacularly unconventional: wild-haired and always dressed in his uniform of sagging jeans, Aertex shirts and sandals, but nevertheless considered the oracle by all the other foreign hacks. His knowledge of Haiti, its history and his familiarity with all the players and their motivations, he dispensed generously and with boyish enthusiasm to anyone who showed an interest in his adopted country. Even the big hitters of the American news media, no matter how self-important, usually found reserves of humility at some point to ask for Greg's guidance as to what was really going on.

The American reporters, for whom Haiti was always a big story, would descend on the Oloffson for that Chamberlain wisdom and illumination and perhaps a drink or a meal. Few had the sense of humour or the reserves of irony required to stay there. They preferred one of the rather neutral hotels just out of town, with full working facilities, and considered the Oloffson to be the domain of the Englishmen. (And, naturally, mad dogs.) But if our American cousins were not exactly envious of Rolf's plumbing, the more imaginative among them were, I think, secretly in admiration of our capacity to tolerate it, if not to find it all rather charming.

For more than a decade, Greg and I became inseparable in our adopted second home with our surrogate family of Comedians.

Richard went as far as to name rooms after both of us, along with those celebrating the more illustrious Oloffson occupants of yesteryear. ('Will you be wanting the Mick Jagger, the John Gielgud or the Graham Greene suite, madam? Oh, just our cut-price Andy Kershaw closet, is it?')

At our favourite perch, the *table ronde* at the far corner of the veranda, next to Richard's office, Greg taught me all the basics. ('Say what you mean, mate.' 'Don't use boring words.'). The round table became our HQ, at which we'd work, conduct interviews, gossip, dissect Haitian politics, drink and eat, often with guests and always with friends. Chief among the latter was my faithful old Creole translator, Milford Bruno, who also owned a souvenir shop across the street from the Oloffson, despite there having been scarcely any tourists for decades to buy Milford's jolly mementoes. We were usually joined, too, by our buddy Jorgen Leth, a suave Dane, resident in Haiti, and Copenhagen's Honorary Consul. Jorgen is also an internationally renowned director of avant garde documentaries about – I am not making this up – cycling.

Recognising each other as connoisseurs of the absurd, Greg and I clicked immediately. It was that fondness for the ridiculous which had led us both – years apart – to become obsessed by the most exhilarating and exasperating country on earth. We also discovered a common history as Leeds University alumni – Greg was there in the early 1960s – and that neither of us owned what are regarded by others as smart clothes. In fact, being of healthy appetite, and in his ill-fitting attire, Greg has the appearance and demeanour of an animated duffle bag.

The seal on our friendship, however, was a shared enthusiasm for plastic bags. Quite independently, before we met, we had both decided that executive luggage was impractical and vulgar. The humble plastic bag was all one needed on most occasions. I also had the extravagance of a rucksack and my trusty BBC box (a robust LP carrying case) but Greg would arrive for a fortnight's stay at the Oloffson and get out of the taxi with his belongings in only a couple of faithful supermarket carriers. And one of those was most likely full of grapes.

* * *

The Comedians – Class of 1993, at the Oloffson. Clockwise, from top left: Monsieur Jacques on his perch on the veranda; veteran Duvalierist, Serge Beaulieu, who once put a gun to my head; my great friend and journalism mentor, Greg Chamberlain, celebrates the naming of rooms in our honour at the Oloffson; Aubelin Jolicoeur, a real-life character from Graham Greene's novel. *AK*

MOST EVENINGS in Haiti would culminate at the Oloffson's wonderful old mahogany bar. It was here, one evening that Serge Beaulieu – a much-feared yet ordinarily charming and expansive veteran Duvalierist who sported a trademark purple beret and Ernest Hemingway beard – growled at me from his stool.

'You are Mr Paul Lashmar,' he began.

'No. Sorry, not me. You've got the wrong guy,' I said, settling with a G&T on to the seat next to him.

'You,' he repeated, now booming, 'are Mr Paul Lashmar.'

'I've told you once: I am *not* Paul Lashmar.'

Just as I was recalling that my friend Lashmar, a British journalist then working on the *Observer*, had been with me to interview Beaulieu on the last occasion we'd met a year before, this sinister and garrulous grizzly bear leaned towards me, slid from his belt a revolver and held the muzzle an inch from my nose. It was a big bugger, in shiny metallic finish and with an uncommonly long barrel.

'Mr Lashmar, you wrote lies about me in the British press.' His finger was on the trigger.

I suppose what Paul had written subsequently about Beaulieu – some allusion to his reputation as a fat Macoute – was not, from Serge's standpoint, a triumph of PR. Beaulieu, though enjoying the fear he commanded and his larger than life reputation, liked to position himself at the plausible and respectable end of Duvalierist violence.

Luckily I had, still with me from a day working around town, the plastic bag in which I carried my Sony Pro cassette recorder, other professional bits and pieces, and my passport. Before Beaulieu had chance to think I might also be going for a gun, I had that identification in my hand. I pushed it towards him, flat along the bar top. Still with the gun pointing into my face he flipped the passport open. Then he roared laughing and slammed the revolver down on the bar.

'Get my friend here a gin and tonic,' he bellowed at the barman. 'A large one!'

* * *

THIS WAS NOT my first nor my last flirtation with firearms in Haiti. My debut as the bloke who is always without one in these situations had come on my first evening in the country with, as a trio of innocents abroad, my pals Jonny Barnes (mild-mannered London solicitor) and Chris Heath (Boswell to the Pet Shop Boys).

'Whatever you do, don't find yourself outside of Port-au-Prince after dark, trying to get back into town,' I had been warned by the only BBC colleague I could find, a reporter at the World Service, who had visited Haiti. This was the one solitary snippet of travel advice I was given before setting off.

After going for a meal up in Petionville, the affluent suburb of Port-au-Prince, in the mountains above the city proper, we found ourselves, naturally, trying to get back into town, and back to the Oloffson, after dark. We flagged down a minibus taxi going our way and jumped in, occupying, as a trio, a bench seat across the centre of the vehicle. On the long twisting descent, and in the darkness of the bus, I became aware that the guy sitting immediately in front of us was very drunk and getting increasingly agitated and loud. An argument with himself developed into an argument with the chap seated behind us. We were, suddenly, and literally, in the middle of a bloody great row, in Creole, between the two. With a yell, the guy in front whipped out a pistol and, mad with drink, waved and pointed it in our faces, swaying to take aim at the bloke in the back. The traffic, meanwhile, bunched up and our minibus slowed to a halt. I saw our chance, grabbed the handle of the sliding passenger door and yanked it hard. Even with the bus pointing steeply downhill, it flew back and I tumbled out, pulling Jonny or Chris after me. We were, all three of us, in a heap on the grass verge and, in a split second, lost to the gunman in the darkness.

It had been quite a day. Soon after checking in at the Oloffson we'd headed down into the city to find the ruins of St Jean Bosco, Aristide's burnt-out church in the slum area of La Saline, down near the waterfront. It was remarkable just how quickly nature was reclaiming the blackened shell. Only just over a year after the attack, already it had the air of an ancient monument with weeds and saplings pushing through the weathered rubble.

I asked an old man sitting at the gates where Aristide might be found. His reflex nervousness lifted when I showed him my BBC card. A taxi suddenly materialised. The old man conferred with the driver. We were urged to get in and off we bumped, back up into the leafier part of the city, not too far from the Oloffson.

By the high wall of a compound in a quiet street we pulled up and the driver pointed towards some heavy steel gates. As I was tapping on them I glanced up to see a familiar bug-eyed face looking down at me from an upper window of the building within. It was Aristide.

A child put his head round the gate. In my O-Level French I explained our presence. We were shown into the yard where we waited under a mango tree. After a couple of minutes, there he was, a tiny fragile-looking figure in an open-necked white shirt, with a thin moustache and thick glasses behind which his eyes looked in differing directions. We shook hands and in perfect English, one of his five fluent languages, he invited us in. The building, he said, was part of a convent. It was from here that he was continuing to run his mission and orphanage for the city's street kids, just as he'd done at the little church. If this was Aristide in hiding, he wasn't making a very good job of his self-concealment.

In a garishly furnished reception room we settled into some easy chairs, I ran a tape and the previously diffident little man hit the ignition. Eyes bulging and speaking in shrill staccato bursts he raged against the plight of Haiti: the violence of successive dictatorships; the predatory and callous elite, pulling the strings of those regimes to guarantee its obscene wealth and to keep Haiti's masses in their place; and the sinister role of the American Embassy. The US, said Aristide, was 'the devil'. (In 1991, and again in 2004, his presidency would be ended by CIA-engineered coups. On the latter occasion, he would be kidnapped by US Special Forces, deposed and dumped into exile in the Central African Republic.)

'Haitians have always had to eat the crumbs that fall from the table,' he said. 'One day we will all sit around the table and share the cake.'

'I've arrived only today in Port-au-Prince,' I told him, 'and I'm astonished by the extent of the graffiti all over the city saying *Titid prezidan*.' (Titid was his followers' affectionate name for Aristide.) 'In the unlikely event of there being held here, in the future, a free and fair presidential election, would you consider standing?' The previous election in 1987 had been abandoned after the Tonton Macoutes massacred voters at a polling station.

'No. No. No. Never,' he said. 'I do not want political office.'

This was December 1989. Just fourteen months later, I was standing below Aristide on the steps of the presidential palace as the sash of office was placed around his neck and more than a million of his adoring dispossessed, beyond the railings on the Champs de Mars, went daft. The tiny but fearless champion of the wretched had won Haiti's first free election by a huge landslide.

At our clandestine first meeting in the convent, I became straight away an Aristide groupie. There was, for me, no other possible human response to the pocket-sized priest's courage and conviction. He was the living embodiment of the folk hero, the little guy taking on, against all odds, and in the most extreme and dangerous circumstances, the big bully, selflessly and on behalf of the downtrodden.

AFTER THAT, I couldn't keep away from Haiti and the amazing midget warrior for justice. For much of 1990, I was flying off to Port-au-Prince as often as time and money would allow. In August of that year I arrived at the Oloffson to learn that Dan Quayle, the much-ridiculed United States vice-president to George Bush Senior, was arriving in town the next day. It was to a journalist what an open goal in the dying seconds of a world cup final must be to a footballer. The next morning, I walked down to the palace for Quayle's speech and press conference.

It is possible that Quayle, on arrival, had to be briefed backstage that he was in Haiti, not Tahiti. The first he knew of his speech may have been when he read it to his audience of grim-faced Haitian generals, me and a few other hacks. But to his credit, Quayle did utter that morning a few words which, I realised in a flash, guaranteed my little pal the presidency. New elections had been scheduled for December 1990. Quayle sent out the signal that the USA, upholders of at least four pitilessly brutal and undemocratic regimes in recent memory, would not tolerate another.

'No coups, no threats, no murders,' stammered Dan. 'The brave people of Haiti deserve democracy.'

From that moment, Aristide was president-elect. And the United States, which had routinely denounced him thus far as a communist extremist must have known that too. Never again did I tell another Dan Quayle joke.

Back at Broadcasting House, I knocked on the door of Michael Green. The saintly Radio 4 Controller put aside what he was doing and listened with me to some of the recordings I'd made in Haiti over the previous few months.

'I think it's a good story,' I ventured, 'following this unlikely little bloke from fugitive to president.'

Michael simply picked up the phone and called Noah Richler, a young producer of Canadian origin who I'd not then met. In the fullness of time, Noah and I would make Radio 4 documentaries in Cuba, Guinea and Malawi during the final days of Dr Hastings Banda. Michael told Noah he was sending me downstairs to see him straight away, and with some remarkable tapes.

'See what the two of you can do with them together. I'd like you to follow it through.'

Noah was rugged, fearless, imaginative and funny. If I'd been a woman, he wouldn't have stood a chance. Instead, we became as brothers, both overflowing hazardously with testosterone. Together we went to Port-au-Prince to complete the recordings for what became that fugitive-to-president feature, a three-part Radio 4 series called *Haiti in Three Acts* (Noah's idea, that title), during that electrifying December presidential campaign.

I CAN SHUDDER now at the fear that seized me every morning when I woke during those two weeks. Dawn on polling day itself was particularly terrifying. I remember hanging over the wooden rail of my balcony in Chambre Onze, as the sky turned from rich purple to orange, wondering what horrors I would witness that day. But once we were out around town, and focused on the work, excitement banished the terror. It was humbling and instructive, too, to watch brave Haitians lining up at polling stations, their memory of 1987's election slaughter still red and raw. More than once I had to tell myself to stop being a big nancy.

We went to delirious Aristide rallies and public speeches at which we expected a Macoute attack at any moment. At least one had been hand-grenaded, killing five. But, foolishly perhaps, I found a security in the solidarity and euphoria and, at his biggest election gathering, I stood alongside Aristide on a chaotic stage on the vast Champs De Mars plaza in front of the presidential palace, holding my humble Sony Pro microphone to his mouth as he went through a spine-tingling call and response routine with a gigantic, ecstatic crowd.

'Why don't we, for a change, turn the tables,' said Noah one morning over our Oloffson breakfast, 'and go and confront the Macoutes?'

We got on the phone to the biggest, most audacious Tonton Macoute of them all, Roger Lafontant, at his base up on the dreary Delmas road. Lafontant had been Interior Minister under Baby Doc and the chief – insofar as they had one – of the Macoutes. But, with Duvalier's departure, he'd gone into exile in the Dominican Republic. There he stayed, still a strong upholder of Duvalierism, until the summer of 1990 when, in the most sinister development before the December election, he'd returned to Port-au-Prince to sabotage an Aristide victory. Few doubted that Lafontant would stop at anything. A warrant for his arrest had been issued back in the summer. It had not been enforced.

'Yes,' he purred down the phone. 'Why don't you come round for breakfast tomorrow?' It would be the eve of polling.

Like most notorious brutes I would meet over the years, Lafontant was charm and urbanity itself. Fresh coffee was served from real china. Warm croissants were handed round while Lafontant, at his desk, flanked by some silent and deeply sinister veteran Macoutes, spoke first of his fondness for British football, particularly Liverpool FC, before turning his thoughts to the election and Aristide.

'The priest he is an ultra-communist,' he said, smirking around the assembled. 'I will fight him.'

'How?' I asked.

'How? Legally!'

Outside in his compound, as we were leaving, dozens of Lafontant's armed enforcers were sitting around sullenly. One, I noticed, was polishing an Uzi sub-machine gun – sleek, black and compact.

Not a shot was fired on election day, a miracle for Haiti. But Lafontant and his lads did not fight legally nor behave themselves for too long. On the night of 6 January 1991, between Aristide's December election and his scheduled inauguration in early February, Lafontant staged an attempted coup. This had been encouraged by the hated Catholic Archbishop of Port-au-Prince, who warned in a radio broadcast that Aristide would run Haiti as a Bolshevik dictatorship. Lafontant's occupation of the presidential palace lasted just a few hours. He had badly miscalculated. The army showed unprecedented loyalty to the democratic will. Following a half hour gun battle at the palace, Lafontant was carted off to jail in handcuffs. He would later be murdered there under circumstances which have never become clear.

The failed coup for Lafontant handed a small, successful professional one to me. I reported it for *Newsnight*, from the vantage point of BBC Television Centre, having returned from Haiti – maddeningly – only a couple of days before Lafontant had a pop.

'ARE YOU THE OWNER?'

The woman who had appeared at the top of the Oloffson's steps and was now snapping at me from half way along the veranda was small, middle-aged, copper-haired, spoke with a posh English accent and was wearing an implausible and rather risky amount of gold jewellery.

'No, I'm afraid I'm just a guest,' I said. 'But can I help you? I almost live here.'

It was sometime in 1993. Aristide, overthrown in September 1991, was in exile. The goons were back in the palace and I had been enjoying, until now, a quiet, solitary afternoon on the Oloffson's veranda. But this being Haiti, and the Oloffson, anything could happen next – and probably would. One afternoon, sitting alone at the *table ronde*, I had looked up to see former US president Jimmy Carter, standing there hoping to spot someone proprietorial. He was, he later told me, in town on a mission for his human rights foundation. I recognised the guy with him to be Andrew Young, Carter's former ambassador to the United Nations, civil rights activist, friend of Martin Luther King and one of those on the balcony of the Lorraine Motel, and in the famous photo, when Dr King was shot. They were looking for some lunch.

'Well, where *is* the owner?' the headmistress apparition was demanding, stepping bossily towards my table.

'I think he's probably having a sleep,' I said.

'A *sleep*? But I want to check in. I've just arrived. What sort of hotel is this?'

'Er... welcome to the Oloffson,' I said. 'Can I get you a drink?'

It turned out I could get her several, but Ann Leslie, doyenne of Fleet Street, scourge of soft lefties like me, and fearless foreign reporter, had a heart of gold. And a *Daily Mail* expense account. She insisted on picking up the tab for our regular gin and tonics, over which we bonded into a most unlikely professional partnership and, in time, good pals.

'Well, I'd like to see something of the city this afternoon,' said the great Dame, as she would later become. 'Do you have a car?'

Richard, now awake, gave me the keys to his pick-up truck and I took Ann off on a tour of the city. We had a row before we reached the end of the drive. (Best to get these things out of the way first.) Ann had been parroting a lot of the right-wing black-propaganda about Aristide, much of it a confection from the CIA's spooks in Langley, Virginia. I hit back with one or two of my fan-club eulogies. On the way into town we agreed to disagree. I drove her past the charred ruins of St Jean Bosco.

That shut her up for at least a minute. Then we turned left through La Saline towards the seafront. Up ahead there, I spotted a crowd, rings of slum-dwellers pressing to look at something on the ground. My instincts for unpleasantness were now finely attuned. I could read the signals.

'Wait here,' I said, jumping down from the pick-up, as though Ann was a novice to these matters.

I squeezed through the outer circle of the throng. Two men, their uniforms suggesting police, were lying face down, dead, in the mud. Each had a black bullet hole in the back of the skull, their hands were tied behind their backs and on the shoulders of both was placed a dead rat.

'Some kind of voodoo thing?' Ann was, of course, already right at my side, totally unfazed by the spectacle.

A number of Haitians, very loudly and all at once, were explaining to us that these were not real policemen but thugs who for weeks had dressed as police to terrorise and extort these streets. La Saline Neighbourhood Watch had finally hit back.

'Bloody hell,' I said. 'Are you crazy? You shouldn't wear all that conspicuous jewellery round here!' Ann was still rattling with gold and sparkling gems.

'What? Oh! It's what I call my Hendon Flash,' she laughed.

Back in the pick-up Ann de-gilded herself and stuffed the lot in the glove box. Then, like all newcomers to Haiti, she asked me the inevitable question.

'Can we go to a voodoo ceremony?'

My heart sank. Could I pretend this wasn't possible? I knew I would have to accompany her.

Voodoo is an official religion of Haiti. Its origins are the animist beliefs of Africa, brought to the Caribbean with slavery and adapted to include many Christian symbols and saints, originally to disguise the practice from European colonial masters. It is often said that Haiti is 90 per cent Roman Catholic and 100 per cent voodoo. Like any other religion, voodoo is a hotchpotch of superstition, the irrational and mumbo-jumbo. Ceremonies are always hugely boring and interminable. No one outside the circle of devotees has the slightest idea of what is going on and those participating are very often spectacularly drunk. Most voodoo rituals are also very banal and benign, disappointingly short on sacrifices, human or animal. The first voodoo ceremony I attended was to mark the departure from Port-au-Prince of a Haitian woman who was emigrating to Miami, and to wish her well. To compound the torment of the visitor, the interior of the voodoo temple (it may be nothing more than the room of a house or even a shed) is always over-crowded, as hot as a foundry and unbearable with screeching, wailing and deafening, relentless drums.

'Yes,' I said. 'We can go to one.' La Leslie, in less than an afternoon, had got me around her heavily-ringed finger.

It was with a voodoo priest, a couple of days later, that Ann decided to have a consultation about her bad back. (As you do.) He prescribed and gave to her a magic potion, a bottle of evil-looking brown-green sludge that, to me, appeared worryingly similar to the effluent in the stagnant sewage trenches along the city's downtown streets. Against my advice, Ann – eager new voodoo poppet that she was – drank it. I saw little of her for the

My idea of heaven. Working on the balcony of my room at the Hotel Oloffson, Port-au-Prince, Haiti, January 1990. *Jonny Barnes*

following few days as she was obliged to take to her bed with amoebic dysentery. Gamely, the old girl emerged later in the week, her back fully recovered, and declaring the voodoo juice to have worked. Evidently.

ALTHOUGH ANYONE, at any moment, might turn up in Port-au-Prince, as Dame Ann had done, life at the muzzle end of self-interest politics has cultivated in the Haitians a keen sense of priority. In February 1992, the Reverend Al Sharpton, ample American activist, was in town and not a single citizen turned out to see him. But I did.

From the Oloffson, I strolled down Rue Capois to the Holiday Inn on the Champs De Mars and at 8am got the Reverend Al out of bed. He had overslept for his previously-advertised, and thinly-attended, press conference. Half awake, and surrounded by his advisors who might have been, for all I knew, a top rap group, he addressed me and nine other glum foreign hacks, in the doorway of the hotel.

Although in Port-au-Prince with the best intentions – to protest Aristide's recent overthrow to the coup leaders and the military government – Al was a little confused. Playing the race card, his reliable standby in the States, wasn't straightforward in Haiti. The baddies here were just as black as the goodies.

'We are here today to deliver this letter to the presidential palace,' he began. Copies were passed round. 'This is the beginning of a battle, erm, to try to help, from an African American perspective, our people here... We must cooperate on an international level with people of colour to end this abuse.'

That said, we set off in a thin straggle, the Reverend Sharpton, bouffanted, fully medallioned and in a flourescent jump suit, to meet the people of colour illegally occupying the palace.

What, I asked, was his general impression of Haiti so far?

'I'm straight outta Brooklyn but this place is straight outta hell. Last night was the first time I remember sleeping that tense, hearing all that gunfire.'

Had he visited the slums of Port-au-Prince?

'The whole city's a slum. I've never seen such poverty.'

Was the impact of his visit diminished by the fact that no one in Haiti seemed to have heard of him?

'I ain't here to get elected. I'm here to get those who were elected back in.'

Big Al got no further than the palace guardroom. We crowded in. He produced his letter, a blank envelope and a pen.

'Now, what's the name of this guy?' he asked the Reuters man.

'Which guy?'

'The general who's taken over.'

The last I saw of Sharpton, he was being driven away from the Holiday Inn for a tour of the capital and flinging dollar bills from his passenger window. In his wake he left uproar: wretched Haitians grappling and screaming in the gutter for torn bank-notes and, hobbling after his pick-up, as it nudged through the congested traffic and around the potholes, an old one-legged beggar on a crutch with his palm extended.

THE SHARPTON CIRCUS was a comedy interlude in a post-coup period of real darkness. It was often very scary and, as always in Haiti, dramatic and unpredictable. There was, for those very reasons, always work to do, and stories to write. I was, without going near the Yugoslavian civil war, cutting my foreign reporter's teeth at the sharp end.

My favourite job was – and still is – to write and file a piece for *From Our Own Correspondent* on Radio 4 and the BBC World Service. As a listener, I had always loved *FOOC* and on the occasion I first got a piece on there, from Haiti during Aristide's 1990 election, I felt I'd arrived, an ambition achieved.

To do a *FOOC* was always a privilege (let's face it, no one would ever do them for the money), to write and broadcast for the most venerable and respected world news and current affairs programme. I loved, too, the discipline of *FOOC*: the requirement to gather one's thoughts, to summon up some analysis, often amid chaos, confusion and extreme stress and sit down to write a colourful and gripping essay which would illuminate the listeners both at home and around the world. It was particularly satisfying when delivered and filed down a crackly line to London.

At the Oloffson, this was ever the case. More than once I found myself alone in the dark, late at night on the veranda or the balcony of Chambre Onze, with a pale Haitian rum in my hand, feeling that sense of a job well done, listening to myself deliver, through the shifting static on my little short wave radio, a *FOOC* I'd written and phoned through to Broadcasting House from Douca's switchboard earlier in the day. The experience of filing one despatch, in 1993, was very Oloffson. And chilling.

The theme of my essay was: *The Bogeymen Are Back*. This was self-evident soon after I got on the phone to London at the reception desk. During that period, in Port-au-Prince, the Macoutes were audacious to the point of arrogance and were even coming up to the hotel to intimidate foreign journalists, an activity previously regarded as simply not on.

No sooner had Douca got me through to London, than one of the regular power cuts killed the lights in the gloomy reception area. Fortunately the phone still functioned. My friend Linda Polman, then working for Dutch radio, went to fetch a candle. I got through to the BBC, *FOOC* rolled its tapes and I began to read my hand-written script from sheets of A4. But Linda's ingenuity hadn't reckoned on candle wax dripping onto my pages and, soon into my reading, large chunks of sentences were disappearing before my eyes. Every now and then I had to stop, apologise to London, pick off the soft warm wax and re-read a paragraph.

It got worse. At one point I looked up to see standing in the shadows, and apparently listening to my speech, two men with machine guns. I stopped and restarted. I stammered and I stumbled. More wax erased more of my copy. Linda was aware of the strangers too. But she was giggling. 'Don't worry,' she whispered, as I stopped again. 'They won't understand English.'

Finally, we got the *FOOC* delivered. In about forty-three component parts. Some months later, I was rather proud to learn that my unedited Haitian Bogeymen despatch was being used at BBC Journalist Training as an example of *Filing Under Difficult Circumstances*.

* * *

OVER THE YEARS, I have been childishly thrilled to be *FOOC*'s man in Haiti, Equatorial Guinea, Congo, Malawi, North Korea, Angola, Romania, Northern Cyprus, Montserrat, Palestine, Kyrgyzstan, Iraq, the Isle of Man, Albania and Lebanon, and the country for which, in 1994, *FOOC* handed me half the programme – Rwanda.

36

RWANDA 1994

IT WAS THE DRONE and hiss that first alerted me. The flies were not only loud and in their thousands: there was something uncommon and alarming about the intensity and agitation of their buzzing. These were flies in full riot. Something, their frenzy said, was very, very wrong. I walked ever nearer, towards the seething swarm, steeled for the worst, or so I thought.

This insect tornado was spiralling on a round hole in the ground. It could once have been a well or a pit-latrine. Taking a last deep breath, I leaned over the edge and looked down. It was a scene of total horror. Fifteen feet below me was a tangle of purple-black swollen limbs and faces, a rotting human mush, bristling with flies. The half dozen bodies that I could see, squeezed together, appeared to be embracing, as though these poor souls had been trying to cling on to some humanity as indignity and death overcame them. A swollen dark blue bottom was jutting upwards, bent over a body below, pants pulled down. From under that, the bloated face of a man, eyes shut, lids blank and bulging, and mouth wide open was turned towards me. For all I knew there may well have been many more bodies below these. I did my best to describe the scene into my cassette recorder. Listeners to the *Today* programme had to excuse my gagging and retching.

Everywhere in Mayange village was the gamey aroma of death and putrefaction. The first time one catches it, without realising what it is, the smell is not unpleasant and – to be truthful – rich and mildly exotic. Only when one has learned to recognise it for what it is does the scent of death acquire an appalling message.

I came across a little bar. The door was open. Everything inside was smashed and overturned. A thick dark brown trail of dried blood was smeared across a cement veranda and over the red dirt beyond, leading into some long grass. In the scrub a man was lying on his back. He had a terrible wound to the side of his head, a crusty black split, crawling with dizzy flies. Again their hum was heavy and constant. The man's abdomen was lifting gently. I jumped. He was alive! But what the hell could I do for him out here? I stepped closer. There was, I saw then, nothing anyone could do for him. Plump white maggots were tumbling from beneath his shirt.

WE WERE NOT supposed to be in Rwanda, my dear friend Geoff Spink and I. The job which *Today* had asked us to do we had completed in neighbouring Burundi in a couple of days, leaving us the best part of a week to amuse ourselves in Bujumbura. The Burundian capital was tense but quiet. Once we had sent our despatches back to London, reporting that the Rwandan horrors were unlikely – for a variety of reasons – to spill over the border there was little for us to do except to sit around the bar of the Novotel and keep the promise we had made to everyone back in London that we would not, under any circumstances, cross into Rwanda.

Geoff had been, until recently, the editor of *From Our Own Correspondent*. During his time, he had always welcomed pieces from me, given generous encouragement and, with his assistant, Lucy Wade, run the *FOOC* office like a youth club. If I'd just flown in from Haiti, or some obscure African police state, I'd head to the *FOOC* office as soon as I could. There I'd meet up with other BBC correspondents, sharp and engaging characters like Misha Glenny, Alan Little, Bob Simpson and Malcolm Brabant. In the early 1990s, they were often just back from an assignment in the Yugoslav war or among the fragments of the shattered Soviet Union. Once our number reached critical mass, Geoff and Lucy would cart us all round to the pub for a session that would become, with the reporters' tales from their trips, a jolly in-person, uncensored edition of *FOOC*. With beer.

Then Geoff had to go and spoil it all by getting himself transferred to a producer's job on *Today*.

On the night of 6 April 1994, I was sitting at the bar of my girlfriend's restaurant in Crouch End. All the customers and other staff members had left. Juliette was cashing up and I was flicking through the news headlines on the teletext of the television up on the wall. I spotted a story that a plane carrying the presidents of Rwanda and Burundi had been shot down near the airport in Kigali, the Rwandan capital, killing both heads of state. 'This means big trouble,' I remarked to Juliette.

For the previous year or so, I'd been noting the worrying escalation of atrocities in Rwanda. I phoned Geoff the following morning and repeated my assessment. Already, he told me, sketchy reports were coming through from Kigali that something very serious was going down: barricades on the streets, vigilantes, killings.

Over the next couple of weeks, although the reporting of what was happening was patchy to say the least, a picture was emerging of mass slaughter of civilians by their own government, its army and militias, and – most shockingly – by other civilians with the encouragement of those agencies. Few in the outside world, even those normally well-informed of African matters, had a real grasp of why. It was also clear that a rebel movement of English-speaking Rwandan exiles from Uganda, the Rwandan Patriotic Front (RPF), had remobilised and, recruiting from those sympathetic to its cause within Rwanda, was moving fast across the country to stop the slaughter and to overthrow the genocidal regime.

In the years since the genocide, I have often been asked why I was sent to Rwanda by the BBC. I wasn't. I was sent to do the reports from Burundi. And I was picked to do that job because at the time Geoff Spink was my ally and a producer on *Today*. He had made it known to the programme's editors that I had knowledge of the conflict next door in Rwanda and, in any case, the attention of the majority of established correspondents and old Africa hands was, in the spring of 1994, on South Africa, the recent post-apartheid election there and Mandela's imminent inauguration as president on 10 May.

It is also undeniable that the Rwanda slaughter did not get the coverage its victims deserved because many foreign correspondents were too frightened to set foot in the country. It was considered to be – correctly – completely out of control, a situation of unprecedented obscenity, madness, ferocity, horror and unpredictability. Journalists were regarded by the government troops, the drunken militias and the gangs of murderous civilians to be an interference and legitimate targets. So, coverage of the butchery in central Africa fell, in part, to your man from Radio 1.

'THESE ARE YOUR TICKETS. Bujumbura via Brussels,' said a veteran *Today* editor, handing an envelope to me. 'Good luck, old man. And do take care.' Had we been in a 1940s black-and-white British thriller, he'd have been played by Wilfred Hyde-White.

In the Novotel, quite a party of anxiety-racked foreign correspondents began to accumulate, among them a team from CNN, another from Channel 4 News. The talk was only of what might be really going on over the border. Another crew rolled in, French I think, who had just escaped from Rwanda's *interahamwe* death squads. They were sheet-white, very badly shaken and understandably thirsty when they reached the safety of our hotel bar.

It was at this bar one night that I was approached by a small softly-spoken African. He asked if Geoff and I were journalists. I told him we were, for BBC radio news.

'My name is Jean-Marie Viamey,' he said. 'I am the Bujumbura representative of the Rwandan Patriotic Front. Would you be interested in crossing into Rwanda?'

I explained that Rwanda itself was not our mission and that I thought it would be too dangerous, even in the company of the good guys, my new friend's pals in the RPF.

A persuasive bugger, Jean-Marie. He assured me that if we

crossed into southern Rwanda at a certain place on Burundi's northern frontier, we would find ourselves in RPF-held territory, which would be quite safe. The rebels, he said, would be happy to host us and look after us well. Furthermore, Jean-Marie would radio ahead to tell the RPF lads to expect us. Everything would be fine. Even without offering 'unbeatable group deals', complimentary cocktails on arrival and *kids-go-free*, he was beginning to make it sound like a most tempting package. Geoff and I went into a huddle.

'Okay, thanks, Jean-Marie. Yes, we'll go.'

Nosiness had won again. And I figured if we could see the reality of Rwanda with the protection of the RPF, who already seemed to be an exemplary bunch, the much diminished risk was worth it. Even at this stage, I felt Rwanda was not being adequately reported.

From somewhere Geoff rented a Mitsubishi 4x4. Its wheels were from a different vehicle, far too small and they lent to it the handling qualities of a blancmange. Still, in these circumstances, it was the best that was available.

We set off on the drive north a couple of days later, with instructions from Jean-Marie to present ourselves at a hospital in a small town in northern Burundi and to ask for a certain doctor. This we did. Geoff was taken into an operating theatre where the doctor, a surgeon and an RPF activist, was in the middle of an operation. He broke off from slicing open his patient to fire up a radio set and contacted his comrades inside Rwanda. He also scribbled for us a note of introduction and accreditation which he said we should present to RPF fighters.

At the last Burundian police post on our designated dirt road, the officers gave us permission to cross and wished us well. 'Just keep going down this track,' one policeman advised. 'After two kilometres, you will find the RPF. Or they will find you.'

'How will I know it's them?' I asked, anxious for confirmation that we would not encounter the Rwandan army or the *interahamwe*.

'Only RPF now, down there,' he said.

* * *

THIS WAS OUR SECOND ATTEMPT to enter Rwanda. We had been through the same emigration procedure the night before but all the Mitsubishi's lights failed as we left the police post. I tried hanging out of the window, shining my torch ahead of us, while driving. It wasn't enough. We turned round, found a guest house just back inside Burundi and embarked on our successful infiltration the following morning.

We rounded a bend in the road, deep red earth with tall grasses on both sides. Up ahead, I saw a scattering of youths. Some were wearing scraps of olive green military attire. Most were shod in wellingtons, others flip-flops or training shoes. A few sported berets. One wore a Michael Jackson T-shirt. All had AK47s. They eyed us calmly. I pulled up a few yards from them and got out, smiling manically and swinging my BBC box with the logo prominent.

'Good morning!' I shouted, walking forward with bogus confidence and extending my hand. It crossed my mind that if we or our RPF contacts in Burundi had made some miscalculation and these lads were not the RPF, I had seconds to live. One of the taller, and I assumed more senior, teenage guerrillas, pointed at my box and smiled.

'BBC?' he asked. The majority of the RPF, having grown up in Uganda, spoke perfect English. I noticed a couple of his comrades were holding small short-wave radios to their ears.

'Yes,' I said. 'My name's Andy.'

Suddenly, it was all handshakes and matey grins. This was, thank heavens, the RPF. It was Tuesday 17 May 1994.

'We listen all the time to the BBC World Service,' said the platoon's leader, a young captain called Innocent Kabandana. 'It is how we learn what is going on here. Do you know Catherine Bond? Lindsey Hilsum?'

Both women had, showing immense courage, and in the absence of others, reported heroically since the start of the genocide just a month before.

A middle-aged officer arrived in a pick-up. Also a jovial cove, he read the note from the surgeon, welcomed us warmly and instructed Innocent and his lads to take good care of 'our distinguished BBC guests'.

We would move off, on operations, explained Innocent, with a truck of RPF soldiers in the lead, our vehicle in the middle, a couple of rebels joining Geoff on the back seat, and another RPF vehicle bringing up the rear.

The first hint of the nightmare to come was a jolly splash of colour in the road ahead, just before Mayange. It was a heap of clothing and shoes, like the aftermath of a jumble sale, much of it brown with dried blood. The colours had attracted a crowd of butterflies which danced over these rancid scatterings. There were smart blouses and high heel shoes. Someone had once been proud of these items and had stepped out with dignity in them.

Standing over these remains, it struck me for the first time just how empty Rwanda was. Apart from our RPF companions, we had not seen anyone in twenty or thirty miles. Neither was there any sound of human activity – only birdsong, which was ubiquitous and incongruously cheery. Just a few weeks before, this had been the second most densely-populated country on earth. Everyone who hadn't run from the killers fast enough over the borders into Burundi, Tanzania or the safety of expanding RPF territory, was now dead. Left behind in the empty villages, bewildered goats and cows wandered among the corpses and the sad belongings dropped by terrified, fleeing families.

We had still not passed a living soul by the time we reached Nyamata. Another trail of clothing there led us to the village church, where again the jumble was piled up. This time, mixed in with it were dried yellow bones and skulls. But there were far fewer skeletal remains than clothes. Someone, or something, had removed most of the bodies.

Explosions had taken place here. The face of a plaster statue of the Virgin Mary by the altar had been part blown away. Dots of bright daylight speckled the ceiling, punched there by shrapnel. The impacts of fragmentation, probably grenades, had gouged fresh wood from the pews.

Across the way we found a makeshift hospital in a school building. Inside, a doctor, an RPF sympathiser from Kenya, was amputating at the wrist the hand of a girl. A machete had hacked it down the middle, irreparably. A Rwandan exile, the doctor had abandoned a good job in Nairobi to return to help the cause.

Waiting next for his attentions was a girl of about fourteen, horrifically injured – a machete again – but sitting calmly on a low wall outside. The heavy blade had cleaved away the crown of her skull, as one might slice off the top of a pineapple. She was smiling at me, weakly. Through the wound, remarkably bloodless, I could see her brain.

The scale and the speed of the carnage in Rwanda, almost a million killed in a hundred days, was achievable only by mass mobilization of a collective madness and a slaughter conducted with neighbour-on-neighbour efficiency. It was far from spontaneous. A clique of hard-line Hutus within the government had been planning it for years. Lists of victims had been drawn up, *interahamwe* ('those who work together') organised and trained. It was also done on the cheap. Guns and bullets were an unnecessary extravagance. In the year before the operation began, the Rwandan government ordered 600,000 machetes from China.

Driving east, we came to a bridge over the Nyaborongo river, about seven miles south of Kigali. It was being guarded by another RPF platoon. The officer in command was standing at its centre. I joined him to lean over the rail and look down into the swirling water, the colour of stewed tea. The area around the bridge, like the territory upstream, had been captured only recently by the remarkable rebels.

'The killing is slowing down,' muttered Lieutenant Henry Nsengiyumva. 'A week ago we were getting nine hundred bodies a day in the river. Now it is down to about three hundred.'

As he spoke, the rigid corpse of a boy, around eight years old, still wearing blue soccer shorts, twirled by, his mouth wide open. A woman was next, floating face down in a floral dress. Her hands were tied behind her back, her pants pulled down around her thighs. 'Sometimes they are shot or hacked to death first,' said the Lieutenant, 'but often they just tie their hands and throw them in alive.'

In the ten minutes we spent with the RPF unit guarding the bridge, nine swollen and stinking corpses passed underneath us.

* * *

The aftermath of the massacre at the church, Nyamata, Rwanda, 17 May 1994.
Around 10,000 people were butchered here on, or soon after, 7 April 1994.
Geoff Spink

THE RPF'S PRIORITY was to stop the slaughter which the rest of
the world had chosen largely to disregard and made no attempt
to understand.

As the savagery ripped across the country, the United Nations,
while maintaining a nominal presence in Kigali, abandoned
shamefully in the capital, and failed properly to supply, its
heroic and principled force commander, Lt General Roméo
Dallaire and his overwhelmed colleagues. (Years later, I met
Dallaire in London, by then almost fully recovered from a post-
Rwanda breakdown. I cannot recommend enough Dallaire's
account of his Rwanda experience. Once you have read *Shake
Hands With The Devil*, you may wish to fling violently your
copy at the next politician who propagates the soothing myth
of 'the international community').

Only the French maintained their full involvement in Rwanda.
A robust ally of the regime which planned the extermination of
the country's Tutsi population and moderates of the Hutu community, France had armed and trained those now carrying out
the massacres, both army and *interahamwe* militias. And as the

RPF pushed the killers westwards, French special forces stepped in again, not to save the innocent but, under Operation Turquoise, to protect and evacuate the guilty behind a cordon in the south-west of the country.

Thousands of others, women as well as men, who had hacked and hammered to death their neighbours and, in some cases, members of their own families, ran from the RPF advance into eastern Zaire. There they were greeted sympathetically by the same aid agencies who had been conspicuously absent in Rwanda where and when they had been really needed. The killers were also received in the black volcanic wilderness of Mobutu's empire by the dimwit reporters and satellite dishes of gormless international television news channels. These had failed, similarly, to alert the world's attention to the real suffering and to hold to account the criminals they now presented to the world as pitiable refugees, deserving of a huge international relief effort. From these camps in Zaire, the *genocidaires* would reorganise to infiltrate and torment Rwanda for years to come and trigger what became known as Africa's World War, which erased the lives of five million people.

The RPF liberators, meanwhile, were regarded by many in the wider world as the bad guys, despite all evidence available to anyone who bothered to look, simply because they were guerrillas of an invading army. But ignorance and laziness were a couple of the genocide's best international allies. In one of my BBC despatches I said, 'A total and swift RPF victory is Rwanda's only hope as the increasingly desperate killer government rushes to complete its final solution. Children are being hacked to pieces right now and the world dithers. Only the RPF is capable of stopping the slaughter.' I was right. And the rest of the world actually did all within its power to hold up that deliverance.

THE GENOCIDE WAS NOT a tribal conflict, although it was routinely presented as such in the international news media. Just as the victims of the genocide were not exclusively Tutsi, neither was the membership of the RPF. Three of my seven immediate RPF guards were Hutus. The bogus ethnic distinction had been institutionalised by the Belgians, Rwanda's former colonial masters, and exploited by Rwanda's Hutu-dominated government to justify and encourage the eradication of the Tutsi population. Equally, the RPF campaign was not a tribal war. They were fighting, they said, for all Rwandans. When we reached the east of the country, the first region to be captured and secured by the RPF, survivors and former refugees had already returned to work in their fields.

Major General Paul Kagame, the RPF's brilliant leader and master tactician, had already overthrown one brutal dictatorship. He had been one of only six original guerrillas who had helped Yoweri Museveni to topple Milton Obote in Uganda in 1986. The son of refugees who had fled massacres of the Tutsis in Rwanda in the early 1960s, Kagame had grown up in neighbouring Uganda. After dealing with the murderous regime in Rwanda – he avoided taking Kigali until 4 July 1994 – and later becoming President Kagame, he then masterminded the removal of Zaire's President Mobutu in 1997. To achieve the latter, against all predictions, Kagame's lads walked from Kigali to Kinshasa, a distance equivalent to half the width of Europe. Within weeks of Kagame's victory in Rwanda, his imaginative strategy was being studied and admired at West Point in the United States.

The RPF fighters I met were certainly impressive, highly disciplined and keenly motivated. The majority also happened to be very young. Innocent, the leader of our escort, was no more than seventeen. The smallest among our bodyguards was Derek, a boy whose AK47, when he stood it on its stock, was only a fraction shorter than he. Always wearing a beret – bright yellow or black – he had the most angelic little face. Derek is still in my thoughts whenever I hear of well-meaning campaigns in the western media against 'child soldiers'. This junior guerrilla claimed to be sixteen. I would be amazed if he were older than twelve. It is an inescapable truth that I owe my life to child soldiers – Little Derek and his adolescent comrades. And many more than 800,000 Rwandans would have been killed had it not been for the courage and selflessness of the RPF's kiddie combatants. They showed they had the mettle

of their leader shortly after we left the bridge over the Nyaborongo.

AS WE ROUNDED a bend on a narrow red dirt track, along the
rim of a valley which fell away to our left, we came up behind
another RPF convoy of three trucks. It was stopped. I got out of
the 4x4 and, to find out what was going on, walked diagonally
across the road in front of our vehicle to the head of the column.
The leading truck was on its side. In the road was the crater left
by the explosion of a big mine. One guerrilla, who I took to be
the driver, was sitting on the grass, stunned and bleeding a little
from his mouth. I asked the commander of this patrol what we
should do. After consulting Innocent, he told me to go back to
our car and wait. There would have to be some shunting of the
vehicles ahead of ours before we could drive on. I walked back
to the Mitsubishi, again crossing the road in front of it. Absurd
though it seems now, Geoff and I carried on with a bit of work
on the back seat, editing some of our recordings, as we waited
for the commander's instructions. So, I wasn't paying much
attention to the truck ten yards ahead, except to be aware that
it had begun to reverse towards us.

There was a tremendous bang and a yellow flash. The flat-
bed flipped over like a beer mat. I looked up to see it twirling
through the air. Even through our windscreen, which amazingly
remained intact, I felt the heat of the blast on my face. Wreckage
and rocks poured down, crashing on our roof. When the smoke
and dust cleared, the deep crater of another anti-tank mine blast
had opened up precisely at the point where I had twice crossed
the road. The truck, likewise, had driven over the device once
without setting it off. Notoriously unreliable devices that they
are, the mine had then exploded when the flat-bed was inching
back over it in reverse.

The shooting from across the narrow valley began immediately. I heard a zup-zup-zup all around us. It was a sound I'd
never experienced before but instinctively I knew what it was.
The broad leaves of banana trees on the edge of the road to our
right were thrashing around as the bullets smacked through

them, a split second before we heard the gunfire from the opposite side of the ravine. It was a textbook ambush.

'Get in the ditch!' I yelled at Geoff, yanking him after me from the back seat.

It is astonishing how rational and calculating we were under fire. At this previously untested level of fear, a weird composure and serenity came over me. For ten minutes or so in the ditch we worked out our chances. It was an awful choice. We could try to escape by retracing our steps. But the Rwandan army or *interahamwe*, said Innocent, were most likely now behind us. Our other option was to carry on down a road that was clearly full of mines to an RPF base some miles away. Taking our 4x4 was, I decided, out of the question. The little knowledge I had of land-mines at the time, demonstrated dramatically a few minutes before, told me that the weight of a person was unlikely to detonate the anti-tank variety. The weight of our vehicle surely would.

Meanwhile, our RPF lads were on their feet, Innocent and Little Derek Yellow Beret standing on the road, in full view of our attackers, blazing and popping away with return fire, incoming bullets whizzing all about them. Every now and then Innocent looked down to reassure us in the ditch.

'Don't mind. Don't mind, Andy, don't mind,' he boomed in a rich, slow voice, his face expressionless, before turning back to blast off a few more rounds.

Geoff and I were resolved to escaping on foot, taking our chances by walking further down the road until the safety of the distant RPF base. I began to work this out. All of our kit and our recordings were still in the back of the 4x4. I was wearing a white T-shirt. It was early evening. The light was starting to fade. I needed something darker, less conspicuous. It was hot and muggy. We'd need some liquid. Also in the Mitsubishi was a crate of tonic waters.

I slithered out of the ditch and reached the back of the car on my belly. I bobbed up for no more than five seconds to open the back door and pull everything out onto the road. Back down on the ground, among our bags, I dragged the lot into the ditch. We cracked open and drank a few tonics as the skirmish rattled away above us. In the top of my rucksack, I found a denim shirt, dirty but dark blue, and I changed into it from my easy target of the white T-shirt. During a pause in the shooting, I told Innocent what we intended to do. He agreed walking was safer. We pulled on our rucksacks, I picked up my BBC box and, on Innocent's signal, with another lull in the firing, we climbed back up onto the road and began to walk. All the RPF lads of our little group stuck with us. We left a £16,000 Mitsubishi on the hillside. Geoff would later have to make a very awkward and apologetic call to the owner in Bujumbura.

It had crossed my mind before we left the ditch that those who'd planted the anti-tank mines had probably laid anti-personnels too. They had. Within fifty yards of stepping out, I saw two. Barely visible, in the grass at the edge of the road, I noticed the metal prongs of what I would later come to recognise as Valmara 69 bounding mines. Brushing a prong causes an initial detonation which fires vertically a package of ball-bearings with more explosive at its core. At chest height, that too detonates, blasting the steel balls to a radius of thirty yards. These shred and kill anything in their path.

Our chances of getting through this I knew were slender. My knees now felt they would not support my own body weight, never mind with full kit on my back. This was fear so intense my motor neurone mechanisms were shutting down under overload. I was mentally ordering my legs to move. It was with some willpower that I got them to obey. Not to walk meant certain death. Innocent was vague about the number of miles to the RPF base. I suspected he didn't wish to demoralise us. And by now it was getting dark.

While the nightfall gave us some cover from the snipers, we could not switch on a torch to look for evidence of land-mines, if there had been any. (Few have the visible prongs of Valmaras.) To do so would have been to create a shooting gallery for those across the valley. All we could do was walk in the tracks of vehicles and hope.

We passed through a couple of empty villages. I could smell the corpses in the blackened and shattered houses from two hundred yards away. As we approached these little settlements, the RPF boys clicked off their safety catches. From the north we heard the boom of the big guns around Kigali and caught their flash against the clouds. Every step towards safety was hell. Every one, I knew, could be my last. We could only walk and wait for the bang.

After about three hours of this torment, at the top of a steep hill I saw blasted gable ends in the headlights of an assembly of trucks. The sounds of human activity from there had a quality that suggested friends and security. Innocent was now laughing at our ordeal but still murmuring, 'Don't mind.'

In the glare of the lights, all I could see were silhouettes of many rebels and more trucks. These RPF fighters seemed very pleased to see Innocent and his boys and they gathered to shake hands with us too. I fell on my knees before the carcass of what had been some kind of shop. Fucking hell, we were alive and safe. From my rucksack I worked free a bottle of single malt and a plastic Thunderbirds mug. I filled it to the brim, took a deep slug and passed it to Geoff.

Within minutes, the RPF had organised our evacuation in a

My friend and BBC *Today* programme radio producer in Rwanda, Geoff Spink, joshing with Rwandan Patriotic Front rebels – the good guys. On the right of the picture is Little Derek. May 1994. *AK*

pick-up. Huddled in the back, we tore along a dark but surfaced road at high speed, the branches of overhanging trees rushing above us. At an abandoned hospital, now a major RPF base, somewhere in the east of the country, Innocent and his unit fed us a hot stew and made up beds for us, thin mattresses on the floor of a former children's ward. There were pictures of teddy bears and other comforting nursery characters on the walls. Despite the whisky, I couldn't sleep. My mind was whizzing over the details of the ambush. I reached up to a shelf of books next to my mattress and took the first volume that came to hand. It was a scruffy old hardback copy of Enid Blyton's *Five Go Adventuring Again*.

SEVEN YEARS ON, in 2001, Geoff was working and living in Kigali, teaching the mysteries of radio to the Rwandans. 'Come down,' he said to me on the phone in London. 'I've found Innocent.'

I knew that at some stage I would have to go back. It would be wonderful to see Innocent again but, that reunion aside, I wanted to see the country at peace and in some state of normality. And I needed to travel down that bloody road once more, this time driving, and in safety.

In Geoff's car we quickly found the small town that had been the RPF base and our sanctuary. From there we picked up the red dirt track and I zeroed the mileometer before trundling off in the reverse direction of our hellish march. At the site of the ambush we stopped and got out for a while. It was perfectly still, beautiful and silent. Rwanda had reclaimed one of the most remarkable landscapes in Africa. Bits of the blown-up truck were still in the long grass. I checked the distance from the village on the instrument panel. We had walked that night down a mined road for eleven miles.

In the southern town of Butare we had an emotional reunion and a lengthy lunch with Innocent, now a major in the new Rwandan army. He brought along Sonya, his delightful fiancee. We all roared laughing when, with my encouragement, Innocent encored a few 'Don't minds'.

'Innocent,' I asked eventually, 'what happened to all the other lads in your platoon? Did they all get through the war?' His broad, rounded face seemed to flatten and fall.

'Not all, no. You remember Derek, the little kid with the beret?' he asked.

'Of course I do,' I said.

'Well, I'm afraid he was killed in battle. Shot, two days after you were with us.'

37

LOONY DICTATORSHIP: THE AK SEVEN-STEP PROGRAMME

ALL BONKERS COUNTRIES are reliable producers and exporters of two commodities. Indeed, the production of extravagant postage stamps and cement is a vital qualification for membership of that exclusive club to which all mad dictators, cult of personality crackpots and military regimes aspire: the Community of Kershaw's Potty Republics.

There are, of course, a wealth of other characteristics. Stuffing one's hand in the till and one's political opponents in jail (or in unmarked graves) are solid first steps. Moving a long-established capital from a city with a historical *raison d'être* and semi-functioning infrastructure to some dusty hinterland village where the president happened to have been born in a shed, always catches the eye of the committee. Ownership of a portfolio of tasteless homes on a number of continents is a help, too. (Applicants are cautioned against any adherence to the notion of less-is-more.) Equally, having an uncontrollable playboy son who shows no interest in politics or succession but demonstrates an impressive flair for crashing Ferraris and pissing his father's money against the walls of Monaco casinos is an advantage. An appalling human rights record is absolutely *de rigueur*. But, crucially, membership of the Potty Republics Club can be pretty much guaranteed, regardless of these other criteria, if the head of state has a fondness for wearing a homburg or, better still, a top hat.

In Haiti, Papa Doc hit the bulls-eye with the bulk of these qualifications, although, cannily, he never left the country after coming to power and Duvalierville didn't really take off. The last time I visited the old man's 1960s showpiece town, the cinema was full of poultry.

In 1993 I came face to face with another top-hatted tyrant. Dr Hastings Banda of Malawi had his own version of the Tonton Macoutes, the Young Pioneers. 'Foreign journalists, tell the truth about Malawi!' screamed the placards they shoved in my face at a rally. Banda, thought to be already a hundred years old or more, arrived sitting on a throne, mounted on top of a Land Rover and waving his trademark fly whisk.

I did tell the truth, as I saw it, about the former benevolent family doctor and his murderous regime, for a Radio 4 documentary Noah Richler and I made in what turned out to be the old monster's final days. I was later sent a copy of the *Daily Times* in which there was a report of presidential outrage over our programme and the news that I was now excluded from the country. This ban I rank among my finest achievements.

THE PROBLEM WITH developing a taste for the more extreme countries is the necessary escalation of that extremity to satisfy my favourite sensation. A flickering career as a foreign correspondent, however, helped me to find a regular fix.

Working for a Channel 4 programme called *As It Happens,* I found myself in Kuwait at the end of the first Gulf war in 1991. The main focus of the programme was the blazing oil wells which had been set alight by the retreating Iraqi army and I spent several days crawling around the desert floor, up to the burning well heads, with teams led by Red Adair and Boots Hansen, in a shower of hot crude. The fires were truly beautiful to behold.

Just south of Kuwait City we drove under a black shelf of smoke, beneath which, even during the afternoon, the desert was as dark as night. This blackness was dotted with hundreds of jets of orange flame and, duplicating the drama, the fires themselves were reflected in mirrored lakes of inky crude oil. To extinguish these flame-throwers, the fire-fighters inched as near as they dared to the roaring geysers and planted explosives around them. The subsequent detonation snatched the vital oxygen from the fire and snuffed it out. To approach the wellheads, crouched behind a steel screen with my film crew in tow, was simply awesome. The heat was ferocious and the ground shuddered with the thunder of the blazing eruptions.

It was on this job that I had my first encounter with land mines. The Iraqis had mined the desert around the oil wells after setting them alight. These mines first had to be cleared before the teams of tough Texans could move in. Years later, after the Rwanda experience, I came home a convert to the anti land mines campaign. I phoned up the Mines Advisory Group in the UK and said I'd do anything to help them in their work to clear mines around the world and in their campaign to prevent their manufacture and distribution. No one, I thought, in countries infested with mines, should have to live routinely every day – in their fields or on their way to school – with the terror and torment I'd known for just a few hours. MAG made me a patron, a position with them that I still hold, although I am ashamed to have given them over the years little more than the use of my name – for what that's worth.

Naïve though I still was about land mines in Kuwait, I knew right then that the position of those who used and profited from them was morally indefensible. One of the mine clearance teams was led by a chap from Royal Ordnance. He showed me, standing in a mine field, some of the anti personnel devices his sappers had lifted from the sand. I noted that these mines had been made by Royal Ordnance, the British arms manufacturer which was now employing my interviewee, and selling his expertise and services to the Kuwaiti government, for mine clearance.

'Well,' said the RO man, brightly, ' business is business.'

* * *

'POISED TO BECOME THE NEW KUWAIT,' was how I described Africa's most obscure and secretive country in a *From Our Own Correspondent* essay in early 1992. Long before Simon Mann and Mark Thatcher had heard of the west African state of Equatorial Guinea, and staged their 2004 attempted coup, I took myself off there simply because no one else ever bothered to go and that it had a reputation for terror, unpredictability and a feared dictator. Teodoro Obiang Nguema Mbasogo (for it is still he) had seized power by having his uncle executed by firing squad following a 1979 trial, held in a cinema, at which Macias Nguema had been sentenced to death '101 times'. Although hardly a community service order, this was a pretty lenient come-uppance for a president under whom a third of the population had been murdered. Alas, Obie (as we Equatorial Guinea insiders know him) hasn't been much of an improvement on Uncle Macias.

I was locked up for a couple of hours as soon as I stepped off a cargo boat in Malabo harbour. The police were after bribes, which they didn't get. The cargo boat had been the only means I could find of getting to the island component of this sinister dictatorship. (The other part of Equatorial Guinea is a speck of land about the size of a pub car park between Gabon and Cameroon.) I flew first to Douala, in Cameroon, the nearest destination on international airline schedules, and hung around the docks there for a couple of days, chatting up sailors, until I found a little coaster which took me, two live turtles, a monkey chained to the railing on the deck, and 108,000 bottles of beer to Malabo.

'Don't get off here,' implored the captain. 'You're crazy. Come with us to Sao Tome. That's a nice place.'

As I swung onto the quayside in Malabo, I put out my hand to steady myself on a length of steel piping about a foot in diameter. I noted that it was stencilled Walter International, Texas. Yes, locals confirmed, there was exploration taking place in territorial waters for oil and natural gas. One night, I left a bar to walk back to my derelict hotel – the only place to stay – and saw the sky to the north of the island was glowing bright orange. The townsfolk were all out on the streets to gawp at this false dawn, for that's what it turned out to be. Equatorial Guinea had struck oil while I was there.

My prediction for a new Kuwait, though optimistic, was mathematically possible, but it overlooked the troublesome detail of a dictatorship. Without its kleptocratic president, Equatorial Guineans, less than a million of them, could have become the richest people on earth.

THE LURE of the potty republic has rendered me a terrible holidaymaker in the accepted sense and to the accepted (and acceptable) destinations. I am not good at lying on a beach and, aside from when I'm fishing, I find relaxation intolerable, an invitation to my great enemy, boredom, and therefore an impossibility. Neither am I, when abroad, very comfortable with comfort.

My then-partner Juliette tried her best to cure me of this disability. After a couple of trips together to Haiti, she suggested we have 'a quiet Caribbean holiday', which itself was a de facto veto of another adventure in Port-au-Prince. She settled on the dreamy-sounding hideaway of Montserrat. All I knew of the tiny island was that former Beatles producer George Martin had run a recording studio there until a hurricane in the late 1980s had forced him to abandon the project. In the spring of 1995, with me under protest and dreading the possibility of running into remnants of Duran Duran, off we went. The island blew up the morning after we arrived.

'What the hell's that?' asked the American owner of our delightful plantation guest house in the north of the island. He and I were standing on his lawn. It was the first morning of Juliette's quiet Caribbean holiday and the owner and I were looking down the coast at a white cloud, a roller of vapour, tumbling off the island into the sea. Then we felt a heavy distant rumbling. The long-dormant volcano of the Soufriere Hills to the south, above the miniature capital of Plymouth, was erupting, and blowing its top in a big way. While devastating for the Montserratians it was, for me, the stuff of journalistic dreams. Here I was, the only foreign reporter on a tiny exploding island,

Swinging my trusty BBC box (mobile office) at the Kipchak Mosque, Turkmenistan, 2005. Loony dictator, Saparmurat Niyazov, was buried here in 2006. *James Parkin*

now suddenly at the centre of world attention, and the airport was closed. All news organisations had to come to your man on the spot.

I got in our rental car and drove south, showing my BBC card to the police at a roadblock, and into what they called the Danger Zone. Hundreds of people were walking north, clutching handkerchiefs or T-shirts to their faces. I found Plymouth deserted and ankle deep in volcanic ash. Bewildered domesticated animals, ubiquitous in disasters, had already reclaimed the streets. On the east coast of the island, I watched a tumble of hot rock – what vulcanologists term, boringly, pyroclastic flow – race down a hillside and hit the sea, causing it to boil instantly. Back at the guest house, I spent almost every waking hour of our tropical break on the phone to BBC radio news and, naturally, *From Our Own Correspondent*.

* * *

FOR AN EARLY family holiday – when our first child, Sonny, was only eight months old – Juliette and I compromised and went to Cuba to take in the May Day celebrations of 1998. This gave the trip a political and journalistic edge to keep Daddy happy and, communist dictatorship though it may have been, Cuba was sufficiently exotic, romantic and tropical to fool Mummy into believing she'd got me on a holiday. (Similarly, I have long had a theory that the durability of the Cuban revolution, unlike left-wing regimes in more inclement parts of the world may, to a large extent, be attributable to the fact that in Cuba the weather is nice and the music's good.)

At the invitation of the Sugar Workers' Union of Havana, a representative of which had introduced himself to us in a bar a couple of evenings before the big event, we marched on May Day with our new friend and his cane-cutter colleagues in a procession more than a million strong through the city and into Revolution Square. The sugar workers insisted we walk at the head of their column where we shared the duties of carrying Sonny on our shoulders and holding high the union banner. When we reached the platform, I lingered for as long as I could in front of Fidel Castro, just a few feet away, and held Sonny aloft in his eye line. Sonny went berserk. I have had my doubts about the boy ever since.

IN THE EARLY 1990s my appetite for the implausible destination was spotted by the producers of a newish Channel 4 programme called *Travelog*. Held together by the wonderfully deadpan Pete McCarthy, as studio presenter, *Travelog* was a holiday programme for people with rucksacks, as opposed to suitcases, and for those who never bothered with booking a hotel before departure. It had a great deal more imagination than its title suggested, as did its two main producers, John Bell and Richard Lightbody, with whom I quickly became good pals and developed industrious and inspirational professional relationships. Likewise with my regular and irrepressible cameraman, Colin Angel.

After my first couple of trips for *Travelog*, I became, unofficially (and certainly not credited as such on screen), their shit-hole correspondent. We made films in destinations unlikely to tempt even the most reckless backpackers: in Mozambique, just as the civil war was winding down; in Lebanon, just at the end of theirs, and where we were lunched by Hezbollah; in a Romania still reeling from its release from the Ceausescus; in Malawi, newly liberated from Dr Banda; in Kyrgyzstan, which no one had heard of at the time (even many Kyrgyz) and in which nearly every male over fifteen was permanently very drunk and heavily armed; and in Albania, in which, erm... nearly every male over fifteen was permanently very drunk and heavily armed and where we were forced to attend three wedding receptions in the same afternoon, one of them at gunpoint.

There was an inevitability about this addiction to the bonkers regime, a momentum towards an unavoidable conclusion, aside from that of wandering around war zones to rack up the level of the *what-the-fuck-is-this?* factor. It was my destiny with the country I'd regarded for many years as The Big One.

In 1995, after pestering the authorities there for five years to get a visa, suddenly and without any explanation for their agreement, they let me in to North Korea. With a *Travelog* film crew.

38

NORTH KOREA:
THE NON-STOP PARTY

IT IS THE MOST VOLATILE place on earth. Panmunjom, at the 38th Parallel, where North Korea meets South, is also the world's last Cold War frontier. Here, the ancient tectonic plates of capitalism and communism still grind relentlessly and terrifyingly together. Concealed in the surrounding countryside, on both sides of the border, beyond the trim lawns, fragrant flowerbeds and ornamental shrubs, is rumoured to be the deadliest arsenal in the world, a concentration of chemical, biological, conventional and nuclear weapons. And all just a minute or two from the gift shop. Panmunjom always guarantees a jolly day out, consistently the high point of a visit to North Korea.

In the spirit of a school trip, we are driven to the border, a hundred miles south of the capital Pyongyang, in a little bus laid on by the state tourism agency – not a terribly busy organisation. The bus, a chummy-looking vehicle, in green and cream, is of the type you last saw being chased by a skyscraper in an early 1960s Czechoslovakian animation. And we are chaperoned by our cheery government minders, a bunch as sophisticated and aware of the ways of the western world as the regime can provide.

The showpiece motorway to Panmunjom – in places six lanes wide on both sides – is, shall we say, unspoiled by traffic. Drivers must be on their mettle, nevertheless, to avoid uniquely North Korean road hazards: deer grazing on the central reservation or a herd of goats being shooed along the fast lane. Giant columns of concrete, dotted along the hard shoulder, stand ready to be dynamited to block the carriageway in the event of an invasion from the South. These are interspersed by military vehicles, always stationary, bonnets up, and with the heads of a couple of North Korean soldiers down inside an expired engine. If North Korea ever does lash out at its southern neighbour, as Seoul and Washington would have us believe is Pyongyang's permanent intention, then the military had better first build up its stocks of string and Sellotape. Meanwhile, in the paddy fields bordering the motorway, giant billboards carry slogans to uplift those working up to their knees in thin mud: 'Unity Is Victory'; 'Let Us Live In Our Own Way'; and 'Long Live The Great General, Comrade Kim Jong Il, The Sun Of The 21st Century.'

It doesn't take long in the People's Paradise to get accustomed to this sort of stuff. In fact, from the moment of arrival in the country, it acquires its own momentum. From Pyongyang railway station, following a rattling thirty-one-hour train journey from Beijing, we are whisked immediately to Mansu Hill to pay our respects at the ninety-foot-high floodlit bronze statue of the Great Leader, Kim Il Sung, which stares out and stretches a fatherly hand over the whole city. (This preliminary is a priority, before check-in at the hotel, even when once my train arrived in Pyongyang at 3.30 in the morning.) From speakers concealed in the shrubbery a military choir sings *Peace Is On Our Bayonet*. And other favourites.

Only with these formalities completed can we then be installed at the spectacular, and virtually empty, five-hundred room Yangakdo Hotel, boasting a spectacular, and virtually empty, revolving bar and restaurant on the 47th floor. Just why this gleaming skyscraper accommodation was built (in the late 1990s) is, like so much of what you see in North Korea, a mystery. On my first trip to Pyongyang in 1995, film crew in tow, I was told by one of my government minders that I was one of only thirty-eight westerners to be allowed into the country that year.

My access to the world's most secretive and least-visited country – on each of my four trips – has been arranged by Nick Bonner of Koryo Tours in Beijing. Nick (like me, Greg Chamberlain, Jack Straw, Mark Knopfler and Dr Harold Shipman) is a former Leeds University student. Upon graduation, Nick moved to China where, spotting a scarcity of travel agents specialising in holidays in North Korea – and apparently untroubled by the reason for that – he went ahead and set one up. Since doing so, he has been kept busy organising tours for ageing unrepentant Stalinists, journalists pretending to be birdwatchers, spooks posing as academics and television and radio crews working with Andy Kershaw, disguised as television and radio crews working with Andy Kershaw.

The Channel 4 documentary was the first, to my knowledge, to be filmed inside North Korea. To this day, I have no idea why we were granted permission to make it when refusal of similar requests is routine. Similarly the programme we made for Radio 3 in Pyongyang in 2003.

DRIVEN BY *JUCHE*, his home-brewed ideology of self-reliance, the Great Leader, Kim Il Sung, ruled the Democratic People's Republic of Korea – the official name – from its foundation in 1948 until his death in 1994. On the night he died, I got a phone call at 3am from the North Korean embassy in the UK, a pre-war semi-detached house in Finchley. The ambassador tearfully broke the news and invited me to call round to sign a book of condolence later that morning. I found the embassy with ease, standing out as it did from the other respectable but unremarkable north London homes thanks to the seventy-foot flagpole in the front garden flying the North Korean emblem at half-mast. Later that day, in the communist world's only dynastic transfer of power, the Great Leader's son, Kim Jong Il – known as the Dear Leader – took control. In 2010, the Dear Leader, now of failing health himself, and apparently turning into Yoko Ono, anointed as his successor his twenty-seven-year-old son, Kim

Jong Un, dubbed provisionally (all right, by me) as the Fat Kiddie. With me so far?

Kim Snr, who was stuffed and is regularly maintained by the same taxidermists who in-filled Chairman Mao, now lies in a crystal case in a climate-controlled chamber in his former palace. In 2002, he was elevated to the office of Eternal President, thus becoming the world's first, and so far only, fully dead incumbent head of state.

Images of, and references to, father and son are ubiquitous and pervasive. In conversation, however brief, with a North Korean, they are routinely and wearyingly credited. ('It is thanks to the warm benevolence and wise guidance of the Dear Leader that we are enjoying this breakfast of cold, fried, rancid flounder...') My tourist phrasebook offers this helpful ice-breaker, among many, in the section called *Sightseeing in the City*: 'The death of Comrade Kim Il Sung is a great loss to the Korean revolution and the world revolution.' And, by way of easy chit-chat, 'Comrade Kim Il Sung was the most distinguished leader of our times.' To overcome any difficulties between railway station and accommodation, the *On the Way to the Hotel* suggestions include, 'Is the hotel far off?' 'The houses are beautiful', and 'Let us mutilate US imperialism'.

The literary section of the Yangakdo's gift shop sells only the works of both Kims – *juche* developed and detailed across dozens of volumes – but the range of CDs demands bulk purchase. North Korean pop, described as 'light instrumental with popular vocal', is lush and relentlessly optimistic top-drawer kitsch, usually sung in a piping voice by a girl who is dressed in a lamp-shade. No serious collector would wish to leave Pyongyang without the following musical souvenirs: *My Country Is Nice To Live In, Song Of Bean Paste, We Shall Hold Bayonets More Firmly, Traces Of Life, I Love An Unmarried Disabled Soldier, Song Of Industrial Rehabilitation For Nation Building, The World Envies Us, Our Ox, The Shoes My Brother Bought Fit Me Tight, Cherishing A Grudge, Song Of Blood Transfusion* and *My Trench*.

A night in front of the telly in my hotel room was more than

That's me in the corner... At the Monument To Victory In The Fatherland Liberation War, Pyongyang, North Korea, 2003. *James Parkin*

just a device to avoid another meal of rotting pickled cabbage and questionable meat. By my second trip, I had it well organised: sitting on the end of my bed, digging corned beef from a tin – a supply I'd hauled with me in my rucksack – with my Swiss Army knife, while enjoying a soap opera about the goings-on within the North Korean women's rapid-fire pistol target-shooting team. Otherwise, the single television channel shows predominantly, in rotation, documentaries about the greatness of the Great Leader and, for variety, others addressing the dearness of the Dear Leader. Those of us who prefer radio, are advised to bring in their own short-wave receivers. North Korean radios have no tuning dial.

'DEAR BOY,' Christopher Hitchens was booming down the phone from his adopted home in Washington, 'I gather you have an understanding with the North Koreans. Can you get me in?' It was the spring of 2000.

I had first met Hitchens a few years before, through our mutual friend, Francis Wheen. On Christopher's visits to London, the three of us had rendezvoused occasionally for a drink. Quite a few of them, actually. Meanwhile, Francis and I had travelled to North Korea together in 1996 and, without the ingestion of hallucinogens, had enjoyed hugely the usual psychedelic Pyongyang experience. Our giggling accounts of the caper had possibly made our friend and greatest living polemicist a little envious. Now Hitch wanted in, too.

I explained to Christopher that the diplomatic skills required to smooth his entry were all Nick Bonner's, not mine. Somehow or other, Nick pulled off the necessary permissions. Hitchens in North Korea I had to see. I signed up, too.

Naturally, Hitchens and I occupied the rear seats of the little bus as we were carted around the endless achievements of leaders Dear and Great. We discovered on these outings that we shared a passion for Bob Dylan, pre-1976 of course, and invented a little game to break the monotony of Kim-related monuments and to test each other on our recall of Dylan lyrics.

'Dear boy,' Hitchens might murmur across the aisle, 'ain't it just like the night to play tricks when you're trying to be so quiet?'

'Well, Christopher,' I'd respond, 'we sit here stranded, though we're all doing our best to deny it.' And so on. The winner was the one who didn't forget the next line.

By about the Wednesday, delinquency was kicking in.

'Mr Chae,' Hitchens bellowed from the back of the bus to my favourite minder, who I am always delighted to have supervise me, 'may we eat dog this evening?'

The minders went into a huddle.

That night, we were solemnly seated in Pyongyang's Dog Restaurant Number 1, eating dog stew, after which we were steered into, of all things, a karaoke club. Leaning on the bar, taking in the scene, I had to confirm to myself that, yes, I was in Pyongyang, sated with dog, and that was indeed Christopher Hitchens plummily warbling and wobbling through *La Bamba*.

'Kershaw and I would like to visit the zoo today,' I heard Christopher briefing the minders after breakfast one morning. Crumpled and dishevelled at any time of the day, the first-thing-in-the-morning Hitchens always looked as if he'd just been set upon by ruffians. It was nothing, however, that a mid-morning rice wine or two wouldn't partially straighten out.

The zoo was not on the itinerary. Another huddle. Another

Suppressing the giggles with Francis Wheen on our supervised excursion to the North Sea Barrage, North Korea, 1996. You really can't beat a visit to a major marine engineering achievement, for a jolly day out, in my book. *Nick Bonner*

conference of minders. We sat on the bus and watched them as Christopher explained to me his unlikely request.

'Tariq Ali was invited here in the 1970s,' he recalled of a visit to Pyongyang, in a spirit of Non Alignment, by his old friend. 'Tariq became sick of the monuments and museums, too. And the relentless references to Comrade Kim Il Sung, the Great Leader this and the Great Leader that. After a few days he was desperate to see something else, anything else. So, he asked them if they could take him to the zoo. That had to be referred upwards. Eventually it was agreed he could go but, of course, under escort. Well, Tariq admired a polar bear here, a tiger there. And then they came up against a cage containing a parrot – a big macaw – sitting on a swing. Tariq looked at the parrot. The parrot blinked at Tariq and said, 'Long live the Great Leader, Comrade Kim Il Sung.' In English.

'Somehow, we know, don't we, my dear Kershaw, that just before Tariq arrived at the zoo, its director had received a call from a panicking head of protocol for overseas delegations to say, "Quick! Get that fucking Russian-speaking parrot out of that cage *now* and shove the English talker in there straight away."'

Hitchens and I were conducted around the zoo but, alas, our parrots failed to squawk their tribute to Kim Jong Il. They have probably since been shot.

ON A SUPERVISED stroll around the city centre one evening, I looked up at a twenty-storey block of flats. All the lights were on and I could see inside every dwelling. With the repetition of a Warhol, the same official and standard-issue framed portraits of Kims Snr and Jnr, positioned alongside each another, stared down into every living room from the same wall.

This absolute uniformity, and the absence of any indications of dissent, however small (and always eventually apparent in every other dictatorship), led Hitchens and I into a discussion about whether curiosity is an innate human characteristic. If it is, we decided, there must be many in North Korea, harbouring in silence and isolation, suspicions that all this is bollocks and that there is the possibility of an alternative way of life in the alien wider world. It is likely these poor buggers are also of the belief that they are unique and alone having these thoughts. They must feel very lonely and live in a constant state of guilt and fear. Even more sinister is the logical conclusion that if a natural human curiosity leads to an awareness of the peculiarity of the North Korean system, and possible dissatisfaction with it, then to achieve complete obedience and uniformity of the citizenry, the regime in Pyongyang must enforce that obedience with some mechanism of terror and punishment so appalling that no one dares to show the slightest flicker of dissent.

Lest we had not fully appreciated the greatness of the Great Leader, we were marshalled around the feet of a huge, white marble statue of a seated Kim Il Sung in the entrance hall of the Grand People's Study House. This ornate sprawling pagoda – ten floors and six hundred marbled rooms – is a public library 'for the study of the works of Kim Il Sung'. It has a collection of thirty million books. In a typical reading room, and under the gaze of the ever-present portraits, dozens of Koreans of all ages sat silently at school desks, absorbed in the works of the old man. Europeans are not a common sight in these parts yet no one even looked up at us.

It was the desks which most excited our guide.

'When we opened the library all the desks were flat desks,' she explained. 'When the Great Leader, Comrade Kim Il Sung came to this room he personally sat at a desk and said that this kind of desk was not comfortable for the readers. So he said it would be better to change the desks into desks with an adjustable, angled surface.' She motioned to the evidence of benevolent desk development, now in use around the room.

'And how many desks had to be modified?' I asked, gripped by this news, in a North Korean sort of way.

'Six thousand,' she said, matter-of-factly.

For students experiencing difficulty with their studies, help is at hand in Room 142, the Question & Answer Room. In this windowless office sits a small middle-aged man, blinking at the wall. His desk is bare, except for a telephone. Those seeking illumination on any subject – philosophy, sciences, the arts – can drop in any time for a consultation. For this, explained our guide, is the Man Who Knows Everything.

We were swept next to the counter where books, ordered from a card index, are delivered. They arrive, bobsleigh fashion, down a chute.

'Let me call for something from our English language collection,' said the guide. Two books hurtled down the chute and landed with a thud on the counter. The first was titled, *Applied Polymer Symposia. Proceedings of the 8th Cellulose Conference – Wood Chemicals and Future Challenges, 1975. Volume 28.* It was like running into an old friend. The same book had appeared as an example of English literature in this stunt on one of my previous visits. As had the other page-turner, a medical paper from Massachusetts: *Deaths & Injuries in House Fires.*

Similarly, I have never tired of the outing, by train journey north, to Mount Myohyang and the International Friendship Museum. In this vast air-conditioned and windowless concrete bunker, also got up artfully as a pagoda, are all the gifts, no matter how humble or outlandish, given to Leaders Great and Dear. All 80,000 of them, displayed in 120 rooms, themed by country of origin.

Joseph Stalin was kind enough to present Kim Il Sung with a bullet-proof limousine. Chairman Mao had topped that with a railway carriage. Thoughtfully, Nicolae Ceausescu had sent the head of a bear, Robert Mugabe a seven-foot-wide etched copper tableau of stampeding elephants. With integral clock. From something called the Lebanon-Korea Friendship Association is displayed a two-bar electric fire with simulated flickering coal effect. Daniel Ortega and the Nicaraguan Sandinistas obliged with a stuffed alligator, standing on its hind legs, grinning, and holding up a tray of drinks. From a former president of Venezuela – and I tried to imagine an occasion when the Great Leader or the Dear Leader might use them – maracas. Maracas from Caracas.

Back at home, moved by my first experience of the Friendship Museum, I sent Kim Jong Il an attractively-priced brass ashtray, stamped 'A present from London', and a bag of cheese and onion crisps. I gather these have yet to appear in the museum's cabinet of gifts from British admirers, the centrepiece of which remains a postcard from a John and Audrey Newall of London to inform the Great Leader that their visit to North Korea back then had been 'unforgettable'.

ON MY VISIT with Hitchens in 2000 I noticed small but significant changes had taken place. There was a striking increase, albeit from a zero base, in the number of cars on Pyongyang's mighty boulevards. The exquisite traffic policewomen on duty at the junctions now had a couple of vehicles to control. Previously, they had spent their shifts twirling and gesticulating frantically at empty, silent streets. A mobile phone network had appeared but only for the party elite, NGOs, diplomats and foreign businessmen. The latter were gradually creeping in to capitalise (crikey!) on a workforce which is the most disciplined, educated and obedient in the world. And very cheap. Over the

The Man Who Knows Everything, Room 142 in The Grand People's Study House, Pyongyang, North Korea, 2003. *James Parkin*

previous three years a number of European countries, including the UK, had opened embassies in Pyongyang and the euro had replaced the US dollar as the favoured foreign currency. A modest market had just opened in the capital and business there was booming, in a bewildered North Korean fashion. And south of the border, president Roh Moo Hyun was maintaining the Sunshine Policy of reconciliation and cooperation instigated by his predecessor, Kim Dae Jung.

'There are signs the regime wants to change things,' said one European expatriate. 'But it wants to do it without losing face. That's very important here. Everyone in Pyongyang is now trying to do business. It's unofficial but it's happening. They're learning quickly how to turn a buck and that's the best hope for a soft landing. The only worry then would be a gulf opening between a relatively rich urban population and a peasantry for whom the currency would still be cabbages.'

The future was looking bright. Before leaving office, Kim Dae Jung made a historic visit to the North. Kim Jong Il met him personally at the foot of the aircraft steps. In his self-designed, utilitarian brown outfit, the Dear Leader was first assumed by the South Korean president's security men to be the bloke who'd been sent to refuel the plane.

'FUCKING HELL, KERSHAW, have you heard?' Hitchens was bustling down the corridor towards my hotel room, a bottle of duty free single malt and a bag of smoked almonds in his hand. It was approaching our Korean cocktails hour.

I had indeed heard. We'd both been listening to the BBC World Service news on our little short waves in our rooms. It had been announced that Bill Clinton's Secretary of State, Madeleine Albright, was to make an equally courageous trip to have face-to-face talks with Kim Jong Il. She was arriving the day after our departure. Jimmy Carter was another hands-across-the-ocean guest of Pyongyang in those Sunshine days. After Carter's visit, the North Koreans agreed to put aside any nuclear naughtiness in exchange for fuel, food and benign nuclear reactors.

It was all going so well. And then George W. Bush took office.

Bush had long before gone on the record to declare his intention to topple the Dear Leader. 'I loathe the man,' he once said, also describing him as 'a pygmy' and 'an evildoer'.

On 29 January 2002, Bush delivered his State of the Union Address in which presidential speechwriter David Frum gave the world the gormless slogan 'Axis of Evil'. Frum later hinted that North Korea had been added to the original Axis membership of Iraq and Iran as an afterthought. Whether Pyongyang's inclusion was glib and casual or not, the utterance of the phrase destroyed all the progress that had been made over the previous five years and brought the shutters down again on any future dialogue.

'Bush, Cheney, Rumsfeld and Wolfowitz have no understanding of the North Korean character,' another nameless European resident of Pyongyang told me there in November 2003. 'Koreans feel personally very insulted to be included in the Axis of Evil. And, post-Iraq, they feel very threatened by the United States but very defiant.'

'Does Kim Jong Il, unlike Saddam, really have the bomb?' I asked.

'I don't know,' he said. 'But whether he has or he hasn't, it's useful to him for the Americans to think he may have. The US knew for certain that Iraq had no nuclear weapons. It was a soft target. They also know this is not.'

Nick Bonner, my effervescent travel agent pal, was also dismayed by regime change in Washington and the reversal of previous policy. It was his belief that Pyongyang needs only kindness and assistance in its fumblings towards liberalisation. 'My feeling is dialogue,' he told me. 'It's the only way ahead. If people just said, "Look, what can we do to help? What do you need?" as opposed to "How can we stop you doing this that and the other?" and stopped telling them what to do, I think big changes would happen here quickly. The attitude we pick up from the North Koreans in the west is a very aggressive one but, in fact, they are very defensive. They don't have ambitions to march off to South Korea, nor any incentive to do so.'

Not having Nick's imagination, US Defence Secretary, Donald Rumsfeld, renewed, in July 2003, Operations Plan 5030, the

Pentagon's war strategy for North Korea. Should its initial objective fail – to destabilise the military, with a provocative action by US forces, which would then overthrow the Dear Leader – the fallback was to be a huge number of nuclear strikes across the country. By the Pentagon's own estimation, casualties during the first hour of a conflict between the North and the allied forces of the US and South Korea would number a million or more.

With that in mind, a tour of Pyongyang's war museum reinforces an understanding of the North Korean siege mentality. In one room is a shocking black-and-white 360-degree photograph of Pyongyang at the end of the Korean war in 1953. Not a single building is left standing. It is a panorama of rubble.

This might also explain the depth of the metro, Pyongyang's underground railway, more than three hundred feet below the city's streets. In 1995, I met an Austrian businessman in the capital's Koryo Hotel. He was setting up a joint venture with the government to recycle plastics. Had I yet, he wondered, travelled on the metro?

'As a matter of fact,' I told him, 'I was down there this afternoon, travelling from Hope to Glory.' (These are names of a couple of the city's garishly ornate tube stations.)

'Did you notice,' asked the Austrian, 'a lot of heavy, unmarked steel doors?'

'Yes, I did. What's behind those?'

'Stairs,' he said. 'They go down as deep again. And they've got factories down there.'

'What?' I said, then suggesting to him a few women sitting at sewing machines in a subterranean sweatshop.

'No,' he laughed. 'They're driving fucking trucks around down there.'

BACK AT PANMUNJOM, I always linger for as long as possible at the Demarcation Line. And that's all it is: a line on the ground, a concrete strip about a foot wide and standing four inches proud of the asphalt. Anywhere else it would be regarded as nothing more than a trip hazard. Here it marks the border between Koreas North and South. There is no fence, no wall and no gate. The People's Army has been locked into a staring match here for almost sixty years with the marines of the 'US Imperialist Aggressor and its South Korean puppets.' If they wish, they can go literally toe to toe and eyeball to eyeball. Sometimes they do, although the Americans prefer to sit in an observation tower (another phoney pagoda), fully thirty yards into the South. The blue glare of their binoculars never leaves us as we scatter about, pose for Polaroids with giggling North Korean guards and openly take dozens of snaps of one of the most sensitive military positions on earth.

On one visit, a jolly North Korean colonel was happy to chat. Did he have a family?

'Yes, I have a wife and two children,' he said.

'Very nice,' I smiled

'But I like big, beautiful girls,' he added. 'My wife is small and ugly.' I nodded solemnly. 'But I am afraid to run away from her.'

North of the border, 2003. Panmunjom, North Korea, where North and South, still at war, go eyeball-to-eyeball. The border itself is the line on the ground behind the North Korean soldiers. The huts, in which infrequent talks are held, straddle the frontier and have a door at each end. *James Parkin*

We'd known each other, the colonel and I, for all of two minutes.

Seven pale blue huts straddle the line. These are the conference rooms of the Military Armistice Commission. North and South Korea are technically still at war. Only a ceasefire was signed to smother hostilities in 1953. There are doors at both ends of the huts. In the middle of each is a green baize topped table. The border runs along the centre of these tables. When the infrequent talks take place, the delegations from North and South enter through their respective doors. And when their inconclusive and unproductive bickering has finished, they return to their opposing countries through those opposing doors.

Back on the bus, it is just a short drive to the Panmunjom gift shop. Here visitors can grab those last-minute stuffed pheasants, blue plastic washing-up bowls, bottles of snake wine or perhaps a postcard showing a photograph of a dog pinning a deer to the ground and tearing at its throat. There is, on the fur of both animals, much blood. The postcard is captioned, 'Dog'.

I chatted here to one of our minders about the threat from 37,000 US troops permanently stationed south of the border.

'Never mind the million strong North Korean army,' I said. 'How would North Korean civilians react to an American invasion?'

'We would fight to every last man and woman,' he told me. 'And if the Americans arrived at my apartment block, I would give out hand grenades to my children.'

'Really?' I said. 'And how old are your kids?'

'Two and four.'

39

THE BOILED OWL VERSUS
THE CORPORATE ZOMBIES

IT OCCURRED TO ME as I walked back up Whitehall towards Trafalgar Square that I may have just been approached by MI6. It was early 1992, years before the British secret intelligence service had its own website, a succession of telegenic directors as sinister as any leading light of the Rotary Club, and a propensity to place newspaper ads saying 'Spies Wanted'. From what I gather, our overseas spooks in those days did not actually articulate the murky business of recruitment. Potential agents were identified and sort of sucked in.

An odd thing had happened just after I got back from Equatorial Guinea. On a Saturday morning edition of *From Our Own Correspondent*, I'd had a dispatch broadcast about the obscure African dictatorship. The following Monday morning, I got a call from the Foreign Office. The chap on the phone wanted to know if I'd mind 'popping in for a little chat' with someone on their west Africa desk. Nothing official, you understand, all very informal and very much off the record. I was intrigued and agreed to an appointment later that week.

At King Charles Street, I was swept along oak-panelled corridors and into an oak-panelled room hung with gloomy portraits, painted in the full spectrum of browns. I was introduced to a most attractive blonde, in a fortyish-older-woman sort of way, who asked me to call her Sarah. She was accompanied by a younger man who carried a spiral bound notepad and a pen. Tea was served in elegant china.

'Not many people go to Equatorial Guinea,' Sarah observed.

While we had no diplomatic representation in the country, it was reassuring to have confirmed that the Foreign Office was fully across every detail of these matters of grave national security. 'True,' I said. 'That's why I went.'

Sarah asked me a lot of questions about what I'd seen there. The young man took notes. Was there much evidence of logging? Could I identify the nationality of the logging companies? And she was particularly curious about my *FOOC* revelation that Equatorial Guinea had just struck oil.

It was all terribly convivial, and more: I probably did not conceal very well that I fancied the arse off Sarah. And Sarah did not flinch from flirting gently with me.

There was nothing I told her that I had not already broadcast on national radio in *FOOC*.

'Thank you for coming in,' she said with a playful smile as she saw me to the door and handed me over to my escort to the street. 'And if you're going anywhere else, do let us know, won't you?'

'As a matter of fact, I'm going to Haiti again next Tuesday,' I told her.

'Oh, really? That's interesting,' she said. 'Well, that's not my patch but do give me a call when you get back. I'm sure one of my colleagues would like to chat to you.'

She handed me her phone number. For the next couple of days, I would pull it out of my pocket and ponder its implications. Could it be I was being asked to spy? Perhaps it was a come on. Did Sarah just fancy a drink? Might there be more in it? Sarah was stunning. Should I call back? An undercurrent of uneasiness won the day. To call back, I decided, would be to cross the line and so, lamenting the loss of possible gorgeous older woman leg-over, I dropped her number into the bin before heading off once more to Port-au-Prince.

SARAH, MY PUTATIVE HANDLER at MI6, possibly escaped my further attentions also because I had, less than two years before, begun a relationship with Juliette, who would remain my partner for seventeen years.

We had met at the end of 1989 when Juliette was – if you'll forgive me – working as a waitress in a cocktail bar, at the end of my street in Crouch End. Within two years she had struck out to open her own place, a neighbourhood bar and restaurant which was an overnight success.

The mechanics and details of business bore me. I have never been driven by money and have no interest in it beyond having enough to be comfortable. I was, therefore, never a formal business partner with Juliette in the restaurant, though my input of creativity and imagination was considerable. She wanted to do something of her own in the crowded Crouch End restaurant market and I helped her to find a focus. I realised that the neighbourhood, although brimming with liberal, sophisticated folk, had nowhere that felt like a natural hang-out for those people. I suggested that she open a place which was, crudely, a bar and an informal restaurant for readers of the *Independent* and the *Guardian*.

I also took care of the restaurant's music, providing a rotation of CDs which might, from one minute to the next, have the diners swept through their starters by perhaps the harmonies of the Louvin Brothers and on to the main course with the classic Congolese rumba of Dr Nico. Memorabilia from my global adventures – revolutionary posters, flags, framed historic newspaper front pages – and rock & roll ephemera decorated the walls. Rock stars dropped in, including one visit by Bob Dylan. Media potentates and celebrities were among the regulars. Motorcycle racing world champions mixed with locals at the zinc bar. To my embarrassment, it was frequently assumed to be, and described as such in magazine dining-out features, as 'Andy Kershaw's restaurant', so fully was it a reflection of my personality, tastes and interests. If this inaccurate attribution irritated Juliette, she did not make a song and dance about it. The restaurant's link to me, and the famous customers that brought in, was good for business. And she deserved all the success that came to her.

Among Juliette's many attributes – sweet-natured, down to earth, physically beautiful – the one for which I admired her most was her capacity for hard work and dedication to her business. I was very proud of her.

IN 1994, I finally surrendered my bachelor existence. Without the nuisance of a tedious wedding ceremony (why drag the church, the state and H Samuel's into it?), Juliette and I bought together a big shabby house on one of Crouch End's grandest streets. Our first child, Sonny, was born in August 1997.

Sonny was given his name not as a tribute to Sonnies Liston or Barger, nor a Sonny from any number of unlistenable jazz musicians, but to recall the affectionate nickname my dad had given me as a toddler and for his fondness of singing to me the Al Jolson weeper, *Sonny Boy*. Dolly arrived in March 1999 and was unashamedly named after Dolly Parton, a female role model I admired above most others. (When our Dolly was three, a historic meeting of both Dollies took place in the singer's inner sanctum, backstage at the Hammersmith Odeon. Ms Parton, clothed in a jewelled gown: 'Oh, my! Dolly that's *such* a pretty dress...' Our Dolly presented her namesake with a wax crayon drawing of the country music legend that she'd done that day at nursery school.)

I took to fatherhood much more readily and enthusiastically than most friends and family members predicted. In fact, the person my position as happy daddy surprised most was me. I was proof, I guess, of Dr Spock's assertion that one knows, instinctively, more than one thinks one knows. I adored Sonny and Dolly, at all stages of their little lives, from wide-eyed, head-rolling spewing machines to adorable toddlers, to insatiably curious infant investigators. To teach them about everything around them, and to observe their fascination, while by no means unique to our relationship, was the most rewarding and heartwarming experience I have known. Everything from 'wiggly worms' to 'Harley-Davidson that go "Bang!"'

An awareness of the fragility and randomness of the children's existence was just one of the wonders of being a dad and, in my dafter moments, I might have been persuaded to keep going. A large family would, after all, have conformed to my most reliable maxim – *If you're going to have one, have a big one*. Fatherhood, like foreign adventures, romances, motorcycles, relationships with pieces of music and friendships could only benefit from going for it full-on.

IT HAS OFTEN been insisted, by freelance bar-stool psychologists, most of whom don't actually know me, that my experiences in foreign hell-holes, Rwanda chief among them, must surely mean I live permanently with Post Traumatic Stress Disorder. This is, of course, nonsense and symptomatic of a modern obsession with special needs and the almost universally held assumption and neurosis that we all need the round-the-clock attentions of the counselling industry to cope with the menace we normal individuals recognise as life.

Being an eyewitness to history and having the occasional encounter with shocking quantities of *what-the-fuck-is-this?* did leave me, however, with a different problem and one which would never occur to the self-appointed experts who have never met me. It was coping instead, after those experiences, with the banalities of everyday life back in Britain. For a couple of weeks after that first trip to North Korea, for example, I did little except to sit at the kitchen table, giggling and going over with Juliette, poor lamb, the details of the absurdities of the trip, just as one might try to recall and analyse a bizarre dream, and seek in it some meaning. (That's the main reason I returned three times to Pyongyang. Could it really have been as bonkers as that?) The downside of the privilege that it is to see extreme events and extraordinary countries, to bear witness to the routine misfortune and misery which is the daily reality for so many people around the world, and to report from those situations, is an impatience it has bequeathed to me with the parochial and the trivial and an intolerance of the small-minded. Frankly, I couldn't give a bugger for what Westminster politicians think of each other. Equally, the small-minded spitefulness and petty obsessions of self-important inadequates in questionable positions of minor authority on, for the sake of argument, the Isle of Man, I have to regard in the perspective of overall experience and priority. That renders, rightly, strutting mediocrities, who have never seen nor done anything noteworthy in their pompous little lives, to the categories of the tragic and the insignificant.

This expanded sense of proportion was to prove corrosive at home. I wasn't screwed up by the civil wars in Angola, Sierra Leone and Rwanda and another dozen madhouses. But those experiences made it that much harder to come home and show much of an interest in what Juliette reported to me over the dinner table of the staff politics at the restaurant. Similarly but professionally, the bickerings within Radio 1, and Peel's perception of their magnitude, only bored me if I even bothered to give them attention. Beyond my eagerness to hold onto my programme, why should I have really cared for the latest insanity some Birtist apparatchik had planned, he or she having returned from another fatuous and expensive corporate bonding exercise? Did I actually give a toss whether the consensus among the children now in producers' jobs had decided this band or that was cool or uncool? I felt I was floating above the everyday world. And it was lonely.

ALTHOUGH I WAS, for the most part, regarded as 'not a proper journalist' and 'really only a DJ', I did, with the help of a few supportive producers, slip occasionally under the radar and onto the airwaves as a foreign correspondent in the disguise of a features presenter.

With Radio 4 producer, Jeremy Grange, I made in 1997 a series of programmes about water crises, current and impending, around the world. Jeremy's idea was visionary. Scarcity of water will lead eventually to conflict. In fact, it already has. The secret agenda of water security is the true reason behind Israel's appalling treatment of the Palestinians. Jeremy and I visited eleven countries in fewer than four weeks, including those remnants of Palestine which other journalists identify as Gaza and the West Bank, dignifying and conniving in the conceit that Israel has effectively erased Palestine as a country, on the map and in reality. I was horrified to see on the ground the daily humiliation and routine brutishness of Israel's treatment of those whose land it was illegally occupying with the help of an international consensus of silence. And all the while, stealing the Palestinians' water from under their feet, draining them virtually dry.

I spent a day with an elderly Palestinian smallholder on his little patch of rocky land near Bethlehem. It was dotted with a few struggling olive trees. The farmer had been obliged to devise and build all manner of elaborate contraptions to catch and store dew. The Israelis had decreed that wells in this part of Palestine – not part of Israel – could be dug only to a certain depth. The water, you guessed it, was not to be found until Palestinian farmers dug a few inches below that limit. My smallholder had done just that, after which he'd had a visit from a number of teenage Israeli soldiers who'd tipped concrete down his well. Meanwhile, on the hill above the parched olive grove, a new apartment block was going up for Israeli 'settlers', the illegal presence of whom would turn political aspiration into geographic reality. I walked up to have a look. A swimming pool was under construction and sprinklers were already drenching the verges and lawns of these as yet unoccupied commuter homes. At the same time, Israel was pumping water from aquifers under the West Bank to enrich the golf courses of Tel Aviv.

MY HOSTILITY TOWARDS religion and, in its name, the infliction of misery – still justified by that adherence to infantile superstition of *all* varieties – came as a surprise to the producers of *Songs of Praise* who, in 1994, wrote to ask me if I'd consider becoming one of their presenters. A programme of televised hymn singing, *Songs of Praise* had been a cosy Sunday evening institution on the BBC since 1961. The letter, offering me this woolly-jumpered position was, I assumed, a joke. It wasn't. When I called the producer he took my assertion that I was possibly the most godless bugger in the whole of the BBC with good humour. He and his team had assumed that my enthusiasm for playing vintage black American gospel music on my Radio 1 programmes indicated that I was a committed Christian and just the kind of groovy evangelist who might bring to the programme an audience which wasn't already, and perilously, nearer to my God than thee.

It was a common assumption, usually among those who had never heard my programmes, that my position as a Radio 1 DJ meant that I would be eager to consolidate and capitalise upon that minor fame by signing up for anything televised, even shows which made *Songs of Praise* seem high-brow.

'What's *I'm A Celebrity, Get Me Out Of Here?*' I had to ask Sonny and Dolly, as I opened the post one morning in 2003. They gave me their synopsis of the newish reality television phenomenon, explaining its mechanism and detailing, as it sounded to me, its protracted tedium. I had been asked to take part in the next series which would have required me to spend a couple of weeks in the northern Australian jungle with Johnny Rotten. For that, they offered me £50,000 in compensation.

'Do it, Daddy!' squealed Sonny and Dolly. And it wasn't about the money. The children's tiny minds, slightly more developed than those of the producers of lowest common denominator television programmes, could not grasp why I was not desperate to be more famous and anxious to appear on a programme on which the participants seemed to be selected necessarily as celebrities on the slide. I turned it down, politely, telling the incredulous producer to contact me again if they were ever commissioned to make a foreign affairs programme, covering the world's hot-spots, called *I'm Not A Celebrity, Get Me In There*.

My late 1990s forays back into television were infrequent, never just for the money, and only for coverage of matters which really fired me up. *Travelog* had long since been killed off by Channel 4. The once stimulating and eclectic network had in recent years eagerly chased the certainties of down-market ratings to the point at which it became – with the honourable exception of the outstanding *Channel 4 News* and one or two other current affairs strands – an ignoble shadow of its former self. I was, meanwhile, over on Sky Sports, happy to put principle aside to take the occasional shilling off Rupert Murdoch, the global pioneer of all that is down-market, but only as one of the presenters of the channel's excellent coverage of my beloved motorcycle racing. On just the one occasion I was in a similar role – your man in the pit lane, wearing ludicrous headphones and bothering the riders – for BBC's *Grandstand*. Then producers of motorcycle racing on all television channels realised the audience-grabbing potential of employing, as reporters, impossibly glamorous girls instead of a bloke who looks like a boiled owl. I was out and went back, very happily, to being again a paying spectator.

Maintaining a manageable and lowish profile was not always successful. In early 1990, *Vogue* called me. Would I care to have my photo taken, they wanted to know, by David Bailey? And, for the shoot, would I wear my black leather motorcycle jacket? As I would become, I thought, the most unlikely fashion icon in the magazine's history and as it's not every day one is asked to appear in *Vogue,* snapped by a photographer more famous than his subjects, I agreed. That, and I thought an overwhelming quantity of sophisticated totty would accrue to me following my full-page exposure in a magazine about posh frocks. At the shoot, Bailey turned out to be so charmless and ill-mannered towards his delightful assistants that I considered telling him to bugger off and walking out. Alas, my one and only fashion appearance, this solitary celebration of AK as a hunk, generated no up-market romantic interest whatsoever. In the summer of 2010, I noted that a second-hand copy of that edition of *Vogue* (March 1990) was being offered on eBay for a pound.

Out there in the weird world of popular taste, only Nick Hornby – an unlikely mainstream success himself – got me right. I am still immensely flattered to have been immortalised in *High Fidelity,* Nick's breakthrough novel. My presence in the book (end of paragraph two, chapter four), in the shadows at a north London pub performance by 'some obscure American folk/country artist' seems to reassure Hornby that the gig will be 'buzzy'. Absolutely. Stick with me, Nick. You'll be alright.

* * *

PURSUIT OF EXCELLENCE, and my prioritisation of substance over style, quality over popularity, recognised by Nick Hornby, was viewed by most of my Radio 1 colleagues as an obsession with the arcane. My refusal to consume hype and image, and my rejection of the latest cowardly consensus of what was and wasn't considered cool, led to my almost total ostracism by the rest of the station's personnel. This reached ludicrous new levels under the regime of Controller, Andy Parfitt, an era also of short-term contracts, job insecurity and fear and loathing.

During this post Year Zero period, Radio 1 vacated Egton House and moved to a nearby building. In this brave new environment, there were no longer individual offices. Everything was open-plan, despite the downright impossibility of listening to music in that environment, except on headphones. The move also meant that Peel and I were split up after twelve years together in Room 318 and repositioned in this wilderness, some distance apart, with a lot of sulking children interposed between us. For these 'producers', enthusiasm was most definitely uncool and, without the courage of their own convictions, they approved only of music endorsed by the *New Musical Express*.

John's coping strategy was to pretend at first that all this was great – a big improvement, in fact, on the previous end-of-the-pier epoch and the security of 318. When I had to point out to him that I had not even been given the courtesy of a chair, desk and CD player in the new office, he tried to persuade me, unconvincingly, of the benefits of hot-desking and that his own incompetent, resentful adolescent producers were just fantastic. Clearly, I'd lost him. I felt very alone. But no more so than on the occasion I walked into the new building one afternoon in early 1998 to find an aluminium sign had been fixed to the outside of the door into the open-plan office. Etched upon it were the names of every DJ, producer and production assistant who occupied that room. Except for mine. I also learned around this time that there had taken place recently the annual Radio 1 DJs team photograph, to which I had not been invited.

With a succession of appalling cut-price kids allocated to me as producers, the shortcomings of the Birtist revolution began to have a damaging effect on what happened live on the air. At that point, I decided this nonsense had got to stop. It was now affecting our output. But my complaints were always dismissed as the awkwardness of 'grumpy Andy' who couldn't readjust to the exciting changes. This was the decoy and the corporate line even when I was given a producer who, with only seconds to go before we went live, admitted to me, after I'd asked her to put the tape of the first session track onto the reel-to-reel machine, that she had no idea how. I had to do it myself, clambering and clattering over the tape decks, while simultaneously greeting the listeners.

'Well,' said a Radio 1 Birtist executive the following day, trying to cover up the producer's inadequacy, 'she does come highly recommended. You do know, don't you, that she used to work for the *Melody Maker*?'

'My partner,' I told him through gritted teeth, 'goes into hospital next week for an operation. To what extent should she feel reassured if the surgeon were to bend over her in the theatre and say, "I've never done an operation before, but my golf handicap is much admired"?'

My protests about this money-saving incompetence, the inevitable reward of a Birtist recognition of the price of everything and the value of nothing – except for when they were eagerly frittering away money on consultants and corporate identity – were countered by Radio 1 black propaganda, most disgustingly that I was 'anti women'. I found myself having to answer this charge to others in the media by pointing out that nearly all my regular producers in television and over at Radio 4 were women, and ones with whom I enjoyed excellent working relationships.

It not only enraged me but broke my heart to see the BBC being destroyed at the hands of these barbarians with their fetish for the bogus internal market (the faddish Producer Choice) before quality of programming. Few among them, with mediocrity as their benchmark, seemed to have any affection for the BBC or any ideological attachment to public service broadcasting. These were, to them, executive jobs, just like the next one to which they would swan off, including Birt himself, once they'd dismantled many of the foundations which had made the BBC so strong and the envy of the world.

FOR MUCH OF 1998, I went on strike. The main condition of my return to Radio 1 was that I be given a producer who – good grief – could do the job. At that stage, to meet my demands, Controller Andy Parfitt had to go and borrow one for me from Radio 2.

Richard Masters was a lovely man and a veteran Radio 2 producer. His appointment brought a serenity and security to compiling and presenting my Radio 1 programmes. I worked with Richard, and his secretary Lisa, out of their office in a Radio 2 building next to Broadcasting House. After we were teamed up, I don't think I set foot in the Radio 1 HQ again. And together, Richard and I made a documentary which is, among all the programmes I have made in twenty-five years of radio, probably the one of which I am most proud.

Since 1971 a Bob Dylan bootleg had been in circulation of an incendiary performance by Bob and the Hawks (later The Band) on their 1966 electric tour. The gig had always been attributed to the Royal Albert Hall although we Dylanologists later identified it as the concert at the Manchester Free Trade Hall on 17 May 1966. It was celebrated not just for Bob and the band at their most majestic but for the most famous heckle in rock & roll history. Throughout the electric set, a sharp and noisy fracture opened up between Dylan fans who embraced Bob's deafening new psychedelic rock music and those who wanted him still to be Woody Guthrie. Just before *Like A Rolling Stone*, the final number, and with perfect timing, the voice of a betrayed folkie yells, 'Judas!' It is a moment of jaw-dropping drama and tension. Dylan, stoned, is for a second taken aback before drawling, 'I don't believe you. You're a liar. You fucking liar!' And with that the band blasts into *Like A Rolling Stone* with the impact of dropping a great Gothic municipal building onto the heckler's head.

In late 1998, Columbia Records finally released the recording officially, clearing the way for me to make the documentary which I'd wanted to make since 1978 when I'd first acquired my bootleg copy of the gig. With the generous and immense help of Manchester academic and fellow Dylan obsessive, CP Lee, who had been at the gig as a youth and had written a book about it, we assembled in the Free Trade Hall many of those who had also been in the audience on the night. Some spoke of a confrontation bordering on civil unrest. The experience of this reunion was very spooky, especially as the grand old theatre, where I had seen my first rock gig, was by then defunct and semi-derelict.

The broadcast of *Ghosts of Electricity* flushed out the Judas heckler, as I had hoped it would. After initially airing the claims of an imposter and chancer, Keith Butler, I received a wounded email from a John Cordwell, living in Cumbria. John, by 1999, was a middle-aged tutor at a teacher training college in Manchester. I went up to meet him and he provided me with enough evidence to convince me that it was he who had been Dylan's teenage tormentor. I was rather proud of having solved one of rock music's great enduring mysteries and to have revealed the identity of someone who had shouted only a single word thirty-three years before. John turned out to be a smashing bloke, by 1999 fully repentant for his 1966 outburst and now a huge fan of the electrified Dylan on the official Free Trade Hall release. He and I became quite pally but sadly John died, prematurely, following a bee sting in July 2001.

John Cordwell, the 'Judas!' heckler at Bob Dylan's 1966 Manchester Free Trade Hall concert, confesses all to me in a Salford pub thirty-three years later. *AK*

Richard Masters and I

– 406 –

Bob Dylan & The Hawks, Manchester Free Trade Hall, 17 May 1966. On the left is bassist, Rick Danko. The drummer is Mickey Jones and lead guitarist, Robbie Robertson, is on the right. This photo was taken by Mark Makin, then a fifteen-year-old schoolboy, in the fourth row of the front stalls. Mark's photos are the only ones known to exist of this infamous concert. *Mark Makin*

never told Radio 1 of our intentions to make the documentary. Neither did we seek the Controller's permission to do so. And we didn't even bother to notify the management that it was going out, as an eighty-minute feature within the breakaway republic that was by then my weekly two-hour programme. Radio 1 did not see fit to put *Ghosts of Electricity* forward for any award. It did, however, get recognition and rave reviews elsewhere and the unmasking of John Cordwell attracted national media attention, even a Robin Denselow report on *Newsnight*.

* * *

THE DYLAN DOCUMENTARY was the centrepiece of my late-90s reinvigoration on Radio 1, for which Richard Masters deserves the credit. The period was also notable for some historic live sessions. Among those was the unforgettable morning we recorded Dick Dale, the King of the Surf Guitar, in a basement studio of Broadcasting House. Dick and his Del-Tones were only half way through *Miserlou* when a shrill, bossy emissary from *Woman's Hour* came bustling into the studio with her hands over her ears to complain that the din was penetrating the adjoining soundproofed wall and interfering with Jenni Murray's live transmission next door.

Joe Strummer and I were reunited, too, for the first time since the Clash gigs at Leeds University. I got a message from Joe on my answering machine one Monday morning asking who the Algerian artist was that I'd played on my show the night before. (It was Rachid Taha.) Joe, like that other soul brother, Robert Plant, never stopped being a music fan. Our conversation led to meetings in a pub near Broadcasting House. At one of these I invited Joe to co-present the programme with me for a night and to bring in a bunch of records he'd like to play. We had great fun on that show, Joe having arrived with nothing but a bag of old reggae and vintage R&B records. Soon after, at a party to launch an art gallery exhibition of photos of The Clash, Joe signed a poster with the preamble, 'To Andy. Without you we wouldn't know nothin'. Rock on.' Clash guitarist, Mick Jones, scrawled alongside that, 'Thanks for the Leeds University gigs.' When I read what they'd written, I almost cried.

In May 1998, soon after Chris Blackwell had signed him to Island Records, Willie Nelson and the entire Family Band came into Maida Vale studios for a live Kershaw session. When, unassumingly, the veteran soul rebel walked through the studio door, I swear to God there was a celestial glow around his wiry frame and ponytailed head.

'What would you like us to play, Andy?' asked one of the twentieth century's greatest songwriters and the maverick custodian-in-chief of real country music, standing before me, the image of humility. I was sitting at a little desk facing Willie and a semicircle of his band members. In photos taken that day,

I look like the invigilator of a school exam, Willie and the musicians a bunch of long-haired and exceedingly mature students.

For a moment, I was stuck for words although I did blabber to Willie that he was welcome to play whatever he liked and for the duration of the whole programme. He did. At the end, Willie held Sonny in his arms. Sonny tugged Willie's beard. (This historic meeting came shortly before I took Sonny down to central London to yell and scream, aged fifteen months, under the private hospital window of General Augusto Pinochet.)

I'd secured the Willie Nelson session myself, by phoning Island Records. My own Radio 1 producer – the last of the amateurs, before Richard Masters – then cancelled it, without telling me, on the grounds that Willie was 'too old'. I demanded it be reinstated, threatening to go public with this oafish decision, while pointing out – though it wouldn't be understood – that Willie had more rock & roll spirit in a single hair of his grey beard than was to be found in the entire lamentable roll-call of the desperate tragedy that was Britpop. Willie's recording was restored, but only at the last moment.

FROM THE MID-1980S to the mid-1990s, at the kind invitation of festival organiser Michael Eavis, I was compère and DJ on the main stage at Glastonbury. For most of those years, Glastonbury was a dream of a festival – partly due to Michael's choice of acts and partly because Glastonbury was, essentially, a gathering of enthusiastic herbalists.

One evening there still amazes me. I watched, close up from the side of the stage, Ry Cooder and David Lindley and, once their set had finished I brought on, as the sun was going down, Black Uhuru, in their original, their greatest and most militant incarnation of Michael Rose, Duckie Simpson and Puma Jones. Riddims, as we reggae insiders know these things, were provided by Sly and Robbie. I was no more than ten feet away from them. At Glastonbury 1987, the Passchendaele of festivals, I stood between Ian Dury & the Blockheads and a crowd which was waist deep in mud and intent on slaughtering the band with flying rocks. Haranguing the assailants, and in a blur of missiles, I turned the rest of the audience against them by warning there would be no more performances from anyone if the violence didn't stop. It did. The Blockheads returned.

I would give up on Glastonbury before the millennium. In earlier years the festival had been like a village fete with world class bands. The backstage bar had been a cosy little space under the main stage, populated by off-duty members of the stage crew and unassuming thirsty rock stars. But gradually this had expanded to a backstage city with corporate hospitality facilities, attracting all manner of oily spivs, and policed not by the usual lads from the village but by bruisers from private security firms. Glastonbury was also discovered, around this time, by the new intake at Radio 1. If these arrivistes had previously held an opinion of Glastonbury it was to express contempt for my fondness for 'a hippy festival'. Now they were crawling all over Worthy Farm and calling it 'Glasto', always the mark of a pretentious Pilton newcomer.

To understand the development of popular music, always follow the drug. That is equally true of festivals, as mirrors of that cultural evolution. Glastonbury changed out of all recognition in the 1990s because the predominant drug among the festival goers changed. What had once been a gathering of amiable dope-smokers became an annual convention of freelance pharmacists. The atmosphere switched from the serene to the wired and I was not the only Glastonbury loyalist who got fed up of having to tolerate these gibbering hordes and their dreary dehumanised dance music.

Trends, thank goodness, disappear as quickly as they arrive and Michael Eavis seems to have gone a long way in more recent years to reclaim some of the spirit of the old festival. In 2009, had I had any money for a ticket, I would have crawled my way to Worthy Farm over broken glass to see Neil Young and Bruce Springsteen & the E Street Band on the one weekend. Again, in 2010, only poverty prevented me from keeping a long overdue Glastonbury appointment with Willie Nelson.

But, whatever Michael pulls off in the future to top those, a performance on the main stage in 1994 will never be matched.

With John Peel in the Radio 1 studio at Glastonbury, mid-1990s. Note my choice of a Roy Smeck album – 1930s Hawaiian guitar music, at the height of Britpop. *Unknown*

When I heard that Johnny Cash was to play on the Saturday afternoon slot, I was thrilled but worried. In recent years that position had been reserved for novelty acts or those making an incongruous appearance at a rock festival. Tom Jones and Rolf Harris had, in 1992 and 1993, satisfied the appetites of tedious post-modern piss-takers. Johnny Cash did not deserve that treatment from a crowd I feared would be too intolerant and too ignorant to realise his true value.

All morning, up on stage, I'd been fretting about how he'd be received and a form of words I might summon to do justice to the man and pre-empt any ridicule. I had to nail it in one short sentence. The hour was drawing near and nothing sufficiently concise would come. I went backstage to find the great man and to introduce myself. I was also looking to get myself off the hook.

I found him in his Portakabin dressing room. There was no security. I knocked on the door and he called me in. The frame was just as imposing as I imagined it would be, more ample than it had been but still he had the shoulders of a fighting bull. He was sitting on a plastic chair, wheezing and sweating. But he had an instant warmth.

'Do you,' I asked, 'have a particular form of words you'd like me to use as an introduction?'

'No, Andy,' he said. 'Just say what you like.'

Oh, fuck. Then he asked me if it was 'all kids out there.' He was worried too about a reception from a chemically-fuelled crowd, not naturally disposed to country music.

'Not all kids, no,' I said not untruthfully. Somewhere on the horizon, I think I'd spotted someone over thirty.

When it was time to go, I'd still not thought of the intro. At the nod from the stage manager, and with the band – minus Johnny – all in place, I set off towards the centre microphone, my head empty and in a state of near panic. I am not a believer and, therefore, cannot claim divine intervention. But when I reached that microphone, the words came from somewhere and someone and it didn't feel like they were from me. Over the gigantic PA, I heard myself say, 'Please welcome, a giant of American music and a giant of a man. Johnny Cash.'

A roar went up. And with that, I turned to head for the wings. But Johnny had appeared at my right shoulder, gazing out. I hesitated. He leaned into the mic.

'Hello,' he said. 'I'm Johnny Cash.'

Hard on those words came the signature twanging guitar intro to *Folsom Prison Blues*. Glastonbury went up like a chippan. I scuttled behind the side-fills. The roaring didn't let up, all the way through that first song. Giant waves of affection were crashing into and breaking over the stage. With the final chord dying away, the swell was immense and overpowering. Cash stood there, humbled, tears rolling down his face. I was in floods too. He was home and dry. It was one of the most emotional moments I have witnessed on a stage and I am still thrilled to have played a cameo role.

MY IRRITATION WITH Birtism's seizure of the BBC ran much deeper than a resentment of its spear-carriers spoiling Glastonbury. When, in 1999, the *Independent* offered me the job of weekly radio critic, I saw it as my chance to hit back publicly.

Never mind the small detail that I also happened to be a Radio 1 DJ at the same time. Bigger and more important considerations were at stake. It was time to defend public service broadcasting. Every week, for more than a year, I relished sitting in front of my laptop, after listening to hours of radio, just as a sniper must relish hunkering down into position. I knew my time with Radio 1 was short. It was just a question of whose patience ran out first, mine or theirs.

My friend Francis Wheen, in his diary in the *Guardian*, called my radio critique for the *Independent*, 'the most suicidal column in the history of journalism.' True, yet it carried more clout for being written by a BBC creature and one who, particularly as a lowly specimen of the Radio 1 DJ, found himself – absurdly – the defender of Reithian BBC values against a corporate zombie onslaught led by, of all people, the BBC Director General.

The column was not exclusively negative, neither was it always a weekly anti-Birtist rant. I heaped praise on quality programmes wherever they were broadcast. Radio 1, in fact, was rarely the target of my criticism, although the column of which I was most proud was the one in which I reviewed the Radio 1 Rap Show, the week after Tim Westwood had been shot on a south London Street. The programme was presented by Funkmaster Flex, a friend of, and a stand-in for, the bullet-riddled son of the former Bishop of Peterborough. Mr Flex did not go so far as to acclaim Westwood's misfortune as, by the measures of gangsta rap, a smart career move, but he did fill the show with back-to-back records which celebrated routine misogyny and recommended, sensitively, reflex macho gunslinging to settle the most minor disputes. I spent eight hours with a tape of the programme going through each record, line by line.

I was ready for the fatuous justification of gangsta values when it came from Controller Andy Parfitt and his lieutenants – one of whom, a middle-aged educated British male, in a managerial role within the BBC, had begun dressing as, and adopting the vernacular and body language of, an escapee from Riker's Island. 'Radio 1 has a duty to reflect the nation's communities and the diversity of contemporary music culture,' Parfitt declared loftily in a statement responding to criticisms of the programme. By 'the nation's communities' he meant black people. The implication was that the Funkmaster's trigger-happy American gangsta pals and advocates of violence towards women were valid representatives of, or role models for, black culture in the UK.

But the most visible proof of the madness of the regime, to which I noisily drew the listeners' attention, as guest presenter of Radio 4's *Pick of the Week*, was when, as part of Birt's 'mission to explain', he hired a graphics company to bring upright the lovely old forwardly-inclined BBC logo, an identity recognised around the world and one of a pleasing elegance and period 1950s optimism. This re-branding – for Birtists had a fetish for that kind of caper, rather than the quality of programmes – you and I could have achieved by giving a ten-year-old nephew a sheet of Letraset and fifty pence for his trouble. Birt paid out £350,000 to have the logo straightened.

After climbing out of the rubble of the BBC in 2000, John Birt later took up an invitation from Tony Blair to apply 'blue sky thinking' (what the rest of us call 'imagination') on behalf of the then prime minister. That, truly, is all you need to know about the pair of them.

Andy Parfitt sacked me from Radio 1 in May 2000. In response, there was a small national outcry. Francis Wheen took up a whole page in the *Guardian* to attack the decision. 'Parfitt,' Francis wrote, 'like all truly ludicrous figures is blissfully unaware of his own absurdity.' With the encouragement of a loyal listener, David Hamer, one of his constituents, the Liberal Democrat MP for Montgomeryshire, Lembit Opik, tabled an Early Day Motion in the House of Commons condemning Radio 1 and citing their decision to drop me as an abdication of BBC public service values. John Peel, meanwhile, was silent.

THE LIVE SESSION guest on the final Radio 1 Kershaw Programme was, fittingly, Warren Zevon, one of my major rock & roll heroes and, like Willie Nelson, a genius misfit.

Before we got down to the recording, I told Warren the story of being surrounded by UNITA in Cuito during the Angolan civil war, and of how I'd been personally armed only with a copy of *Lawyers Guns & Money*. This amused him no end. He saved the anthem as his last·song of this live set and, grinning at me as he whacked his twelve-string, spontaneously changed its words and the location of his predicament. '*I was gambling in Havana...*' became, '*I was gambling in Angola, I took a little risk. Send lawyers, guns and money. Get me out of this!*'

Warren and I had never met before the session. By the end of it, he was giving me his home phone number in California and saying the next time I was planning to go to Haiti I should let him know. He'd not been there but said the country had long fascinated him. He thought it would be fun to go together. Alas, poor Warren developed mesothelioma soon after our only meeting and died in 2003, aged just 56. His death was a real tragedy. Warren Zevon was still at the peak of his creative zeal and still had much more to give. In 2007, while I agonised for weeks over hundreds of pieces of music, all worthy of inclusion among my eight records for *Desert Island Discs*, my selection of *Lawyers Guns & Money* for castaway stimulation was never in any doubt.

My last Radio 1 programme, featuring the Warren Zevon session, was pre-recorded and, on air, it finished at one o'clock in the morning. I listened to it go out at home and felt a sense of finality and accomplishment. I'd lasted longer than most Radio 1 DJs and, in the words of Brian Eno, for whom I have huge respect, I'd 'made a difference'. It was also satisfying to go out in the company of Warren Zevon, another square peg in a round hole.

The phone rang a couple of times when the programme ended. Francis called to say 'well done' and Ray Lowry, the great cartoonist and a keeper of the rock & roll flame, phoned in floods of tears. Ray, as usual, had dined well.

40

HEY, HO! LET'S GO!
BORN AGAIN ON RADIO 3

INSIDE A FORTNIGHT, I got a call from a stranger. A chap called Roger Wright, claiming to be the Controller of Radio 3, was asking me out to lunch. He even asked at which restaurant I'd like to eat. We met at the Gaylord, my favourite of all Indians, close to Broadcasting House. Before we'd got through the onion bahjis, Roger seduced me.

'Do you know what I liked about your Radio 1 programmes?' he asked. I couldn't for the life of me imagine. 'I never knew,' he continued, 'what was coming next.'

It was like a light going on. He got it! Roger *understood*. In that moment, he had me. When, he wondered, would I like to start on Radio 3? I was astonished. My programme? A dog's dinner of a music policy, among all those very particular classical programmes? I told him that, while very flattered, I'd like a few months to rest and spend some time being a good dad before going back on the CD listening treadmill. We agreed on the spring of 2001.

For weeks, leading up to my return to the airwaves and my Radio 3 debut, I agonised over what should be my first record. Events, early in the week of that first programme, took matters out of my hands. If any listeners predicted the track would be something elegant and spiritual from, say, the Sahara, as a statement of world music sensitivities, they got a rude jolt. The premature death of Joey Ramone a couple of days before the show left me no alternative. Not only was it a fitting tribute to Joey but my opening record for Radio Quiet announced rock & roll values were now in the house. Straight off the back of the solemn announcer's introduction of 'a new programme here on Radio 3' I banged in *Blitzkrieg Bop* ('Hey, Ho! Let's Go!').

My arrival was greeted by surprisingly little outrage among the traditional Radio 3 listeners. I was grateful for their generous accommodation. My own Radio 1 following moved over with me mob-handed. Within Radio 3 itself, I felt reborn. I was suddenly working with bright, enthusiastic, curious, amusing, energetic people – chief among them producers James Parkin, Roger Short and Iain Chambers – who, equally, seemed to value me. This was astonishing, given what I had been obliged to tolerate for the previous five years or so at Radio 1. My enthusiasm, which had been on a life-support machine, came surging back. The attitude of my new colleagues and friends made me want to work hard. And, given my liking of Roger Wright, the faith he had shown in me and his bravery to import what might have been seen as an invasive species, I wanted to repay him with excellence.

'I'VE ALWAYS THOUGHT one of your great strengths is the combined travel and music documentary,' Roger said to me soon after I'd joined his network. 'Where would you like to go?'

'Iraq,' I said, without hesitation. He laughed. And I laughed because he laughed. But where could a chap go for a bit of *what-the-fuck-is-this?* after three trips to Pyongyang? This was 2001. Iraq was still under the rule of Saddam Hussein. I wanted to see it. Was it possible, I needed to know, to buy Kenny Rogers records in Baghdad? (It was!)

The next I knew, I got a call from Roger Short to ask me for dates when I'd be available to go with him, as producer, to make some Radio 3 documentaries in Iraq. We were off.

In fact, I went twice in 2001 to the most demonised country on earth, the second trip in the company of the MP, George Galloway. I had always admired Galloway's sense of principle and his fearless drive to expose injustice and hypocrisy. Our mission was to look at the effects of UN sanctions on Iraqi civilians. From Baghdad, we flew down to Basra, where, after touring the city's hospitals, I wrote half a page for the *Independent* about the surge in cancers and horrific birth defects in southern Iraq, possibly arising from the use of depleted uranium shells by the American and British forces in the first Gulf War. At one hospital, I was shown around the wards by the city's leading oncologist who, with admirable sense of proportion, chain-smoked as we chatted to his terminal patients. On the flight back up to Baghdad, our civilian aeroplane was tailed by an American F16 fighter, which radioed our pilot to say that unless we immediately vacated 'the United Nations no-fly zone', he'd shoot us down. This warning ignored the detail that the no-fly zone was not UN authorised but imposed by the United States and the UK. We got out of it nevertheless.

In the capital, we were obliged to attend some dreary government presentation in an ugly concrete conference centre. I went along, hoping we might be addressed by Saddam himself. He did not show up, alas, but I got the consolation prize when I slipped out of the main hall for a cigarette in the corridor. I was alone there until an unmarked door onto the corridor opened and out stepped Tariq Aziz, the Iraqi Deputy Prime Minister and plausible international face of the regime. With him – and, wherever I go, I don't seem to be able to get away from the bugger – was former Zambian president Kenneth Kaunda. The three of us chatted for a good ten minutes. I was able to tell Dr Kaunda how much I'd enjoyed his last single, *Tinyende Pamodzi*, and that I'd played it quite a bit on Radio 1. (It's not widely known outside of his own country but Zambia's Father of the Nation is also a singer-songwriter and guitarist.) Kaunda seemed delighted to have had some airplay. I invited him to come in and do a Radio 3 session for me next time he was at a loose end in London. Tariq Aziz was just as urbane and charming as I would have expected. He has, of course, recently been sentenced to death.

WITHIN A COUPLE of years of Roger Wright taking me in as a genuine asylum seeker from the horrors of Radio 1, I was piling up the Sony Radio Awards outside his office door. At the Sony ceremony in 2002, I repaid Roger's faith by winning three in one night, two golds and one silver. In addition to that, and with the Controller's encouragement, James Parkin, Roger Short and I soon visited all three Axis of Evil countries on our Radio 3 foreign adventures. Documentary-making trips to Iraq, Iran and North Korea (the first to be made inside the Hermit Kingdom) were only a part of our global outreach programme, which still goes on. In those early Radio 3 years we also bothered the locals in Algeria (against British Foreign Office advice), Mauritania, Haiti, Turkmenistan, Ethiopia and Mali for the *Festival in the Desert* there in 2003.

In Mali, what had begun as an annual gathering of the nomadic Tuareg people from across the Sahara had turned into a small music festival, about a hundred miles north of Timbuktu. Attendance by Europeans was still thin in those days. The site, in the middle of the desert, could be reached only by 4x4s, using local drivers. There was no road. In front of a small stage, among the peach-coloured dunes, gathered an audience predominantly of Tuaregs, on camels, swathed in indigo cloth so that only their eyes were showing. Most had AK47s slung across their backs. So did the main band that year. It was my first encounter with the remarkable and menacing Tinariwen, a bunch of former guerrilla fighters for Tuareg independence from Mali. For me, it was love at first sight – and sound. Tinariwen had a gang attitude, a militancy and a rebel stance I had last seen in The Clash. Musically, too, they had that rare quality of instinctively knowing how to roll rather than to rock.

The bill-topper of the festival was my old friend and local hero, Ali Farka Toure. Meanwhile, the celebrity European visitor happened to be Robert Plant. It was an opportunity I couldn't miss. Turning my hand to shuttle diplomacy, I beetled between Ali's tent and that of Robert for a couple of days, encouraging the two to get together. They were camped at opposite ends of the site, Ali most imperiously, with entourage, in some grandeur, as befitted his regal status in these parts. Eventually, around a camp fire one night, I brought the two great bluesmen together. They had an impromptu jam, Ali picking at his acoustic while Robert howled at the moon. We recorded it and our resulting documentary about the festival won another gold Sony Radio Award.

A SENSE OF FINALITY seemed to be building in the early 2000s, despite my renaissance at Radio 3. We had lost Walters to a sudden heart attack in the summer of 2001. His death was a shattering blow: the loss of my confidante, my advisor and my inspiration. Other role models and heroes tumbled in what felt like rapid and tormenting succession and every death was premature. So many certainties were collapsing like dominoes.

Joe Strummer dropped dead in December 2002 from a heart condition he didn't know he had. His breathless performances with The Clash were, we now know, all the more remarkable for a man of cardiac fragility. At Joe's cremation in north west London, I was reassured to note he was the rebel until the end. A sticker on his coffin reminded us to 'Question authority'.

Warren Zevon died in September 2003 without getting anything close to the recognition his genius deserved and without the pair of us remaking *Lawyers, Guns & Money* together in Port-au-Prince. Johnny Cash went five days later. Ali Farka Toure succumbed to cancer in March 2006. Eighteen months before Ali, John Peel died in Peru.

The last time I saw John was shortly before his South American adventure. We had bumped into each other in the street close to Broadcasting House. His awkwardness, arising from his guilt for not having supported me in my battles some years earlier with Radio 1, still lingered. But I had moved on. Now it was John who was in trouble and needed an ally. He poured out to me his weariness and the details of his mistreatment. Radio 1 had pushed his programmes later into the night. I told him that this was Andy Parfitt's cowardly strategy to get rid of him. Parfitt did not wish to be remembered as the Man Who

Can't quite put my finger on what it is, but something tells me this photo was taken on the streets of Iraq... Making a Radio 3 documentary in Saddam Hussein's Baghdad, 2001. *Roger Short*

Sacked John Peel and so, to avoid getting John's broadcasting blood on his hands, he was adopting instead, I suspected, a tactic which would marginalise and demoralise John to the point at which he would throw in the towel and sack himself. I reminded John they had tried it with me for years. But my response, which they had not anticipated, had been to dig in my heels and fight.

I urged him to walk into Broadcasting House immediately and demand an audience with Jenny Abramsky, Controller of Network Radio, and Parfitt's boss.

'Tell Abramsky that unless she directs Parfitt to treat you and your audience with a little more respect, and makes him restore your programmes to a civilised time, you'll walk out on *Home Truths*. That will really frighten her.' By this stage, *Home Truths* had become a national institution.

'Oh, no,' he murmured, 'I couldn't possibly do that.'

His last words to me, before he shambled away towards Oxford Circus, were, 'It's killing me.'

I was alarmed by what I saw of John that day. He looked drained and beaten. He was more overweight than when I'd last seen him. He'd been diagnosed with diabetes a few years before and, for a man with those conditions, probably should have curbed a little his fondness for red wine. He was also, that afternoon, even scruffier than usual.

So concerned was I that I phoned Sheila, John's wife, as soon as I got home. She confirmed John was at a low ebb and hurt by the contempt with which Radio 1 was treating him. I urged her to get him to press the *Home Truths* button with Abramsky, and, if that didn't work, that John should phone Roger Wright and defect to Radio 3, where he'd be valued. And I advised her to take him away for a while on a holiday, although relaxation was an activity in which John was almost as unskilled as me. I offered her the use of our family holiday cottage which, by then, Juliette had bought in Peel on the west coast of the Isle of Man. John adored the Island, an affection he'd developed during our trips together to the TT Races. ('I love Peel,' he once confided to me, strolling down one of the former herring-fishing town's narrow streets. 'And not just because I share its name. It's the atmosphere: the aroma of the kipper smoking sheds; the comforting smell of the coal fires; and how charming it is that so many of the children here still have rickets...')

'Thanks,' said Sheila, 'but we're actually going away already. We're off to Peru in a few weeks.'

'Peru?' I said. 'I thought he had a fear of flying? Where in Peru? How high up are you going?'

Sheila told me they were going to Machu Picchu, to realise an old ambition of John's to see the Inca ruins. It worried me deeply. I recalled my experience of crossing the Andes in 1989 from Bolivia to Chile for BBC2's *Great Journeys of the World* with Billy Bragg and the strains of altitude I'd felt, even as a wiry lad of twenty-nine.

On 25 October 2004, in his hotel bar in Cusco, Peru, having a drink with Sheila, John had a heart attack and died. He was

65. Just minutes before he was struck down, John sighed to Sheila, 'I do miss Walters.'

AN UNEXPECTED LETTER, in 2005, arrived from Leeds University, and provided a happy finality to my unfinished life in academia. Perhaps prompted by the honorary Doctorate bestowed upon me in 2003 by the University of East Anglia, at the suggestion of some kind academics there who were enthusiastic listeners to my programmes, Leeds had decided to award me that missing degree. All was forgiven. A new administration was in charge, whose members were drawn from the rock generation. Professor Michael Arthur and his right-hand man, University Secretary Roger Gair, wanted to recognise the contribution I'd made not only to broadcasting but to the rich rock & roll history of Leeds University. At last, those who ran the university could see that heritage as an asset and one which attracted students to Leeds, just as it had drawn me there in 1978.

In a ceremony in the University's Great Hall on 15 July 2005 I was presented with an honorary Doctorate of Music by the Chancellor, Melvyn Bragg. The writer, Bill Bryson, joined me on the platform to receive a Doctorate of Letters, well deserved if only for what he had once written about Iowa farmers and their casual attitude to appalling self-inflicted agricultural injuries. I even wore a tie, kindly loaned to me by Jon Snow, award-winning connoisseur of these things, peerless presenter of *Channel 4 News*, and that most humane of foreign reporters.

The citation for the Doctorate spoke of my achievements and enthusiasms, and also, I was delighted to note, did not overlook the fact that I still owed the Politics department a number of essays, dating back to the summer of 1980. Afterwards, the University held the post-ceremony buffet on the famous stage in the empty Refec. I was hugely moved by this. They knew how much those scruffy boards on that rusting frame meant to me. They'd even set up a bar on the stage and, for a wonderful and rather surreal lunchtime, I found myself – Doctor Kershaw – drinking Tetley's bitter with Lord Melvyn Bragg, Bill Bryson and lots of old Ents pals. Professor Arthur wandered over.

'Andy,' he said. 'I thought you'd like to know: we've finally applied to the city council to have a blue plaque put up on the front of the Refectory to commemorate The Who's *Live At Leeds*.'

Just a couple of weeks later, I was at the WOMAD festival, chatting with Robert Plant in his marquee dressing room after his headlining performance. We were joined by Robert's manager, Bill Curbishley, also the veteran manager of The Who. I told Bill the news of the *Live At Leeds* blue plaque. He was pleased.

'Hey, Bill,' I said after a minute or two. 'There are really only two blokes who are qualified to unveil that plaque when the ceremony takes place. Townshend and Daltrey. What do you say?'

'They'd be honoured,' said Bill. Perhaps a minute went by before I decided to press home the advantage.

'Bill,' I said. 'And while Pete and Roger are up there, unveiling the plaque...'

I didn't have to finish the sentence. Bill did it for me.

'They'll do it,' he said. 'Let me know when.'

That night I phoned Professor Arthur. The Vice-Chancellor was, it turned out, on holiday and answered his mobile on a ski slope in Colorado. 'In that case, Michael, you'd better find a snowdrift to sit down on,' I told him. 'The Who are coming up to unveil the blue plaque and, while they're at it, they're going to do *Live At Leeds Again*.'

To my delight Paul Crockford was roped in to help run the gig. Saturday 17 June 2006 was a day that crackled with a sense of history in the making. With the help of the University's Chief Press Officer, Vanessa Bridge, I tracked down, and invited as VIPs, many Ents veterans from the era of the original *Live At Leeds* concert. Simon Brogan made an unprecedented return to the Refec from his sheep farm on Orkney. BBC News 24 carried live for fifteen minutes the plaque unveiling ceremony and speeches by me, Pete Townshend and Roger Daltrey.

'Dr Kershaw, I am so excited about this,' Townshend said. 'And it's all your fault.'

At sound-check time, I walked to the back of the Refec. It was empty apart from some distant figures on stage at the far end,

Crockers leaning against a pillar, and the silhouettes of technicians on the lighting and sound desks. Just as I was taking in this moment, Townshend slashed out the opening riff to *Substitute*. Zak Starkey kicked in the drums and, by reflex, I dropped my bag and went running, cartwheeling and yelling down the length of the hall.

I'd resumed my old position, a couple of hours later, against the panel of house lights, at the top of the stairwell by the stage steps. The Who were ready to go. On the given signal, and as he squeezed past me, Townshend put a fatherly hand on my shoulder.

'Thanks,' was all he said. It meant the world.

IN THE SUMMER of 2007, I would persuade Townshend to bring The Who to play in a field in our adopted home town of Peel on the Isle of Man.

'He looks a bit small to stand out there,' Pete said, electric

Live At Leeds Again – The Who on stage in the Refectory, Leeds University, 17 June 2006. *Richard Hanson/Leeds University*

guitar in hand and nodding at our Sonny, then aged nine. We were grouped at the bottom of a ramp, behind the stage. Dropped suddenly into darkness in a vast tent, the crowd was roaring its anticipation.

'Fetch him on stage,' said Pete. 'Just follow us up the ramp when we go. Stand behind those speakers.'

For Sonny's first proper rock concert, he stood within a few feet of Pete Townshend, at the great man's invitation.

Our adoption of that Isle of Man home had occurred just a year earlier. I was sitting on Peel beach during the 2005 Manx Grand Prix. Juliette and the children were in London and I was staying at our holiday cottage for the races. My eye had been caught that morning by a substantial Peel property in the window of an estate agent.

For a year or two, I'd felt we should move out of the capital. Secondary education for Sonny and Dolly was looming. Over my dead body were they going to a north London state school. Their primary school was bad enough. Manx schools, on the other hand, had a fine reputation. Already we knew and loved the Island. I had a long history there. For kids, it was an idyllic environment in which to grow up; healthy, outdoor, crime-free, classless, spontaneous and safe. I had also had my fill of London's default selfishness and rudeness. The Isle of Man, meanwhile, and particularly Peel, had a sense of community and neighbourliness that had not been known in London since VE day.

'Get someone to look after the kids,' I urged Juliette. 'Catch a flight to the Island tonight. You've got to see this house. You'll adore it.'

She did.

We sold up in north London and, in the first week of April 2006, in three removals trucks, one carrying just my record collection and its shelving, we moved full time to the Isle of Man.

41

LONESOME FUGITIVE

WHEN I WAS A CHILD, of about four or five, I had two recurring bad dreams. These were not nightmares in any ghastly sense. The horror lurking in these dreams was implicit rather than explicit. In the first, I was falling down a cliff. There was no beginning to my fall and I never reached the bottom. I was just falling. Black, jagged rock rushed past my face. During this endless descent, I would look down. A little girl was always there, sitting on the sand below, an angelic child of about my age with dark curls, in a pretty summer frock, white and dotted with flowers. She was a picture of innocence and serenity, looking up and smiling as I hurtled towards her. And she was always whispering, 'Don't worry. You're going to be all right.' But, it being a dream, her reassurances were terrifying and her whisper was deafening.

In the other, I was lost and very frightened. Not in a dark wood, populated by goblins and witches, but in a street of respectable red brick pre-war semis. It was the utter plausibility and ordinariness of it all that made the location sinister. It looked like half of Rochdale. But it wasn't my childhood home town. At some point, I was always approached by a concerned stranger, although they never offered me any help. They spoke to me kindly but only to confirm that I was in Ludlow, Shropshire. Subconsciously, I must have picked up the town's name on the news.

In the autumn of 2008, after falling metaphorically down that cliff-face, I found myself in Ludlow, on that street. I don't know why I was there or how I got there. And, though I'd never harmed a soul, I was on the run from the police. A UK-wide warrant had been issued for my arrest. I'd learned of that a couple of mornings before when I'd opened a copy of the *Independent* in the Somerset village where I'd been staying with my friend Tessa and her children and seen my photograph attached to a news story which revealed the Isle of Man arrest warrant had gone national. I was the subject of a man-hunt. This nightmare was getting even worse. I had to scarper again.

Now I was roaming the streets of Ludlow. All I knew was that I'd stepped off a train. From where, I couldn't remember. Its destination was anywhere. Ludlow must have claimed me, finally and after all these years, because I'd been desperate for a cigarette. I was also exhausted, hungry, anxious, hung-over, lonely, and missing my children and my home. I found a quiet pub, bought a pint with my dwindling money and flopped in a corner. I had nowhere left to go.

How had we arrived at this position?

I'D ROLLED UP at our new home on the Isle of Man the day after Juliette and the kids had flown out from London. It had been my job to drive over, bringing on the ferry the family car loaded with valuables, breakables, the children's hamster and their aquarium fish in buckets. As I pulled up at the kerb on Peel promenade, I saw Juliette in my wing mirror running towards the car, her face alight with joy and excitement. We were starting our new life on our island paradise.

The removal men were almost finished unloading. I helped them with the last few boxes and then marched them to a pub along the promenade to buy them all a drink. Juliette joined us. After half a lager she got up to return to the house. She had a thousand domestic jobs to do and looked thrilled to be setting about nest-making. Our domestic phone line was not yet connected, she said. Her mobile battery was flat. Could she borrow mine? No problem. I never gave it a second thought as I bought the removals men another beer.

Half an hour later, I came home to find the house empty. On the kitchen table was my mobile. Its screen was displaying a text message. At first, I didn't recognise it. Then I remembered. It was from a woman with whom I'd had a one night stand at the Womad Festival almost a year before. Although it alluded to leg-over in the Reading area, it had been of such little significance to me that I had not gone to the trouble of deleting it. Had it been a relationship which was ongoing – an affair – I suppose I would have been careful to cover my tracks. But, this time, I had compounded the insult of an infidelity with arrogance and carelessness.

I found Juliette on the promenade, staring out to sea, her face a mixture of grief and anger.

For the next few months we staggered along, Juliette in a state of understandable and unrelenting bitterness. She was not to be convinced any longer of my fidelity, not even by my eager migration away from my old life and my old ways in London. Neither was she persuaded that moving meant a new life and a fresh start for all of us, especially for me and her.

It was entirely my fault, a culpability to which I consistently pleaded guilty. I went about doing everything within my power to atone and repent. In the August of that summer of 2006, I gave up drinking totally. Not that this had become an issue between us at this stage but I hoped to make myself more attractive by losing my beer belly. I did. And I stayed off everything for the next eight months.

My efforts were too little too late. In October 2006, Juliette moved out of our new dream home to the old holiday cottage which she still owned in the next street. She announced that she had decided to become a 'strong independent woman.'

For the next few months, Juliette drew up timetables for the children, specifying which home they would be in on which evenings, and we kept up a working dialogue. That 'civility' collapsed when she met a visiting biker at the TT in June 2007. Shortly before, in March 2007, I had appeared on *Desert*

Island Discs. Ordinarily, this would have been affirmation that I had made it, a recognition far more meaningful than those handed down in the Honours List. But in my case, while thrilled to be asked to pick my eight records as Radio 4's castaway, I knew that my world was actually falling apart. One of my musical choices was the sublime Gram Parsons and Emmylou Harris duet, *The Return of the Grievous Angel*, which I dedicated to Juliette, 'the love of my life', revealing I carried it with me on all my travels as it reminded me of her. Which was true.

A few days after the broadcast, she summoned me for a cup of coffee to the refreshment kiosk on Peel breakwater.

'You were fantastic on *Desert Island Discs*,' she said. 'It was a classic Andy performance.'

I was really pleased and I thanked her.

'But what you said about me was a load of crap,' she continued. The blow of this, after the positive preamble, was almost physical. But she was probably correct.

One morning, later that spring, a letter from Juliette was waiting on my doormat when I got back from the shops. It was her declaration that she was never coming back.

THE APPEARANCE OF the new boyfriend at Juliette's side around Peel was agonising but a humiliation which I tried at first to contain. He was, at this stage, only visiting, although regularly so from Scotland where, according to a tabloid exposé, he was still married with a step-daughter, having left a previous long-term partner for his current wife.

Meanwhile, I was sinking deeper into depression. The children's time was no longer equally shared between parents. The boyfriend was in Peel more frequently. The timetable of visits was by now no longer being issued by Juliette. The next one I received was sent by a firm of advocates in Douglas. I dropped the letter in the bin, refusing to have my contact with Sonny and Dolly decreed by some faceless lawyer who had never met me. I carried on phoning Juliette about contact. In return, I got a visit from the police who warned me not to approach again the mother of, and gatekeeper to, my children.

Juliette applied to the court in Douglas for a Restraining

Order. This was granted readily. Significantly, it barred not my contact with the children, only with their mother and her new partner. I had never harmed anyone. Nor was I likely to do so. Juliette was fully aware, from a seventeen-year relationship with me, that I have no tendency whatsoever towards violence. No one needed protection from me.

Shortly before the Restraining Order was handed down, realising that this could not go on and that a big gesture was needed, I sent a text to Juliette suggesting we call a truce, bury the hatchet and that we should meet in a local pub where I would buy her new partner a pint and shake his hand. It went unanswered.

To maintain contact with the kids, and to avoid accusations of harassment, I went out and bought Sonny and Dolly their first mobile phones. I had to get Barbara Shimmin, my saintly next door neighbour, to deliver them. Dolly, then aged eight, wrote me a thank-you note to say it was the happiest day of her life. But after a while, unhappy with text messages I was sending them, Juliette took the phones away. Denied any alternatives, I continued to phone her about access to Sonny and Dolly.

For this, the police turned up again to issue me with a caution for harassment. This time, I had broken the law by violating the Restraining Order. And I carried on phoning, on occasions very angry and the worse for drink.

I was now drinking to achieve oblivion. Reality – the shattering of our Isle of Man dream, on day one of our new life, itself the result of my stupidity and selfishness, the loss of my partner of seventeen years and the withdrawal of contact with Sonny and Dolly – was too much to endure. I was, on many days in the summer and autumn of 2007, waking up hung-over, nauseous and depressed. The only way to feel anything approaching normal and able to function was to top up again with booze. Often, to that end, I was slumping in a local pub at twelve noon and putting away three or four pints to guarantee the anaesthetic of sleep on the sofa for the rest of the afternoon and the early evening. By that time, I was awake and heading for the supermarket to buy a bottle of red wine to drain before bedtime to banish the insomnia. This soon became two bottles of red.

It was cowardly but, in the short term, effective. One of the many sinister aspects of excessive alcohol consumption, about which your doctor will never tell you, nor agree with you upon, is that nothing he or she can prescribe to you, nor anything you can buy from the chemist, dispels anxiety as fully and efficiently as having a drink. Beyond the stage of what-the-hell (and judgement is the first casualty of boozing) lies the merciful release of sleep. But in the medium and long term, drinking only racks up the overall level of anxiety and poor judgement, requiring more and more to keep those torments suppressed. It was in this manner that alcohol got it claws fully into me.

There were, nevertheless, many days of sobriety if not abstinence, but only for as long as these were necessary for me to do the work to compile my weekly programmes for Radio 3, fly to London, record the shows and fly home. The broadcasting, however, did not last much longer. In early July I had to call Roger Short and James Parkin, my producers and good pals at Radio 3, and Roger Wright, the Controller. I couldn't carry on. The boozing surely was not helping but more daunting was the expectation that I should go on the air, under these pressures and torments, and entertain.

In August, exasperated by my lack of contact with the children (I'd had to ask Barbara, again, to deliver Sonny's tenth birthday present), I turned up at Juliette's house, demanding to see them. I was drunk but there was no violence. I was arrested, thrown in police cells overnight, brought before the court and pleaded guilty to breaking the Restraining Order. I violated the Order again, by text, within days. On that occasion, I was sent to jail for the first of three spells over the next five months.

IT MIGHT BE argued that, given the colourful life I had led thus far, it would have been downright negligent of me had I not, at some stage or other, been thrown in jail. And aside from a few days I spent in one cell overrun with vermin and with a broken window, through which knifed a northerly gale, in February, the experience itself wasn't too bad. I got a bloody good rest and in my longest stretch, forty-two days (half of a three month sentence), I read more than thirty substantial books – mainly history, politics and foreign affairs – sent in by friends. These included both books then written by a relatively unknown American politician called Barack Obama, and I got terribly excited in my cell when I heard on the radio of his unexpected victory in the South Carolina presidential primary. The prison's own library was permanently closed.

Reading, and listening to Radios 3 and 4 (I was always struck by the irrelevance of the weather forecast) were my main survival mechanisms, to keep at bay my old enemy of boredom. I have often been asked since if I kept a prison diary. But about what? Nothing happened to put in a ruddy diary. My other activity was writing letters to Sonny and Dolly, to friends and in reply to supporters, many of whom I had not known before but who had written to me very caringly.

A particularly sympathetic note arrived unexpectedly from Terry Waite. On learning of this, Bernard Bateson, a jolly prison officer who I liked very much, then lent to me Terry Waite's autobiography, which I read in a day. If Terry could take it from Islamic Jihad, for more than four years in their solitary confinement, I reckoned I could get through six weeks of lying on my bed, chain-smoking and reading Robert Fisk – although I don't recall Terry mentioning he'd had to cope with the constant clatter and rumble of a pool table and the deafening roar of football commentary, or yet another action movie, blasting from the communal TV room.

From the music world I received moving letters from Martin Carthy, Norma Waterson, Steve Tilston and Sid Griffin. These pals have maintained their contact and support ever since.

One day, an officer came into my cell and started to count my books. He was apologetic.

'I'm afraid I'll have to take some of these away. You've got more than ten.'

'Yes. So what?' I asked.

'If you have more than ten, we have to take some off you. It's a rule, I'm afraid. They say it's a fire risk.'

With the exception of just a trio of blokes along my landing – Big Eric, Little Colin and his friend John – I hadn't much in common with the other prisoners, mainly hard drug dealers and those inside for violence. They were, however, all very affable towards me – and me to them. Most expressed surprise that I was in custody as I had not harmed anyone. The prison officers, equally, were sympathetic and all were easygoing and likeable.

The morning I returned home from my first spell in jail – just the long weekend, a sort of Custodial Bargain Break – there was an envelope on my door mat. It contained a lovely card from a woman, an Island resident, I'd met as long ago as the TT races in 1992 but had not seen since. She wrote that she really felt for me, had been through the relationship mill herself and, giving her phone numbers, said if I'd like to talk I could call any time. I sat in the sun in my back yard and read it several times.

Catherine had been a TT competitor for much of the 1990s. She was slightly younger than me, very beautiful, and irresistible back then with long dark hair tumbling over her red racing leathers. She was also highly intelligent, huge fun, and at the top of her real profession. Her note revealed she'd been married for thirteen years, was now divorced and was a single mum. I called. We met that night. She was still irresistible. And, for both of us, it was love at second sight – after a seventeen-year gap. That feeling was reinforced for me when I saw her bookshelves, occupying two walls, floor to ceiling, in one of the living rooms of her beautiful period home.

We became instant soul mates. And we sparked. Catherine made me feel valued and valuable for the first time in two ghastly years. I worshipped her. She had the measure of me, too.

'Do you know what your trouble is, Kershaw?' she announced one evening.

'No,' I said, although I could have given her a monologue.

'You've got no off switch, that's your trouble,' she said with a big smile.

'You're right,' I said. 'But it's also my greatest strength.'

Catherine laughed. She knew that too.

Catherine wrote beautiful letters and sent books to me every day I was in jail – on and off – over the next five months. That love, and mine for her and for Sonny and Dolly, were everything I then had to look forward to. She organised, and paid for, a small welcome home party at my local Indian restaurant for the evening of the day of my release from what was my final incarceration, 29 February 2008.

I LEFT MY HOME on the Isle of Man in the first week of March of that year. I just had to get away for a while, not least from the attentions of newspaper reporters and photographers who had set up base camp in a pub along the promenade. But I was not, as reported by some tabloids, ordered by the court to leave the Island.

The first few weeks of my recovery were spent with Our Elizabeth and her family in rural Northamptonshire. There, as the spring unfolded, I went fishing every day on the Grand Union Canal or my beloved River Tove. I didn't drink any alcohol. I made myself useful as Elizabeth's handyman and I wrote several times a week to the children, still on the Isle of Man with their mother and her new partner, who was now permanently installed.

Almost two months went by. Despite all my letters, each vetted by Elizabeth to ensure they contained nothing to which their mother could object, I hadn't had back from Sonny and Dolly a single letter, postcard, email, text or phone call. I couldn't ring them myself. Although the Restraining Order did not prevent my contact with the children, its terms barred me from contacting 'in any way whatsoever' Juliette and her partner. If I were to phone their house, if only to speak to my kids, I'd be violating the Order once more and, according to the judge at my last court appearance in Douglas, any further transgression would guarantee me a whole year in prison.

Eventually Elizabeth picked up the phone to find out why I was getting no response from Sonny and Dolly. When she told me that Juliette had said she would not let the children have my letters and didn't think it was a good idea for them to be communicating with me, I hit the roof. And the bottle. Juliette has since said that she read all my letters to the children and claims she has never said otherwise. But on the night of 30 April 2008 I broke the Order again, calling the house to let rip at both mother and partner. Then I compounded my onslaught with a bombardment of hugely abusive texts. The next morning, knowing the police would soon be round, I had to become a fugitive.

John Cooper – Britain's most gifted and popular professional motorcycle racer of the era between the supremacies of Mike Hailwood and Barry Sheene – is a kind man who years before had assumed the position of my surrogate uncle. John, without being asked, came to my immediate rescue, driving down from his home in Derby to collect me from Elizabeth's. But I could stay with John and his wife, Rosie, only for one night. They had a grown-up daughter, who was about to leave hospital and coming to stay with them for convalescence. They needed their spare room. It was a fine summer evening. John took me to a country pub just outside Derby. There I got chatting to a chap called Colin Law, a friend of John's. Colin told me he'd been following my plight in the newspapers, that he'd been through a messy divorce himself, but was now happily remarried and that he sympathised with me.

On John's doormat the following morning was a note from Colin. He'd not been able to sleep, he said, thinking of my situation. He and his wife Debbie had discussed it long into the night and they'd decided I could stay with them, and their daughter Alice (of Dolly's age), at their home on the other side of the city. Colin had driven over to John Cooper's house to drop off the note in the early hours.

It was with the mixed emotions of gratitude, humility, and embarrassment that I arrived at their lovely home in the Chaddesden neighbourhood of Derby. I was a total stranger to these good Samaritans. And an emotionally fucked-up, alcohol-dependent one at that. Debbie was the embodiment of sweetness, sympathy and wisdom. Little Alice took my presence – which must have been scary – bravely and generously in her stride. Had it not been for the kindness of these strangers, I possibly would not have lived.

Our plan was for me to lie low, get off the booze and demonstrate to the Manx authorities that I was not routinely harassing my ex. Everything was going nicely until one Sunday afternoon in mid-May when there was a knock at the front door. I was in the back garden with Debbie. Colin walked through to say the police were on the doorstep. I was arrested by two officers and taken to the city's main police station. There, I was asked to wait in a room crowded with bruised and bleeding football hooligans. Eventually, I was brought to the desk where another officer tapped away on a computer keyboard. He studied the screen.

'You've done what on the Isle of Man?' he asked.

'Broken a Restraining Order,' I said.

'Ha! Thumped her one, did you? Or the new boyfriend?' he asked with a laddish grin.

'No. I've never laid a finger on anyone. I broke it with some phone calls and texts last month,' I said.

More keyboard tapping. His brow began to furrow. 'Oh, dear,' he said. 'It looks like the Manx police haven't filled in this warrant correctly. They'll have to re-submit it.' Then he looked up at the arresting officers.

'Run him back to where he's staying,' he said. 'I don't know what they have to do on the Isle of Man but we have real crime to deal with.' He wished me good luck. I almost lunged over the counter to hug him.

In the patrol car, on the way back to Chaddesden, the Derbyshire Constabulary's sensible approach to policing reached new levels of enlightenment.

'The Manx police will probably send a new warrant, properly completed, within a day or two,' said one officer. 'Me and my mate here will then be obliged to come back here to look for you again.'

I was left in no doubt that it would be wise to move on.

THAT NIGHT, after phoning my old University Ents friend, Al, at his holiday home in Trearddur Bay, Colin put me in the back of the family camper van and drove me to my new hide-out in Anglesey.

Al and Josie were just as generous and accommodating as my pals in Derby. So was their next door neighbour and permanent resident, Simon Howard, who I knew well and liked very much from my previous Trearddur visits. With Al, Josie and Simon I had the companionship and security of old friends and the distraction of fishing and messing around in Simon's boats. But while all that was a comfort, our daily gathering on the terrace of Simon's cliff-top home for evening drinks, was also poignant: we would sit listening to The Band or The Flying Burrito Brothers and I'd be staring out to sea, longing for my children and my home, just over the horizon, to which, without going to jail for a year, I could not return.

Wherever I was sheltered, I was permanently anxious about overstaying my welcome and putting my friends in a difficult if not illegal position. I yearned to be alone in a place I could call my own. In the UK, I still had half of such a place, the one-bedroom flat Juliette and I had bought jointly, and outright, in Crouch End – as her base when she was there on restaurant business and mine for BBC work – when we moved full-time to the Isle of Man. I travelled down from Holyhead to London by train on a sweltering day with a heavy rucksack. I had not been in Crouch End for more than a year. I arrived at the flat exhausted and, with huge relief, unlocked the door off the street and climbed the stairs to the flat on the first floor. But at some point in the previous twelve months, the lock had been changed on the flat's internal door. I sank to my knees, engulfed by despair, exhaustion and anger: the flat was still just as much mine as Juliette's.

Across the road, in the garden of a pub, I called a few London pals, looking for a floor or a sofa for the night. It was summer school holidays. Everyone was out of town, except for my friend Florence on the other side of the capital. I set off for south London and fell asleep at Florence's kitchen table before I'd finished my first beer. I will never forget her kindness. Similarly, and separately, I was given shelter from the storm by two other generous and caring London friends, Judy and Helena.

I'd become the Merle Haggard or Jerry Lee Lewis character in *Lonesome Fugitive*, one of my favourite country songs, only it wasn't terribly romantic now to be living it. At one point, I headed from London to Our Elizabeth's in Northamptonshire to find she and her family were away on holiday in Spain and I had no key to her house. Instead, and with nothing else to do on a beautiful, warm summer afternoon, I walked for miles through farmland along the nearby and idyllic River Tove until I flopped down at the isolated spot, by a waterfall and a pool, which had always been a favourite picnic location for me, Juliette and Sonny and Dolly. Here was where I'd been Daddy at his best, the father fulfilled, where I'd taught the children how to fish, showed them the creatures of the river and amazed them by demonstrating how to catch freshwater crayfish under the stones and minnows with bread in a bottle. Now, not even the extraordinary sight of two Spitfires circling overhead, no doubt practising for a display that coming weekend, could divert me from the sense of loss and overpowering grief. I lay on my back and wept buckets, crying out the children's names.

I was making my way back to Trearddur soon after and found myself, as ever that summer, at Birmingham New Street station. Railway stations, with the likelihood of a police presence, were always a bit dicey. I had become alert quickly to the flash of fluorescent yellow jackets. Consequently, I spent much of my time on the run ducking from the view of oblivious workmen and a lot of Health & Safety officers. Shuffling across the concourse – exhausted, heavily-laden, unshaven, needing a shower and a haircut, jangling with anxiety and a hangover that felt like a head full of bluebottles – I came upon an advertisement, to attract visitors, which had been crafted in the floor with a colourful mosaic of vinyl tiles. 'The Isle of Man,' it read, 'Set Yourself Free.'

Sonny's birthday in late August was particularly painful. Back in Trearddur Bay, Simon Howard had kindly stepped in and fronted £20 for me to send my little lad a present. On the day itself, Buster – our adorable standard schnauzer, the dog I had bought for Sonny and Dolly when we moved to the Isle of Man, and my constant fugitive companion – was out with me for a walk along the cliff tops and around the wide sweep of the bay. (Buster, in appearance and personality, is more Paddington Bear than dog). We were sitting on the beach. Buster was at my side. From a distance of about a hundred yards, Buster stiffened when he spotted two children, a little boy and a girl, splashing in the low tide. They were about the same size and age as Sonny and Dolly, who Buster adores. He sprang up and went tearing off towards them. But when he got within a few yards of the children he stopped. His muscles sagged visibly. He turned and walked back up the beach to rejoin me.

It began to rain hard. Except for me and Buster, the beach cleared. I got to my feet and, with Buster circling me, I scraped in the smooth hard sand *Happy Birthday, Sonny* in letters thirty feet tall and facing the Isle of Man.

Buster and I moved on from Anglesey, at the invitation of Simon Broughton, my old BBC radio producer, and his wife Kate, to join them at Kate's mother's holiday cottage in the isolation of Exmoor. It was lovely. Simon and Kate were reservoirs of wisdom. But soon their holiday was at an end and I was on the road again, this time to the Somerset Levels where I stayed with my friend Tessa Munt and her two delightful teenage children. For a few weeks, I occupied myself taking some load off Tessa – she was a busy local Liberal Democrat councillor, now an MP – and I enjoyed most cooking for us all, when I wasn't fishing on the stream which ran past the house. Buster, now having the company of Tessa's three rescued mongrels, a big fenced garden in which to run around, and his first experience of a membership of a pack, thought he'd arrived at doggie Butlin's. I was even invited to join the local pub skittles team, another member of which was a police officer.

Catherine, with whom I'd restored tentative telephone contact, flew over to see me from the Island. We spent a wonderful day together, pottering around nearby Wells. Lying on the grass, in front of the cathedral, in the autumn sunshine, Catherine confirmed we had a future together if I stayed off the booze, came back to the Isle of Man and got the ridiculous police and courts business out of the way. I was so happy. And I steeled myself to do just as she asked.

The trigger for that return came about a month later when Buster and I were back with Debbie, Colin and Alice, the heat in Derby then having lifted. I learned that Juliette intended to leave the Isle of Man and take the children to live with her new partner in Scotland.

This was a cruelty too far and one I was determined to fight by returning to the Isle of Man, arrest warrant or not. I knew, too, that I would have to be ready for a legal battle for which I could not afford a lawyer and I would, therefore, have to be in peak mental shape to represent myself and the best interests of Sonny and Dolly. For that reason, above many other valid motivations, and with the support of Colin, Debbie and her friend Phil Almond, who worked with those with similar problems, I gave up alcohol completely.

On the evening of 15 December 2008, I flew home to the Island from Birmingham airport. When I saw the tears flooding down Debbie's face as she waved me off from her doorstep, I was doubly resolved I would win all my battles – and crucially the one on behalf of the children. I would now not let down those few people who had stuck with me through all this, chief among them this wonderful family I had not known a year before.

BACK IN PEEL, I'd not been inside my own home, nor slept in my own bed for nine months. As I fumbled for my front door key in the dark, Sonny came around the corner, on his way to the youth club next door. He looked astonished and frightened. I got the door open and the light on.

'Sonny! Sonny! It's me, Daddy,' I said and hugged him. 'Come in!'

But he wouldn't cross the threshold and melted quickly into the youth club with his friends. There, I learned, he called his mother – understandably – to break the news of my return. Even though she and her new partner were off the Island, visiting the UK, she called the Peel police. I was arrested again, within ten minutes of coming home, at my kitchen table. I spent the night – without any justification for detention – in the freezing police cells in Douglas, from where, convinced I was on my way to jail for a whole year, I was taken to court in a police van and brought before the High Bailiff, Michael Moyle, the following morning.

At the hearing, Moyle asked the police prosecutor to clarify when I had last contacted Juliette. The prosecutor was obliged to confirm that the police had received no complaint since April, more than seven months earlier. There was, it was finally becoming clear to all, no pattern to my behaviour that could be regarded as harassment. There never had been. My approaches, which had violated the Restraining Order on half a dozen occasions, were always specific responses to specific events.

I pleaded guilty, once again, to transgressing the Order. Because I had done so. Mr Moyle sent me on my way with the minimum he could hand down, another suspended sentence.

I was immensely relieved and grateful for his judgement and his evident grasp of reality. A year before, among a number of penalties he'd handed down to me, was a ban for a fixed period from all licensed premises on the Isle of Man, although I had never caused any problems in a pub. News of the ruling got into the tabloid newspapers, creating the hugely damaging national impression that I was some kind of bar-room brawler. But now the High Bailiff seemed to have sensed that my case was not simply one of my being 'hell-bent on self-destruction' nor that of 'a Greek tragedy', two of his previous characterisations, and that provocation, when I had previously transgressed, may possibly have played a part.

Despite those earlier pronouncements, I actually liked Michael Moyle. A bit of a performer and a humourist, his hearings were consistently entertaining. At one, after handing me a suspended sentence, he thanked me for having played so much Phil Ochs on my radio programmes.

It did not yet, however, occur to the court, which had imposed the evergreen Restraining Order, that it was the Order itself which was actually the cause of all the problems – and my criminalisation – not the solution. Not once, in the months of upheaval and during previous court appearances, had my reaction to what had happened been looked upon in the obvious terms of simple cause and effect. The police, the courts and the press jumped eagerly to the conclusion, it seemed, that I had woken up one morning, blinked at the ceiling and said to myself, 'I know: instead of going fishing today or working on my radio programmes, I think I'll go off the rails, have a nervous breakdown and take up excessive drinking. Recreationally.'

I was instead directed to attend an 'anger management' course. I didn't go, arguing my presence there would be valuable only if I were allowed to teach it. By this stage, after my return from the UK, I was the living embodiment of anger management.

The eagerness of the authorities to look away from the real problem was, at least, consistent. It had also, following my first court hearing more than a year before, been recommended I see a psychologist. She, alone among so many experts, was able to identify the blindingly obvious, albeit with the medical diagnosis of 'severe reactive depression due to serial trauma.'

'I did not spend four years at university, like I daresay you did, studying psychology,' I said to her. 'Does your diagnosis mean I am distraught because of the collapse of my family, and my dream, and that I can't see my kids?'

'Yes,' she said.

More than once throughout this fiasco, it crossed my mind that the authorities, the media and the public would not for a second contemplate treating someone with a physical condition, even one partially self-inflicted – some forms of cancer, for example – in the way they treat those with a psychological illness.

From this final court appearance, I caught the bus back to Peel. It had been a long, hard journey, staying on the run until it became unarguable that I was not harassing anyone. But on the top deck that morning, deflating with relief that I was a free man, I didn't anticipate that the toughest journey still lay ahead.

That began when I got home, and looked around the house in daylight. I realised it had, during my nine month absence, been ransacked. Twice.

42

OFF THE ROPES

TOMORROW WOULD BE Christmas Eve. I had electricity still but no heating oil, coal or gas. I had no food and no money. Worst of all, without the certainty of jail, I had no way of contacting my children, who were living just up the road, at yet another Peel address, with their mother. Aside from birthday cards they had sent to me, care of Our Elizabeth in November, I had had no contact with Sonny and Dolly since March of that year, 2008. I had never stopped writing letters to them. But still they went unanswered. For now, all I had was my freedom. At last.

The house was filthy. Every room was upside down. Someone else's greasy sheets were on my bed. I threw myself into cleaning and tidying the whole place room by room. Now, on the eve of Christmas Eve, I'd reached the children's bedrooms. I'd left them till last, not really wanting to step into them at all. Their mother had removed their little beds even though they had beds at the other homes around Peel she had occupied with the children over the previous two years. I was on my knees in Sonny's room, sobbing and holding open a black garden refuse sack, dropping into it once-treasured, now abandoned toys – some of the former wonders of previous and happy Christmases.

Once I'd finished, I told myself if I could get through that I could get through anything. I found some bottles of beer in an alcove in the kitchen. I drank the lot, perhaps half a dozen and, with the curtains drawn and a fan heater to keep me warm, I fell asleep on the sofa in what had been the TV room before the television had been stolen. It was to be my last lapse into boozing.

I was woken the following morning by a crash of glass outside. I went to the door. There, lying in a puddle in the pouring rain was the shattered wood and glass of a picture frame and – creased, crumpled and soggy – at the centre of the wreckage was my prized poster for a Clash concert at Leeds University. It had been hung on the wall of the TV room. I had noticed, when I returned from the UK, that it had, like so much from my home, been stolen while I was away. Now, someone had returned it but made a point of smashing it on my doorstep.

Scraping the broken glass and wood from the pavement, I heard a friendly voice. There stood my old friend Dave McLean, formerly the local pharmacist and a fellow music fan. Dave asked what had happened. I told him I had no idea but the poster was among my most valued possessions. He helped me lift the sodden paper sheet into the house where we laid it on the floor of the living room to dry. Straightened out it was remarkably undamaged.

'It's good to see you're back,' said Dave. 'And Lizzie and I were really pleased to hear good sense prevailed in court last week.' Lizzie is Dave's wife. They live in a large house on the edge of Peel with what seem to be dozens of children and grandchildren of all ages.

'What are you doing for Christmas?' asked Dave. I'd been dreading the question. I told him I was staying put, that I was just glad to be home after nine months, to be free and so relieved not to be hunted any longer. Dave must have sensed the cold and damp of a long uninhabited house.

'You're coming to ours,' he said.

A couple of hours later, I was propped up in an armchair by a crackling log fire, being fed by Lizzie all manner of frivolous Christmas treats and watching one documentary after another on the History Channel. But again, and especially on Christmas Day itself, I felt awkward, helpless, embarrassed and an imposition on those whose kindness I was not able to return. I was not part of their family, no matter how welcoming Dave, Lizzie and their children were. I was missing my own family terribly, especially given the season. The McLeans, doubtless sensing that, gave me the best possible present under the circumstances – love, care, warmth and security.

The day after Boxing Day, Lizzie drove me home and bought for me at a petrol station a bag of coal. I sat by the fire, listening to the BBC World Service and felt proud of myself that I'd not had a drink for three days. At Dave and Lizzie's hearth, I'd quietly sweated out the chemical dependency. Now it would all come down to willpower and the breaking of habit. It was a breeze. I had, in securing the future of Sonny and Dolly, the incentive. There was also the high bar which Catherine had set for me, on the grass at Wells cathedral, which over the coming months I would more than clear. But Catherine, alas, did not come back.

I began a check around the house for missing belongings. Some items had been removed, legitimately, by Juliette as jointly-owned possessions. Most had not. There was no reason I could think of for Juliette to take the television, for example, or my bicycle and all of my tools. No break-in had taken place. The culprit had to be another key-holder but surely not Barbara, my guardian angel next door. That left someone I had considered to be a friend. This chap had phoned me during my months in the UK to say he'd been kicked out by his wife. Was my place unoccupied? Could he please stay there for a while? Feeling compassion for him, someone in a position similar to my own, I agreed and told him to get the key from Barbara. I said he could stay there rent free, as I'd be glad to have someone looking after the place.

I learned soon after my return that he and another bloke of my acquaintance had been the thieves. They'd even boasted in a local pub that they were helping themselves. So much had gone: from my working model of a steam engine, which my mum and dad had given to me for my tenth birthday and which had, more recently, thrilled Sonny and Dolly, to my olive tree in a huge tub in the back yard. The value of my final audit of stolen property was around four thousand pounds.

I went to report all this to the police, with a list of the missing items and, in the case of expensive electronic equipment, photos of the devices copied from the instruction manuals. I also gave them the names of my suspects.

'There isn't enough evidence,' the most senior officer in Peel told me when, after hearing nothing from the police for a week or two, I made an appointment to see him.

From another officer, I was given the excuse that nothing could be done because the removal of property from my home could not be considered theft if it had been carried out by someone with a key.

No one was ever arrested or charged for the robbery. Some months later, I got a letter from the police to say that, as no further lines of enquiry had become available, they would not be pursuing their investigations unless and until I could bring new evidence to their attention.

FROM JANUARY TO OCTOBER 2009 the legal battle over the children's removal from the Isle of Man to Scotland rumbled through the Family Court. Only for the most crucial of the hearings did I hire a lawyer. For the rest, and for reasons of poverty, I represented myself. It was a battle that should never have taken place, and which I lost. Despite having been told that I had no job and very little money, the judge awarded all costs against me – which amounted to some sixty thousand pounds.

Meanwhile, I played the long game to become reunited with Sonny and Dolly. I let a few months go by after my return before making my move. This would give the children – possibly still jumpy about the family disintegration, my criminalisation and my absence in the UK – sufficient time to adjust to the news of my return. They would also learn from other people in Peel that I was in fine shape.

Knowing she was more self-confident than her older brother, it was to Dolly's school playground that I first turned up, at going-home time on 17 March 2009. She stopped dead in her tracks when she first saw me and burst into tears. I crouched before her, smiling and crying with my arms stretched open. She ran into them and we hugged and hugged, sobbing.

Authority intervened again at this point in the shape of the

Family Court Welfare Officer. She told me I would have to have my future meetings with my daughter at the Isle of Man Children's Centre, in Douglas on Saturday mornings, where I would be supervised by one or more of the centre's staff. But I had never harmed nor been a threat to my children. For three weeks I went along with this farce. For Dolly's arrival and departure I was locked in a side room. Dolly and I were studied and eavesdropped as we chatted awkwardly in a lounge painted that obligatory shade of institutional yellow and piled with tatty backcopies of celebrity chat magazines.

The final straw came when I insisted, on the third week, that Dolly and I would not be sitting in that room again for two whole hours. It was a lovely morning. Dolly agreed we should go for a walk. The Court Welfare woman protested but, as daughter and daddy, we just set off. From a distance of ten or twenty yards, we were tailed by the official, all the way through Douglas, even into a sweet shop, and down onto the beach. After that, I refused to attend any more of these supervised sessions.

For the next few months, following our March reunification, Dolly divided her time between my home and her mum's, staying over with me from the week we were back together. I felt so proud of her the day she turned up at mine, carrying a pathetic little camp bed she had brought down the hill from her mother's. She carefully made it up in her old room to replace her original, missing bed. With every visit, Dolly was reporting back to Sonny that Daddy was fine, that we were having a lovely time and that he should join us.

Fully battle-hardened by the spring of 2009, there was nothing that could scare me any longer. (Okay, I'll admit it: only landmines and Mrs Shimmin at number 30.) Those who have lost their fear cannot be intimidated. But even on this war-footing, I did not expect the next blow, the latest betrayal and humiliation, to come from a familiar and, I thought, friendly quarter – BBC Radio 4, for which I had given long and distinguished service.

In April 2009, I was invited to appear on the programme *On The Ropes*, in which those who have overcome adversity and perhaps controversy are cross-examined by John Humphrys. During our interview for this, my attitude was only positive and optimistic. There was no anger. I did not use it as an opportunity to blame anyone. Neither did I mount a score-settling attack on the injustices which I believed had been dumped on my children. Our chat finished with Humphrys asking how I felt after all I'd been through. 'I'm ready to rock and roll,' were my final words of the recording.

My conversation with Humphrys should have been an announcement to the listeners that I was fully recovered, in great humour and very much back. It felt cleansing. As we left the studio, the great interrogator slapped me on the shoulder with the words, 'I think you got the tone of that just right.' The producer was leaping around saying it was the best *On The Ropes* they had ever recorded.

The programme, I learned later, was cleared by BBC lawyers – a check which is routine for *On The Ropes* – on the day we had recorded it, the Thursday before scheduled transmission the following Tuesday. Over that weekend it was heavily trailed on Radio 4. On the Monday night, I got a phone call from a stranger, a Radio 4 executive editor of factual programmes, to say the programme had just been pulled, the night before broadcast, by Mark Damazer, the Controller. Damazer had neither the moral courage nor the courtesy to phone me himself.

It transpired that my ex or her advocates had contacted Radio 4 on the Monday morning, after catching the trails over the weekend, in which I was sounding strong and optimistic. Despite BBC lawyers having no difficulties with the recording, Damazer pulled the programme on the grounds of 'concerns for the children'. He had listened to it. He knew I scarcely mentioned in it my ex and spoke only with great warmth for Sonny and Dolly. And he was unable to tell me, when I finally reached him on the phone, what I had said to Humphrys which had given him those concerns. Yet here was the Radio 4 Controller affecting publicly an attachment to the welfare and privacy of my children, superior and more intimate than my own. He was also assuming an expertise on the laws of privacy more reliable than that of the lawyers he hired. Most worryingly, he was – instead of showing backbone and leadership – handing over for the day the job of Radio 4 Controller to a member of the public who was complaining about a programme she hadn't even heard.

On The Ropes ought to have been a turning point for me, a national advertisement that I was again, after all my troubles, on fine form. Instead, its cancellation sent out a very damaging signal, encouraging a widespread assumption that it must have been pulled because I had gone into a studio and been out of control, making a programme so full of slanders and anger that it was unfit for broadcast. Far from it.

Mark Damazer has since moved on to a new career in academia. My edition of *On The Ropes* has never been transmitted. It was the first and only programme John Humphrys has had pulled in more than fifty years of broadcasting.

As we DJs tend to say, the hits just kept on coming. My dad died at the end of July 2009. I was distraught. I wanted him to see me win my battle for the future of Sonny and Dolly. Nevertheless, I did have the small consolation that he saw me just a couple of weeks before his death and was much cheered by my recovery and by my impressive physical and emotional condition. But he would have been truly thrilled to have seen me and his grandchildren happily together, and properly for the first time, on our Isle of Man home, a place for which he also had long and huge affection.

On 25 September 2009, I went to find Sonny after school. He was playing on some swings in a nearby park. We were instantly and joyously reunited. The following day, a Saturday, we were out in our boat together for the first time in almost three years. We went to sea again, doing dad and lad stuff, on the Sunday.

Only one month later, I made the children one of their favourites for lunch, chicken korma. At three o'clock their mother arrived to sit, staring straight ahead, in her car across the promenade. I kissed and hugged both children more powerfully than usual. I watched them climb into the car. Waving until I was out of their sight, they were gone to Scotland. Already I had missed two years of their little lives, a lot at their age, and they had missed that irreplaceable time with their dad.

THE STRUGGLE TO SURVIVE has been long, a daily humiliation and often terrifying. I was so poor at one point during that summer of 2009, that I walked the ten miles to one of the hearings in the Family Court in Douglas. I couldn't afford the bus fare. Only by bumping into a friend afterwards who was driving back to Peel was I spared a ten mile walk back home. There have been winter nights when I have slipped out, under cover of darkness, to collect old timber from around Peel or driftwood on the beach that I had spotted during the day.

At other times, I kept going by selling off valuable belongings – treasured rock & roll and motorcycle racing memorabilia. And there were occasional loans from generous and supportive pals. A dear friend on the Island, Frank Coates, gave me the money I hadn't got to travel to my dad's funeral. I had the heartbreak of having to advertise my record collection. I just managed to hold on to my fishing boat, even though I could afford petrol only if pals offered to buy a gallon or two in exchange for a fishing trip. I never asked for this. Having the boat was therapeutic. It was also, at times, a means of survival. For much of 2009, I lived off what I caught. From one Family Court hearing, I came home hungry but with the cupboards again bare. I checked what remained of the catch I had stored in the freezer.

'Oh, bloody hell,' I thought to myself as I sat down to eat that night. 'Not ruddy lobster again.'

The horrors of poverty alone, experience taught me, were enough to drive anyone mad, leaving aside all the other torments I had endured. Yet, remarkably, and perhaps because I was weathering everything, I noticed by the late spring of 2009 that I had more energy, optimism, ambition, efficiency and a sharper sense of humour than I had ever had. A friend half my age in Peel dubbed me Duracell Man.

And despite what I'd occasionally still read about myself in the papers, I knew emphatically that I wasn't insane. Confirmation of this came one morning that spring, when I walked up the hill from my home to the supermarket on the shopping street in Peel. Passing the window of the jewellers, there among the full range of hideous nick-nacks, my eye was drawn to one particular specimen. It was a porcelain mouse dressed as a fireman. I took this in for a moment. What on earth inspired, I wondered, some designer in a fancy goods sweatshop in, perhaps, Dandong to think, 'I know...'? But more troubling is who, and under what circumstances, at this end says to themselves, 'Ooh, I really must nip out this morning and buy a porcelain mouse dressed as a fireman...'?

I reached the Co-Op, self-confidence soaring. It wasn't me who was nuts.

For the most part, the people of the Island, and particularly those of Peel, could see that too. Many were immensely and movingly supportive. Old ladies, who I did not know by name, would – without warning – grip my arm in the street and say, 'Keep going, son. We're right with you.' Or similar. My neighbours Audrey and Tony Mansell became surrogate parents. Without their wisdom, advice on strategy and their moral support, I would never have got through. Similarly, Debbie Law, my protector in Derby, phoned me every single night for more than a year after I returned to the Island just to chat and to make sure I was okay. Barbara Shimmin, next door, was a constant rock. Reliably, Peel friends, Vic and Pam Bates, Nigel and Nicky Kermode and Colin Fenton were always there. Just up the road, my pals Anglin and Jen Buttimore fed me regularly, probably knowing I hadn't had enough to eat in days. So did Jackie O'Halloran – most generously over Christmas 2009. My friend and neighbour, Jenny Alford, gave her time and gardening expertise freely and regularly to help me look after my yards. It was a great tonic. And although they are irregular visitors to their holiday flat overlooking Peel harbour, my friends Jane and Bob Taylor, near Birmingham, have always been at the end of the phone.

IN JULY 2009 I was summoned to London for a lunch with Roger Wright, Controller of Radio 3. The BBC paid for me to fly over. Dear old Roger took me back to the Gaylord of India, the location of our first date. He was, I believe, checking me out, to have confirmed that I really was back in great shape. I didn't confide it to Roger, but this was my first proper meal in weeks. Over our lunch, he told me about his plans for a Radio 3 series, to be recorded all over the world throughout much of 2010, and called *Music Planet*. He wanted me as one of the presenters. I dissolved into quiet sobs.

While Roger had not kept up daily contact with me since I'd had to abandon my weekly Radio 3 programmes, following my nervous breakdown in 2007, he had never shunned me and always left open the door for my return. He had kept the faith and now, apparently, the figure in front of him in the Gaylord, looking years younger than when he'd last seen me, had repaid that faith. I silently resolved to be for Roger, and for *Music Planet,* on the broadcasting form of my life.

By the following March, 2010, I was back on the road with my old Radio 3 producer pals, James Parkin and Roger Short. They too had always stood by me, checking regularly on my welfare and progress. Both had even advanced me small loans when it looked like my electricity or phone would be cut off.

Now, in one week, I was on top of a jungle-covered mountain in the Solomon Islands with Roger, teasing music out of a community of reclusive marijuana farmers whose way of life was still Stone Age. Next, I was with James in Cambodia, combing through the ashes at the spot where Pol Pot's body had been burned by his Khmer Rouge comrades in 1998 and interviewing one of the few musicians to survive that madness. A few weeks later, I was sitting in the dereliction of the stadium in Kinshasa in which Muhammad Ali had fought George Foreman in their 1974 *Rumble in The Jungle* – and filing an essay about it for *From Our Own Correspondent*, my first *FOOC* in five years.

In just eight days on that trip, Roger and I had recorded remarkable music around four African countries. In the maximum security wing of Pretoria Central Prison, a choir made up largely of murderers gave us the most uplifting gospel. For their inevitable finale of N'Kosi Sikelele Afrika, I couldn't hold back from bellowing along with them. In Zulu. I went hunting with the Bushmen of the Kalahari in Namibia and recorded their songs. On other adventures, we recorded the hunting calls of shark fishermen in Papua New Guinea, I discovered Siberia can be scorching in the summer and heard enough throat singing there to see even me, Mr World Music, through my new life-

Back on the job and back to Africa. Resting on a baobab tree in the Kalahari desert, Namibia, September 2010, during one of our trips to record the *Music Planet* series for BBC Radio 3. *Marvin Ware*

time. So it went on. Professionally, I was firing again on all six. I was thrilled to be back. More importantly, my producer pals seemed just as elated.

IN MAY 2010, James Parkin and I ended a breakneck tour of Indo-China and south east Asia, recording Radio 3 *Music Planet* documentaries, in Bangkok. It was from the Thai capital that we were due to fly home two days later. Unusually for these trips, but because we'd worked so hard and so efficiently, we had those two days to kill. James being James was looking forward to some well-deserved leisure time by the hotel pool. Nothing wrong with that. But I had other ideas.

It is not often, as the instinctive foreign correspondent, that one is flown, by coincidence, into the biggest news story in the world. That happened to me with Bangkok. The Red Shirt Revolution had been building up for months and I had monitored the intensifying popular crescendo whenever I'd managed to get near rolling television news or switched on the BBC World Service on our travels around Cambodia, Burma, Laos and Thailand. The consensus among most reporters on all networks over that week or so was that 'Red Shirt City is completely sealed off.'

The anti government demonstrators, organised as the UFDD (the United Front for Democracy Against Dictatorship) and drawn mainly from the rural poor, had occupied much of Bangkok's downtown business district. There had already been deaths at the hands of the army and police. I wanted to know why the demonstrators were so angry and prepared to go to these desperate lengths. And what was life like inside Red Shirt City?

I dropped my rucksack into my room at our Bangkok hotel, and rendezvoused with James in reception on his way to the pool. I told him I'd see him later. He just grinned.

Out the front of the hotel, I was able to approach a motorcycle taxi driver with words I had only dreamed of.

'Take me to the revolution,' I said.

Within an hour of arriving in the capital I was in the centre of 'completely sealed-off' Red Shirt City. I got on my mobile to

Katherine Butler, the foreign editor of the *Independent*. Would she like a piece?

'You bet,' said Katherine. '1500 words? But be careful.'

AS I SPOKE TO HER, I was already sheltering from a sniper. She could hear the gunfire in London. With every rifle crack, chips of asphalt were leaping up off the road surface, just ten feet in front of me.

I had not realised until my motorcycle taxi pilot and I pulled up on a broad, empty, dual carriageway – after twisting through side roads, and hurtling along deserted boulevards, past indifferent police and army positions, gun shots cracking the evening torpor – that we had entered the Red Shirt zone. But a burnt-out bus nearby suggested we were no longer in the Bangkok of my arrival, only an hour before.

At our second stop, where a side street met a main thoroughfare, locals urged us to scamper to join them in the shelter of an empty market stall. Many, although not motorcyclists, were wearing crash helmets. On the corner, just thirty yards away, black-clad men were leaping out to fire small rockets – fireworks – along the road. Between menacing pauses, the response came as sharp, measured, rifle cracks, rattling among the office blocks. An army or police sniper was firing from behind and above us. Pressed back into our shelter, I had no way of knowing who or what was responsible for a series of explosions which followed. But these were detonating close enough to be felt as well as heard. Advice to evacuate, and to escape by another insane motorcycle dash, came from a youth swathed in a black headscarf and carrying a night-stick. At no time did I see a Red Shirt, even these apparent UFDD militia men, carrying a gun.

Red Shirt City was indeed a city – albeit a spontaneous one – within a city. When I reached its centre, I was astonished to find an impromptu, though well-established, infrastructure. There were full civic amenities. Volunteers from among the protesters were carrying out rubbish collections and street sweeping. There were tented shower blocks, mobile toilets, makeshift temples and pavement food stalls.

In a marquee, behind a stage on which an Elvis impersonator was entertaining a crowd largely comprising middle-aged ladies in deck chairs, I sat down with Dr Tojirakarn Weng, one of the Red Shirt leaders. Why, I asked, had the Red Shirts rejected the government's offer of new elections in November?

'We say "yes" to the proposal,' he told me. 'But first the rule of law must be upheld. The deputy prime minister must be arrested over what happened on 10 April. [The deaths of several Red Shirts]. And the soldiers must draw back to their camps.'

And if that doesn't happen?

'Well, this government can have war or peace. If it is war, we will wait here until they come and kill us.'

The possibility of imminent slaughter did not appear to be troubling those beyond the marquee. In all directions, under shelters fashioned from plastic sacking on scaffolding or bamboo poles, families stretched out on raffia mats, reading the newspapers, dozing, cooking, washing their clothes, chatting and playing draughts with bottle caps.

In most areas, Red Shirt City had the atmosphere of a rock festival. Think urban, oriental Woodstock – without the nuisance of Crosby Stills & Nash.

I went back in again the next day. This time I hooked up with Andrew Buncombe, Asia correspondent of the *Independent*. Andrew was most generous to me, a chancing freelancer who'd parachuted onto his patch and was writing for the same newspaper.

We got talking to a couple of the protest's more senior ladies, Mrs Jindar Intarahutti and Mrs Pimtong Pattarakomol. Both were from central Thailand and had left their homes and families to up sticks for the capital, sleeping under the stars and enduring self-evident discomfort and danger to make their feelings known about corruption among their rulers and poverty among the ruled. Mrs Intarahutti was ready to do this despite, in her case, being infirm as well as middle-aged. They had met and become friends at the demonstration two months earlier. They had been living here ever since, sharing a straw mat at a central crossroads, close to the stage. Both were prepared to camp out indefinitely – because they were angry. It was an anger arising from a sense

Top: Watching the motorcycle races on Bray Hill, Douglas, Isle of Man, with Sonny and Buster, 2010. Buster loves the races. And, yes, before any fusspots write to complain, he is on his lead. *Shaz Nicol* Below: Dolly with Buster on our boat, looking for basking sharks off Peel, Isle of Man, summer 2009. *AK*

of deep injustice and despair. 'We will stay here until the Prime Minister, Abhisit, resigns,' they told me.

Neither lady was frightened of what might happen next. Enduring gunfire and explosions (and occasional cabaret crooners), they sat on their mat, serene and cross-legged. 'We are not afraid,' said Mrs Pattarakomol, 'because there is a shrine here with a Brahma [Hindu god] guard.' She motioned towards a miniature plastic temple, in simulated gold and adorned with a mug of burnt-out joss-sticks, which perched on the pavement nearby. Mrs Intarrahutti, maybe less spiritual than her companion, was no less resolute. 'We will not run away,' she said matter-of-factly. 'I will give my life for democracy.'

I wrote and filed from my hotel room that night. James and I were flying home to London the next day. As I packed my rucksack the following morning, I saw from my window black twisters of smoke rising between the skyscrapers in the direction of Red Shirt City. The long-anticipated military assault had begun. When my plane was climbing out of Bangkok, four hours later, I looked back through the window, over my shoulder, to see much of the downtown on fire.

At Heathrow later that day, I bought the *Independent* from the first shop beyond the barrier. My Red Shirt City piece covered two of the foreign pages and was flagged up on the front as an exclusive. I was also to discover, soon after I landed, that twenty-five protesters had been killed, with another eight hundred injured, as I was flying home. And Andrew Buncombe had been shot in the leg, just as I, the departing dilettante, was having hot towels pressed upon me by handmaidens of Royal Thai Airlines.

FOUR DAYS LATER, on the Isle of Man, I was making my way home from watching the first session of practice for the TT motorcycle races. It was a beautiful early summer evening. My mobile rang. It was Sonny.

'Dad,' said his little voice from Scotland, 'I'm coming home.'

He was back with me on the Island permanently, and with his mother's written consent, before the end of TT race week. We watched the main event, the Senior, together. It was the first time in four years we'd enjoyed the races as father and son. Dolly came over for it too.

IT IS NOW just before Christmas 2010. Sonny has been home for six months. Dolly is still in Scotland, understandably feeling the attachment of a little girl to her mum. She visits us as often as her mother allows and we speak on her mobile every night. Dolly will be joining us here next week for Christmas, the first the three of us have had together in four years.

If there are any doubts still lingering that I am not now as strong as a monkey's tail, a perception maintained and reinforced by persistent tabloid characterisation of me as a 'shamed DJ' or 'troubled DJ', Sonny and Dolly should be consulted first. They are the ones who are best placed to judge their daddy. Their judgement is the only one which matters to me.

And should the day come when I can afford the treat they both deserve, I have promised I will take them to Zimbabwe to see the Victoria Falls, the most spectacular natural wonder in the world. After that, Dolly will fulfil her fantasy to go shopping in New York City. There she will buy everything that is pink on Fifth Avenue. We will then fly from New York to Houston where Sonny, especially, will be filled with the same wonder as me at the Lyndon B Johnson Space Museum with its Saturn V rocket, all 364 feet of it, laid out to greet visitors on the front lawn.

Then it will be time to feed the children's growing interest in potty republics and to sharpen their own developing sense of *what-the-fuck-is-this?* I have not yet been myself so, for a holiday, we shall head, finally, to Belarus, the last truly bonkers country in Europe. A family fortnight in Minsk. What more can a father do?

INDEX

CREDITS

LYRICS

The author is grateful to the copyright holders for permission to reprint the following lyrics:

"Something In The Air" by John Keen © 1969 Fabulous Music Ltd. International Copyright Secured. All Rights Reserved. Used by Permission.

"Dixie Fried" by Carl Lee Perkins and Howard Griffin © 1956 Hi-Lo Music, Inc. © Renewed 1984 Carl Perkins Music, Inc. All Rights Administered by Wren Music Co., A Division of MPL Music Publishing, Inc. and Hi-Lo Music, Inc. All Rights Reserved. Used By Permission.

"School Days" by Loudon Wainwright III © 1970 (Renewed) Frank Music Corp. All Rights Reserved. Used By Permission.

"The Free Electric Band" by Albert Hammond/Mike Hazlewood © 1973 Imagem Music. All Rights Reserved. Used By Permission.

"Lawyers, Guns & Money" by Warren Zevon © 1978 Zevon Music (BMI). All Rights Administered by BMG Chrysalis. International Copyright Secured. All Rights Reserved. Reprinted with Permission of Hal Leonard Corporation

PHOTOS

All images are copyright of the author, except as noted in the captions. While every effort has been made to contact copyright-holders of illustrations, the author and publishers would be grateful for information about any illustrations where they have been unable to trace them, and would be glad to make amendments in further editions.